It takes st
lives. This st
others, but ev
  Personal e

MW00987448

the face of these demands smooths our passage. To get centered means to sense our place in the grand scheme and to trust the rightness of all experiences that beckon.

It is our hope that these brief daily meditations will help you find your place and thus help you summon the forces to see you through the days ahead. We both follow a Twelve Step program for sane living, and openness is an integral part of this approach. Healing, help, and wisdom may come from anywhere, so we gathered these quotations from men and women of many lands and times, and let them stimulate our own reflections.

Taking responsibility for our own lives, trusting in the rightness of a plan—however we may define the higher power that is its source—and nurturing ourselves to be the best we can; these are the tasks that renew our energies even as we perform them.

The words we have chosen remind us that women and men in every place and time have pondered, struggled, succeeded, and failed in much the same way as we. In every case, they had the drive to begin their journeys anew, day after day. They are like all of us. We are like all of them: journeying forth courageously one day, tentatively the next. The real importance of the journey is simply that we're making it, alone and yet mysteriously together.

—the authors

One faces the future with one's past.

— *Pearl S. Buck*

We are never divorced from our past. We are in company with it forever, and it acquaints us with the present. Our responses today reflect our experiences yesterday. And those roots lie in the past.

Every day is offering us preparation for the future, for the lessons to come, without which we'd not offer our full measure to the design which contains the development of us all.

Our experiences, past and present, are not coincidental. We will be introduced to those experiences that are consistent with our talents and the right lessons designated for the part we are requested to play in life. We can remember that no experiences will attract us that are beyond our capabilities to handle.

All is well. I'm ready for whatever comes today. My yesterdays have prepared me.

One cannot collect all the beautiful shells on the beach, one can collect only a few.
—Anne Morrow Lindbergh

Our lives are a series of selections. We select projects to do, activities to participate in, friendships to cultivate. And often we'll have to forego some of the selections we've made because time and energy run out. Full commitment, total involvement with singular activities and few friendships, is far better than partial attention to many. Rapt attention to the moment and all of whatever it contains enriches our lives; nothing less than full attention can do so.

The talents we each have been blessed with can only be developed if we use them fully to benefit the lives of others as well as our own. Thus, when our selections are vast, our attention is sporadic and our talents aren't fully developed. The fullness of our lives individually and collectively is proportionate to the depth of the relationships developed between ourselves, our friends, and our activities.

I can't be everywhere today. Nor can I attend to the needs of everybody I meet. I will carefully choose where to give my attention and then offer it totally.

• JANUARY 3 •

> *. . . goodness cannot adopt the form of blind passions, even in the act of defense and offense, and even when it refuses to tolerate evil. . . .*
>
> —Benedetto Croce

Willful blindness can't be good. To shut out any sight from the mind's eye is to exclude part of life. Any action blindly taken is likely to do unintentional harm.

It's not easy, when we're in the grip of any strong feeling, to stop ourselves from acting on blind impulse. It's not easy, but it's wise. Yielding to an impulse, without giving ourselves time to "see" it through clearly, can set us up for guilt or regret.

We needn't know everything in order to act; we merely need to know ourselves. "Blind passion" hides most of ourselves from view. Passion may move us to great selflessness, but never to great clarity, and good actions come from the clear-seeing soul.

I can trust myself to mistrust blind passion, and to wait for clarity before I take action.

Faith is not, contrary to the usual ideas, something that turns out to be right or wrong, like a gambler's bet; it's an act, an intention, a project, something that makes you, in leaping into the future, go so far, far, far ahead that you shoot clean out of time and right into Eternity, which is not the end of time or a whole lot of time or unending time, but timelessness, that old Eternal Now.

— Joanna Russ

Isn't it amazing how some people contrive to live in the present? They seem not to worry about the future; they seem not to regret the past. "Two days I can't do anything about," runs the saying, "yesterday and tomorrow."

We love to fantasize about the past and the future: What if Napoleon had died in infancy? Where would I travel in a time machine? But we get into trouble when we forget that "the past" and "the future" are inventions; the only reality is the present. Yes, past events contribute to our now; yes, the present will help to determine the future. But we can't do anything about them; the past and the future are out of our reach.

It seems, oddly enough, that it's people with a strong faith who are best able to live in the present moment. Enjoyment of the present, care for the quality of life: these are a kind of reverence, a kind of faith in life itself. The present is valuable, this faith tells us: it is all we have.

Let me swim in the present, reverential and unafraid. Let me be sustained by the water of life.

Nothing on earth consumes a man more completely than the passion of resentment.
—*Friedrich Nietzsche*

Our obsession with controlling other people, and our failure to succeed with our attempts, are most likely consistent attempts, the fodder for the resentments that we garner. It's human to want to control others, to try to control outcomes to favor us. But the resentment that develops begins controlling us, and this situation leads only to frustration, at times panic, always unhappiness.

If we're feeling resentment toward anyone, or because of any situation, we are not able to recognize the opportunities presenting themselves to us today. And when we don't respond to the invitations for meaningful involvement, our personal growth is jeopardized.

We give our power away when resentment swallows us. Our identity becomes enmeshed with it. Responsible action eludes us. Fortunately, we can take back our power just as soon as we decide to get free of the resentment.

The lesson I must learn is simply that my control is limited to my own behavior, my own attitudes. Today can be my new beginning.

It is not what we see and touch or that which others do for us which makes us happy; it is that which we think and feel and do, first for the other fellow and then for ourselves.

—Helen Keller

Our attention to someone else's needs is spirit-lifting, both for that someone and for ourselves. We need to move our focus away from the self to experience our well-deserved emotional health. The more frequently we honor another person's needs above our own, the greater will be our own strides along the path to health and wholeness.

When we peer beyond ourselves, we remove our attention from whatever our present personal problem is and it dies from neglect. We keep a problem a problem when we indulge it by obsessing over it. Switching our focus offers a perspective that's new, and thus destined to be beneficial.

All around me today are people whose needs are greater than my own. Personal health is enhanced when I forget myself.

I'm not sorry for anyone's being poor; I'm only sorry when they have no work.

—Helena Morley

Human beings have been described as animals with language, animals with laughter, tool-using animals, animals that play. But we're pre-eminently animals that work. Small children's play is imitation of the work they see adults doing. Fortunate adults put the same energy and devotion into their work as children do into their play.

Work—although we sometimes curse it—is a blessing. Work, the work that is a real expression of the spirit, focuses our energy and allows us to be whole. Maybe our real work isn't our job; maybe we feel whole when we're carpentering or cooking or writing, and we think of these as "hobbies" or "just stuff I do." If we could bring to our jobs the concentration and pride with which we turn a chair leg or roll up sticky buns, we would exalt our working days.

The jobs we do, the work for which we're paid, are deeply important to most of us. When we find work we can love, and do it as well as we're able, we've earned a victory in life.

I will try to be able to say of my work today, "I would do this even if I weren't paid for it."

All writers are vain, selfish and lazy, and at the very bottom of their motives there lies a mystery.
— *George Orwell*

For the most part, we receive too much information. We're bombarded with print, sound, images. Many of us cultivate a healthy skepticism: we consider the source. What does this person, this agency, this network, this advertiser, or this elected official stand to gain from telling me this information?

But we cannot doubt everything. Humans need to believe in something, even something wildly implausible on the face of it. Thus, cults and causes abound. In this age of widespread corruption and cynicism, faith also is widespread.

Faith is healthy; it is an affirmation of human worth and continuity. Fortunate are those of us who have both strong faith and good judgment. Belief in the essential goodness of our fellows and in the basic rightness of our world can renew our vitality and remind us to treat others with the respect due their humanity. In turn, others will respect our belief in them.

Sometimes, faith is betrayed; sometimes, we stumble. But the delusions or mistakes of others need not sour us; they are part of the mystery.

I will believe in my own capacity for goodness, and all will be well.

When a man leaves off believing in imaginary property, then only will he make use of his true property.

—*Leo Tolstoy*

The original meaning of property is "belonging to the self." In this sense, land, houses, money, paintings, jewels, cars, cannot be our *property*; they are all things, and we enjoy using them, but they have nothing to do with our *selves*.

What then is our true property? It's our moral and spiritual qualities; our capacity for love, our commitment to honesty. These are what make a difference in who we are. The difference between a lie and the truth is vastly greater than the difference between a bicycle and a Mercedes. When we appreciate this distinction, we can begin to develop our spiritual selves.

We all know that things can't make us happy; only a loving heart and a clear conscience can do that. Yet often we act as though the piling up of things was important in itself. A little reflection can restore our balance and return our imaginary property to its true place in our lives.

True property is what nothing can take away from me.

A private railroad car is not an acquired taste. One takes to it immediately.

—Eleanor R. Belmont

The hunger for solitude visits each of us at various points in our development as whole, healthy human beings. It's in our solitude that we come to know ourselves, to appreciate the many nuances that distinguish us from others. It's in the stillness that we detect our soul's inclinations. The privacy of silence offers us the answers we need. The distractions that stood in our way no longer fetter us when we've invited solitude to be our guest.

We need time away from others, from the chaos of our job, families, and society if we are to find, once again, the clarity we need to make the best forward movement. We cannot hear "The Director" call to us when all around is the clatter of voices and anxiety.

I will relish the moments of silence today. They'll reward me with sure guidance and clarity of thought.

Children require guidance and sympathy far more than instruction.

—Anne Sullivan

Children are not just the people under ten. We are all children at heart. And in many of the activities that call us we are as uncertain of the steps to take, as unsure of the course of the outcomes as any ten-year-old. No matter the age, what we all need in the midst of any challenge is soft comfort from a loved one and gently probing questions that serve to guide our choices as we move ahead with the task.

Giving someone explicit directions about how to proceed can deprive them of opportunities for discovery. Stumbling is part of the human experience. Picking ourselves up allows us an additional glance at the landscape on which we tripped. In the second glance comes a new understanding and thus the growth the gift of life has promised us.

I'll comfort another child today and willingly accept the guidance offered by my own mentor.

Freedom means choosing your burden.
—Hephzibah Menuhin

Everyone of us is haunted by fears of some measure. That we learn through pain and grow beyond our fears we can only appreciate in retrospect. During the moment of painful confrontation or the spell of overwhelming anxiety we learn only that we're feeling no joy, no peace, and probably no security. However, we must remember that no painful burden, be it immobilizing anxiety or a relationship in which we've become victimized, has "happened" to us without acceptance—no matter how passive. We are free to reject all burdens and all unhealthy conditions. That we don't relish our freedom from all pain is a fact of the human condition.

Looking anew at the struggles that confound us and accepting responsibility for them doesn't lessen them, perhaps, but it does restore our personal power. We are not powerless, worthless individuals at the mercy of our friends and co-workers. We are in partnership all the way, and any moment we each have the power to rewrite the terms of the contract.

_____

I am free today to be who I want to be. To grow or not to grow. To feel joy or pain.

Our reality is influenced by our notions about reality,
regardless of the nature of those notions.
—Joseph Chilton Pearce

How we greet today will color the returns of this day. Further, our expectations will be manifest, which means we have the personal power to determine the course our minds and thus our actions will take. It's both awesome and thrilling to understand that we are each responsible for our affairs. Moreover, we will handle them with ease or experience turmoil as is our habit.

What we perceive at any moment is equal to our vision of that moment. If we want more laughter, greater freedom, further attainments, they lie within our power—they can't elude us unless we let them. But first we must define our direction for movement and then coach our steps along the way.

I go where I want to go. I see what I want to see. Everything can change in a flash of the mind's eye.

*Perhaps this very instant is your time . . . your own,
your peculiar, your promised and presaged moment,
out of all moments forever.*

—Louise Bogan

"This very instant" is all we have. We make plans for the
future, we invoke memories of the past, but really, all we
have to deal with and to act in is the moment at hand. We
cannot stop its going; we cannot hurry the next moment on
its way. Like everyone else in the world, we're partners in
the dull, humdrum, dazzling, fabulous, totally unpredic-
table moment.

And if we have a time that is "our time," it's right now. It
has to be, because there isn't any other. Maybe we've had
times in the past that were special for us; maybe the future
will hold precious moments. But the only time that is truly
"our time" is this time, where we are, right now. And what
we do with this time is ours to decide.

*Each moment is mine, to make as beautiful or as painful as
I choose.*

When the most important things in our life happen we quite often do not know, at the moment, what is going on.

—C. S. Lewis

Retrospect offers us what no one moment, in the present, is capable of doing. There is a pattern to the events of our lives, and even what appear as the most inconsequential occurrences are contributing their input to the larger picture that's developing. There is no question but that every event has meaning. No experience is without its impact. Time will reveal the reason for the baffling or troubling situations that have dogged our paths along the way.

Whenever the road feels rocky or we are confused, we need to trust. Our lives are not happenstance. There is a performance being staged.

How helpful it is to understand that we are all "players" sharing the same stage. All of us are needed for some acts, and there will be a concluding scene making clear the intricacies of our many earlier scenes. As life progresses, our understanding grows. Our finales are assuredly appropriate to our life plan.

Today's happenings will have their impact. Sometime—in some way. All moments, all events are part of my sacred pathway.

We are partakers of a common nature, and the same causes that contribute to the benefit of one contribute to the benefit of another.

—William Godwin

Ecology, the study of how all life fits together, has an emotional dimension. We all know people who are emotional polluters. Bullies, gossips, or self-pitiers spread a noxious influence; no one wants to be around them.

Often they're gifted people, and sometimes they're in positions of power over others. It's difficult to keep our own clarity among the belching smokestacks of an emotional polluter. But our ecology—our interconnectedness—means that, potentially, we influence them as much as they influence us. If we can stay out of their poison, refuse to play, we can help to clean up the atmosphere.

Our ordinary notions of politeness often lead us to encourage emotional polluters. We may not see that our tacit acceptance and cooperation harms both us and them. Let us use our faith in our common nature to behave cleanly; we will thereby help others to clean up their acts.

I'll try not to confuse politeness with pollution.

If we seek to be loved—if we expect to be loved—this cannot be accomplished; we will be dependent and grasping, not genuinely loving.

—M. Scott Peck, M.D.

We receive love when we give love, with no strings attached. Bargaining for love is sure to disappoint us. It's human nature, when bargaining for anything, to hope to pay only half of what something is worth. Expressing this attitude in our relationships guarantees that we'll be shortchanged.

No one of us is free from the need for love. And most of us search for reassurances of that love from the significant people in our lives. However, the search will be unending until we come to love ourselves. Love of self is assured when we understand our worth, our actual necessity in the larger picture of the events that touch us all.

When we realize our value and see that life's mysteries have reasons, we'll no longer doubt ourselves and we'll be free to love and understand another's value too. We need never grasp for love when we sense the real meaning of the lives that surround us.

I will love someone fully today and I'll understand their meaning in my life.

The true wonder of the world is available everywhere, in the minutest parts of our bodies, in the vast expanses of the cosmos, and in the interconnectedness of these and all things.

—Michael Stark

Let's take a moment and look around ourselves. All that we see has its connection to us and to all other parts of this vast universe, and there is a universal rhythm with whose beat all life is in tune.

Our existence, all existence, is to be marvelled at. How perfect is the rosebud, the baby's toenails, the dog's sense of direction. We are not alive by accident. The beat of our hearts is necessary to the continued beat of the Universe. The whole is maintained by the combination of all the parts.

Life is sacred, all life. Friends and enemies are sacred. Lovers, children, parents are sacred. When we've come to understand this fact, understand it to the depths of our being, we'll know love; we'll know ourselves. Most of all we'll feel the peace that accompanies faith in the vastness and the rightness of the Universe and all it contains.

Everything as far as my eyes can see and heart can feel is contributing a part to my personal existence today.

Imagine that we conjure up a world that is safe for mothers and daughters.

—Louise Bernikow

The question of violence and danger in society occupies a lot of time, breath, and printer's ink. The possibilities of peace and safety take up very little. It is common for us to think of containing violence by greater violence: the violence of weapons, of prisons, of riot squads. And yet the teachers whose wisdom we prize above all others tell us that one cannot answer force with force; that only peace and detachment can meet violence and draw out its poisons.

No sane person wants war. Yet we are so locked into violent patterns of thinking that many of us believe we should prepare for it. How would we go about preparing for peace? What are the first steps we could take? What is peace, anyhow? We seem to know very little about it.

A world that is safe for mothers and daughters would be safe for fathers and sons as well. Let us search our hearts to discover what we know of peace, and let us talk to one another, work together to realize our knowledge.

I shall not study violence anymore; instead, I shall discover as much as I can about peace and safety—for in my life, peace begins with me.

It is not fair to ask of others what you are not willing to do yourself.

—Eleanor Roosevelt

Equality is a state of mind. When we value our own self-worth, we are comfortable with the achievements and the well-being of our friends and associates. The symptoms of a punctured ego occur when we criticize others and make demands we don't want to fulfill ourselves.

Most of us experience wavering self-confidence on occasion. It may haunt us when a big task faces us. Or it may visit us when we least expect it. It's a facet of the human condition to sometimes lack self-assurance. At times we need to remember that life is purposeful, and the events involving us are by design.

Almost daily we'll face situations we fear are more than we can handle, and we'll hope to pass the task off to another. It's well for us to remember that we're never given a task for which we're not prepared. Nor should we pass on to others those activities we need to experience personally if our growth is to be complete.

I must do my own growing today. If I ask others to do what I should do, I'll not fulfill my part of life's bargain.

Let me listen to me and not to them.

—*Gertrude Stein*

Our ears would fill with advice, if we listened to it: advertisers, evangelists, publishers, educators, all clamoring to market their products, try to get us to conform to their notions of what we should be.

One of the dangers of a democratic society is confusing the individual and the mass—using statistical data to define persons instead of trends. "Trendiness" is a way of avoiding individuality. To choose for ourselves means taking responsibility for our choices, saying, "I do this because I want to."

Each of us has an interior voice that knows what we want. We know—even if the knowledge sometimes causes us pain—that we're unique individuals, with goals, programs, and behaviors distinct from others'. Acknowledgment and enjoyment of our full humanity means owning our differences—listening to our own voices.

I am the expert on my own life. Today and every day let me be wise enough to consult myself.

All our resolves and decisions are made in a mood or frame of mind which is certain to change.
—Marcel Proust

When we are alert in the here and now we are constant collectors of new information. Consciously and subconsciously we sift through it and file it away—not to be forgotten, however. Our opinions, our attitudes, and our responses to life are influenced and expanded by those moments in which we absorbed new information, moments that in turn enhance our credibility as flexible, thoughtful decision-makers.

It is much easier to keep our minds closed and our attitudes and behavior rigid. Venturing into uncharted territories need never be risked. Each day becomes predictable and dull—in time, not really worth living.

Life's joys lie in adventure. We're promised adventure every moment of the day if we open our eyes to it. The currents that flow from the activities around us are charged with reasons for reformulated plans, new opinions, advanced enlightenment. That we're fully contributing members of the universe is evidenced in our flexibility when called for by changing situations.

I can change my mind today with pride, if new information calls for it.

No person could save another.

—Joyce Carol Oates

We encounter the experiences we need in our lives. It's sometimes hard to believe that when we're grappling with disappointment, anger, or loss. Yet everything that comes our way is material for our growth.

Many of us entertain a fantasy that some person can complete us. We don't believe that we're complete in ourselves. Only when we do will we become able to share in a life-enhancing partnership with another person. Only when we love ourselves can we love others realistically, instead of seeing them as fantasy figures, projections of our own desire.

No one can hurt us emotionally unless we allow the hurt. We're full partners in everything that we do, and taking responsibility for our actions and our desires is our first step toward being fully lovable.

The only one who can save me is me.

He has the right to criticize who has the heart to help.
—Abraham Lincoln

Our negative judgments of others very frequently inform us of our own shortcomings. In other words, what we dislike in others are often those things we hate about ourselves. Much better than criticizing another's abhorrent behavior is a decision to look inwardly at our own collection of traits and attitudes. Our desire to criticize, to pass judgment, offers an excellent mirror of who we truly are. And the image we see reflected can guide our movements toward becoming healthier, happy individuals.

We can feel a bit of gladness for what our negative reactions are able to teach us—but we must be willing to learn from them. How exciting to contemplate that every hateful moment actually is offering us a positive opportunity for change.

It's human to find fault, and we shouldn't be overcome with shame. However, we hinder our own personal growth every time we quickly criticize another rather than rejoicing that we've been given an additional opportunity to move closer to the person we're being called to become.

Today I'll look beyond others' faults and recognize my own.

Is there any stab as deep as wondering where and how much you failed those you loved?
—Florida Scott Maxwell

Treating our loved ones as we hope to be treated is our assurance against failing them. And if we listen to our inner voice, we'll never falter in our actions toward others. There is always a right behavior, a thoughtful response, a respectful posture.

Let us be mindful that we're sharing our experiences with others who need the talents we have to offer. It's not by coincidence but by design that we're given opportunities to treat those close at hand in some manner. We'd do well to let the choice be loving.

How we treat another invites like treatment. Actions from our heart will soften our own struggles. Also, spiteful, critical treatment of others will hamper our steps. We teach others how to treat us by our gestures and words.

The inner voice can be heard if I choose to listen. It will never guide me wrongly.

I came into this world, not chiefly to make this a good place to live in, but to live in it, be it good or bad.
—H. D. Thoreau

To live is to open ourselves to possibility, to rule out nothing. There is no way we can spare ourselves, or those we love, the pains of living, because they are inseparable from the joys. How grandiose we are when we think we can save the world.

All we can do—and it's quite a lot—is to live the best way we can, achieving a balance amid the forces that pull on us: pleasure, responsibility, power, love. If we can live so that we respond to all of them, rule out none of them and yet enslave ourselves to none, we will have the best the world can give.

One quality all great people seem to share is humor—the capacity to see our struggles and triumphs with detachment. Not that our life is unimportant, but that it's only a part of the huge web of life on this planet.

If we can keep our lives in balance, we won't get puffed up by any little triumph, or squashed by a defeat. We'll keep on with our lives, confident that we're doing our best.

Let me not forget—my chief business in life is living.

*I feel we have picked each other from the crowd as
fellow travelers, for neither of us is to the other's personality the end-all and the be-all.*

—Joanna Field

It's not mere chance that we gravitate toward those who
become our friends. Nor is it only happenstance that we are
piqued by others. We are, in fact, on a journey and have
much to learn. From our friends and even more so from
those not so friendly, we are destined to learn what our souls
yearn for. The journey is the process of enlightenment for
which we all have gathered. From one another we are receiving that which we're ready to learn. All of us students.
Each of us a teacher.

How comforting to know that the pain of a particular experience, or the confusion over a set of circumstances, will
become understandable with the passage of time. All experience plays its part. All of our acquaintances share destinies
overlapping our own. There is security in knowing that our
journeys are necessary and right for us.

*I'll not discount the value of any person or any experience that
circumstances offer today.*

A truth that's told with bad intent
Beats all the lies you can invent.

—William Blake

The quality of our relationships with others depends heavily on our motives. If we're trying to change our friends, to correct their behavior or to improve their lives, we'll ensure a poor quality of friendship.

The only life we have power over is our own. Trying to fix other people isn't only futile, it's disrespectful. Chronic "fixers" are likely to attract people who seem to cry out for their services. Over time, the situation usually proves to be a set-up for frustration and anger.

Self-respect begins inside ourselves. Real consideration for others demands that we treat them with the same respect we'd like to receive.

There is no such thing as my telling someone something "for their own good."

I come from nothing, but from where come the undying thoughts I bear?

—*Alice Meynell*

Nothing is new under the sun, except each day as it dawns. The thoughts that visit our brains have all been thought before; the freshest, brightest, best ideas and inventions all have their roots in ancient visions of human possibility.

Yet this day is new because it is our January 29. The elements that make it up may be immortal. They have not ever come together in just this way before. We feel at home in the timelessness of our spirits and the sense of the unique possibilities of today. We will be given many chances, today, to be the person we want to be.

We have no power over the events of today, except our power over our own behavior. If we act from our knowledge of what is right for us, all will be well.

I am unique, and I have inherited the rich medium of thought.

Maturity is the capacity to withstand ego-destroying experiences, and not lose one's perspective in the ego-building experiences.

—*Robert K. Greenleaf*

Our emotional health is proportionate to our willingness to take personal responsibility for thoughtful responses to the myriad circumstances in our lives. We are not powerless over our attitudes or over behaviors, even though we are generally powerless over the events themselves. The most troubling of times need not diminish us, unless we let them.

Likewise, the flavor of the most pleasurable situation retains its long life in proportion to our willingness to assimilate the experience gradually, letting it enrich us but not overwhelm us. Overreaction to any event casts a spell over us, inhibiting our ability to perceive accurately the moments, hours, perhaps even days of experiences that follow.

Finding the balance between overly emotional reactions to people and circumstances and disinterested passivity takes effort and a commitment to emotional health. And that balance is the real key to experiencing a life that's joyful.

No event need throw me today. And yet, every situation offers me a chance to practice healthy living.

It seems to me that in the long run it is impossible to maintain a democratic society unless you can spread the benefits and burdens of being an American citizen reasonably evenly.

—Felix Rohatyn

In our relationships, in our work and play, do we assume an equal share of the burdens, and do we get a reasonable amount of benefits in exchange?

There's no way to calculate the burdens and benefits of living. But our own inner awareness is a pretty accurate measure: if you feel ripped off and resentful, then something's wrong; if you feel guilty, as though you were getting away with murder, something's wrong.

Often we're reluctant to track down the source of our guilt or our resentment; we're afraid that what we find may force us to change the way we live and work, and change is painful.

Letting go of a source of pain can be as difficult as losing a source of pleasure.

I am the only one who knows just what is going on in my life, and all such choices are mine.

You are a child of the universe no less than the trees and the stars; you have a right to be here. And whether or not it is clear to you, no doubt the universe is unfolding as it should.

—Max Ehrmann

There is a patterned sequence to the events surrounding us, attracting our attention, inviting our personal involvement. We must accept this as a given, and then attune ourselves to the rhythm of the ordered flow. This will augment our personal growth and facilitate our contributions, which are both needed by other players in this sequence of events.

We need not understand the full picture of the pattern we're each woven into. We need only trust that it's a design which will comfort us—if not today, then tomorrow.

I can go forth today—sure that events will move me in the right direction even though I can't see what's around the corner. There will be no unplanned event in the big picture.

. . . we ourselves are only fragments of existence, and our lived life does not fill the whole of our capacity to feel and to conceive.

—*Paul Valéry*

Our feelings are bigger than we are. The love, sorrow, fear, or rage that any one of us feels at any moment is just a thin slice of a great stream of feeling that runs through all of humanity. To experience strong emotions in a crowd, for instance, takes us out of ourselves.

Mob anger can be viciously destructive. Mob joy can be transcendent. The difference between one individual and the mob is that each one of us can choose, every moment, what we will do with our emotions. We can feel rage and choose to express it without harm. We can feel sorrow and survive it. We can choose to dwell with feelings that console and enhance our spirits, and we can choose to let go of those that diminish us.

With feelings, as with everything else, the law of life is change. We shall not always feel as we feel now. If we accept our feelings as they come, and try to feel them fully as we're able, we shall become more unified with our fellow human creatures, and with all existence.

Pressure builds up behind a dam. I will let my feelings flow.

. . . fear makes strangers of people who should be friends.

—Shirley MacLaine

Life is sterile and stifled when we close ourselves off from the smiles or swift glances of others. The opportunities we have for personal contacts are not mere chance. We draw to ourselves experiences and thus acquaintances which will lend meaning to our lives.

Our fear of others is generally tied to our sense of personal inadequacy. How frequent are our suspicions that others are smarter, more capable, destined for greater success. However, we fail to gain the growth promised by another's presence in our lives when we give in to the fears that haunt us all at times. Those strangers in our lives are not without purpose. Their growth, as well as our own, is dependent on the removal of the barriers separating us.

A stranger lingering in my life is not here by chance. I will gain from opening myself.

No one can make you feel inferior without your consent.

—*Eleanor Roosevelt*

Self-talk is powerful. It will develop a healthy ego. Likewise, it can trigger ego deterioration. Our strength in times of trouble can be doubled or eroded depending on the commitment we've made to positive self-worth.

A secure self-image and unwavering self-confidence are characteristics we all long for. They need not elude us; they are our birthright. However, most of us fail to understand we need only to claim them to own them. Instead, we doubt our abilities, question our self-worth, and discover that our strength and our potential are exactly what we think they are.

Belief in ourselves precedes achievement. Our successes are always within our power if we understand our responsibility for them. We are self-talking every moment; the words we use are our personal choice.

I'll be conscious today of my self-talk. My experiences will directly reflect my thoughts.

It's important to know that words don't move moun-
tains. Work, exacting work moves mountains.
                                        —*Danilo Dolci*

Exercising our spiritual muscles for the arduous and exacting work of faith is a new thing for many of us. Our culture doesn't seem to put the same value on spiritual power
as it does on muscles or intellect. Yet a strong and agile
spirit, the kind that can do the work that moves mountains,
is possible for us all.

Like the muscles of our arms and legs, the spirit swells
and grows with use. Small acts of faith will show us
the way. As we grow increasingly secure, we are capable of
greater and greater leaps of faith. Real prayer, real meditation, means touching and using that inner core of faith, and
the more we do it, the stronger it grows.

The fullest life is possible for those whose powers are the
best developed. If we choose to move mountains, we must
be prepared to work. Even achieving freedom of choice in
our lives means developing our spirits.

My spiritual power matches the task at hand. As I become
stronger, I can accomplish greater things.

In this world everything changes except good deeds and bad deeds; these follow you as the shadows follow the body.

—*Ruth Benedict*

Our identity, our being at any moment, is a composite of all we have been in the past. Some of our actions have made us wiser. Others haunt us because we didn't put forth our best effort. All of our deeds contributed in some measure to our growth, however, and they can guide our choice to behave honorably today.

Acceptance of who we are, our total self, is necessary for our emotional maturity. Shame for past actions will keep us stuck. Our restitution for the past is best made by responsible behavior today. How fortunate that each waking moment offers us opportunities to become our better selves.

Today, just like every day, I'll make choices to behave in ways that will fill me with pride or shame. I pray for thoughtfulness today.

*With history piling up so fast, almost every day is the
anniversary of something awful.*

—*Joe Brainard*

"History" is mostly a record of awful events—war, famine,
conspiracy, oppression, betrayal. But surely, every day is
equally the anniversary of something wonderful. It's all in
how you look at it.

Perhaps a calendar of wonderful anniversaries would be
an antidote to depression: this is the day I first heard tender
words from someone dear; this is the day I stopped smoking; ten years ago on this day I committed myself to a program of positive living and spiritual growth.

Keeping such a calendar, even for a short time, gives us a
record of spiritual progress. Even to be able to say, "How
different I am from what I was five years ago" can be a truly
cheering thing. Why let the tyranny of history depress our
spirits? Let's make our own.

*I will treasure the private record; the public one will keep track
of disasters.*

He who angers you, conquers you!

—Elizabeth Kenny

It's by choice that we let others control our emotions. When we make that choice we have abdicated our personal responsibility for growth. Deciding to feel how we truly want to feel rather than giving someone else control is free-ing, exhilarating, and nourishing.

When we let someone anger us, we have decided to make them the object of our attention, and any intention to do what needs to be done is gone. Anger consumes us. With it we become preoccupied and the growth and con-tributions we were created for come to a standstill. Our personal power to think creatively and to take action are lost when we choose anger instead. For this way, the object of our anger decides who we are.

Today I'll be in charge of my growth if I choose to determine my own emotions.

Imagine there's no country. It isn't hard to do.
Nothing to kill or die for. And no religion, too.
                                    —*John Lennon*

If we let go of all conventions of life as we know it—the laws, religions, customs, and other institutions—we could train our imagination to build new ones, perhaps based on different values of work and wealth and play.

What is our image of an ideal society? Perhaps it is one in which there is no money. Or one where all work is done by computers and people are free to play. Perhaps our model is military or tribal.

How would we define crime or punishment in our Utopia? What would be the criteria for success and failure? Would we redefine the family as we know it? How would we reward our heroes? Whatever our ideal society is, it's likely to express our most deeply held values.

To find out what I hold most precious, I will try to imagine giving it up.

Limited expectations yield only limited results.
—*Susan Laurson Willig*

Our thoughts determine our actions, and when our thoughts are negative, our successes are few. What we hold in our mind is certain to be reflected in the day's activities. And we are capable of fueling our thoughts positively, if we choose to.

Positive self-assessment and uplifting pep talks can become habitual if our desire to live up to our potential is great enough. The expectations we privately harbor, be they small or far-reaching, will set the pace for the progress we make today, and every day.

We can greet a challenge with eager anticipation when we've grown accustomed to believing in our capability for success. First, we must expect to handle, with poise, whatever confronts us.

No one but me determines my course today. My success begins in my mind.

SERVICE. A beautiful word fallen upon bad days.
— Claude McKay

Silver service; military service; tennis service; evening service. The word has so many different connotations that we lose the thread that connects them; something done *for another*. Whether it's our profession or our gift, service is our offering of skill or care to a fellow being.

We now have the term self-service, which mostly connotes convenience in shopping. Do we ever truly serve ourselves, in the sense of offering our best to our own benefit? A high quality of self-service is an important part of self-esteem. By taking time for ourselves, treating ourselves gently, we demonstrate our belief that we deserve love.

Quality self-service doesn't only mean caring for our bodies, although that's important. It also means forgiving ourselves, letting mistakes remain in the past, and nourishing our spirits with good thoughts, good words, good deeds. If we're to earn tranquility and joy in life, surely we can learn to serve ourselves with kindness.

Today will abound with opportunities to serve myself and others. I'll be open to them.

For have you not perceived that imitations, whether of bodily gestures, tones of voice, or modes of thought, if they be persevered in from an early age, are apt to grow into habits and a second nature?

—Plato

What does it mean to act "as if"? When we feel angry and unforgiving, it means we act *as if* we forgave someone who stepped on our toes, or took our parking place, or ruined our paintbrush; when we feel cold and self-pitying, it means to act *as if* we were warmly interested in the child or friend or spouse who has something to tell us. It can be a wonderful exercise. If we really give ourselves to the performance, we can act *as if*, and the mood we imitate becomes real.

Oscars will never be given for acting *as if*, but the rewards are far more useful. Acting *as if* can salvage a bad day; it can repair or prevent a quarrel. Act as if we didn't have a headache, and often the headache disappears. Act as if we weren't in a hurry and often we will have time for everything.

When we were small, adults said to us, "Don't make a face or you'll freeze that way." Now that we're grown, we can learn how to imitate, flexibly, what we want. Instead of freezing into negative postures, we reach for agreeable ones—and so often "*as if*" becomes "*as is*."

Today I shall practice acting as if I were serene; perhaps it will grow into a habit.

Every truth we see is one to give to the world, not to keep to ourselves alone.

—*Elizabeth Cady Stanton*

Sometimes we feel that we are the guardians of a fragile, threatened civilization: if it weren't for us, all would be lost. Such feelings are a signal that we need to check out our reality, to test our perceptions of the world against those of someone we trust. We are seldom in sole possession of the truth!

But shared commitment to truth is powerful; it enhances our spirits. Most of us feel a need to express this commitment, whether by sharing worship or simply talking with friends. Often the truth is a process, a relationship between ourselves and others, and sharing it gives it roundness and luster.

I need courage to face the truth; and the truth will strengthen me.

It is not the things we accomplish that are important,
it is the very act of living that is truly important.
　　　　　　　　　　　　　　　　—Dr. Bill Jackson

We've been invited to participate in this life, to be present, one to another, and that's all that's expected of us. Our successes may bring us personal joy, but our value as persons lies only in our being.

But living fully is more than just making an appearance, here—today. It's celebrating our oneness—our ties to one another—our need for one another's presence to complete our own. And we can be a celebrant only when we're involved and fully focused on the experience. We capture life's gifts, its riches, when we are intent on the moment's fullness. We miss what we most need when our hearts and minds are distracted.

All that's asked of me is rapt attention here, now, to others. And I'll find the good life.

I had often occasion to notice the use that was made of fragments and small opportunities in Cranford. . . . Things that many would despise, and actions which it seemed scarcely worthwhile to perform, were all attended to. . . .

—Elizabeth Gaskell

Our lives are full of "fragments and small opportunities." Bouquets of wild grasses, shells and pebbles from the shore, a half-hour visit to a convalescent home, small acts of kindness, found poems—anything that enriches the moment, for ourselves or for another, is worth performing.

And it's the busiest people who seem to have time for these fragments, time to smell the flowers. It's often a shock to realize that doing something nice for ourselves might involve a small deliberate kindness to another. But the more we are good to ourselves in this way, the richer our lives become.

The moment is mine to cherish and to share. When I share a kindness, I double it.

You can't cross a chasm in two steps.

—*Rashi Fein*

When a small child hides her eyes, she means, "You can't see me." We sophisticated grownups sometimes have trouble getting rid of magic thinking. We tear petals from daisies, one by one; we tell ourselves that anything we eat standing up has no calories. We know one must leap across a chasm, but still we think, "If only I could change feet in the middle!"

The important thing is getting to the other side—tackling the problem on its own terms. Playing magic games is one way to stay stuck. There's nothing romantic or admirable about futile efforts; they're an admission that we don't want to succeed.

Every problem teaches us how to resolve it. If we can't see the solution, then we're not ready for it, and instead of sputtering vainly we should set that question aside and address ourselves to our appropriate tasks.

I will remember that wishing almost never makes it so. Wishing and working almost always do.

. . . concern should drive us into action and not into depression.

—Karen Horney

If a situation in our lives causes concern, be it mild disgruntlement or serious frustration, we should understand that our concern indicates that we need to act, responsibly. Events that attract our attention need our action.

Our actions can take many forms. Occasionally we will be called upon to take charge of a situation. More often, offering emotional support to another is all that's needed. Perhaps most frequently, our prayers are enough.

There is always a proper response to any circumstance that causes us concern. If we choose no response, our inaction will only heighten our concern. And preoccupation will hinder the day's activities.

My actions today should reflect my concerns and be appropriate to the need.

If the only tool you have is a hammer, you tend to see every problem as a nail.

—Abraham Maslow

When we can take a long view of our problems, we can sometimes see that we're using inappropriate tools to try to solve them. What's necessary for us to do is to move away, to detach. That may show us a whole new context into which our problem fits—and in which it may not even be a problem.

Detachment is hard to achieve when we're deeply hooked into a situation. When we send ourselves drastic messages like "now or never!" we're pressing our noses right up against the problem—a position in which it's difficult to maintain a balanced view. To stop and say, "If not now, then perhaps some other time," unhooks us and lets us remember that life is richer and more varied than we thought when we were hooked.

Crisis thinking can be like a hammer—it flattens everything. This can be our way of trying to control the outcome of our individual struggle. But when we remember that we make up only small parts of one grand and beautiful design, we can surrender our problems to it.

To be a competent worker, I will seek out the tools that are best suited to my task.

Eyes, what are they? Colored glass,
Where reflections come and pass.
Open windows—by them sit
Beauty, Learning, Love, and Wit.
                    —*Mary Elizabeth Coleridge*

How we appear in others' eyes can become an obsession. Do they see me as I see myself? Or do they see the Real Me—and is that worse, or better? Are the eyes of others mirrors, in which I'll find my own reflection? Or are they windows, through which I can touch the spirits of those I love?

We can never know the real lives of others, but we can trust that they are not so different from our own. The experiences we share are more powerful than those in which we differ; others struggle with the same temptations and surrender to the same destiny as we do.

If we esteem ourselves, we won't worry about others' opinions. Of course we want to be respected, loved by those we love, accepted as a fellow traveler on life's journey. But our main concern is our own spiritual growth—and it will be the key to how we are perceived.

Today, I'll look within and seek to please myself.

Do not dream of influencing other people. . . . Think of things in themselves.

—*Virginia Woolf*

One sort of plan is doomed to almost certain failure: the plan we have for someone else. An experienced breeder can predict a pedigreed puppy's future with reasonable accuracy, but a human child is quite a different matter. Any relationship that is built on our expectations for another turns into a bitter struggle, a disappointment, or both.

There is one person, and only one, on whose life we can have a strong, positive influence, and that is each one of us. What's more, we deserve our own support. We'll richly repay our efforts in our own behalf. Anything we can do for ourselves will stay with us; the more we learn, the wiser we'll become.

"Things in themselves" are the actual things in our lives, now: our work, our play, our relationships, our spiritual growth. These things deserve our best efforts. As we become more and more the persons we want to be, we will discover the spheres we are meant to inhabit, and learn to welcome those who share them with us.

My efforts in my own behalf are never wasted.

*Although the act of nurturing another's spiritual
growth has the effect of nurturing one's own, a major
characteristic of genuine love is that the distinction
between oneself and the other is always maintained
and preserved.*

—M. Scott Peck, M.D.

Those we love must be free to love us in return, or leave
us. The honest evidence of our love is our commitment to
encouraging another's full development. We are interdependent personalities who need one another's presence in order
to fulfill our destiny. And yet, we are also separate individuals. We must come to terms with our struggles alone.

One gift of life available to each of us is security, the
sense that accompanies the recognition of our spiritual
center. Helping someone else discover their spiritual gifts
strengthens our own. Nothing is too difficult when we act
in unison as separate entities, relying on the spiritual core
that strengthens us to meet any situation.

*My own spiritual center will be strengthened if I help someone
else develop theirs.*

Happiness is the meaning and the purpose of life, the whole aim and end of human existence.

—Aristotle

We find happiness with our friends, if we expect it there. The workplace guarantees it, too, if we go in search of it. Happiness visits us in our solitude and in our myriad involvements. Wherever we are, so is happiness, unless we've chosen to keep it out. Our attitudes are powerful, and will prevail in all matters, with all people.

Happiness is contagious. It spreads quickly when shared freely. When it catches up with us, the cares of the day are immediately lightened. We have lessons to learn in this life, and we have essential contributions to make, contributions that will ease another's burdens, foster happiness in another's heart. Likewise, someone else's lessons may well encourage our own happiness.

Every struggle is eased by laughter. I am never left to struggle alone, unless by choice. Today will be joyful and eventful if I live in the laughter.

When we think of cruelty, we must try to remember the stupidity, the envy, the frustration from which it has arisen.

—*Edith Sitwell*

Our outer behavior matches our inner state of mind and emotional well-being. Our expectations of others are consistent with our personal expectations. When we feel less than adequate because of our imperfections, we treat others like failures, too. How someone treats us today indicates how that person feels about herself or himself.

Self-love is lacking wherever people criticize others destructively, and self-love is necessary before we can offer love to any of the people in our lives. Developing self-love requires discipline. Our existence verifies our value as human beings. Understanding that our lives do have purpose contributes to our ability to love ourselves.

Today is day one for me to develop my loving behavior.

If you shut your door to all errors, truth will be shut out.

—Rabindranath Tagore

Since so much of the world remains mysterious, how can we rule out new possibilities? It's very human to want to cling to the little bits of truth we're sure of; but we mustn't use those bits of knowledge to keep us from the possibility of further discoveries.

True wisdom includes the humility to acknowledge what we don't know. The careful scientist and the experienced physician are humble before the immensity of what they don't know.

New experiences, new relations and connections can reveal more and more, if we are open to them. Once we decide we know something—and close our minds to the possibility that we don't—we're keeping ourselves willfully ignorant. Filtering out life's richness robs us of our birthright—experience. Nothing is true that can't stand to be tested against life's flow.

Even welcome visitors can only enter through a door I've opened.

Relationships are only as alive as the people engaging in them.
—Donald B. Ardell

We receive from every experience in proportion to what we give. In other words, the richness of our lives is necessarily dependent on the depth of our commitment. Reserved involvement guarantees only limited rewards, while wholehearted efforts promise full-scale returns. In all aspects of our lives, we'll find this to be true.

Our relationships gift us justly. These experiences with others are woven together, and their beauty is equal to the beauty we bring to one another's company. However, if we bring only criticism and bleak hopelessness to a relationship, we'll find despair rather than joy. Every relationship is the sum and substance of the partners involved. No relationship is more fruitful than the efforts of those doing the pruning.

How much do I give to the relationships I deem meaningful? They bless me in just proportion to what I give. Today gives me a chance to make a greater contribution.

Self-determination does not mean exercising intellectual mastery at all times over bodily, earthly processes, though the capacity for that mastery expands our human possibilities.

—Linda Gordon

Growth means learning the limits of our will. What appears to be mastery—flying in an airplane, for example—is merely cooperation with natural forces. Human intellect does not *master* natural processes; we tap into them, learn them, bring our own aims into harmony with them.

The world is not a jungle, to be hacked, cleared, or bulldozed. Human beings are learning not to clear jungles that way either. The world is us extended over the globe. We can spend our whole lives discovering the wonderful oneness of creation.

The awareness of this unity expands our human possibility, for each case is an example of our growing harmony with nature.

I will pray for harmonious resolution of my human possibilities with the great forces of nature.

God creates. People rearrange.

—Joseph Casey

Being alive is our invitation to act in fresh, inventive ways. All it takes is concentrating on our inner vision in combination with external reality. The components for accomplishing any task are at our fingertips, awaiting discovery.

Our burdens are lightened when we understand that all situations are resolvable—no mystery need leave us in the dark for long. Just as surely as we each exist, so exists every element we need to solve any problem or chart any new course. Our purpose in life is to select those elements that will satisfy the need. We each have been blessed with this capability for proper selection.

The day promises challenge and many choices. I can successfully handle all possibilities.

I want somehow to tell the story of how the dispossessed become possessed of their own history without losing sight, without forgetting the meaning or the nature of their journey.
—Sherley Anne Williams

To use the past without being controlled by it—that is our responsibility to history. Because the past is irrecoverably vanished, it's sometimes tempting to forget it or to falsify it. But being true to ourselves means being true to our history.

Past cruelties can remain powerful in our lives—yet to take possession of our history means to free ourselves of bondage to past events. Nothing can ever change them. If we are to make the future good, we'll learn what the past can teach us. But our freedom requires us to make choices based on the needs of the present, not the past.

I can act at every moment in such a way as to honor the past and enhance the future.

Patience is a particular requirement. Without it you can destroy in an hour what it might take you weeks to repair.

—*Charlie W. Shedd*

Enjoying the moment, in its fullest, makes possible a peaceful and patient pace. Progress is guaranteed if our minds are centered, in the present, on the only event deserving of our attention. We can be certain that error and frustration will haunt us if our attentions are divided.

Patience will see us through a troubled time, but how much easier it is to savor patience when it's accompanied by faith. We can know and fully trust that all is well—that our lives are on course—that individual experiences are exactly what we need at this moment. However, faith makes the knowing easier and the softness of the patient heart eases us through the times of challenge and uncertainty.

Patience slows me down long enough to notice another, and to be grateful for the gifts of the moment. Patience promises me the power to move forward with purpose. Today's fruits will be in proportion to my patience.

*It is time to show the strength of water and flow away.
. . . To stand is to be crushed, but to flow out is to
gather new strength.*

—Marge Piercy

Water is one of the strongest elements on earth: it can't be broken; it can assume many shapes; it joins easily with itself. When it reaches a certain mass, moving water presents an irresistible force.

We might do well to learn to acquire the strength of water temporarily; to be able to lose ourselves for a time, in concert with others, and then to reclaim our identities. We needn't fear their loss. We are unique personalities, and our selfhood is intact.

How successful I would be if I could use the strength of water when I need it; the purity of air, the solidity of earth, and the appetite of fire.

One's mind may be given readily and it may be given with zest. Not all control is oppression. Sometimes it is release.

—Gilbert Ryle

Our most dangerous delusion is that we can control others. The hard-won truth is that we can control only ourselves— and it may take us a lifetime to learn this. Self-control means release, however; release from the bondage of uncontrolled and thoughtless behavior. When we recognize that our only legitimate power is over ourselves, we become free to grow spiritually and to increase that power.

Lack of control is not freedom; it is chaos. Conflicting impulses squander energies instead of controlling them and directing them toward growth. We can't subdue our unruly selves by fighting them: accept them, love them as part of our human imperfection, our superb and jagged individuality.

As we come to recognize the benefits of self-control, we'll choose it more and more often. We'll become more fully in control of our lives, better able to direct our energies and do what we want to do.

Only by choosing self-control will I achieve freedom.

*Love is mutually feeding each other, not one living on
another like a ghoul.*

—Bessie Head

Real love is compromise. It's sharing and taking turns.
It's putting someone else's best interests first. Love wears
many expressions and is demonstrated by many gestures.
Offering love to someone, when the offer is genuine, benefits the giver as much as the receiver. Our calloused souls
are softened by the gentle nature of our love. No one of us
develops mentally and emotionally to our full stature if we
cultivate isolation rather than intimacy.

We learn who we are through our involvement with
others. We come to terms with our defects and have opportunities to enhance our assets while experiencing the
strengths and shortcomings of others. What time and
patience teach is that love is generally slow to develop but
will result when there is a mutual decision to live and grow
in one another's company. Each person we genuinely love
makes our own survival easier.

*My love is best expressed when I help someone else live life more
comfortably.*

The art of pleasing consists in being pleased.
—William Hazlitt

Others' pleasure in our company becomes our pleasure. If we can set aside our self-conscious anxieties and simply enjoy being with others, they will enjoy us. As lovers know, there is no aphrodisiac like a loved one's desire.

When we give one another our full attention, we enhance one another's humanity. Much of life consists of routine transactions, in which people hardly recognize each other as human. Even intimate relationships can come to suffer if we withhold ourselves.

When we discover pleasure in each other's company, we kindle a spark of joy that illuminates far more than the moment.

Today I will decide to be fully human in all my encounters.

. . . you don't get to choose how you're going to die, or when. You can only decide how you're going to live. Now.

—*Joan Baez*

The responsibility we each are charged with for our individual development is awesome, particularly when we look ahead to our whole life stretching before us. It's not uncommon to be immobilized with the fear of making a wrong decision, heading down a dead-end path. It's with great relief that we realize that the tomorrows will take care of themselves if today is well lived.

Lives well lived, a hope that's cherished by us all, are not beyond our simple grasp. Attention to the demands of the moment only, coupled with the decision to behave in ways that will fill us with pride, will ensure that our experiences are generally smooth. The attitude we carry into any situation will influence the outcome, our growth, but most of all the quality of our whole lives.

I need to concern myself with today, only. And live it well.

"Freedom ain't nothing but knowing how to say what's up in your head."

—*Ralph Ellison*

The freedom to speak our minds is a precious gift. Throughout the world, throughout history, it has been and is a rare privilege. The privilege should oblige us in return to broaden and strengthen our minds, so that what we speak is worthy of free people.

The obligation is not to be perfect; the search for truth proceeds by trial and error. It is to be generous, forgiving, and honest. A moment's thought before we speak might save us and those around us many petty words.

We can't choose our feelings. From time to time we'll be swept by feelings that we wouldn't choose. But we can choose our actions. We can always choose to speak or not. Often it's wiser not to speak out of negative feelings. If we remind ourselves that free speech was a hard-won right, we may have more respect for the way we enjoy it.

A moment's reflection may keep me from abusing my rights— or others'.

Nothing happens to any man that he is not formed by nature to bear.

—*Marcus Aurelius Antoninus*

Reflecting on the past reveals that indeed we do find the strength and the ability to cope with whatever experiences ripple our calm. Moreover, we have come to accept that the tides of turmoil wash in new awarenesses, heightened perceptions, measurable calm.

Tragedies are guaranteed to trigger first pain, then perceptible growth, and finally, tranquility. Over and over again we pass through these stages that are designed to nurture our fuller development as healthy human beings. Over and over we see that the tough times teach us what we're ready to learn.

We can look to the day ahead fully expecting to be strengthened enough to handle whatever we've been readied to experience. Nothing will present itself that can't be coped with.

Today I can be certain of growing. I will meet the challenges in unison with my inner strength.

". . . you never get over bein' a child long's you have a mother to go to."

—Sarah Orne Jewett

For most of us, our mothers were the first love, and the quality of our relationships throughout life is influenced by that earliest one. A mark of real maturity is the ability to see our mothers simply as human beings—lovable, fallible, interesting, and imperfect, just like ourselves.

Some or us have suffered a mother's early death; some of us cope bravely with her long illness. Few of us have a simple, easy relationship with our mothers. Too much is at stake. The infant who needs its mother's arms lives on within us all.

Few of us have such a continuous bond with our mothers, but we're fortunate if we can have an adult relationship that includes the love and nurturing we crave, because we never get past the need for it. The most successful intimacy seems to be based on reciprocal nurturing, for we need to give as well as to receive.

The child I was lives within me, and so does the mothering caretaker I first loved.

All great reforms require one to dare a lot to win a little.

—William L. O'Neill

Unfortunately, life does not come with a money-back guarantee. Going after what we want, especially if we're up against established interests, is likely to demand the commitment of our best energies—with no certainty of getting it.

Oddly enough, some of the happiest people we are ever likely to meet are those who devote their lives to seemingly hopeless causes. For such people, daring a lot can mean staking their lives on a belief. The outcomes are bound to be small in proportion: failure, perhaps. At best, limited achievement.

But none of this seems to matter. In fact, a happy person with a cause seems to have totally let go of the outcome. The joy is in the struggle, in the process. They learn so much; and by living for something outside themselves, their own small problems miraculously fall into line.

Today I'll keep in mind that achievement is risky, but dedication wonderfully liberating.

One cannot have wisdom without living life.
—Dorothy McCall

Understanding circumstances, other people, even ourselves comes with the passage of time and our willingness to be open to all the lessons contained within a moment. We must be willing to participate fully in the events that have requested our attendance. Then we can discover the longed-for clarity about life and our role in it. Immersion in the moment accompanied by reflective quiet times promises a perspective that offers us wisdom.

We all long for happiness, an easier life, and wisdom. We learn so slowly that both happiness and the easier life are generally matters of attitude. Therein lies our sought-after wisdom. How much simpler it makes living through even our most feared experiences when we have acquired the wisdom to know that the mind we carry into the moment, any moment, will be reflected in the outcome.

It takes patience and willingness to live fully enough to reap the benefits that accompany wisdom.

Today I'll practice patience.

What most of us want is to be heard, to communicate.
—Dory Previn

The need to know that we count in the lives of others, that our presence has not gone unnoticed, is universal. Few of us are blessed from birth with full knowledge of our connectedness to all life. Instead, we falter and fumble our way through our experiences, uncertain of our worth and meaning. Acceptance by others is our want. Unconditional love is our due.

Since we all share this same need to be acknowledged, it's best we each offer acknowledgement to those sharing our experiences today. They aren't unlike us; their needs and insecurities match our own. We'd all survive the harsh bumps of life with so much greater ease if we felt the comfort of others. In the company of others nothing is too much for any one of us to handle.

Today I'll remember that others need my comfort and willingness to listen just as much as I need theirs.

There are two tragedies in life. One is not to get your heart's desire. The other is to get it.
—George Bernard Shaw

Desire is strong; we all feel it. Desire can impel us toward positive, life-enhancing experiences, or it can fasten on vain and unproductive ends. Material things will never satisfy desire; only a serene spirit and a detachment from outcomes will enable us to live peaceably beside the torrent that is our desire.

In itself, desire is neither good nor bad. How we direct our desire, and whether we join it to our love or to our anger, determines the effect it will have in our lives.

If our desire is continually unfulfilled, perhaps we should examine, deeply and honestly, the direction we've allowed it to take. If achieving our desire leaves us feeling hollow, we should do the same. Desire can nourish us if we understand it as a continuous process, a part of our spiritual growth.

Let me be sure that what I desire is worthy of my best self.

The best thing for you, my children, is to serve God from your heart, without falsehood or shame, not giving out to people that you are one thing while, God forbid, in your heart you are another.
—*Glückel of Hameln*

We pray for wholeness of the spirit: to be able to live cleanly, with no shame, and to meet every aspect of life with the same serene face. It isn't easy for most of us. We fuss. We trip ourselves up. We may find ourselves telling lies, creating emotional turmoil to escape what we see as even greater turmoil.

The first step toward wholeness is for us to admit that we are human. No, not perfect; yes, about as flawed as everybody else. Once the knowledge is part of us that we're part of suffering, seeking humanity, a lot of falsehood and turmoil shears away.

There isn't any big secret to protect; there's just you, just me. However different we may appear, we're more than kin. And we can keep each other honest. The habit of honesty, once formed, is harder to break than the habit of lying.

I shall resolve to show the same face everywhere, and I'll become serene.

My children weary me. I can only see them as defective adults . . .

—Evelyn Waugh

If we expect children to behave as adults, of course we will find them tiresome. If we expect water to be milk, we will be continually disappointed. But—since we can control and direct our expectations—why should we set ourselves up for such inevitable annoyances?

But we do. We are constantly expecting things unreasonably, and then being disappointed, shocked, heartbroken, and betrayed. It would be so much more rational simply to take things as they come, without expectations.

But that would involve a degree of detachment that most of us would find impossible—even repulsive. It would mean unhooking our feelings from other people's behavior. "But I *care* about her," we say. "Of course I want her to . . ." It doesn't much matter what we want her to do; get married, get divorced, brush her teeth at night, or come in before midnight.

What matters is our involvement, our expectations. We can care about her and still not feel hurt by her actions that may not be what *we* want. Hurtful actions are another matter; but she has a right to be who she is, just as we all do.

My expectations today will be only for myself.

Gold, for the instant, lost its luster in his eyes, for there were countless treasures of the heart which it could never purchase.

—*Charles Dickens*

The mysterious thing about "treasures of the heart" is that they are "countless"—boundless, self-renewing, inexhaustible. When we love and are loved, trust and are trusted, this reciprocal relationship gives us and those who love and trust us a literally endless wealth.

Only when the relationship is one-sided do we feel drained by our commitments. Love that is based on mutual understanding and respect will never drain us of our resources; our fund of love is replenished even as it flows out of us, as though the act of loving generates more love.

Fear can impede this miraculous process. In general, we have to know ourselves pretty well and be quite secure in our own skins before we can make to someone else the glad and unconditional gift of ourselves. Love entails risk—the risk of being completely open, and completely self-forgetful. But all success involves risk; and in this case the rewards are the greatest possible.

I will not let fear keep me from the treasures of the heart.

Within our dreams and aspirations we find our opportunities.
                                        —*Sue Atchley Ebaugh*

Our dreams invite us to broaden our horizons to reach beyond our present goals. They are much more than whims. They are probably calling us to those opportunities for which our talents have been readied. Most of us need this encouragement to attempt new ventures.

We've each been invited to this present moment by design. Our lives are joined like the tiles of a mosaic; none of us contributes the whole of the picture but each of us is necessary for its completion. More importantly, the depth, the richness of the picture in its entirety, is enhanced by our fulfilled dreams.

With joy and excitement we can anticipate our frequent aspirations, recognizing them as the guideposts offering directions for our daily travels.

Today I will welcome my dreams. They indicate tomorrow's successful ventures.

Every outlook, desirable or undesirable, remains possible for anyone, no matter what his present outlook is.

—Dr. George Weinberg

The attitude with which we greet the day, approach a situation, or respond to a friend or co-worker is fully within our control. We exercise absolute control over little in our lives, but our attitudes represent personal choice each moment.

Recognizing the power inherent in personal choice is exhilarating. It means we are free from domination by others, if such is our choice. Freedom to act, to think, to dream our own dreams is ours when we exercise it.

I celebrate my power today. I am free to choose my every response to each encounter. Hallelujah!

Life is curious when it is reduced to its essentials.
　　　　　　　　　　　　　　　—Jean Rhys

Life is always reduced to its essentials. We're frail creatures: without water and shelter, we can't survive. We may not think of our lives in these minimalist terms, but accidents of many kinds can disrupt our fragile web of protection.

It makes sense, then, to assure ourselves of the best quality of life while we have it. This does not mean luxury or plenty; a high quality of life accompanies a high standard of behavior and relationships.

Clarity and honesty in our dealings with others will assure the quality of our lives. Simplicity is more satisfying than complexity. The less we get in our own way, the more clearly we can see these elegant essentials of life—elegant in that they are never extraneous. Life is indeed curious in the way it engages our full attention.

Like a curious child, life presents me with the most interesting questions. I'll be patient, and the answers will come.

We are apt to call barbarous whatever departs widely from our own taste and apprehension. But soon [we] find the epithet of reproach retorted on us.

—David Hume

Judging others is a hazardous game that's likely to backfire. Labeling others is a form of judgment. It's a way of sticking people into pigeonholes and saving ourselves the effort of thought. Do we really want to be thoughtlessly tossed by others into some category not of our choosing?

The world's rich texture holds much that each of us will love, and much to which we'll be indifferent. How much more pleasant it is to look for—and to find—what we like, than to sneer at and judge what we don't. A need to judge others is a sign that we lack confidence in our own taste—an indication of shaky self-esteem.

Our personal growth asks us to look positively at life. We want to find occasions for rejoicing, not disapproving. The thoughtless and intolerant teach others that they themselves are not worthy of respect.

I will set aside my judgment of others and concentrate instead on freeing myself.

> *. . . you must remember that an arbitrary power is like most other things which are very hard, very liable to be broken.*
>
> —*Abigail Adams*

Sway is built into tall buildings so they won't break. Rigid structures are never as strong as flexible ones. The strongest minds are also the most nimble, the most ready to change and to include new information.

We only see one little slice of reality. How can we know what's right for others? Our spirits will be strong to the extent that we can keep them flexible, ready to incorporate new energies and to make fresh associations.

To be flexible doesn't mean to be wishy-washy or indecisive; often people who refuse to grow will say they want to "remain flexible." But one can be flexible and still have strong direction, generosity, and broad tolerance for others' growth. What cannot bend may break.

I'll respect the truth of your living, growing spirit. Your reality can be your gift to me.

If our species does destroy itself, it will be a death in the cradle—a case of infant mortality.
—*Jonathan Schell*

Compared to rocks or to termites or ginkgo trees, our whole species is a very recent passenger on this Spaceship Earth. We've had a busy time of it, for the few thousand years that there have been enough of us to make a difference. But in time as geologists measure it we have barely entered the history of the planet.

If we eradicated ourselves with the lethal means at our disposal, we wouldn't be the first species to disappear. But wouldn't it be a shame? We humans have the capacity for transcendence as well as destruction. Surely we're adaptable enough to guide our own development away from our current preoccupation with deadly toys.

Written history gives us just a tiny glimpse of life on earth. Let's live so as to guarantee that human existence lasts out its full chapter.

I am one of the earth's children. I will treat my parent with respect.

It is good to have an end to journey towards; but it is the journey that matters, in the end.
—Ursala K. LeGuin

Our goals lend direction to our lives. Without them we flounder, often uncertain of who we are. They provide substance for our self-definition and they motivate us, at times even deeply exhilarate us. Nevertheless, it's the many steps, the myriad activities, the unexpected barriers along the daily journey that give real meaning to our lives. We are so much more than our completed achievements, and the process is what develops the person within.

It's far too easy for most of us to miss the moment and its richness because our sights are on a particular journey's end. How often do we fail to appreciate the many occasions for feeling satisfaction over a task well done? We seldom grasp the full joy of living because our sights are glued to the future.

It is a hard but easily forgotten lesson that a goal completed is always followed by a letdown. The joy resides in the process.

Can I stay with the moment and the activity before me, just for today?

When I trust and respect myself enough to be myself honestly, others respond with trust and respect.
—*John Stevens*

We can greet all situations today with ease if we have committed ourselves to lives of integrity. Having made the decision to be fully honest at all times eliminates our uncertainty in responding to others, and thus we don't cloud issues and confuse our contemporaries with inconsistencies.

Without fail we recognize others' integrity as ours is recognized. It goes without saying that each of us is more at ease with those we trust.

Honesty invites honesty. Self-respect encourages respectful behavior toward others, and like a boomerang, it returns to the initiator. We teach others how to treat us. With every action we take, every word we speak, we are informing others of our personhood.

I will set the tone for my day by my behavior toward self and others. Over this I am all-powerful.

Being human is itself difficult, and therefore all kinds
of settlements (except dream cities) have problems.
—Jane Jacobs

A sure cure for rage at the minor irritations of daily life is
to sit back from the traffic jam, the broken appointment,
the lost vital information, and say, "Being human is itself
difficult." It may not cure our frustrations for long, but it's
worth practicing.

Many of our troubles stem from forgetting just how difficult it is. We often have impossibly high standards for behavior, especially our own. We are complicated, marvelous
creatures who have many skills, but we thwart our own
capacity for enjoyment by expecting that we will be perfect.

Being human is difficult; we perform it imperfectly. And
when we combine our effort with others'—building a building, performing a play—we multiply our imperfections as
well as our skills. Yet we need each other.

If we can detach ourselves from anger and disappointment and reflect on how wonderful it is that we can do
anything at all, we may remember to love ourselves and
others for our human complexity and simplicity.

Nobody's perfect; such is the nature of my humanity.

. . . we will be victorious if we have not forgotten how to learn.

—*Rosa Luxemburg*

There is no goal beyond our grasp, no achievement beyond our attainment if we reduce our natural barriers against new information and new perspectives. Our victories accompany perseverance, fearless learning, openness to the unfamiliar.

Each of us is experiencing a particular period with a select group of people, by design, not by chance. Myriad situations call us, and messages secure our attention because they contribute to our potential for victory. What's asked of us is rapt attention to the moment, intense openness to its richness, and a willingness to be edified or humored or perhaps simply nurtured. We will gain from every moment's offering whatever we need for our continued growth and ultimate victory.

Learning is forever in my control. The decision is personal and perhaps must be made each day, anew. The choice is mine.

*When you have become willing to hide nothing, you
will not only be willing to enter into communion but
will also understand peace and joy.*

—*Anonymous*

Keeping secrets is synonymous with keeping stuck. Our
human potential is stifled by our stuffed feelings, attitudes,
ideas. Conversely, the more we allow others to really know
us, the greater will be our opportunities for growth and
happiness. Our secrets burden us.

The choice to shield our inner selves from others is ours
to make. Risking vulnerability takes strength, and a great
deal of courage. We can never be certain that our audience
won't betray us. However, we can be certain that words and
thoughts hidden will haunt us.

The gift of total honesty and openness is profound intimacy. It's this gift that makes possible a level of friendship
that dispels self-doubts, that gives rise to a euphoria that
turns all situations into opportunities for greater happiness.

*I may be tempted to keep some secrets today. I will remember
that sharing them will relieve me of a burden that weighs
me down.*

. . . we do not always like what is good for us in this world.

—Eleanor Roosevelt

Today will call each of us to make our particular contributions to the moment. There is no guarantee that we will enjoy every experience, but we can be certain each one of them will teach us something we're ready to learn because "when the student is ready, the teacher appears."

Little reflection is necessary for us to realize that our most troubling times have generally been responsible for our greatest growth. Our achievements are always accompanied by periods of frustration, occasional loss of direction, even momentary despair because the actual results miss the mark of our hopes. However, the passage of time makes clear that these actual results benefit us far more than those we'd hoped for.

Our personal vision is narrow and limiting. We can't really imagine what's in store for us. The most we can do is trust that our experiences have our best interests in tow.

I'll remember: Today I'm a student and my experiences are my teachers.

The person who fears to try is thus enslaved.
—Leonard E. Read

Immobilization is fear's result. In its grip we fail to move forward. We fail to think new thoughts, live new experiences, chance new personalities. All that life is prepared to offer us goes ungreeted.

Let us remember, we have been given the gift of life and we are obliged to test our wings and spring forth, displaying the message that's within. Even when fear crouches close at our heels, we can elude its grasp if we remember this message that eternally accompanies us: "All is well."

Life is a series of opportunities for emotional, spiritual, and intellectual growth. No opportunity for action is beyond our capabilities.

I will look to this day only. I will be invited to participate in those experiences designed for my particular development. All is well.

A house is no home unless it contains food and fire for the mind as well as for the body.

—Margaret Fuller

No matter how full our social and professional lives are, we all need a base, a place where we are at home. Whether it's a studio apartment furnished from secondhand stores and garage sales or a luxurious country retreat, one of our basic human urges is the need to make a home. And our spiritual fulfillment asks that our home nourish us.

Look around: in our choices for our home we reveal what nourishes and inspires us. Perhaps we opt for the comfortable and well-used: old books, chairs that speak more to the back and bottom than to the eye. Perhaps we are restless and change the way our homes look frequently. We all use our homes to express our desires.

Are we neglecting "food and fire for the mind"? Sometimes we misinterpret inertia as comfort. Are we giving our minds a wholesome environment?

Fuel for my spirit is never wholly consumed. Today, I will look to my supply.

If you can imagine it, you can achieve it.
If you can dream it, you can become it.
                                        —William Arthur Ward

Our dreams and our aspirations are our invitations to set new goals, attempt new tasks, dare to travel uncharted courses. We each have gifts to offer our fellow-travelers, but most frequently need encouragement to recognize our own strengths and talents.

Seldom do we rise in the morning fully eager to join in the opportunities that await us. More likely we have to prepare our minds, center our emotional selves, nurture the inner person who may fear the experiences the day promises.

It's normal—completely human—to be conscious of our incompetencies while lacking awareness of our abilities. To them we give scant attention, generally blocking out the praise they elicit. To our failings, however small, we compulsively devote our attentive minds. We forget that today's abilities were last year's incompetencies.

Achievements today will be many, and they are indications of past dreams. My hopes today guide me toward future achievements. My failings are few and help to keep me on track.

Freedom is like taking a bath—you have to keep doing it every day!

—Flo Kennedy

Nothing stands still. Change is the law of life. We may sometimes feel that our personal gains have to be won over and over again. But looked at from another perspective, that's not so: our solid personal gains are the ones that no one and nothing can take away from us.

They are tools for continued growth. Jobs, lovers, houses may change, but serenity and freedom of spirit are within our power to achieve—to maintain—or to give away.

Freedom means choice; our choice of what we do with our bodies, our money, our lives. If we decline to choose, the choice will be made for us. If we don't use or claim our freedom, we are giving it away. Our lives need our active, creative participation every moment.

Like bathing, I must daily exercise my freedom. No one can do it for me.

In the transformation and growth of all things, every bud and feature has its proper form.
—Fritjof Capra

Our lives are a series of unfoldings. Our struggle to be perfect at every stage of life is a common element of the human condition. What comes with age and wisdom is acceptance of our imperfections. We see that we develop at every stage of life.

We can rejoice that we're unfolding according to the needs of our existence. Each day is ushering in new growth, subtle changes. Our transformation is lifelong and according to specifications known to the inner self—our connection to Universal Wisdom.

The changes we'll experience today are compatible with the new growth we adapted to yesterday. And likewise, what will come next week, next year will have been prepared for by the tiny transformations accumulated on this road to maturity. We are developing exactly as we need to each step of the way. And our fit, yours and mine, one with another, is perfect at every moment.

I am changing, growing, maturing at every moment—according to plan.

We must assist natural processes that serve the function of reunification.
—*Joseph G. Hancock*

Some families in mild climates have begun to experiment with unified living: recycling wastes, growing food, and using only renewable sources like the sun and the wind for power. Seen from the twelfth floor of an apartment building, in sub-zero weather, this is a radical gesture. Yet it's a conservative way of living, asking for little, spoiling nothing, and putting back into the earth everything that's taken out.

We can all put back what we take out, but are we as careful of our emotional and spiritual processes? Or do we sometimes block them or try to erase them or hoard them up? The universe is one sphere. Energy flows through it, through polar bears and bacteria and Republicans and cranberries. Surrendering to the flow is our only way of achieving personal reunification.

I can assist natural processes by giving my assent, freely choosing unity.

Time is a dressmaker specializing in alterations.
—Faith Baldwin

We are learning as we go, and the experiences shed light on our own plans for proceeding. The steps we are taking, in unison as well as on separate but parallel paths, enhance the particular movements of us all.

We often expect perfection from ourselves, forgetting that we're all beginners in life. The best we can do is willingly acknowledge our errors, grateful that we can always begin again on any task—grateful that we have the experiences of others to help guide us.

Life is process. We learn, we grow, share burdens, reformulate ideas, and restructure our values. Every change we make alters the steps we take, altering in turn someone else's movements, too.

Today I'll discover a change I need to make, one that will reach further than my own task.

He was the victim of his own rage. . . .
—Paule Marshall

Our negative behavior always turns on us. So does our positive behavior. Obviously, it's better to have joy and peace rebound on us than violence. Then why don't we consistently act peaceful and joyous?

It probably takes an idiot or a saint to be consistently positive in this world of cynicism, cruelty, and corruption. However we may strive to free ourselves of preoccupation with things beyond our control, we all find ourselves reacting to certain events with rage, envy, fear, or other painful, destructive emotions. But knowing we have a choice can free us from bondage to this pain.

We can choose to respond ragefully or enviously—or we can choose to feel the feeling and then to let it go, so that the negative feeling doesn't control our behavior. Successful living involves learning to control how we behave; if we hide or deny our feelings, they're with us forever. It's only by letting them go that we can be truly free. And it's only by experiencing them that we can let them go.

I can only spread joy if I stop being a victim of my own despair.

If you would be loved, love and be lovable.
—Benjamin Franklin

We all desire to be loved. Our common human characteristic is our need to count in someone else's life. At least one other person needs us, we tell ourselves, when we feel least able to accept life's demands. How alike we all are. The paradox is that our own need for love is lessened when we bestow it on others. Give it away and it returns. A promise, one we can trust.

The reality about love and its path from sender to receiver and back again is often distant from our minds. More often we stew and become obsessed with the lack of love's evidence in our lives. Why isn't he smiling? Why didn't she care? Has someone more interesting taken our place? Choosing to offer love, rather than to look for it, will influence every experience we have. Life will feel gentler, and the rewards will be many and far-reaching.

Loving others promises me the love I desire. But I can't expect it if I don't give it first.

. . . [I]t was not so much that they drifted, as that in the presence of a boat the world drifted, forgot. The dreamed-about changed places with the dreamer.
—Eudora Welty

Dreams can be so potent and mysterious that many of us, at one time or another, have felt that they put us in touch with some other level of reality. Sometimes we wonder if we're dreaming our waking lives, too. Some of us have had the fantasy that we're characters in someone else's dream, or in some great world-dream.

Sometimes our dreams show us what we want; or what we fear. Dreams are like messages sent from one part of us to another: scrambled messages in which the people, places, and happenings from many epochs of our lives come together.

Sometimes we may dream a great happiness, or a wonderful solution to a problem. Such dreams cast a rosy glow over our whole day; as a nightmare can make us feel uneasy for a long time. Such dreams may be messages about feelings we're not feeling. The dreamed-about—fear or joy—does seem to change places with the dreamers, who have shut the feeling out of their waking lives.

Owning our dreams, cherishing them, is part of fully accepting ourselves. However silly, scary, sexy, or confusing a dream may be, it is our dream, we made it.

I don't need to crack the code to get the message.

Speak kindly today; when tomorrow comes you will be in practice.

—*Anonymous*

Behavior is habitual: we thoughtlessly brush our teeth, set our alarm clock, start our car, or dress in order. We create rituals in our lives, and they free us from thousands of small decisions, leaving our minds less cluttered for the more important choices. However, every action we choose sets into motion a behavior that may become habit. We should be wary of habits that harm ourselves or others.

We have the personal power, with every decision, to choose to act in ways that promote well-being—our own and others. For instance, a tense situation might be better served by a smile and a deep breath than by a harsh response. Knowledge of our freedom to choose such a response exhilarates us. We should be mindful that every response that is frequently made is approaching habit, and our habits determine the ease with which we greet and adapt to the conditions life offers.

I am a creature of habit. The power is mine to create positive habits. I will make careful choices today.

I refuse to pronounce the names of possession and nonpossession.

—Monique Wittig

New relationships require new names. If we want to stop behaving in a customary way—as an adversary, as a victim, as a bully, as a martyr—then we need new words to describe our new behavior.

Perhaps we glimpse the possibility of a new relationship to power—that one might use power, yet not subjugate others. Perhaps we glimpse the possibility of sharing, of lateral extensions rather that hierarchies.

It's clear that if we are to change the world, we must begin by changing our relations with others. Perhaps we don't want such a grand project as changing the world, but we might want to change old ways of using our skills. Let us be fearless and trust in the knowledge of our hearts.

The only way I can discover the consequences of change is to change.

Make yourself necessary to someone.
—*Ralph Waldo Emerson*

We are each positioned, not by chance but by design, within the context of home, job, friends, and acquaintances. Our involvement with life around us, the myriad experiences that confront us, guides our growth. The gift of life obligates us to contribute our best efforts, our talents to the situations involving us. From them we'll gain exactly those lessons we are ready to handle.

Creation is interdependent. Every element, every human, every organism is necessary to the completion of the whole. How comforting to know that our existence is not mere chance. The space we take here, now, is advancing the development of all aspects of life. We never need to doubt our value, our importance to others. Being alive is the ultimate proof that each of us is necessary to the many persons in our lives. Gratitude for them, and for us, will strengthen our understanding.

I will look upon my many human contacts today with real understanding. I am here by design.

*If an idea, I reasoned, were really a valuable one,
there must be some way of realizing it.*
—Elizabeth Blackwell

These words were written by the first woman who earned a medical degree. They're useful to anyone who fears that their most precious dreams are doomed to failure.

If our dreams are valuable ideas, they will be useful goals. If they're childish fantasies, they won't, although those can be fun. It's important to distinguish the ones we can achieve from the ones we can't. The first kind will nourish us, like bread; the others, like candy, won't.

We have a responsibility to those nourishing dreams, because they come from what's best in us. Our responsibility is to live so that the dream might be realized. When dreams become goals, they have a way of calling us forth. Goals organize our lives, so that we may reach them.

———

Reaching my goal is never as important as the progress I make toward it.

Happiness is not a matter of events; it depends upon the tides of the mind.

—Alice Meynell

It's all too easy to blame a friend, spouse, or co-worker for the uneven quality of our lives. If only others would behave according to our plans and dictates, then all would go well, we think. What seldom is remembered or even understood is that each of us has an individual perspective on any single event—our own. We need to stretch our minds and hearts to understand an experience from another's point of view. However, we need never fully understand how another perceives life. We need only to accept that another's perspective is legitimate.

Our happiness is not dependent on the perceptions or the actions of someone else. Nor is it dependent on attention, or lack of it, from a loved one. Our occupation may be challenging and fulfilling; however, the joy we get from it depends on the attitude we carry to the job. In every way, whether in the company of others or by ourselves, we make our own happiness.

My opportunity for happiness is guaranteed if I opt for it today.

We must be true inside, true to ourselves, before we can know a truth that is outside us.

—*Thomas Merton*

Integrity is not a given in everyone's life. It is the result of self-discipline, inner trust, and a decision to be relentlessly honest in our response to all situations in our lives. We are quick to recognize this quality in others, and hope to acquire it ourselves. However, we must cultivate risk-taking and cast off fears of rejection and derision if we're to discover the serenity a fully integral life offers.

Recognition of truth in others, realization of the appropriateness of decisions or the aptness of choices is made easier when we're certain of the truth of our own lives. The inner turmoil dissipates and we are quiet within when we choose to live lives full of truth. And in the quiet we discern all truths. How much softer the edges of experience when we're guided by truth. How much easier every decision, every choice, when we've committed ourselves to a course of total honesty.

My level of peace is my responsibility. I will find just as much as I need.

You can have your cake and eat it. But my God, it will go rotten inside you.

—*D. H. Lawrence*

When we try to hang on to another person or to any part of life, we impede the natural flow. To be in harmony, we must let go. "You must lose your life in order to find it." Real strength, real self-respect, is achieved only by setting the hungry self aside.

It's human to want to hold on to what's precious. But life's real treasure is found in achieving the rhythm of ebb and flow. Joy can't be a constant state. Glory is part of a cycle that includes defeat.

Accepting imperfection, accepting change, is part of accepting our humanity. We obey the same cyclic laws that govern the universe. Success in living depends on accepting that one day we'll eat cake and the next we won't. Fear tempts us to hoard the crumbs of our success, but wisdom lets us brush them away.

I will remember that joys recur just as sorrows do.

We must build human relevance into the paradigms of science itself.

—Steven Rose and Hilary Rose

Science itself is not to be feared. We fear what science is capable of—just as we fear what human beings are capable of, when they act on their violent feelings, without control or choice. Science is a powerful tool of the human mind, when it's used with respect and tenderness for the unity of life.

It isn't human relevance we need so much as relevance to this seamless unity. As our capacity for knowledge grows, we glimpse more clearly how interrelated all human efforts are with the great rhythmic processes of the planet. The paradigms of science are the models it makes of the world. When scientists make a model that ignores relevance, they risk using their knowledge stupidly, or harmfully.

We need to recognize that science is part of our human endeavor—not more nor less than art or agriculture or raising children, but part of all of them (as they're all part of science). We must remember how broad a definition of human relevance we need, when we contemplate the unbroken beauty of the world.

There is a choice in all activity; so I will prepare to choose well.

Promises that you make to yourself are often like the Japanese plum tree—they bear no fruit.
                                        —Frances Marion

Promises are merely empty words if they aren't backed up by action. And action is generally preceded first by deliberate resolve, then verbalized commitment (often to someone besides ourselves), and finally, a carefully laid out plan of steps to be taken. Promises that are made, but not kept, quickly hamper any progress we dream of making. They hang like weights on our shoulders, reminding us of our weak resolve.

Only actions can fulfill our promises. Perhaps we'd do well to make a promise, any promise, only for a day. We can always renew it tomorrow.

The additional and unexpected gift is that a promise kept, no matter its magnitude, enhances our self-image. And since we can only live one day at a time, no promise need be made for longer. All of us can manage to fulfill one promise, for one day, if we believe in it and in ourselves.

Today offers me the opportunity I need to feel better about myself.

I am ashamed of these tears. And yet
At the extreme of my misfortune
I am ashamed not to shed them.

—Euripides

Shame is a little whip we always carry with us. We can shame ourselves easily; the little whip stings. We often use it to punish our feelings, because they evoke the helpless children we were. So we learn to suppress our feelings of fear, or rage, or desire. We would rather not feel at all than feel the sting of shame.

Why should we punish our feelings? Everyone feels much the same things. Why should our humanity shame us? Perhaps somewhere we acquired the notion that it's wrong to be human; that an inhuman perfection is the only proper public image.

Love can heal the pain of shame. Self-love and self-acceptance can make us strong enough to discard the little whip. We're much more lovable when we acknowledge our humanity and let go of our shame. We're also better able to love others. Shame shuts us up; love opens us to joy.

———————

I m grateful for my feelings; they're close to my capacity for love.

Noble deeds and hot baths are the best cures for depression.
—*Dodie Smith*

Preoccupation with ourselves exaggerates whatever condition presently haunts us. The temptation to dwell on our pain is so great, it takes strength and a serious commitment to emotional health to move our focus to another's needs. We are slow to learn that our own pain is soothed each time we offer comfort to another in pain.

Periods of depression will foster compassionate thoughtfulness, if we're willing to take advantage of the natural inertia that accompanies the blues. Our moments of stillness give us time to take note of another's condition. And it's through consideration for another that our wounds are cleansed and healed.

Rarely do we offer rapt attention and sincere concern to the troubled individuals in our lives. And yet, each one traveling our same or parallel pathway needs the attention that only we can give. Our own spirit is nourished every time we offer love to someone else.

Well-being, my own and someone else's, will be fostered by my actions today.

. . . Fatherly and motherly hearts often beat warm and wise in the breasts of bachelor uncles and maiden aunts; and it is my private opinion that these worthy creatures are a beautiful provision of nature for the cherishing of other people's children.

—Louisa Mae Alcott

Nature has beautifully provided that all humans can love all other humans. We don't have to be related by blood, nationality, or even language. Unlike the great apes, we have no unbreakable patterns of rivalry and aggression; we're free to choose love as our means of relating to the world.

Many people choose a sort of great-ape behavior, instead of enjoying the miraculous freedom of their power to cherish others. The choice of mistrust, rivalry, and aggression sometimes threatens to imprison us all in a zoo, surrounded by fences and patrolled by guards.

The choice is ours: can we leave the apes behind? Human love looks risky, from a cage. Let's dare to be human today.

I can choose to bestow the gift of my love.

The edge of the world does not look far away,
To that I am on my way running.
                    —*Papago Indian song for a young girl*

All things seem possible to us when we're young. The world's problems look solvable; our optimism and our immense youthful energy combine to make us hopeful and impatient. Why didn't anyone see it before? It's all so simple: if people would just love each other . . .

As we grow older, we learn more about the complicated system the world is. We learn that everything is interrelated, and that none of our simple youthful solutions even addressed the problems. In fact, we learn that they aren't problems, they're how the present system is working. If we want to change those features that we thought of as problems, then we have to be prepared for everything to change.

If we're wise, we also know how to keep that rapture; how to rekindle the belief that all is possible. Not because we believe in our power to change the whole world, but because the vision is beautiful and gives us the energy.

The end may be in sight, but today's journey is all I really have. Let me make the most of it.

Every great mistake has a halfway moment, a split second when it can be recalled and perhaps remedied.
—Pearl S. Buck

We make mistakes because we are human, we are imperfect, we are frequently out of touch with the rhythms of the moment. When our minds are one place, either still trapped by the past or in limbo due to fear of the future, we fail to revere the experience of the present. And only when we salute completely the moment do we respond accurately to its meaning.

Seldom is a mistake as important as we allow it to be. Always we can rechart our steps; never is a task completed without some modifications along the way. Perhaps we'd do well to consider all mistakes as simply modifications in the original plans. Corrections triggered by mistakes may well be responsible for better outcomes. In fact, mistakes may be part of the process necessary to keep our spiritual program focused. Their role in our lives may be of greater significance than we'd ever imagined. However, we shouldn't dwell on the mistake but, rather, on the remedy.

Today I'll have to modify my steps, probably a few times. And that's to be expected.

Courage is fear that has said its prayers.
—*Karle Wilson Baker*

No one of us is always courageous. With trepidation we embark on many journeys. Fear is dispelled each time we rely on our inner strength and trust that our lives are in good hands.

Self-talk is powerful and will prepare us to meet whatever lies ahead today. Self-talk is like prayer and quiets our fears, making it possible to give our full attention to the events transpiring. Self-talk, when positive, cultivates a healthy self-image, one that offers security, even in the face of disaster. We all carry on a dialogue with ourselves much of the time. Taking charge of the messages—making sure they enhance our personal well-being—is an option always available to us.

No situation is more than we can handle. Whatever courage or strength is needed is as close as our willingness to go within, to commune with ourselves.

I must own my fears before I can let them go. Courage follows closely on their departing footsteps.

She walks around all day
quietly, but underneath it
she's electric angry energy inside a passive form.
The common woman is as common
as a thunderstorm.

—Judy Grahn

Many people spend their days in anger and aren't aware of it. The conditions of work and life make many of us angry; we feel powerless to change them, and our frustration angers us more.

The Serenity Prayer asks for "the serenity to accept the things I cannot change, the courage to change the things I can, and the wisdom to know the difference." If we examine our lives fearlessly, we may find many things that are in our power to change.

Since we cannot change, or do not choose to change some things, we'd do well to accept them, instead of spinning our wheels in unproductive anger or turning the anger in, against ourselves. And when we summon the courage to change the things we can, our lives will bless us.

Today I'll look at anger as something I've chosen, instead of something inevitable. Is it covering fear? How can I resolve it?

One often learns more from ten days of agony than from ten years of contentment.

—Merle Shain

Pain pushes us, sometimes gently, sometimes forcefully. It pushes us to make or accept changes in our lives. We do not always welcome change. Often the change even seems to intensify the pain for a spell. But in time we'll clearly see the need for the change.

The peaceful periods in our lives have their purpose, too. They give us time to rest, to grow accustomed to the changes, to nurture the "new self" that the changes made.

Accepting all experiences as necessary to our development removes the negativity we are likely to attach to these experiences. We might instead choose to celebrate those difficult times, recognizing their worth to our human potential.

A positive attitude today will enhance the value of every experience. The choice is open to me.

I have learned silence from the talkative; tolerance
from the intolerant and kindness from the unkind. I
should not be ungrateful to those teachers.
—*Kahlil Gibran*

Every situation we experience, every individual we encounter offers us valuable insights about living life more
fully. We learn what we appreciate in people by confronting
what disturbs us. We are certain to learn more about ourselves when we acknowledge that which displeases us in the
experiences that enjoy our attention.

It's all too easy to label "of no value" experiences that, on
the surface, bore us. We also discount persons whose life
experiences are different than our own. It takes a decision
followed by concentrated effort to recognize the value of
every moment. Each one is serving us a lesson that deserves
our full attention, and it's frequently true that the lessons
most helpful are the ones least appreciated or understood in
the present.

I can be certain that whatever situations disturb me today are
also guaranteed to offer me unexpected growth.

[In the 16th century] one has only to consider the difficulties involved in feeding a baby if the mother's milk ran dry.

—Philippe Airès

Scientific progress has brought our society to the point where such a natural disaster as a milkless mother need have no consequences for her or her infant. Clean water, sewage disposal, immunization, and a widely available varied diet ensure relatively good health for millions. Sometimes this tempts us to look at the past as if it were another planet or the history of another species.

People had the same feelings four hundred years ago as we have today. Life was brutally hard; no families expected that all the children born would survive to maturity; people were old at 35 and often dead at 45. But they loved, feared, raged, and sought spiritual peace as we do.

Visiting old cemeteries is a moving experience, and an exercise for the imagination. Here is a man who buried three wives; here a family that lost four children in four years. We can reconstruct a different world in an hour or two and give ourselves an occasion for gratitude.

Imagining myself into the difficulties of the past can broaden my sympathies for the present.

It is more profitable to turn away thine eyes from such things as displease thee than to be a slave to contention.

—Thomas À Kempis

Focusing our attention incessantly on matters that disturb us, keeps us disturbed. And our obsession with our problems leaves no room for their solutions. However, we are only powerless in the face of difficulties if we choose to be. We are always free to search for the good which is lost in a tangled situation. We can be certain that our progress in life is equal to our capacity to let go of our problems and move ahead with the momentum of a positive attitude.

All too frequently, we fail to recognize opportunities for growth and success because we have chosen to be trapped by circumstances that are beyond our control. We may not **realize** this but we are never tied to problems. Solutions are always within our grasp. However, we must let go long enough to gain a responsible perspective on the situation.

Problems need not stifle my growth today.

All the strong things of her heart came out in her body, that had been so tireless in serving generous emotions.

—*Willa Cather*

We're always fascinated by beauty, and we see it as the outward sign of goodness. For young children, anything that brings pleasure is good: soft fur, music, colored lights, candy. What a disappointment to find that the soft kitten has claws that scratch!

As we mature, our notions of beauty and pleasure deepen and become more complex. We see that beauty in people often is a reflection of their spiritual selves—and that physical beauty is a little shallow and unsatisfying unless a generous spirit accompanies it.

That's what we call straightening out our priorities: deciding or discovering that virtue isn't boring, it's essential. Honesty, dependability, and truth are what we look for in others and what we strive for in ourselves. They wear better than clothes or cars.

There's a saying, "In middle age, we have the faces we deserve." Everyone has seen the wreckage that selfishness or dissipation can leave on the faces of old beauties. When we have strong, durable, compassionate spirits, we will be good to look at.

Strength and tenderness are more beautiful than high cheekbones or curling hair, and I deserve them in my relationships.

A soft answer turneth away wrath but grievous words stir up anger.

—*Proverbs*

Our treatment of others in the home, at work, or at play is our invitation for similar treatment. In fact, our every action, be it overt or covert, is noted by someone. We are always teaching someone how to treat us.

Anger is a seductive teacher. Unwanted tension, missed opportunities, stifled growth, are all we can expect if we're trapped by anger. Our chances for creative fulfillment will be unnoticed when our attention is sapped by anger. But we can change our basic response to life. All it takes is a decision.

Just as powerful as negative behavior is a positive, friendly approach to situations and persons. We can decide to love life. And we'll find that smiles invite smiles. Respect generates respect. A serene attitude lessens tension in others. Each of us is responsible for our own actions, and we each have the power to positively influence all experiences we share with others.

How I'm treated today will mirror how I'm treating others. Will I be proud?

I too am born and
grown to be this thing only;
to be Anna in the world.
                    —Anna Rydstedt-Dannstedt

In all the world there is no one like you or like me. Even identical twins are not wholly alike. The sum of genetic information, experience, learning, desire, and memory that makes up each individual is absolutely unique. At any given moment we represent that sum—and the next moment the sum is different.

It follows that each of us is best in the world at one thing—being ourselves. To let go of competition with others is to release within ourselves the creative energy to be the best we can. We need never stop growing; the task of developing our individuality lasts our whole life. Fortunately, it's an absorbing task, and one that each one of us happens to be uniquely suited for.

To be ourselves in the world is a glorious thing. We should stretch our spirits so that we inhabit our lives fully, and we will learn all we can.

Let this day be my teacher, and my mirror.

*In nature there are neither rewards nor punishments—
there are consequences.*
                                    —Robert G. Ingersoll

In life, as in nature, we experience the consequences of
our actions. Some consequences benefit us in very positive
ways. Others teach harsh lessons. But no action avoids having some effect on our lives and on the lives of other people,
too. It is fortunate that each of us has personal power over
our actions. Individually and collectively we are in control,
every moment, of the actions that culminate in good or bad
consequences for all humanity.

It is easy to overlook the ramifications of our haughty
attitude toward a co-worker, or our temper tantrum because
we thought a loved one let us down. We easily justify our
treatment of others, and seldom take responsibility for the
consequences we triggered. And yet our emotional maturity
and our personal happiness are directly related to our commitment to behave in a responsible manner. We not only
adversely affect others by our negative behavior, we hamper
our personal progress, too.

---

*My actions are far-reaching, as are their consequences. I will
take care to make them positive today.*

The body repeats the landscape. They are the source
of each other and create each other.
                                        —Meridel Le Sueur

The beautiful correspondences that structure the world—
from the five-pointed star in the core of the apple to the
snail-shell spiral of our inner ear—can be a source of great
comfort to us. When we feel most alone, most abandoned,
and out of sorts, the simple forms of beauty can remind our
eyes of the world's unity and our place within it.

Our path through the world is a part of it. We add our
individual voices to the chord that is language, that is history. No matter how desperate we may feel, or how hopeless
our lives may seem at times, the fact remains that loss and
sorrow are a part of life, and the law of life is change. Unless
we choose to cling to sorrow, it will flow through us. The
next wave of feeling may bring us joy.

The hexagonal cells of the honeycomb recall the shapes of
insects' eyes, snowflakes, geodesic domes. We fit into this
grand design. We're here for a reason—for many reasons.
Let us treat ourselves as gently as we try to treat the other
parts of the delicate web of life.

*I stand in a reciprocal relationship with the world, part of it as it
is part of me.*

Resolve to be thyself and know that he who finds himself loses his misery.
—Matthew Arnold

How confusing the issues in our lives can be when we try to accommodate all the views of the persons in our midst, persons who share few opinions in common. Agreeing with first one and then another is dizzying, and makes us suspect in the eyes of others. "Who is she really?" "What does he honestly believe?" We quickly become ill at ease in the company of those whose opinions we share only when it's convenient to do so.

We can be at peace when we've thoughtfully determined a course of action, and a world view that's compatible. Our attitudes, our opinions, and thus our responses to the currents of life will be consistent. When we develop integrity and strive to maintain it, rather than being in constant internal conflict because of our fluctuation, we discover a smoother passage over the bumps each of us can expect in life.

Today will be much less stressful if my actions reflect my inner self.

Our doubts are traitors,
And make us lose the good we oft might win
By fearing to attempt.

—William Shakespeare

Our own doubts are our greatest barriers in any endeavors. We are only free and able to accomplish what we think we can. When doubt arises, defeat is not far behind. However, that principle is just as strong in reverse. When we believe in ourselves, nothing can hold us back. Our accomplishments are many when we've developed the habit of self-assurance.

We must take personal responsibility for our beliefs, whether they be positive or negative. No one else is capable of putting thoughts in our minds. We have chosen those that are there. Far better that we coach our minds along positive paths. Only they can lead to the accomplishments that will give us satisfaction, today and every day.

We can anticipate our victories with excitement in this life. They will reflect what we've coached ourselves to attempt.

What I feel myself today will very much influence my achievement.

• MAY 4 •

The most prophetic utterances have emanated from the most poetical minds.
—William F. R. Stanley

What we call poetry is a capacity to use language so freely, so beautifully, and with so much imagination that it transforms ordinary words. What we call prophecy is the ability to see through the complex machinery of the present into the true nature of events. Both the poet and the prophet seem to be touched with magic—with more than human powers.

They tear aside the veil of ordinary reality. Both reveal a vision more intense than ours. Yet we can learn from poets and prophets, if we wish. Their vision is available to us.

All we need is humility and a willingness to let our minds play freely. Great prophets and poets speak to our human condition. Their vision can challenge or console us, if we consult them.

Truth is truth; I can recognize it where I find it.

He that knew all that learning ever writ
Knew only this—that he knew nothing yet.
—Aphra Behn

It's true that the more information we have about the world, the more clearly we see the shape of what we don't know. It's also true that we don't need to learn anything at all in order to deal fairly with others and to walk gently in the world.

The wisdom that we need is inside us. Before our schooling teaches us to forget it, we know instinctively how to treat others because we know how we wish others to treat us, and we know that all people are one.

This primitive knowledge mustn't be buried under the classifications and analyses we pick up along the way. We can, if we try, de-school ourselves to the point where we can listen to our spirits, trust our bodies, and revere the world for the seamless whole it is.

If I cherish my original wisdom, then learning can help me to be comfortable in my ignorance.

Fear is only an illusion. It is the illusion that creates the feeling of separateness—the false sense of isolation that exists only in your imagination.
—Jeraldine Saunders

We are only alone in our minds. In reality, we are each contributing and necessary parts offering completion to the wholeness of the universe. Our very existence guarantees our equality, which, when fully understood, eases our fears. We have no reason to fear one another's presence, or to fear new situations when we realize that all of us are on equal footing. No one's talents are of greater value than our own, and each of us is talented in ways exactly appropriate to our circumstances.

Freedom from fear is a decision we can choose to make at any time. We can simply give it up and replace it with our understanding of equality with all persons. Taking responsibility for our fear, or our freedom from it, is the first step to a perspective promising healthier emotional development.

If I am fearful today it's because I've forgotten the reality of my existence. I am equal to all the people in my world, and we are necessary to one another.

There is no cardinal who does not aspire to the papacy.

—*Stendahl*

When we think of it, there is something truly remarkable in the fact that practically all human beings want to be better than they are. What a hopeful reading of the human race— four billion people, all eager to improve themselves!

For many of the humans on earth, self-improvement has an economic basis—to be able to eat two or three times each day, perhaps, rather than once. We are fortunate to be able to understand improvement in a moral and spiritual sense. Increased income or possessions cannot truly augment us; our real growth is inward.

However we understand our spiritual selves, most of us agree on how to foster them: through peace, silence, and beauty, in meditation, and in what some of us call prayer. Just as every bud aspires to be a flower, and as the flower holds the secret of the fruit, so we enfold the beauty of our spirits. If we nourish the spirit, we can grow to be our better selves. If we allow nothing to hamper its growth, our spirit will unfold.

I shall set my eyes on the clear path toward my spiritual unfolding.

Our true age can be determined by the ways in which we allow ourselves to play.

—Louis Walsh

Too few of us laugh as heartily as we might. We often fail to see the humorous side of our lives. We respond gravely to most situations, certain that a serious perspective is called for. We are unaware, it seems, that we're charged only with living responsibly. Never are we asked to be solely serious.

Any situation is easier to handle if our response is lighthearted. Laughter and playfulness ease the tensions inherent in certain circumstances. Taking life less seriously doesn't mean living less responsibly. Rather, it means freeing ourselves from the negative forces that may well encumber the circumstances facing us presently.

It's difficult even to recall what tripped me last week, and this fact alone should bring relief while I'm looking at today's potential hazards.

Breaking through the foreground which is the Playboys' Playground means letting out the bunnies, the bitches, the beavers, the squirrels, the chicks, the pussycats, the cows, the nags, the foxy ladies, the old bats and biddies so that they can at last begin naming themselves.

—Mary Daly

Racial and sexual stereotyping, casual put-downs that consign another person to non-human status, is so demeaning that it's hard to believe the speaker really means it. We've become so habituated to the put-down that it's hard to be aware of how disrespectful this can be, to ourselves as well as others.

This competitive attitude keeps us jockeying for position, leads us constantly to measure where we stand, and assumes that there's only a limited amount of rightness in the world.

We're both all right, and if we're going to have a relationship that lets us be self-respectful as well as respectful of one another, we'll act as if we're both all right. We won't call one another chicks, pigs, big apes, or foxes. We won't call each other by our body parts or our ethnic groups, either; we'll recognize each other's full and individual humanity.

I will live today in honor of my name, and thus honor others.

There are as many ways to live and grow as there are people. Our own ways are the only ways that should matter to us.

—Evelyn Mandel

Letting other people grow, develop, live their own experiences as they must takes courage and acceptance of the knowledge that our responsibility in this life is to our own healthy development—not to controlling someone else's.

It's not easy to let go of someone with whom we want to share a particular path in life; however, no two of us are destined for exactly the same lessons today or any day. We must each find our own way and develop those opportunities we meet that are certain to enhance the lessons our souls have been created for.

Our need to control someone else generally results from our own insecurities about life's meaning. Because we lack understanding of our own personal worth, we look for it in someone else's devotion to us—a devotion that, in time, we squeeze the life from.

We cannot control another's behavior, and yet we try. And the more we try the greater the barriers between us become. Trust is all we finally have that each of us is progressing, according to our own pace, in rightful company. We cannot force what is not meant to be.

My own pace and direction are all that I need to be concerned with today.

• MAY 11 •

The distance doesn't matter; only the first step is difficult.

—Mme. du Deffand

Life continually presents us with opportunities for achieving what we desire. "Only the first step is difficult." Each time we sense the possibility of a new direction in our lives, we are being given a chance to grow.

Sometimes the first step is a big one; sometimes we start to take it almost without noticing: a dream, a book, a conversation. Sometimes growth may come from *not* taking what looks like an opportunity. Whatever choice we make we can be challenged to grow.

"The distance doesn't matter." Our road has many branching paths. What we work and pray for is the ability to see those paths clearly, and the strength to take a difficult first step.

Today my first step may be surrender.

Hope is a good breakfast, but it is a bad supper.
—Francis Bacon

Each day we hope for accomplishment and satisfaction, and we'll achieve these when we scale our hopes to our real capacities. There's no more satisfying feeling than finishing a project we've set up ourselves, tailored to our abilities, and worked at with patience and care. Our lives can be filled with such successes.

Learning to live means learning to keep ourselves in the present. This day is all we really have to work with. Of course, today will be influenced by what has already happened; and its influence will extend to tomorrow, next week, and beyond. But all we can make or do lies here, within this window of space and time.

May my supper be contentment. I'll breakfast on hope again tomorrow.

To keep your character intact you cannot stoop to filthy acts. It makes it easier to stoop the next time.
—Katherine Hepburn

Good habits are as easily formed as bad ones. It's quite likely that most of our daily activities are routine. With little need for forethought, we make our necessary motions every day. And if we've behaved toward others in disrespectful ways on many occasions, we may thoughtlessly repeat those acts today.

Yet we should be grateful that we are in full control of all actions we choose to take. No one else has power over our behavior. No one else can push us into actions for which we'll feel shame or remorse.

Responsibility for who we are, in all respects, is our birthright. Perhaps we don't always rejoice over this fact. And yet, it is the one absolute that guarantees we each have the power to become who we wish to become.

I'm creating behavior patterns today. Will they make me proud?

However much we guard against it, we tend to shape ourselves in the image others have of us.
—Eric Hoffer

Our sense of how someone else perceives us is a compelling influence in our lives. At such times we've often chosen not to rely on our personal power, which can forge the posture we want to present to others. We must put forth the effort, however. Passively letting others decide who we are gives us who we deserve!

We are not powerless in any situation. It's true that we cannot control others, but the reverse is likewise true. Unfortunately, too often we let another individual decide our worth, our capabilities, our very personality. Domineering parents may have done it in the past. A hateful boss or a too-critical spouse may do it presently. We are always responsible for our participation in someone else's underestimation of us. We are who we want to be. The question we must answer is, why do we choose to satisfy someone's negative image?

Self-talk will help me maintain the self-image I choose today. I will accept personal responsibility.

A man is rich in proportion to the number of things he can afford to let alone.

—H. D. Thoreau

Conscious, careful selection of those activities, situations, or people to whom we'll devote attention is all that separates centered, serene people from harried men and women. All of us are bombarded by myriad requests for some form of personal involvement. The temptation is great to attend to first one thing and then another, passively and superficially. However, our lives are enriched only when we commit ourselves to a deeper level of involvement, and to the few, rather than the many.

The talent given each of us shines forth if it's been nurtured, coddled, encouraged. We must become immersed enough in a project or an experience to lose self-conscious reservations if we're to discover the real weight of our talent. We know ourselves fully only when we're able to let the talent within define the posture without.

I can't be all things to all people today if I'm to be the person I need to be for me.

I am determined to maintain the perpendicular position.

—Lucy Stone

Perpendicular lines make right angles; they make possible extensions of both height and breadth. Right angles are weight-bearing. We speak of asserting something "squarely," making perpendiculars.

People who speak their minds freely and assert their individuality feel perpendicular; the corners they create, by their points of view, are sturdy and open. Others can use them to build structures on.

It's important to claim the perpendicular, even though we may feel pressured into curved or parallel positions. If we're centered in ourselves, others won't throw us off balance. Each of us needs to find our own center so that we can occupy our own place. Others will recognize us. Together we'll build high and wide.

My remotest ancestors dared to point their spines upright. I'll carry on the project they began.

Who cannot give good counsel? 'Tis cheap it costs them nothing.

—*Robert Burton*

Other people's problems are so easy to solve. Isn't it amazing how much better we are at their lives than our own? Of course, other people's lives don't hook us emotionally, by means of love or guilt or precious delusions. We can look at them wisely, with detachment.

Detachment is the key to solving our own problems, too, except that the detached intelligence may see a solution we're unwilling to use—especially if it means changing our behavior. Then we may feel despair. We're stuck, between the rock of our intelligence and the hard place of our reluctance to change.

Whether we stay stuck depends on us. We can choose to live as hybrids, a little wise, a little infantile; a little happy, a little miserable. Or we can risk change and growth. Within us is the knowledge and power to get what we want, if we'll believe in ourselves.

My problems are like other people's. Whether I solve them or not is up to me.

Memory is the power to gather roses in winter.
                                        —Anonymous

What a marvelous capacity we each have to capture and savor the bliss of past moments. They serve to comfort us while we're enduring the pain of the present. However, it's this present experience that has called us to attention. Within its context we'll be challenged to tackle the lessons for which past memories have prepared us.

Notwithstanding the comfort of the past, we'd do well not to hang on to past memories unrelentingly. Only by flowing with the present and absorbing how these events punctuate our lives, are we grasping the full experience our lives offer. There are too many people who live half-lives, and thus find half-joys because they fail to give up the past for the fuller measure that is offered in the present.

Fortunately, we are blessed with the power to live here and now, or in the past, if we so choose. Freedom of choice is the special gift of the human condition.

I'll appreciate my gift of choice today and linger in the past only as it benefits the better part of the present.

Everything's got a moral, if you can only find it.
—Lewis Carroll

To say that life is full of meaning is not to say that meaning is fixed or magical. Signs come to us from within, not from outside; the morals we can draw from the little dramas in our lives have to do with our own growth.

We can learn from negative experiences as well as positive ones, and we need to applaud our own progress (it's likely no one else will). Only we can know how far we have travelled when we overcome a fear of speaking in public, or joining a volunteer telephone campaign. Or perhaps we've learned to say "no" to the constant demands others make of us; we're the only ones who recognize that advance, and we deserve to congratulate ourselves for it.

Finding the morals in daily events can be an adventure. It's good to take stock periodically; it helps us to see what progress we've made and to scale our expectations to the real pace of our growth.

Today I'll hold a private viewing of some of my recent successes; I'll be my own best audience.

Our deeds still travel with us from afar,
And what we have been makes us what we are.
—George Eliot

Changing cities, countries, jobs, or partners can't change what we are; that change only comes from within us, from deep searching and redirection of our values and behaviors. Yet many of us blithely hope that a physical move will work a spiritual change. Still others trust in the delusion that a new relationship can transform the self that has developed slowly over our whole lives.

If we like ourselves pretty well, we can acknowledge our past. We'll own the choices we made at this or that juncture, and we can see the results. But if we're dissatisfied with how we're doing, if we feel the need to change our lives, we must recognize that hard work will be involved, hard choices and some pain.

Feeling the need is usually painful in itself. Often it means we're ready for those hard choices, and much of the work is already going on, deep within. Only a little more spiritual housecleaning, absolute honesty about our motives, and we may accomplish what we seek to change.

Wherever I am, in the twisting road of my life, is where I'm meant to be.

Obstinacy in a bad cause is but constancy in a good.
—*Sir Thomas Browne*

Faults, when they're closely examined, often turn out to be the other end of virtues. Carelessness in one situation might be generosity in another; secretiveness might turn out to be an extension of tact. In most of us, positive and negative attributes are related to one another like positive and negative photographic prints. The way we see the image depends on the situation and the light.

Quickness to anger can also mean quickness to forgive, to understand, or to move quickly in emergencies. A slow reaction time may go along with thoughtful caution. Understanding of ourselves will grow when we come to see ourselves along a continuum, where the traits that hold us back in one situation may be advantages in another. As we understand ourselves, we learn to love ourselves better, as we deserve.

Today I will look at my behavior to see whether a fault I don't like about myself might not be the other end of an asset.

*The ego is a self-justifying historian which seeks only
that information that agrees with it, rewrites history
when it needs to, and does not even see the evidence
that threatens it.*

—Anthony G. Greenwald

One of the larger struggles facing us is relinquishing
the need to be right always. Only when we've given up the
struggle do we understand that the battle is finally won. We
come to see nonresistance as the quintessence of the power
play. However, our need to be right is the point of real concern, and in order to let go of this need, clarity regarding the
human condition is in order.

Few of us are sure of our worth, our necessity to the better functioning of the human universe. We falter and fear
our mistakes, certain that they will enlighten our fellow
travelers about our inadequacies. And so we bully others,
covertly or with great poise, into accepting our viewpoints.
We believe that ideas shared by others are more valuable,
and thus our own value is assured. No one is served by the
exercises in truth.

*Might the time finally come when I will understand that my
individual existence is all the proof I need that I am right—
without the struggle? I can practice this belief today.*

"Living in the forest" would mean sinking into one's innermost nature and finding out what it feels like.
—Marie-Louise von Frantz

Our innermost nature—that fearsome place where our dreams dwell—what would we find there? Crude passions, lust, rage, and selfishness, or a void, a sadness without end? Many people do fear themselves, and their personalities are built on a shaky foundation of mistrust.

These are people who don't seem to confront their feelings very successfully. They may have trouble acknowledging resentments or desires, out of some sense that they ought to be above such human impulses. Unfortunately, it is often the very people who have such unrealistic expectations of themselves who surprise everyone with sudden violence. "They were such nice quiet people," everyone says, after the scandalous divorce or the suicide.

Getting to know our inner geography, our own pattern of needs and fears, is never dangerous. The danger lies in refusing to know. We can't build solid self-confidence on ignorance and mistrust of ourselves; only by loving ourselves and acknowledging our kinship with needy, fearful humanity can we grow as individuals.

My roots in the forest will keep my head out of the clouds.

Toleration is the greatest gift of the mind.
—Helen Keller

With immeasurable ease we are able to pass through difficult times if we are tolerant of the people and circumstances that are beyond our control. Toleration is an acquired trait, but one that's cherished once it's securely developed.

Toleration comes more easily when the real nature of our existence is understood. Our lives are purposeful; however, no two lives share exactly the same goals or path. Each of us is fulfilling a destiny that's designed only for ourselves; others' activities or manners will be fitting only to them. Peace of mind is our due, but it will elude us if we're ever trapped by our desire to direct another's steps.

Freedom to live the day fully accompanies a tolerant attitude. Precious moments that could enhance personal development need never be wasted on fantasies of controlling others—fantasies that can never become realities.

My achievements today can be many if I'm not wasting precious moments anguishing over persons I can't control.

. . . my grief was too deeply rooted to be cured with words.

—*Orinda*

We give enormous power to words in our culture. Most of us have given words the power to hurt us, at times, and we have also given them the power to heal. Many of us say prayers that have a special meaning, invoking deep comfort and putting us in touch with our spiritual essence.

Life deals wounds that can't be healed even by these precious soothing words. For many of us there will be times when all our strength is needed simply to endure, to live from one moment to the next. At such times, silence has more power than words. We're fortunate if we've developed our capacity to meditate to empty ourselves, and seek the still point.

The wounded spirit shrinks from words. They can never say all we mean, and words always carry the world with them. We must cultivate the serenity that lies beyond words. It has a nourishing power.

Today I shall remember that silence can heal the wounded spirit.

. . . the absence of love in our lives is what makes them seem raw and unfinished.

—*Ingrid Bengis*

Love expressed softens the harsh cutting edge of any experience. Whether we're the recipients of love or the givers, we still share in the promised rewards, the greatest of which is the knowledge that we belong, that others know us. We know we're not alone when we feel another's love, and when we have someone to give love to.

Independence and self-reliance are worthy attributes, and may prepare any one of us for survival in hard times. However, if they interfere with our awareness of and praise for the interdependent nature of the world, we'll discover that our personal survival is at stake. Our emotional, intellectual, and physical development is enhanced by our involvement with others.

The alienation any of us feels at this moment can be quickly dispelled if we'd but offer the hand of love and willingly receive it in turn. Our lives are rich and fulfilling in proportion to the love exchanged among us.

I will let someone else know I love them today and cherish the good feeling it gives me.

It is impossible that anything should be produced if there were nothing existing before.

—*Aristotle*

Everything comes from something. All the organic compounds in our world come from four elements: carbon, hydrogen, oxygen, and nitrogen. From these simple ingredients have developed the marvelous chains of self-replicating proteins that fill the planet with jungles, gardens, farms, the swarming life of the sea, and four billion people.

Each of us contains all human possibilities within ourselves. Nothing that we do comes from nowhere; we all have the capacity for great goodness as well as great selfishness and blindness. The choice, at every moment, is ours. What will we use, out of our formidable repertoire of responses?

Most of us have a pattern of response that we are comfortable with. Our habitual behavior saves us from the discomfort of always having to make a choice. But in exchange for comfort, we give up a little bit of our spontaneity. Every once in a while, it's good for us to become aware of what our habits are, and what determines our usual behavior.

Today I'll take myself off automatic pilot and navigate the whole course in person.

Happiness is a by-product of an effort to make someone else happy.
—*Gretta Brooker Palmer*

Self-centeredness aggravates the natural flow of circumstances surrounding us; too much attention on ourselves distorts whatever might be troubling us. However, focusing on others' needs diminishes what we'd perceived as our own pressing need. This is a simple principle we might all consider adopting.

None of us is free of problems. That's one of life's givens. Through their resolution we grow and ready ourselves for the next group of challenges. Each group survived enables us to offer better assistance to someone else who will confront a similar problem. Perhaps we'd do well to see all our problems as preparation for guiding someone who will come into our life. Helping someone else is certain to lift spirits and foster happiness, but the unexpected reward is that the helper reaps even greater benefits than the one helped.

My happiness is guaranteed if I help someone else find it today.

*People noticed and respected families that included
many old people, knowing that in those families must
be industrious, wise, and spiritual women who
gathered good foods, prepared meats properly, and
made daily offerings and prayers to the spirits.*
—Mary Louise Defender

Until the recent past, the health of her extended family
was a woman's responsibility. Perhaps the American Indians
were unusually wise in appreciating the health-giving qualities of both good nutrition and spiritual practice. We sometimes forget how important a tranquil spirit is to our overall
health.

Health, as a positive quality, expresses how well we in-
tegrate with the world. It's measured by the success of our
detachment from those things we can do nothing about, as
well as by our engagement with those things we can. A
healthy organism cooperates with natural processes and
throws off insults.

More and more, we are taking responsibility for our own
health. If we live to a ripe old age, it won't necessarily be
because of our daughters-in-law or our nieces, but because
we've learned to respect the balance of the body and spirit.
"Daily offerings and prayer," that is, daily meditation and
spiritual cleansing, is something we can all incorporate into
our lives. Whatever our life span, it will be richer and
happier if we nourish our spirit along with our bodies.

*Many sources of wisdom are available to me, and the strong
voice of the spirit sounds in them all.*

To live in dialogue with another is to live twice. Joys are doubled by exchange and burdens are cut in half.
—Wishart

We live in one another's company for a reason. The talents any one of us is gifted with are most pleasurable when used to benefit many. And each of us is talented in ways unique and yet burdensome if not shared.

Our personal growth and development are dependent in part on the contributions made by those we're in company with. We live better because of others' presence and talented contributions to situations affecting us all. Likewise, others are equally benefitted by our positive involvement in their lives.

We need one another to diffuse the pain and sorrow in our lives. Sharing lessens the weight on a single pair of shoulders. Sharing also reminds us that none of us is burdened in ways unfamiliar to others. Laughing together multiplies our appreciation of someone else's involvement in our lives. Every aspect of life promises more meaning when shared openly with another. We could even say that no event is really integrated into a life if experienced in isolation.

I'll find meaning today in the company of others.

"Yes," I answered you last night,
"No," this morning, sir, I say.
Colours seen by candle light
Will not look the same by day.
    —Elizabeth Barrett Browning

Circumstances alter cases. We all know that important decisions require time and preparation, yet many of us make them impulsively or on inadequate information.

When was the last time we made a mistake in judgment and admitted it? Whether it has to do with the color of our walls or the terms of a contract or the person we said we'd marry, admitting that we've changed our minds is far more honorable than going through with a wrong decision.

There used to be a saying, "It's a woman's prerogative to change her mind." It's everyone's prerogative, because nobody's perfect. We are all influenced "by candle light." To be too proud or inflexible to alter a decision, even when we've changed our minds, is a good way to set ourselves up for misery.

Joining the human race is much preferable to fighting it. I will be human enough today to admit my mistakes, and free enough to change my mind.

The tail of the kite, it is true, seems to negate the kite's function: it weights down something made to rise . . .
—Cleanth Brooks

Without its tail, the kite would fly off in the lightest breeze. The tail serves as a rudder, to steady the kite and allow it to be directed. Every force needs a counter-force to channel it effectively.

Ancient philosophers looked on the body as ballast for the mind. Without our physical anchor, they thought, our desires, our imaginations, our ideas would run away with us and the world would go to wrack and ruin.

Our minds and our bodies aren't two different things. They're made of the same stuff. They make up one being. We can never say where one leaves off and the other begins, nor can we say that one weighs down the other.

We can say, though, that we contain within ourselves all sorts of contradictions, checks, and counter-forces. This makes life interesting. Looked at positively, it means that we can understand any human possibility because we contain them all.

Contradictions only bother me before I can see them as parts of a larger whole.

Our grand business is not to see what lies dimly at a distance, but to do what lies clearly at hand.
—*Thomas Carlyle*

First things first. How much more simply life could evolve if we'd but focus our attention on the obvious situation confronting us, looking always for our direction from within the situation's elements.

How little point there is in worrying about what may come, and yet we expend incalculable amounts of energy in just such activity. What lies before us is all there really is in our lives—today. Nothing confronts us without purpose. Whatever the situation, it has called us forth to act. Our action will benefit us if we choose to transcend the ego that invites our worry, our smallness in thought and behavior.

Today stands before me, awaiting my involvement. I will go peacefully, addressing only those situations that invite my attention, and I will give it, fully.

Maybe if I listen closely to the rocks
Next time, I'll hear something, if not
A word, perhaps the faint beginning
   of a syllable.

—*Phoebe Hanson*

Everything in the world has something to say to us: rocks, garbage, even our disappointments and failures. For everything belongs to the vast, pulsating pattern that is the earth. Nothing that exists does not belong; if we find this or that piece of the pattern troublesome, it's because we haven't perceived its contribution to the whole.

Sometimes, when we're feeling down on ourselves, nothing seems to fit. What we're really feeling is isolated and sorry for ourselves—"out of sorts," that is, unmatched. Why do we do this to ourselves—pretend we're different, pretend that no one can understand us? It's a childish game, really; we're surrounded by pattern pieces that we match like lock and key, even the rocks by the cabin door.

I will listen closely. Who knows? I might hear something I need to learn.

No person in the world ever attempted to wrong another without being injured in return—some way, somehow, sometime.

—William George Jordan

Whatever our actions today, they will repay us in kind. Our choices will be many, as will our opportunities. Kindness fosters kindness. Respect elicits respect. A positive attitude clears the way for smooth sailing.

We create the world we find by our every action. No thought escapes the ripple effect. Each response we make to another, or to a situation, sets in motion a new wave of activity that will find its way back to us, in time.

To each moment we owe attention, and we have total power regarding the form and the manner of our attention. We can be certain that whatever confronts us today has its roots in our own past action.

I can be certain that to invite positive opportunities in my tomorrows means meeting those of today with kindness of spirit.

Anyone can blame; it takes a specialist to praise.
                              —*Konstantin Stanislavski*

True praise is a form of love. Mystics and saints have seen the whole living, breathing world as a hymn of praise to the Creator Spirit. This spiritual vision implies that praise is both a natural act and an art; simply being can be a form of praise, and so can the most intricate skill.

When we praise another insincerely, we are often concealing other utterances—perhaps jealousy or fear. When was the last time we spoke praise with all our heart?

Blame is easy because we all know what it is to fail. And if we feel blameworthy ourselves, we like to enlist company, to point out others' failings. Why should we be so grudging of praise? Praise doesn't diminish us; to the contrary, it augments our spirit. We might seek out occasions for praise as a way of expanding our lives.

I will do what I can to become a specialist of praise.

Rudeness is a weak person's attempt at strength.
—J. Matthew Casey

How others treat us indicates the self-assurance attained by those persons. Confident, content, self-respecting people are ably respectful of others. We often doubt our ability, either physical or intellectual, because someone has heaped criticism upon us.

The converse is likewise true. How we treat others at any time clearly reveals our personal contentment. We are not powerless over our reactions, even to pressing situations or pushy personalities. We can decide to behave admirably, which in turn nurtures all personalities and soothes every situation.

The adage, "we teach others how to treat us," is a wise reminder when we contemplate our actions and reactions.

My behavior today is an open invitation to others for treatment in kind. I will find responses that are complementary to my own.

Life is no argument. The conditions of life might include error.

—*Friedrich Nietzsche*

We've all known people to whom it was terribly important that they always be right. Perhaps some of us *are* those people, at least part of the time. Life under these conditions is an unrelenting struggle against sloppy thinking, dirt, carelessness, and the general slipshod stupidity of the rest of the world.

When we think this way, it is well to wonder how it is that we are right, while everyone else is wrong. We may find that our behavior is based not on rational thinking but on fear—the fear that if we relinquish control even for a moment, we'll fall into chaos.

How sad to be held hostage by such fears! The chaos we imagine at these times is no more real than the order we struggle to impose. What we need is self-acceptance—the humble but joyous recognition that we are human, just like everyone else, and that human beings might include error in their lives.

Perfection is an ideal, not a real phenomenon. Only by accepting my imperfection can I become fully human.

Doubt indulged soon becomes doubt realized.
—*Frances Ridley Havergal*

Self-confidence is not a given in our lives. It must be developed, often painstakingly, one task, one account, one deadline at a time. And each day that we court indecision and doubt, we erode not only this development in process but the level of self-confidence that had already been attained.

There is very little in our lives that we have full control over. We can affect the outcome of a situation. The dynamics of a relationship reflect our input. But in most instances of our lives, we offer only a contribution. We do not have the power to totally control the outcome. However, in one area we do have full power. That area is attitude. And the attitude expressed on any occasion will profoundly affect the dynamics of the situation.

A confident posture in one instance makes easier the same posture in instances thereafter. Likewise, doubt breeds itself. The attitude we choose to express teaches others what to expect from us.

What posture will I assume today? The one I choose will directly affect all outcomes. I can move forward with assurance.

The solution to my life occurred to me one evening while I was ironing a shirt.

—Alice Munro

We all receive flashes of illumination, messages like shafts of lightning from one part of our brain to another. *This is the answer! This is the meaning of life!* Mathematicians tell stories of equations solved in a dream; we cling to the notion that an apple beaned Isaac Newton.

We all experience moments that seem like the brilliant knitting together of our fortunes. At such a moment, we are happy. We wish this could last forever. But the moment, like the illuminating flash, fades in intensity and is gone. The next moment holds something new.

What we may not remember is that these revelations and these moments of joy are prepared for, day by day. The slow building up of ordinary acts and thoughts prepares us for the flash of blinding clarity. The solution to our lives isn't a meteor; it's a mosaic, made up of many ordinary acts and choices, plans and reflections. And oh, how sweet the flashes, when they come!

Because I am the source of the questions, I really do know all the answers.

The worst sin towards our fellow creatures is not to hate them, but to be indifferent to them; that's the essence of inhumanity.

—George Bernard Shaw

The greatest gift we can give is rapt attention to one another's existence. Of one thing we can be certain: we each are in this world by design. Further, we are in one another's daily travels by invitation. We share a destiny, and our understanding and joy will be proportionate to our sincere attention to those we're obviously accompanying.

No opportunity for an exchange of words, simple gestures, quiet thoughts should be discounted or denied. Each moment of our lives offers us the necessary experiences for our full potential. We need one another's presence, contributions, even tribulations in order to move forward together as well as individually.

I go forth today alone and yet in good company. Everyone here in my life now is part of my destiny. Our trip is planned for today.

The mind is a baby giant who, more provident in the cradle than he knows, has hurled his paths in life all round ahead of him, like playthings. . . .
—*Robert Frost*

Sometimes we are bewildered by the options open to us. We feel we have no way of knowing which course would be best. But when we reflect calmly on our choices, we usually find very few that are realistic, that are in tune with our personalities and consonant with the rest of our lives.

It sometimes seems that a choice made, or an option dropped, when we are very young, can determine our whole lives. This is probably an illusion. Perhaps we believe that our fate was forever altered by missing a train ten years ago. Late at night, we might talk wistfully of what might have been, "If only I'd caught that train!"

Most likely, though, our lives would have turned out pretty much the same. What happens to us, and what we choose, seem to follow the same pattern—a pattern that is true for each one of us. We've marked out our paths, whether we're fully aware of them or not.

Sometimes I am indecisive because I desire to remain open to life's choices. Today I will act freely and strengthen that freedom by making responsible decisions.

Two may talk together under the same roof for many years, yet never really meet.
—Mary Catherwood

Conversation does not always assure, or even imply, self-revelation. Trading words is easily, frequently, and safely done; however, it doesn't introduce us to the one-another that resides within. Knowing one another can only be fostered by soul-baring.

Each of us needs to be wholly known by another. Only then, in the act of total self-disclosure, do we honestly confront ourselves. We learn in the process that our fears and our shame about our secret selves are far greater than is warranted. Silence about the "me" within distracts our perspective. Meeting another person fully reveals to both a new reality about life.

We cheat ourselves of the real pleasure in living when we hold ourselves back from someone close. Tearing down the barriers that separate us is exhilarating. Only when those barriers are down do we experience the full measure of the moment.

I will have a chance today to be whole and open with someone close. I'm guaranteed a reward when I take this opportunity.

Memories, like olives, are an acquired taste.
—Max Beerbohm

We've all learned to like different things as we've grown: different flavors, different colors, different music. There's no such thing as just naturally liking hockey or jazz; even if we're barely aware of doing so, we had to discipline ourselves to find the pattern of rewards in the game or the music.

It's no accident that the greater the effort we expend on acquiring a new taste, usually the greater the pleasure it gives us. Bridge is more fun than gin rummy; Bach wears better than Mantovani. It's true for other behaviors as well; the more of ourselves we invest, the greater the rewards.

This is nowhere so true as in relationships—the more we put in, the more we receive. A truly high quality of personal relationships is something we all deserve and too few of us get. We may settle for less than we deserve out of doubt or pity or the sneaking feeling that perhaps we don't deserve the best, after all.

The first and most important element is us—our own investment, the honesty and openness we bring to others, and the trust we are willing to bestow. Quality attracts quality; if we have trouble with our relationships, we'd do well to reevaluate the tastes we've acquired.

I'll look at my part; the only person I'm responsible for is me.

There's a period of life when we swallow a knowledge of ourselves and it becomes either good or sour inside.
—Pearl Bailey

None of us is all good or all bad. Each of us takes pride in some of our actions and suffers shame for others. To be human guarantees upheavals; we are assured of shortcomings, and we can count on glad tidings too. Taking all of life's ebb and flow, smoothed by our own personal responses, leads us to a mellow maturity.

Self-acceptance is mandatory if we are ever to experience the sweetness of serenity. This acceptance must be whole and unconditional, not selective. We are who we know how to be at the moment, nothing more. But we are in a continual state of becoming. Whatever we've said, thought, or done combines in untold ways to enrich our experiences and the lives of those we touch. Let's not be soured by the self of the past, of yesterday even. Humbly accepting that portion of the whole will sweeten the rest.

I can avoid personal shame today if I think and feel before acting or reacting.

At Oran, as elsewhere, for lack of time and thinking, people have to love one another without knowing much about it.

—*Albert Camus*

What is time for? How often we say, "I don't have the time for—"meaning our marriages, our friends, our children, our hobbies, our parents, ourselves. Just what is important, anyway?

Some people seem to do everything in the margins of their lives, without thinking or knowing much about it. They go to school, get married, have children, get divorced, experience losses, get jobs, all rather offhandedly. Their attention always seems to be somewhere else.

All of us are preoccupied sometimes. And sometimes, in the middle of our lives, the preoccupation clears. "I woke up this morning and took a long look at my life. What have I gotten myself into!" Suddenly, somehow, our full attention is turned on the matter at hand. Suddenly, we have time to think. What's revealed then is the pattern of our lives. Did we make choices at random, irresponsibly? Now that we can see, are there parts to do over?

I'll endeavor to write my life story in the center of the page, not in the margins.

Hold fast to dreams for if dreams die,
life is a broken-winged bird that cannot fly.
                                        —*Langston Hughes*

Our dreams are our invitations to perform the dance we've been gifted with. Dreams are full of purpose. They mean to inspire us, acting as markers along the paths to our destination. Had we no dreams, we'd quickly lose the will to live.

The twenty-four hours ahead will be filled with dreams as well as actions. The actions we take today are no doubt inspired by yesterday's or last week's dreams. Dreams help us to image that which our souls desire us to do. This imagery is powerful, helping us to be prepared for any situation that requests our involvement.

Through our dreams we feel the pull of the inner self— that center we each have which knows our needs, our talents, our proper course and destination. We need to nurture the tie to the inner self; we can be grateful for our dreams.

My lifeline to tomorrow is through today's dream. I will respect its call.

The desire to believe the best of people is a prerequisite for intercourse with strangers; suspicion is reserved for friends.

—Mary McCarthy

How often we find ourselves treating our acquaintances with exquisite courtesy, while our friends and loved ones get our yawns, our sulks, our tantrums. We may pride ourselves on treating everyone alike, but most of us lapse into rudeness with our intimates. "It doesn't matter," we say. "They know me."

If someone doesn't know us, we behave with generosity. Why? To convince the stranger that we are nicer than we really are? Which is the ideal person, the one who is courteous to strangers, or the one who is rude to friends?

Mistrust of ourselves is the basis of these false values. Most of us fear, at one time or another, that we won't be liked, loved, or respected for ourselves alone. So we try to appear different, usually better. Once we're assured of approval from another, we feel comfortable enough to drop the facade.

Sometimes, perhaps, we even punish the new friend a little for the strain of our good behavior. Wouldn't the best behavior be a comfortable respect?

My friends deserve my courtesy as well as my love. Today I will welcome them gratefully to my life.

The greatest danger, that of losing one's own self, may pass off quietly as if it were nothing; every other loss, that of an arm, a leg, five dollars, etc., is sure to be noticed.

—*Søren Kierkegaard*

Loss of self can threaten us at every juncture in a relationship. Self-love and self-acceptance serve as valuable antidotes. None of us is without the need for love and attention from others, and the temptation to buy that love by denying our own needs or goals is great. Dependence on someone else's acknowledgment of our value can be addicting.

We can build self-love. We can create habits that will foster a strong self-image—one that doesn't rely on another's attention to ensure its survival. Self-talk is one tool that promises a changed attitude. When self-talk is positive, we will discover a more secure person. Another tool is imaging. When we image ourselves whole, happy, and at peace in our relationships, we prepare ourselves for the eventuality of that state of mind.

Today offers time to practice becoming a stronger self. My words and my thoughts are my protectors.

I think I must let go. Must fear not, must be quiet so that my children can hear the Sound of Creation and dance the dance that is in them.

—*Russell Hoban*

Often we hold fast to our fear, and it prevents us from growing. Life's ordinary rhythm carries us through good times and bad, but sometimes we fear the bad times so much that we try to hold back life's forward motion. This also means that we won't leave ourselves open to the good. The only constant truth is that everything changes. If we can believe in that, it will help us to relax our grip.

Our fear is even stronger when we think we are responsible for others—our children, for example. We want to spare them pain, and so we forget to listen to the Sound of Creation. No one learns from someone else's mistake. If we respect others, we must recognize that they have a right to their own dance. Their own spirits will guide them.

It is often hard to watch another stumble or fall. "I could have spared that tumble!" I may think. But I am wrong. I will trust in others' respect for life.

Change of scene has no effect upon unconscious conflicts.

—Edmund Bergler, M.D.

There's no running away from the internal strife. Whatever haunts us must finally be confronted and resolved if we're ever to grow and thus contribute to our world its due. When we keep secrets locked away, the secrets begin to keep us locked away as well.

It is folly, and yet entirely human, to think a new location, a new job, a new lover will cure whatever troubles us. The truth is, however, that whatever trips us up is at the same time trying to edge us forward to new awareness, and thus the next level of growth. Our troubles are tools for a strengthened foundation. Without them, we'd soon crumble.

When we consider the conflicts we encounter as opportunities for further development, they excite us rather than provoke anxiety. Changing our perspective can make the same scene appear quite new.

As I look out upon "the scene" today, I can control my response to it. I can relish it and grow.

May the new week come to us
For health, life and all good;
May it bring us sustenance, good tidings,
Deliverance and consolations.
　　　　　　　　—Women's Sabbath Prayer

Our life constantly renews itself; we celebrate the new year, the new week, the new seasons. New babies, new jobs, new homes give us occasion for rejoicing; the reunions with old friends and family, the strengthening of old bonds, remind us of other cycles of renewal.

For some women, their menstrual cycle provides a silent rhythm of renewal. Some people chart their biorhythm, hoping to tap the ancient springs of life-cycle energy that power the universe. Recovery from an illness, completion of a long project, harvesting a garden, even making a new garment, remind us of our place in the long breathing rhythms of life.

When we are at the end of a cycle, we sometimes forget that renewal always comes. When our energy ebbs, when all the trees are bare, when any effort seems fruitless, we may believe that we have fallen out of the pattern. "I'll never smile again," we think; "the sun's gone out—nothing is worthwhile." Depression for some of us is part of the cycle, and like hibernations or the shedding of foliage, it permits us to gather our strength for the next creative leap.

When things look bleak, I will remember that change and renewal are a law of life.

. . . all humans are frightened of their own solitude.
Yet only in solitude can we learn to know ourselves,
learn to handle our own eternity of aloneness.
—Han Suyin

Being quiet with ourselves lets the inner person surface. Acknowledging the inner voice invites the comfort it can offer. Acknowledging also gifts us with certain guidance needed by our uncertain steps. Our quiet times away from others nurture the soul struggling to safeguard our journey.

In solitude we find serenity securely nestled in the recesses of our mind. We begin to understand that all is well. We begin to see that our way is being lighted. Only in our quiet times can we fully hear the voice assuring us to move forward, not alone, but in concert with it.

In solitude we find our sanity when the world around us seems insane.

I will go within today in search of rest and peace. I will discover myself.

*All weddings are similar, but every marriage is differ-
ent. Death comes to everyone, but one mourns alone.*
                                            —*John Berger*

What wonderful creatures we human beings are—so alike,
and yet so different! We can work together; we have built
the Pyramids, the Great Wall, the great cathedrals of Europe,
the temples of Peru. We can play music, make quilts, run
hospitals, program computers. Yet we can also work alone.
Each one of us has the power to think, to plan, to carry out
projects that are distinctly ours.

We are both interdependent and independent—and both
of these characteristics can give us both joy and pain. Sometimes we feel burdened and oppressed by other people. They
need us, they weigh on us. We think that if only they would
leave us alone, we could realize our true potential.

At other times we feel desperately, achingly alone. Un-
supported, abandoned, at such times we may think that if
only we had someone on our side, if only someone cared, we
would succeed. True freedom, however, like true security,
lies within us. We cannot get them from others; we must
find them in ourselves.

---

*I will accept either good company or solitude as the condition
necessary for self-fulfillment in today's endeavors.*

The grand essentials to happiness in this life are something to do, something to love and something to hope for.

—Joseph Addison

Focusing our attention outside of ourselves on hobbies, on goals, on friends, steadily bathes us with inspiration and enthusiasm for moving forward. And this movement, in turn, rekindles our commitment to all our attention-drawing activities.

It is true that happiness lies within us, but our discovery of this is only made possible by our willing involvement in the lives and experiences surrounding us. Those who lead narrow, self-seeking, self-serving lives fail to discover happiness. It lies beyond their reach because they've failed to reach beyond themselves.

Each day is as full and as ripe with adventure and meaning as we choose to make it. Where we look, what we see, do, and plan for, are in our control.

I am personally responsible for the happiness I discover. I'll help my search today by getting truly interested in what others are doing.

The woman I am
is not what you see
I'm not just bones
and crockery
　　　　—Dorothy Livesay

As our bodies age, our spirit remains young. When we look at old people, too often we see only the "bones and crockery," the disturbing image of brittle frailty that lies ahead for us all. Seldom do we take the time to evoke the ageless spirit of an old person.

Yet those of us who are privileged to have close relationships with old men and women see beyond the mask of age. What we often find there is a distillation of experience, sometimes wisdom, always keen memory, and almost always a fresh and ruthless impatience with hypocrisy and lies.

Old people are wonderfully shameless; they have no time for false pride or prudery. In the process of living so many years, whatever pretensions they might have had seem to have dried up and blown away, like corn husks or last summer's leaves. This quality is as bracing as sea air.

The very old share it with the very young, who are too new in the world to be polite. The lessons that old people can teach us aren't written anywhere.

Today I will become both old and young by seeing beneath the surface.

The universe is transformation; our life is what our thoughts make it.

—Marcus Aurelius Antoninus

It's awesome, the power we each wield in the life that unfolds before us. The inclination of our thoughts invites that which we encounter, which is that which we expect to find. What we can become or experience is limited only by our imagination. Our dreams shine like beacons in the dimness of our minds.

Just as our thoughts can nurture positive experiences and outcomes, negative episodes might be drawn to us, too. We can be sure, though, that we use this individual power to create the flavor of each day as it's met.

Our attitude is the by-product of our thoughts. It is in our attitude that we discover strength or weakness, hope or anxiety, determination or frustration. Alone, we determine whether our attitude will be loving or jaundiced.

The breadth of personal power is awesome. Today will be what I choose to make it. No more and no less.

• JUNE 27 •

Science probes; it does not prove.

—*Gregory Bateson*

We crave security. Even the most restless and adventurous among us has a need for bedrock certainty about something. Religion fills this need for some; politics or ideas satisfy others. When this need is answered, we can achieve a measure of serenity.

Where does this need come from? Nothing in nature is fixed or constant. We know that our bodies, our surroundings, the air we breathe, are made up of chemical compounds that are always changing, renewing, building up, and breaking down. Change is the only constant. And yet, if our inner reality mirrors this change, we may feel chaotic and unquiet.

All great philosophies and religions share the image of a still point, a final proof. The purpose of meditation is to quiet the mind, to find this still point. It is a human need to imagine something beyond changing reality that is the real certainty, the real assurance.

In a world of shifting, slipping reality, where it sometimes seems that our identity is just part of a data base that one computer error could erase, where city streets and national boundaries change their shape every year, we need all the inner stillness and serenity we can find. Belief in constant values can anchor us. Truth is truth, love is love, and we are what we are. These things are always true for us.

I will cultivate my inner serenity; I will attempt to find my constant truth.

Anyone who limits her vision to memories of yesterday is already dead.

—Lily Langtry

The breadth and attitude of our vision for today's potential or tomorrow's dream will profoundly influence what we see at this moment. We have the personal power to chart our course, to set our goals and to take the necessary steps for their attainment. We also have the option to walk backwards, stuck in yesterday's lost hopes.

Imaging the person we strive to be, coupled with clear details of the path we feel pulled to travel, is powerful preparation for the actual trip to our destination. Conversely, our progress to "anywhere or nowhere" is a direct reflection of our shortsightedness.

The strength of our power to create that which can be is awesome, thrilling, and demanding.

I look to this day with hope and determination to say, "Yes, I can leap forward."

God did not make us to be eaten up by anxiety, but to walk erect, free, unafraid in a world where there is work to do, truth to seek, love to give and win.
—Joseph Fort Newton

Today stands before us with promise. It invites us to fully participate in experiences. That we are alive, that we stand present facing this day, guarantees that we are qualified to handle every challenge that snags our attention. And we need have no fear. The world and all that's in it is spirit-full. We are safe and secure if we'd but believe it.

When we look toward the day with confidence, we tap the inner strength that is ever-present. The more frequently we turn to this strength, the less often we are haunted by pangs of anxiety. Our trust in that strength heightens our faith and our understanding that all is well—always and forever all is well.

Giving up fear offers a freedom that will exhilarate us. Faith, trust, confidence will ready us for any challenge, all experiences.

Nothing needs to make me fearful today. I am here. Therefore, God is here too.

My life, I will not let you go except you bless me, but then I will let you go.

—*Isak Dinesen*

There is something noble in the spirits of those who battle death, who cling to life. We are all moved by their struggle, yet perhaps it is nobler still to let life go when the time comes.

This makes sense only if we think we can look back on a life lived to the fullest. We wouldn't want to die without knowing we had stretched our limits, inhabited them as largely as we could. Not in a worldly sense, perhaps; spiritual breadth can be as exciting as travel, sport, romance, or achievement. It's the limits of our brain and heart we want to test; for that, we could live in one room

Not everyone is blessed with robus physical health, but we all have the capacity for spiritual health and adventure. Self-examination and meditation are the tools for self-knowledge and serenity. Unknown adventure awaits us when we seek to know ourselves.

My spiritual journey is the real one in my life. On that road, the true blessings are encountered.

A Feather . . . might accomplish it . . . or a Trifle done in the right Spirit . . .

—Djuna Barnes

Sometimes it seems as though a decision truly hangs in the balance, with such equal values on both sides that the weight of a feather might tip it either way. "I was that close to saying no—or yes—" we say, holding thumb and forefinger a few microns apart.

But that's probably not an accurate version of how we came to make our decision. *That close* may not be close at all; we knew all along what was appropriate. If we let ourselves be still and listen to our private inner voice, we usually know what's right for us to do.

If we find ourselves faced with a lot of decisions that seem only a feather's weight apart, maybe we're not acting according to our ideas of what's right. It might be time to reappraise our values. If we're believing one way and acting another, it might be time to change either our behavior or our belief.

Any obstacles to knowing the right course of action are within me, and so is the right course.

When once estrangement has arisen between those who truly love each other, everything seems to widen the breach.

—Mary Elizabeth Braddon

Intimacy is a bonding agent that softens our exteriors while it hushes the inner rumblings and creates a need for itself. None of us is spared that need. Having at least one other with whom we are intimate heals us, keeps us honest, and strengthens us for whatever lies ahead.

When intimacy is absent from our lives, it's terribly easy to lose ourselves—to lose clarity about our identity, to lose confidence and self-assurance. And these losses contribute both to a strong need for intimacy once again, and to a heightened sense of the risk involved in being open and intimate.

Any time we break the intimate bond, we impede our progress as growing, healthy persons. Mental and emotional health is directly proportionate to how close we allow another person to be to us.

My emotional health today is in my control. I'll let someone in.

That has not half the power to do me harm,
as I have to be hurt.

—William Shakespeare

Each day is steaming with activities around which we choose attitudes and reactions. Any one circumstance might anger us today, even though yesterday it triggered laughter. No event, within itself, has the power to determine our feelings or our reactions. How fortunate that this is so. However, we often pretend exactly the reverse. "He makes me mad!" "You've really hurt my feelings." With ease we refuse to take responsibility for whatever mood we're in.

A sure sign of mental and emotional health is acknowledgment of our personal power—power over our feelings, our attitudes, our behavior in every instance. When we celebrate this power, we are energized; we anticipate, confidently, the situations moving toward us, secure in the knowledge that we can make them beneficial to our growth if we so choose.

How much easier it is to face each new day knowing that it has no power over us.

I go forth today ready to take control of my attitude and my behavior. My day will be just as good as I make it.

> *I also had nightmares. Somehow all the feelings I didn't feel when each thing had actually happened to me I did feel when I slept.*
>
> —*Andrea Dworkin*

Dreams are messages that we send ourselves about things in our lives that bind deep feelings. Often we find ourselves dreaming scenes from our daily life, ordinary situations that may make us anxious. Sometimes our dreams are images like newspapers, account books, or video screens to show us our fears.

When the events in our lives are dangerous and destructive, we may numb ourselves so that we won't feel the fear or pain they provoke. But our dreams know; our nightmares are an outlet for feelings that we've chosen not to feel.

Our dreams will guide us, if we honor them. We don't have to interpret every last detail of a dream to be able to understand it. The symbols in our dreams are coded, and only we can break the code. When a dream brings us strong feelings, we can usually—if we're honest with ourselves—determine what it's about. Then it's up to us what we do about our lives.

My dreams tell my personal story, and all the feelings in them are mine.

There is after all no obligation to answer every passing fool according to his folly.

—Elias Canetti

Often we behave as though we were in other people's power—as though we were bound to act in certain ways because others expected it from us without their even asking, or our ever checking.

Perhaps we have a deep need to please the authority figures in our lives because we fear we're not worth much. Let's say, further, that our boss stays late in the office every night. We may feel compelled to stay as long as, or longer than, the boss, out of some wish to prove our loyalty and productivity.

Most of us realize that a challenge doesn't mean we have to fight; an invitation doesn't mean we have to accept. But sometimes, especially when it hits a sensitive or insecure area, we find ourselves blindly reacting to someone else's unreasonable actions. We feel sucked in, manipulated, powerless.

We can depend on our own power when we trust in our innate value as humans, and we will make decisions that leave us comfortable with ourselves.

I will remember to guard myself against irrational compliance.

Of course, fortune has its part in human affairs, but conduct is really much more important.
—Jeanne Detourbey

Our behavior in small, mean situations is ultimately as grave in its impact on the whole of human relationships as a major action taken in response to a large-scale crisis. No action or expressed attitude is void of effect. Though it may go unobserved at the time, it will be felt and it will influence another's response at another time.

Our influence on others, on immediate situations, on the future, is profound. When we accept responsibility for all of our actions, as well as our attitudes, our choices will reflect a widened perspective. The power inherent in even the barely perceptible thought is awesome.

My conduct toward others, my unspoken thoughts and unexpressed attitudes will have their effect. My impact today can be positive.

What loneliness is more lonely than distrust?
—*George Eliot*

Becoming fully trustworthy individuals, living up to our own ideals, makes easier the decision to trust others. And when there is trust, intimacy is possible. With intimacy comes self-love, then other-love, and finally joy.

Isolation from others is a choice, one that breeds new levels of insecurity. Familiarity with isolation hinders our movement toward others, a movement that offers the risk of self-disclosure. And it's this risk that nurtures the friendships that comfort us.

Self-acceptance and self-disclosure are intertwined. Our rough edges are softened and easier to love after we've owned them, held them up for inspection, and patted them before tucking them away.

Today offers new hope to the hopeful. Being rid of the burden of distrust will lighten my day.

Love is when each person is more concerned for the other than for one's self.

—David Frost

Loving ourselves is a healthy and necessary attitude if we are to garner the strength and confidence to move into our world of experiences each day. Self-love, when it is honest and nurturing, fosters compassion toward the others who share our experiences. Preoccupation with self is not self-love.

How distorted our perceptions of life are when, with incessant rigidity, we force our personal selves to the center of every experience. When we focus only on how a situation relates to our own lives, too often we lose sight of the lesson we might have learned. To look instead with compassion upon the needs and frustrations of those sharing our experiences will usher in solutions and will invite an exchange of gratitude which makes all expressions of love easier.

When we look outward with love and acceptance toward our fellow travelers, we inwardly feel greater love, too.

Any expression of real love today—toward anyone—will multiply my possibilities for loving.

It was only after the advent of the white man that we met people who did not understand about the uniqueness of human beings.

—*Good Day*

Human beings have been known to act toward other people as though they were things, objects, instead of subjects like ourselves. Men sometimes act this way toward women; parents toward children; the young toward the old. This behavior has been most obvious and brutal toward the original inhabitants of some territory that others wish to colonize.

As the world runs out of secrets, and no place is left open to colonial assaults, we must guard against this tendency among ourselves. We can see it in military organizations and in industrial production, in bureaucracy and in mass movements. It's called disrespect for the individual, and it's always dangerous.

Each human being is precious and unique. It injures our spirit to forget that, even for a moment. And when we remember it, we're better able to act in concert with our self-respecting fellows.

In respecting ourselves fully, we show others how to treat us, and as we treat them respectfully we acknowledge and enhance their humanity. The quality of human interaction can be so wonderful; why should we deface it by forgetting others' uniqueness?

I'll look for the same respect from others, today, that I show them.

By education most have been misled
So they believe, because they so were bred.
The priest continues what the nurse began,
And thus the child imposes on the man.
—John Dryden

In the early years it often seems to the growing human child that most of civilization consists of saying "No!" Parents and teachers sometimes act as if that were so. Everyone who has ever raised, taught, or cared for small children knows what a totally involving commitment it is, and knows, too, that it is impossible to do everything right. Parents struggle with their children over trivia; teachers may punish small infractions and ignore large ones. Humans raise humans; if it were possible to do it perfectly, surely we would all be angels by now.

Often we are fully grown before we're able to let go of some of the rigid rules we learned. Often it may seem that our task as adults is to *unlearn* what we learned as infants. The "housebreaking" that has made us considerate to one another and peaceable in adjusting our differences may also have squelched some of our capacity for feeling.

We can recover our feeling selves, without violating the rules of society, if we can remember not to be afraid. Feelings are only frightening when we repress them; when we let them out and let them sweep through, then they are gone.

My feelings may be strong, but they are not evil. How could they be? I am a child of the universe.

Persons who habitually drink water become as fine gourmets on the subject as wine drinkers on wine.
—Alexander Dumas

How fortunate are those among us who have the ability to turn things around—to transform liabilities into assets. Life deals them lemons: they make lemonade, lemon pie, candied lemon peel. They seem to be able to assess the needs of the moment accurately and turn them to advantage.

We are all different. Success in life probably has more to do with expressing our uniqueness fully than with suppressing it and trying to resemble everybody else. Who is "everybody else," anyway?

We can't respond authentically to the moment if we're concealing the truth. The truth for us involves our own unique package of qualities, our own experience and energy, our own way of looking at things. Freedom, for us, depends on the choices only we can make. The proper appreciation of water is a pleasure that demands discipline. We're totally unable to experience this pleasure if we are wishing for wine.

Human beings share many characteristics. One of the most important is difference. Today I will cherish these differences as one of the bonds that joins me to others.

. . . he yearned to package for each of the children, the grandchildren, for everyone, that joyous certainty, that sense of mattering, of moving and being moved, of being one and indivisible with the great of the past, with all that freed, ennobled.

—Tillie Olsen

In childhood we glimpse the dear connectedness of life. The delicious sense that life is a grand adventure mustn't be put away with our roller skates or high school diplomas; it remains as true for us today as it was when we first sniffed freedom and greatness in the air.

Life holds so much! Every morning we can open a package of "that joyous certainty." Each day, as we trace our paths, we're connected with all that has gone before, and all that is presently in the world, and we are preparing the future. Yes, we matter; we matter enormously, each one of us as much as any other; our unique and precious consciousness matters above all things.

The part we play touches all of life. Sometimes we choose to join our personal strength with others'; sometimes we act alone. But we are part of the whole, linked by our lives and our choices to all the others on earth, as they are linked to us.

Today I'll be true to my heritage of freedom and nobility.

• JULY 13 •

It seems that there is a direct connection between creative thought and involvement in life and the production of epinephrine by the adrenal gland. When the challenge stops, the supply is turned off; the will to live atrophies.

—*Norman Cousins*

Living on the fringes of activity is a choice we can make. Always holding back, rather than becoming fully intimate with another in conversation is a choice we can make. Partial attention rather than wholehearted involvement with the task at hand, whether it be reading a report, chopping wood, or preparing a meal, is also such a choice. Each moment we choose half-involvement we are also choosing partial death. The soul is nourished only by the rapture of fully experiencing the myriad vibrations surrounding us.

Attuning ourselves to "all that is" elevates the mind, heightens gladness, nurtures the creative act. Each task we undertake today will benefit ourselves and others only to the degree of attention we give it.

The joys today offers are tucked inside the experiences that invite my attention. Living on life's fringes won't bring joy.

If we try too hard to force others to live in our world, because we think it is the real world, we are doomed to disappointment.

—William Glasser, M.D.

The desire to control other people, all situations and each outcome to benefit ourselves is a human compulsion, and one destined to foster frustration. Our need to control others is addicting, but our condition is not hopeless.

"Letting go" is a learned behavior. Like any habit, practice will make it a natural response. Freedom to fully respond to any experience can only be attained when we have sacrificed the outcome to whatever the bigger picture dictates.

To be enthusiastically, creatively alive means responding to the pulse of the moment, which means following the unself-conscious inner urging rather than the self-protecting and consciously manipulative ego. Our burdens are lightened each time we act free from the weight of the ego.

Letting go of others will lift my own spirit high today.

Our ordinary mind always tries to persuade us that we are nothing but acorns and that our greatest happiness will be to become bigger, fatter, shinier acorns; but that is of interest only to pigs. Our faith gives us knowledge of something much better: that we can become oak trees.

—E. F. Schumacher

Most of us struggle at times with a sense of worthlessness. Sometimes this sense of being good for nothing leads us to self-destructive behavior; sometimes it is accompanied by self-pity. At such times, other people's lives appear infinitely attractive, and we may fancy that there are easy solutions to our problems. "If only I had two nice children, an adoring spouse, and a house in the suburbs!" we may think, or "Oh, to be single and on my own in the big city!"

The truth is, and we know it when we're not in a funk, that our solutions, like our problems, lie within us. We all tend to blame other people and circumstances for our own shortcomings. That's human. But we let go of blaming if we want to grow.

We have the power to transform every situation. If we feel trapped by a job that seems dull or a relationship that seems lifeless, we can redefine our sense of the trap. What do we want? What prevents our going after it? What opportunities have we overlooked? If we're frightened by a prospect that seems dangerous, we can turn it into a challenge, and at the same time plan realistically how to protect ourselves.

I will remember that every seeming problem is an opportunity for growth.

Sharing a burdened heart with another who has the wisdom, strength, and knowledge to carry it, frees us from its weight long enough to focus on solutions.
—Liane Cordes

Our obsession with a problem, any incessant problem, keeps it a problem. Our focus on it destroys the balanced perspective that is necessary for a solution to become apparent. Sharing a problem's details with an interested friend clarifies the muddle. It also doubles the chances that a solution will emerge.

Holding onto problems, like keeping secrets, keeps us stuck. Our emotional health is proportionate to the freedom with which we willingly share ourselves with the people close to us. Sharing our joys doubles them. Sharing our burdens diminishes them. But more than that, it promises the discovery of their solutions.

Today I will share a problem, perhaps my own or someone else's. A solution will be apparent, nevertheless.

You had better live your best and act your best and think your best today; for today is the sure preparation for tomorrow and all the other tomorrows that follow.

—*Harriet Martineau*

What's done is done. What's been said is said. We can't undo the mistakes of yesterday. And occasionally they create the barriers blocking us today. However, we can make sure that our behavior today doesn't contribute to unnecessary problems for tomorrow.

A negative attitude toward other people and toward life's circumstances becomes habitual. Fortunately, a positive attitude does as well. The choice rests with each of us to respond in ways fitting to the preferred attitude.

How much easier all situations are when we are respectful, hopeful, and interested. Likewise, the trivial matter can become a major catastrophe when we struggle unnecessarily and with carping egos. We make the world we find, at home, at work, and at play.

Today is mine to make. Let me choose my attitude with care.

*Man is a pliant animal—a being who gets accustomed
to anything.*

—*Fyodor Dostoyevsky*

The ease with which we adapt to our surroundings is, to
some degree, a very positive trait. It means we are generally
flexible. However, our pliancy may allow us to adjust to situations that harm us. We learn with too much ease to accept
painful situations—maybe believing that time will ease us
away from it, or that a bit of magic will transform the people
and the situation, thus eliminating the pain.

Knowing when to adapt to circumstances and when to
make a personal choice to move away takes mature assess-
ment. It also takes attunement to our inner self—the "knower"
of all right action. Development of this relationship with our
inner selves takes practice, courage, patience, and the willingness to detach our minds from external stimuli for a time.
Responsible choices are never accidental reactions, and
they will sometimes usher in a radical action, at other times
easy acceptance.

*Today will offer opportunities to "go along with" a situation. I
will be thoughtful rather than always pliant.*

. . . [I]f you listen carefully, you get to hear everything you didn't want to hear in the first place.
—*Sholom Aleichem*

What are those things that we don't want to hear? Mainly, we don't want to hear disagreement from people who are important to us. We don't want to hear that our children are making choices we wouldn't make; we don't want to hear that our partner believes we are anything but perfect; we don't want to hear that our friend, our parent, our teacher, our boss, sees anything in us to criticize.

Poor us! We know we aren't perfect, but we can't tolerate hearing it from someone else. Why should that be? We know other people aren't perfect, either. Where did we get the idea that we're supposed to be error-free?

To accept our own imperfection is to make a giant step toward peace of mind. To accept that the world is full of people who disagree with us—some of whom even love us very much—is to begin to achieve maturity. Perhaps we think, or used to think, that we would be happy when we rubbed out our last traces of imperfection. That is not happiness, that is to become marble—hard, cold, and breakable.

True spiritual progress begins with my acceptance of my imperfections.

Our soul makes constant noise, but it has a silent place we never hear.
—Simone Weil

In an unjust, difficult world, our soul is often in pain and weeping. Sometimes it makes a joyful noise. But the silent place, the still center, is one we may neglect. Like white light, this silence of the soul contains everything, yet it transfers the warring jumble of noise and color into a peaceful blankness.

Call it acceptance or surrender. The stillness of the spirit is the stillness of communion with truth beyond change. It's silent because it doesn't belong to the world of the senses. We have spiritual knowledge that's ancient, if we let ourselves listen to it, and it will nourish us, if we permit.

For some of us, it's a great effort just to learn to listen to the noise of our souls. We've spent years blotting out pain or joy with alcohol, other drugs, or rationalizations. We feel we've made enormous progress when we learn to hear our own soul's noise. But be assured, the soul's great silence can be achieved. It's our choice.

My spirit can grow infinitely. I trust where it will take me.

Grief can take care of itself, but to get the full value of joy you must have somebody to divide it with.
—Mark Twain

We share this planet that supports us. We share it with other living creatures, each one offering a necessary ingredient that nurtures and sustains the continuation of the whole. Every experience that involves one of us, involves others who also need what the experience may teach. We are not alone, ever. We are traveling a path in concert with others whose needs are similar to our own.

We can expect to discover joyous occasions and will undoubtedly be visited by grief in our travels. The latter will be eased by the knowledge that others, too, have known grief. Joy, on the other hand, is doubled in intensity when we acknowledge the occasion giving birth to it and then celebrate it with others. No day passes without giving us many occasions to shout for joy. Too often, feeling alone and lonely, we close our eyes to the wonders that could excite us. The most fruitful lesson we can learn is that we have fellow travelers among whom joy abounds and multiplies when shared.

Today I'll look for the joy in my life.

As contagion
of sickness makes sickness,
contagion of trust can make trust.

—*Marianne Moore*

Attitudes give birth to themselves. Fresh ideas foster fresh responses to old and new situations. Each of us is favored with responses from others that generally match those we've shared, too. We should never be surprised by how others treat us. We have been their teachers in every instance. Giving love invites it. Expression of honesty encourages that, too. We must only expect that hatefulness and dishonesty will greet us if we've offered nothing more to others.

We should always be aware of the power of our attitudes and behavior toward others. They will bring favor or disfavor upon us. We should be mindful, too, that joy is contagious—as are respectful behavior, a trusting attitude, and gratitude. We are charged with the responsibility for creating a better world in which to live. Peace and happiness begin here, now, with each of us.

Peace, joy, and good fortune will accompany me on my trip today if I do my individual part to spread it.

Not the fruit of experience, but experience itself, is the end.

—*Walter Pater*

The end can never justify the means; the means is life, as we live it, in the present moment. When we read of aged paupers who die on a bare mattress stuffed with cash, we recognize their delusion; but at times we can lose that clarity and find ourselves justifying practices that we know are undesirable in the service of a desired end.

Means that involve injustice or deprivation are never justifiable. We cannot ignore experience. We may have our sights set on a law degree or a sports car, but the experience of law school and of budgeting for the car are what we live. The quality of our life isn't measured by our degrees or possessions but by our behavior. If we have love and fulfilling work, nothing else matters.

Let's concentrate on today; it's all we have. Within this day, we have many choices and a rich texture of experience. We can't control the outcome; the moment is within our grasp. We must seize it, savor it, learn from it; it is life itself.

If I were meant to live in the future, my eyes would have telescopic lenses.

*Two great human institutions were apparently in-
augurated together, proprietary marriage and the
division of society into masters and servants.*
—Emily James Putnam

Just as every generation must invent sex for itself, so every
committed relationship must invent equality. The concept is
an old one; histories and civics books are full of it; but most
of us have precious little experience of it in our lives.

Unfortunately, most of life is some variation of a
dominant-subordinate relation. However loving our parents
and teachers, they definitely have the upper hand. We play
games to win; we're ranked in school and at work. We learn
to jockey for position, to manipulate, to get what we
want from those we perceive as above us and below us on
the scales.

For many of us, intimate relationships present a new
challenge: how to get along as an equal. With no assumption
of superiority or inferiority, sometimes we're at a loss. How
does one act with an equal? Who gets to decide? What are
the rules?

Emotional openness, honesty, and willingness to take
risks can bring most of us to the point where we can share
equally—or, at least, discuss the issues with a partner. It's
hard to let go of our old place on the ladder—to decide to be
neither a master nor a servant.

Rare is the experience of equality. I will let myself be open to it.

The question is laid out
For each of us to ask:
Whether to hold on
Or to drop the mask.
                    —Martha Boesing

Do you ever feel you are wearing a mask? It's a strange, uncomfortable feeling. We mistrust our own face; we don't even know what it looks like, because we put on the mask so young. But sooner or later we must drop it and face our reflection.

Perhaps the mask is silent, and behind it we feel like screaming. Perhaps the mask is festive, and our own eyes weep.

The mask chafes and confines us, but it gives protection, too. We're naked without it; we have nowhere to hide. To summon the courage to drop the mask, we must believe in ourselves enough to trust our naked vulnerability.

We may take courage in knowing that everyone is vulnerable and afraid. By wearing our own faces proudly, we show that it's possible. Soon, masks will be dropping all around.

Today I will risk showing myself as I really am.

The principle of life is that life responds by corresponding; your life becomes the thing you have decided it shall be.
—Raymond Charles Barker

The attitude that we carry with us into a particular setting will greatly influence our perceptions of any event. Our attitude also influences, positively or negatively, personal interactions, and not just those involving ourselves. The effect of our message is this: our personal power is profound. We have explicit control over our own perceptions. We determine our own attitudes. Every moment of our lives we are deciding what we want to see, to think, to feel. And reflections will inform us that our expectations are firmly fulfilled.

How exhilarating to become aware of our freedom to think and to feel as we wish. However, with this freedom comes responsibility. We're barred from blaming others for our troubles. Each of us is charged with the responsibility for deciding our own fate. How we prepare ourselves for this experience or this day is individually chosen. Every minute we are in control of our perceptions, our attitudes, our responses.

Today is mine to mold. My attitude, my thoughts and responses will decide my fate today.

Whoever is interested in life is particularly interested in death.

—*Thomas Mann*

In this biological world we can see clearly that death is a stage in the life cycle. In our human case, we cling to the precious consciousness that seems to set us apart from the rest of the natural world, and we see death with different eyes—as an ending, often cruel, and sometimes unendurable.

We do ourselves no service to make an enemy of death; it is a presence within our life, and by denying it, we deny a part of ourselves. Our deepest knowledge includes a knowledge of death. To experience loss and to grieve it are the great common human experiences, and to deny them is to make ourselves less human.

We live in a beautifully balanced system in which death is a part of everything that lives. The pain of our personal loss is ours; within the greater whole, nothing is lost. Perhaps it is too much to say that we will ever understand death; the fruit of time and pain and healing is that we will come to accept it.

Let me open myself to the knowledge of wisdom, to which death belongs in equal measure with life.

If you find your inner conversation running along negative lines, you have the power to change the subject, to think along different lines.
—Martha Smock

Most of us carry on a continual inner dialogue. At times we're sizing up our co-workers or perhaps strangers entering the room. At other times we're being critical of our appearance, or a piece of work we've just completed, or of our capabilities to handle a new challenge that's in our path. If we were to log the minutes of self-talk and categorize them, many of us might discover that few moments of the inner dialogue are supportive or filled with praise. In fact, we often verbally abuse ourselves and others—a behavior we can ill afford.

Determination to change our inner thoughts is our first step, if we want to find greater peace and happiness in this life. We are under no one's power but our own, and we have chosen negative thinking for whatever payoff it offered. Time will prove to us that the payoffs from positive thinking are far greater. We tend to become the person our thoughts prepare us to be.

I will celebrate my personal power and use it to my advantage. Today!

. . . we have
grown into one as we slept and
now I can't jump
because I can't let go your hand.
                              —Marina Tsvetayeva

Long, intimate relationships often confuse us. We may lose the sense of where our individual boundaries are. We confuse our desires and our pain with another person's—our spouse or lover, our parent, siblings, or child. When that relationship changes, when the other person dies or leaves or forms another intimate bond, we may feel wounded and desperate, unsure of who we are.

The blurring of boundaries is never healthy for us—although we may not feel the damage at first. Sound relationships are carefully made; we enter into them without giving away our own authentic responses to life. When relationships change, of course we may feel pain; but we need not feel the awful confusion that comes from having given pieces of ourselves away.

I'll adjust my focus so there are no blurred areas in my relationships. For me to love well, I need to know where I stand.

Everything has its own perfection, be it higher or lower in the scale of things; and the perfection of one is not the perfection of another.
—John Henry Newman

There is no "perfection" in the world, yet in another sense, everything is perfect. Everything has its part to play in the world's great unfolding.

Everything in our lives serves its purpose for us. Everyone we meet today will bear some message that we need to hear—just as we'll bring messages to others. We're all partners in this dance. Each move we make affects the whole pattern, and we respond to the changes made by one another.

Sometimes the message is a need for change. That message is perfect, too. At each moment we are where we need to be, and the path before us can be clear. If we don't see it, it's because we've chosen not to.

When we grasp the reality of choice and change, when we learn to live in the moment, we come to understand perfection not as a frozen, changeless state, but as a part of our perpetual becoming. May the next perfect moment carry us to ever more satisfying choices.

Today I'll strive to clear my path and to appreciate the perfection of each moment that I choose.

*We are whole beings. We know this somewhere in a
part of ourselves that feels like memory.*
—Susan Griffin

When we study biology, we learn that in every cell of our
bodies we carry our whole genetic program, the complex set
of chemical instructions for building us: our skeleton, skin,
hair, eyes, muscles, brain, genitals, guts. Every human being
is born with a set of capacities and responses that are as
much a part of him or her as the capacity to grow fingernails
or to heal cuts.

Yet deep in our language and culture is a habit of speaking about ourselves as though our intelligence, our feelings,
and our will could be separated from the rest of us. We
talk about "a body/mind split," as though our bodies or our
minds did not fully belong to us. And all cultures have the
myth of a golden age when humans were fully integrated.

Much "civilized" behavior is bad for us—we eat and
breathe stuff that no self-respecting animal would tolerate.
Our lives can make us ill: immobility, anxiety, and stress
show up as ulcers, hypertension, skin rashes, heart disease,
obesity. We need to learn to respect ourselves as animals, and
not to deny that we have bodies. Our lives, like ourselves, are
all of one piece, whether or not we understand.

My real golden age is now, because it is the only time I have.

Keep your face to the sunshine and you cannot see the shadow.

—Helen Keller

We can make of our experiences what we choose. We can focus on the traffic snarls while traveling to work, or we can smile because we have a job to go to and a car to carry us there. We can be angry because the washing machine broke down, or grateful that we've been free, for a while, of the laundromat hassle. Every experience offers us an opportunity to respond, and our response is always a reflection of our emotions.

We choose to be angry, depressed, or afraid. We can just as easily decide to be trusting, happy, or confident. And the exciting realization for us is that we are free to choose whatever pleases us. Even though we've gotten mad for years over traffic jams doesn't mean we can't give up the anger. How liberating it is to claim control of our emotions, our attitudes, our reactions to the full panorama of our experiences.

Today can trip me up or I can run with it, leading all the way.

*Old folks—and here I'm talking about myself—need
more than anything else to feel they are needed, that
they have a purpose in life.*
—Ruth Youngdahl Nelson

Believing that we count in the lives of others, that others
need us and appreciate our contribution in the workplace,
the community, and at home is a universal need. In those
times when reassurance from others is lacking, we must
simply remember that every one of us is unique, and created
to contribute to our surroundings in individually inspired
ways. At every moment we are leveling an impact on the
physical, mental, and emotional environment of the community that surrounds us.

We are not without purpose. The daily activities which
invite our attention are the paths to growth and fulfillment
which are fitting for the contributions we are called on to
offer. We are obliged to do our part.

---

*My involvement in life has meaning. I may not wholly under-
stand the part I'm playing but I can trust that I'm being invited,
today, to participate in matters influencing a bigger picture.*

Any idea seriously entertained tends to bring about the realization of itself.
—Joseph Chilton Pearce

There is magic in believing in our capabilities at the moment, believing in our future potential, believing that we are worthy human beings with a purpose for being alive. Those ideas we hold in our minds, be they positive self-appraisals or negative personal assessments, will influence our behavior and as a consequence will invite others to form like-minded opinions. We tell others what to think of us by our actions and reactions, silences and outbursts.

However, the chance is present every moment to realize new dreams, to progress to new heights, to switch whatever course we are presently traveling on. All it takes is a changed attitude, commitment to a new idea, and the accompanying belief in the idea's potential. Any idea held in our mind can become a reality.

I'll have a chance to practice believing in myself and my potential today. It will open new doors.

Rivers and roads lead people on.

—*Georgia O'Keeffe*

Life is flowing and continuous; it is full of crossroads, tributaries, and sudden bends. To live is to travel, and navigable space attracts us. We want to follow the road or the river to find what lies around the next bend, over the next rise. The mere fact that they exist seems to tell us that we should follow them.

No one has ever lived our lives before us. This moment we are in a space and time that have never been traveled. Many past events prepared us for this moment, and we may often feel as though we were following a track that has been laid out for us; but at other times we feel as though we were strapped to the nose of a rocket, plunging through space where no one has ever been.

Then, at times (and we wish they were less rare), we become one with our path, immersed in our lives unquestioningly. This is the condition we prefer; when the river that leads us through life simply flows.

I will endeavor to accept my life; it is taking me where I need to go.

You cannot shake hands with a clenched fist.
—Indira Gandhi

Each person we welcome into our lives blesses us in ways that only the passage of time can validate. To invite someone in, however, takes an honest extension of the self, an open-armed posture which implies that we will risk being open.

How short and bland life seems when we cut ourselves off from the myriad experiences and acquaintances that present themselves to us. When we back away from the persons who have curiously crossed our paths, we back away from the lessons for which earlier experiences and persons have prepared us. Our progress and our success in life is both measured and nurtured by the number of genuine contacts we make with the men and women who are sharing our space in time.

Will I offer myself freely to today's experiences and personalities? The choice is mine.

So get a few laughs and do the best you can. Don't have an ideal to work for. That's like riding towards the mirage of a lake.

—Will Rogers

Human societies seem to go from crisis to crisis, fraught with injustice, oppression, and deception. But comedy is a gift of the human spirit. Sometimes it is the only weapon we have against official absurdity. Doesn't it often seem as though those who most clearly understand the dangers that face us are the ones who can play most wholeheartedly?

Laughter and play don't mean carelessness. Each of us must make our way through these serious times, carefully ordering our priorities and doing what we need to do to safeguard our spiritual growth. One temptation that besets many of us is to take ourselves so seriously that we begin to attach great weight to unimportant gestures. Humor is a wonderful tool for shaping us back down to size.

Sharing play is sometimes the only way we can touch another human being. Let us be grateful for the gift of true humor wherever we encounter it. It gives us strength to continue.

Today's events will remind me who I am. I will accept them with humor.

There is guidance for each of us, and by lowly listening, we shall hear the right word.
—*Ralph Waldo Emerson*

Perhaps it was only yesterday or the day before that we doubted our value to society, or to our family or friends. We often lose our direction. That's normal and consistent with the human condition. However, the length of time we spend floundering, uncertain of ourselves, is proportionate to the time it takes us to acknowledge the guide within. We need not be lost or full of doubt for long.

Going within ourselves may not be a spontaneous reaction for many of us, but we can learn to respond in this way. And when we're open to the inner urging and willing to follow it, we'll discover the benefits. All that's asked of us is the decision to listen.

I can quiet my thoughts today, long enough to sense the necessary direction to take. I can be certain the guidance is right for me.

Everyone has a talent. What is rare is the courage to
follow the talent to the dark place where it leads.
—Erica Jong

Our lives are purposeful and the dreams that mold our
actions or tease us down new avenues are not coincidental.
Our dreams are messages from the inner self, who urges us
to fulfill the purpose for which our talents have been given.
We each have talents to be employed in a fashion uniquely
our own; however, all too many of us opt for the half-life,
never fully giving our attention to the occasion at hand.

We can never know our talents or when to utilize them
when we pass through life on the fringe of activities. We cut
off our awareness of the inner urging when we don't enter
into the present, when we step back from ourselves, when
we refrain from offering rapt attention to the "talent scouts"
among us. And we'll never experience the joy we deserve
until we favor the inhabitants of our world with our talent.

My dreams are my guides but I must follow them.

. . . there are many sham diamonds in this life which pass for real, and vice versa, many real diamonds which go unvalued.

—W. M. Thackeray

It's high praise to say that someone is "genuine—the real thing." We use the image of jewelry when we talk about character: "Pure gold—14 karat—rings true—a diamond of the first water—a pearl." The qualities of beauty and rarity make gems precious to us, and by using the same language to describe people, we imply that real personal worth is equally beautiful, and equally rare.

Yet it's within everyone's grasp. We all agree on the valuable character traits: honesty, loyalty, openness, courage, humor, and the capacity for love. Everyone has them, and everyone can have them. Imitations won't do.

I needn't worry about whether someone else's qualities are genuine. I know what I admire and I have plenty to do polishing my own.

It is possible to be different and still be all right. There can be two—or more—answers to the same question, and all can be right.

—Anne Wilson Schaef

We're accustomed to thinking there are two sides to a subject: right/wrong, Democrat/Republican, walk/don't walk. This binary mode of thinking may lead us to disregard many possible solutions to our problems. "That's what makes ball games," we say, as though life were a competitive game. Relationships are an area where many of us fail to recognize that a question can have many right answers.

We may find ourselves locked into behavior patterns that guarantee we will be unhappy. We may set ourselves up as victims: "Everything happens to me!" or as bullies: "They all *obey* me, but no one *likes* me."

If we look at our own part, we often can see that if we had behaved differently in a situation, the outcome might have been different. We often act as though we were programmed in a simple binary mode, yet we have the power to choose a new mode at any moment.

———————

Today I will be true to my reality, which offers me an infinite range of choices.

When you are offended at any man's fault, turn to yourself and study your own failings. Then you will forget your anger.

—*Epictetus*

We take note of others' shortcomings and frequently record them in our minds, and then rely on these memories to feel superior. Seldom do we perceive our own failings as clearly. It takes courage and determination to inventory all our traits, both the pleasant and the unpleasant. It also takes an honest desire to know ourselves before we can fully assess the value of our traits. We can be certain, however, that the shortcomings we've noticed in others, we'll discover in ourselves.

It might well be a worthwhile exercise in personal development to let what bothers us in others guide our own attempt at self-improvement. For instance, if another's cynicism triggers negative feelings in us, we can be fairly certain we, too, respond cynically on occasion. Then we can make the decision to clean our own house. We aren't perfect, but we can strive to like ourselves, and others. Self-improvement and self-love will make it easier to accept someone else.

If I don't like something someone is doing today, I will take an honest look at myself.

. . . words are more powerful than perhaps anyone suspects, and once deeply engraved in a child's mind, they are not easily eradicated.

—May Sarton

Some of our greatest adult sufferings are owed to the many innocent abuses inflicted upon us as children. Harsh words, demeaning punishments, too many silent treatments, taught us who we were. Many of us remain disheartened, even diminished because of these powerful memories. When we accept criticism as accurate and deserved, it molds our characters, and eventually we live up to these assessments.

The good news is that we are in control of our own thoughts and attitudes, and in this respect we are all-powerful. The decision is ours to cast aside another's criticism, replacing it with positive self-talk. However, to successfully undo the harm others' words have caused takes daily dedication to our own positive reinforcement. Those who are confident and assured have internalized a positive dialogue with themselves.

Today is a new beginning, and I can make a fresh start by believing that I am a worthwhile person and my contribution is necessary.

*. . . it is only by labour that thought can be made
healthy, and only by thought that labour can be made
happy, and the two cannot be separated with impunity.*
—*John Ruskin*

We all require a balance of thought and labor, intellectual
and muscular effort in our lives. The work that most of us
do doesn't exercise either our brains or our bodies fully.
Most of us aren't scientists or scholars, or farmers or dancers;
we spend our working lives doing routine tasks and our
leisure time on passive amusements.

It's within our power to enhance the quality of our health
and happiness. If we look around, the world is full of challenges to our minds and bodies. We need only open ourselves to them. Other people will welcome what we can
give—physical effort, mental gymnastics, or any combination of the two.

Ideas that aren't applied or tested tend to become anemic;
and work that isn't examined and evaluated tends to become
stale. We can't really separate our minds from our bodies
without injuring them both. Our knowledge that we are
whole, integral beings is precious; let it illuminate this day.

*My spiritual well-being depends on living deeply with both my
thought and my labor.*

To find the good life you must become yourself.
—Dr. Bill Jackson

The more we run away from ourselves, the greater is our disenchantment with all the opportunities each day offers. When we live far from our own center, we ensure distance from all the persons in our life. Happiness in all things eludes us when we become distant from self and others.

Finding ourselves, closing the gap on the distance created, is a by-product of a personal inventory. We must *know* our wholeness before we can celebrate ourselves. And with celebration comes relief, freedom, and a readiness to tackle the opportunities presented to us.

Self-acceptance fosters self-love—the necessary prerequisite to the discovery of a good life. It's within reach. We must decide to move wholly toward it.

I can be excited about the chance to celebrate myself today. My qualities are special and deserve recognition.

If politics may be broadly defined as "the way we are with each other" then anything that affects how we connect with each other is political.
—Phyllis Jane Rose

There's a word for someone who is democratic with strangers and despotic with intimates, and the word is hypocrite. One of the important lessons of our time is that the personal is political. Our behavior reveals our true beliefs and what we truly are.

"Politics" may sound like too heavy a word for our behavior with our families, lovers, friends, and co-workers. Yet it's accurate. If we oppress or manipulate those who are close to us, bribing and threatening instead of asking honestly and negotiating for what we want, then it doesn't matter what we say, or how we vote. Our weakness and lack of maturity reveal us to be unstable.

Our politics is our lives: how we connect with one another, how we use resources, even how we think about things. How we deal with the smallest details is how we really are, and others are apt to deal with us in kind. If we're abusive or insincere, we're going to encounter abuse and insincerity. Let's bring our behavior into agreement with our beliefs.

Today I'll tune in to my political broadcast and make sure it reflects my platform.

Any path is only a path, and there is no affront, to oneself or to others, in dropping it if that is what your heart tells you.

—Carlos Castaneda

Our inner guide, our conscience, desires to be heard every step of our way today. And the choice to listen is easy if we've developed trust in those messages from our heart. There is no absolute path we need to follow in this life, but some will be more advantageous to our destiny than others. And some paths will weave themselves more smoothly among the paths of other travelers. We are all moving toward the same destination.

How thrilling it is to recognize that there is a message center within that has foreknowledge of our needs today, of the direction most fitting to the growth that's in store presently. We are not lonely, forgotten figures in this universe. We have purpose. And we can fulfill our purpose if we are acting in concert with our heart's message. When we move softly through the day, we can be certain of hearing the words forming within.

I'll take slow, sure steps today and know I'm on the right path.

We only do well the things we like doing.

—Colette

When you were a child, did you feel you had to do everything you were told to do? If you didn't perform all tasks equally well, did you feel that something was wrong with you?

When we were young, many of us were never told that we were doing as well as we could. Or if we were told, we didn't know how to hear it. It has taken some of us years to learn that to do something well often means to do it as well as we can. And somewhere inside us, those children still groan over tasks they can't do easily.

It helps to remember that we are not alone. Something we find difficult to do may have all sorts of repercussions for us and for others. We can always ask for help. Other people are pleased when we ask them to share their skills. When we know how to console the child within, we need never feel inadequate.

I'm working toward the day when I can truthfully say, "I like everything I do because I do everything as well as I can."

. . . the healthy, the strong individual, is the one who asks for help when he needs it whether he's got an abscess on his knee or in his soul.

—Rona Barrett

It is not meant that we should shoulder our problems alone. We are in the company of others by design, and the growth that each of us needs to experience is tied closely to both the sufferings and the celebrations that come to us all.

We each have the capacity to nurture and guide another's wavering steps. But the invitation to help must be extended. Perhaps we need reminding that each of us carries within us the remedy for another's ills. Likewise, someone among us awaits our call for help. We are accompanying one another on this journey because together we can smooth away the rough spots that would cause us to stumble if we were traveling alone.

Many calls for help will be made today, and some of us will be ready to respond. All of us need to remember that one of our greatest gifts is offering comfort to our stumbling friends.

Others need to help me—just as much as I may need their help.

A truly total history would cancel itself out—its product would be nought.

—*Claude Lévi-Strauss*

The world has always been as rich and varied as it is at this moment. Wealth and poverty, joy and pain, peace and struggle, have always existed side by side. The history of human life is the history of each person's journey from birth to death.

When we study history, we're always reading someone's interpretation or argument. The total history could never argue a point or prove an interpretation. We each can tell many true stories about ourselves by selecting facts from our personal histories. Yet our total history will cancel these stories and show us to be neither saints nor villains, merely seekers.

There's much we can learn from others' stories. They can illuminate our path; they can persuade us of the wisdom of one choice or another. Yet to be fully human is to escape the neat outlines of such a story. We immerse ourselves in life; we are surrounded by it.

I will try to respect everyone's reality, and to remember that much of the world lies outside my range of vision.

The liar leads an existence of unutterable loneliness.
                                                    —Adrienne Rich

All human interactions are built on agreement. Language itself depends on agreement: we agree, broadly, on the meaning of friend, blue, danger, cold. We agree on times of meeting, rules of procedure, and appropriate behaviors for many situations.

To lie is to break some of those agreements. "I returned your call" is a harmless lie, we might think, but if we didn't return the call, then we're lying about our intentions and our actions. It would be so much simpler for us to say, "I meant to return your call." So why don't we?

One important motive for telling such lies is to make ourselves look good. "I returned your call"; "I don't know how the paint got chipped"; "Someone stole my gloves"; all these are small falsehoods in which we claim that our performance was error-free—whatever slippage occurred wasn't our fault.

Human beings aren't error-free. We forget things, mislay our gloves, back into telephone poles. We're human. Pretending we're not isolates us from the rest of humanity. Not only do we break the agreement at the base of language; we set ourselves apart from each other. We pretend we are more perfect than someone else; we condemn ourselves to loneliness.

Let us admit our imperfections; they are part of our humanity.

Geese lower their heads when flying under a bridge,
no matter how high its arches may be.
                                    —*Julius Caesar Scaliger*

Old fears oppress us. They can hamper our growth; we learn nothing from them. Yet many of us continue to be afraid, for reasons we have long since forgotten, or never knew. Our bodies sometimes carry the weight of these old fears; a cringing of the shoulders or a knot in the gut may be part of the legacy.

Our growth as free beings may depend on shedding these old fears. They are as real as viruses, and they make us ill in similar ways. We need to examine our actions, to be sure that we aren't just ducking our heads every time we fly under a bridge. Am I behaving appropriately? Am I meeting this situation in this moment, or am I letting the past govern me? Am I acting or reacting?

When we discard old fear, we have a sense of liberation. Whatever wound that old fear was protecting can heal. We are ready to face life as it comes, not as we fear it might come.

Healing myself empowers me to shed the fears that limit my growth.

Gentleness is not a quality exclusive to women.
—Helen Reddy

Our options for how we respond to the men and women in our lives are vast. Being critical is one option open to us. Indifference and gentleness are others. The way we treat others reveals our own state of being. When we feel at peace, we generally respond peacefully to others. Conversely, when we feel worthless and full of self-doubt, we're likely to be sarcastic toward others. However, we can pull ourselves out of the self-imposed dungeon of despair. The method is this: In spite of personal feelings, be warm, kind, and gentle in every personal exchange with another, and your own dark mood is sure to be lifted

Again we are confronted with the reality that we make our world. Our treatment of others treats ourselves simultaneously. Our friends and co-workers mirror the self we often think we're hiding away. A conscious decision will guarantee the happiness we long for when the decision is to be gentle, loving, and caring toward all the people in our lives.

Today I'll be as happy as I want to be.

Our greatest happiness does not depend on the condition of life in which chance has placed us, but is always the result of a good conscience, good health, occupation, and freedom in all just pursuits.
—*Thomas Jefferson*

Opportunities abound each day of our lives for respectful, thoughtful actions toward others. It's within our power to apply serious effort to any task securing our attention. Being concerned with our physical health and emotional well-being is also a choice. And we discover the level of happiness we attain in this life is in proportion to the considerate attention we give to others, to our personal needs, and to the activities occupying us.

The blessings we receive in this life are measurable by those we bestow upon the lives of those with whom we're traveling. There really are no surprises in store for us. We each must assume responsibility for our own happiness and good fortune; and there's no time like the present for opening our minds to this reality.

We sit at the controls today, and our perspective on the situations we experience will make them pleasant, productive, or problematic.

The choice is my own. I'll find happiness and good will if I foster it.

If love does not know how to give and take without restrictions, it is not love, but a transaction.
—*Emma Goldman*

Many people form primary relationships before they've had a chance to live alone, to be on their own, to test themselves out in the world. Sometimes, in fact, it's fear of testing themselves that drives them prematurely into a relationship. So a lot of early relationships dissolve. And if the people involved in them are motivated by fear, they're likely to form new relationships before they've given themselves a chance to heal or grow from the old ones.

In a healthy relationship, both partners give and take without restrictions. Love is a process, an unfolding intimacy between adults. It's no substitute for a mortgage or a Band-Aid. It's difficult to conduct this kind of relationship when we're young and unsure. We need an enormous amount of trust to be nurturing and vulnerable. After we've knocked around in the world a bit, we're more likely to have the strength to form a real love bond.

Today I'll remember to promise only what I can give freely.

*. . . the greater part of our happiness or misery depends
on our dispositions and not on our circumstances.*
—*Martha Washington*

A light heart eases a hard struggle. A sense of humor
takes the sting out of troubling circumstances. Likewise, a
hateful attitude takes the luster out of the brightest moments. We have the power to control the flavor of the circumstances which will invite our involvement.

Accepting responsibility for our own happiness frees us
from others' control. And it heightens our moments of
pleasure. We are in control of the level of our joy and sorrow. In any situation we may choose to give others control
over our feelings, but making that choice guarantees that
we'll live half-lives with little real happiness.

*Knowing that happiness is always within reach if I extend my
hand for it strengthens my grasp. I'll practice taking charge of
my own happiness today.*

Life is terribly deficient in form. Its catastrophes happen in the wrong way and to the wrong people.
—Oscar Wilde

Villains get punished and heroes triumph in well-made plays and books. In life it's not easy to say who's who; most of us are heroic sometimes and villainous other times. Our lives are an uneven mixture of triumph, reward, and hanging-in. Unjust events happen: children die, airplanes crash, rivers flood. The world contains starvation and abundance, violence and gentleness, in its pattern.

The strands of right and wrong, good and bad, are mingled; there's no untangling them. What contributes to our personal progress is our ability to accept this bewildering complexity. To live wholeheartedly, yet to detach ourselves from the outcomes of our actions is the secret of serenity.

When a catastrophe strikes, we may be unable to turn it over, to find any good in it. We don't know all there is to know; we see only a part of the world's pattern. Hanging on to a disaster multiplies its effects. We must feel our feelings and let them go.

I will work for surrender and acceptance; the days to come will hold brand new possibilities.

Every time a man unburdens his heart to a stranger
he reaffirms the love that unites humanity.
—Germaine Greer

Intimacy is the gift that bonds us to one another. We understand our likenesses and can acknowledge our differences in this process of sharing ourselves. We can see how similar our fears and our hurts are, and in seeing we gain strength.

Becoming intimate with someone else unites us, enlarges our capacities to nurture the people in our lives. Our emotional growth is proportionate to our attempts at intimacy.

Too often we hold back from telling others who we really are, fearing that they'll think less of us if they know the person we hide within. Only the experience of self-revelation can assure us that others won't think less of us. Our unity with another is possible only if we share the person who lives within.

I must find unity with others if I am to have the strength to withstand whatever befalls me. The people around me can be trusted with knowledge of my inner self. I'll reach out today.

. . . to have a crisis, and act upon it, is one thing. To dwell in perpetual crisis is another.
                                    —Barbara Grizzuti Harrison

Misery is an option available to us every day, over any situation. We can linger, befriending despair. It is also possible to take life's rough currents in stride, responding to them sanely, thoughtfully, trustingly. The rough times, we can see in retrospect, teach us the most.

Crises become too familiar to some of us. They push us into overdrive and an elation accompanies them, an elation born from the energy inherent in the crisis. However, this same energy is inherent in calm, sensible responses to life if we'd learn to cultivate it. Crises ultimately burn us out, while measured, balanced responses to turmoil rekindle belief in ourselves, and our ability to handle the gravest conditions.

Dwelling in crisis allows us to avoid forward movement. However, if we want to grow and find the real happiness we deserve, we must move ahead to the challenges that promise us our due.

A crisis may protect me from unknown opportunities today. It will also prevent growth. My choice is open.

We do not weary of eating and sleeping every day, for hunger and sleepiness recur. Without that we should weary of them. So, without the hunger for spiritual things, we weary of them.

—Blaise Pascal

A great spiritual hunger is a hallmark of our age. Our age, however, is such a secular one that any of us do not recognize this hunger for what it is. We feel an emptiness and we try to fill it with consumer goods or exercise workshops. Our restless narcissism takes up one fad after another but, since we were not truly hungry for them, we weary of them.

Spiritual nourishment comes only with self-forgetfulness. This seems paradoxical; and yet transcending ourselves is the greatest gift that can be bestowed. Haven't we noticed that the people who seem most at peace in the world are those who live for others?

When we find a true source of spiritual wealth, we can learn to satisfy our hunger. And it will recur! Our needs for refreshment of the spirit will be more focused, better defined, and we will know how to satisfy them. We can never nourish our spirits by concentrating on ourselves.

I will strengthen my spirit by endeavoring to achieve selflessness in my dealings with others.

Don't do nothing you can't share, and be prepared to discuss everything that you do.
—Martin Shepard, M.D.

Secrets diminish self-respect; they foster paranoia, and they make it impossible to have honest and open communication. Self-disclosure cleanses us; but an even greater benefit is that a commitment to it triggers careful forethought, and a needless or perhaps hurtful action can be avoided.

It takes only a moment to reflect on the possible ramifications of an intended action. And that moment's reflection can save us from apologies, shame, and embarrassment. Being committed and prepared to inform others of all that we are nurtures the growth of our better selves. No greater encouragement for self-improvement exists than the decision to share absolutely all.

I will think before acting today and find freedom from shame.

The reward of labour is life.

—William Morris

Almost everyone complains about work: the price of fertilizer, the drudgery of housework, the bureaucratic details, and the long hours. Whether we're mechanics or physicians or keypunch operators, most of us complain about the work we do.

Yet without work, where would we be? How could we derive a sense of ourselves as connected to the world if we weren't involved in it through our work? Work is the fiber of our lives. It nourishes us and provides us with a measure of ourselves. When we're productive, we feel good. When work loses its meaning, we feel bad.

We owe it to ourselves to find work that fulfills us. We need the rhythm of tasks begun and completed for our spiritual health. When our work violates us, we suffer. Then we need to look for creative solutions to end our pain—changing the work we do, taking risks.

Work is our blessing. Today I'll be grateful for good work; what I do, I'll do well.

What is this life if, full of care,
We have no time to stand and stare?
—William Henry Davies

Souls, like animals and plants, need air. Do our lives have enough empty space in them to nourish our spirit? Living in cities, plugged into networks of jobs, friends, and projects, we sometimes neglect our standing-and-staring needs.

They're quite specific: we need to be outside, in pleasant weather, with nothing much to do. We need to let the world go on its way without us for a while. We need to have things pass before our eyes: clouds, or boats, or waving grass.

Blessed idleness! Blessed inattention! When we slip back into the groove, we're refreshed by our passive interlude. Let's remember the recipe and find some time to stand aside and stare.

If I don't take the time, it will take me. I'd rather the choice was mine.

*I believed what I was told and not what my own
eyes saw.*

—*Margaret Drabble*

Children see a flat world and are told it is round. We are
trained very early to disbelieve the evidence of our senses.
But there comes a point when we begin to question what we
are told and to feel that our own vision is probably as keen
as anyone's.

Independence of thought can be an admirable quality. It's
also a quality that distinguishes those we call crackpots.
Where do we draw the line?

It's important always to try to disentangle what we want
to believe from the evidence of our senses. Wanting events
to have a certain outcome can blur our view of what is
actually happening. We can delude ourselves to the point of
denying the reality we perceive in favor of some ideal, some
fantasy.

Testing our beliefs against what our own eyes see and the
opinions of those we respect will keep us balanced between
skepticism and delusion. Life is rich and baffling enough
without our fantasies to complicate it.

My uncorrected vision sometimes distorts my reality.

The great thing in this world is not so much where we are, but in what direction we are moving.
—*Oliver Wendell Holmes*

We may feel idle, but we are not. We are moving along some pathway at every moment, and each of us needs to accept responsibility for our movement and determine our course. For when we are not moving forward toward our desired destination, we are moving away from it. We are moving, always.

Having a goal inspires concrete action. It fosters planned movement, a focus for the day. Additionally, it facilitates decision making. Living without goals diminishes the joy that's inherent when we respond advantageously to an inviting opportunity. Further, we can only truly recognize essential opportunities when we are in command of our direction.

It may be difficult to look forward to the days ahead if we have no dream to shoot for. Perhaps a goal for some of us is simply to choose a goal.

I never stand still. I will take charge today of the movement that's guaranteed. I will go where I want to go.

It is only when there is nothing but praise that life loses its charm, and I begin to wonder what I should do about it.

—*Vijaya Lakshmi Pandit*

We lose our appreciation for joyful times when they become a matter of course. Compliments lose their delicious quality with overuse. Balance in all things offers the greatest satisfaction.

It's not likely that we realize the full value of variety in our lives. Probably we long for easy times, the absence of struggle, and certainty regarding outcomes. Were life to treat us in such manner, we'd soon lose our zest for the day ahead. The sense of accomplishment that we hunger for is nestled within the day's rough ripples.

Our experience in this life is purposeful, which means there are matters we'll be asked to attend to. Not every involvement will provide pleasure. Some, in fact, will inflict pain, but we'll discover elements that will enhance our self-awareness. Through this knowledge we'll find lasting fulfillment.

Today will be a mixture of joy, boredom, perhaps both pain and sorrow. Each element will give me reason for growth.

*I accept life unconditionally. . . . Most people ask for
happiness on condition. Happiness can only be felt if
you don't set any condition.*

—Arthur Rubinstein

When life offers you lemons, make lemonade, so the
saying goes. It's simple and true. No matter the circumstances of our lives, we can maximize the positive events.
More importantly, we can learn from the negative ones. In
reflections on the past, we are frequently surprised to discover that the lemon made possible the deliciousness of a
present experience.

All events of our lives are threads, weaving a pattern that
is unfolding by design. Each experience is equal to every
other experience. We shouldn't cling to any one of them, or
shrink from any. It's their sum that makes us who we are.
Each of us is a mosaic unto ourselves. And yet, by design,
our patterns, our lives intersect.

An expectation that an experience is a necessary part of
our design will foster gratitude, even in the moment that we
must swallow the bitter fruit.

Today I'll be faced with some lemons. Can I make lemonade?

*A depressing and difficult passage has prefaced every
new page I have turned in life.*
                                        —*Charlotte Brontë*

What would it be like to shed our old skin, like a snake,
when it grew too small? Perhaps the discomfort we feel
at each new stage of growth is something like that feeling. Truly, each new page or stage of life has a difficult
introduction—but if we can only remember that, it may help
us through the bad times.

Too often, in the grip of change, we lose sight of what we
are becoming. Did you ever wonder how it would feel to be
a grub and then turn into a winged creature? It helps us to
endure the depressing passage if we can remember that we're
being prepared for a new stage of our lives, one in which,
perhaps, we will leave our old selves as far behind as the
dragonfly leaves the larva.

With time and wisdom comes the knowledge that some
pain always accompanies growth. We can accept the pain
more gracefully if we remind ourselves that we are preparing
to turn a new page.

My spirit, like my body, holds the secrets of growth and change.

Tomorrow doesn't matter for I have lived today.
                                    —Horace

The twenty-four hours lying ahead is all we have been promised. With that promise is a guarantee that we will greet opportunities for growth that have their roots in yesterday. Our evolution is not without purpose and design; therefore, we need not concern ourselves with the future. It will educate and comfort us as it becomes the present.

When we understand that the situations inviting our responses today have purpose, our anxiety is eased. Fear is allayed when our understanding is complete. Our life experiences are not happenstance, of this we can be sure; there exists an interdependence. Events are woven together for our greater good. Moreover, no one event offers more than a glance at the whole picture. So what we see today enlightens us about yesterday and last week, even last year, perhaps. Tomorrow will do likewise. But today is our only concern. It will provide exactly those opportunities we need to weave the next portion of our chosen design.

I am peaceful. Today will take care of my needs.

To dream what one dreams is neither wise nor foolish, successful nor unsuccessful. No precautions can be taken against it, except, perhaps, that of remaining permanently awake.

—Margaret MacDonald

Dreams, like desires and feelings, simply happen. They happen to everyone from early childhood to old age; they're part of the life of the human mind, and we can't really control them. All we ever can control is our behavior—how we act on our dreams, our desires, and our feelings.

At times some of us try to control the uncontrollable, and stay "permanently awake," to fence out or repress the sadness, desire, or rage that we don't want to feel. By doing this, we make ourselves doubly unhappy; for human beings are creatures of feeling and fumbling. To try to engineer the unruly parts out of our lives is just to create another way to feel bad, for the attempt is doomed to fail.

Accepting our roughness, the violence and vulnerability that live within us, is to let go of shame. Why be ashamed? All others are the same as we. We can't choose our feelings, but we can choose how—or whether—we express them.

If I fence out my dreams and feelings, I turn them into enemies.

When we cling to pain we end up punishing ourselves.
—Leo F. Buscaglia

Painful situations, relationships that hurt us, memories of experiences that pinch our nerve endings, need not imprison us. However, we are seldom very quick to let go of the pain. Instead, we become obsessed with it, the precipitating circumstances, and the longed-for, but often missed outcome. We choose to wallow in the pain, rather than learn from it. And we salt our own wounds every time we indulge the desire to replay the circumstances that triggered the pain.

Pain can't be avoided. It's as natural as joy. In fact, we understand joy in contrast to the experiences of pain. Each offers breadth to our lives. And both strengthen us. Our maturity is proportionate to our acceptance of all experiences. In retrospect we can be grateful for pain, for it offered us many gifts in disguise.

I can see pain as part of a bigger picture, if I so desire.

I was tender and often, true;
Ever a prey to coincidence,
Always I knew the consequence;
Always saw what the end would be.
We're as Nature made us—hence
I loved them until they loved me.

—Dorothy Parker

Did Nature really make us so that we despise those who love us? Groucho Marx's joke, "I wouldn't belong to any club that would have me for a member," implies the same thing. But this can't be; we're children of the universe, each of us exactly as lovable and fallible as all the others.

Many of us go through years of upheaval in which we want only what we can't get. If we should get it, heaven forbid, it turns to rubbish in our hands. Some people call this the "reverse Midas touch," and it's common enough so that we all recognize it.

This is a symptom of self-mistrust, of self-dislike. If we believe in ourselves, we'll evaluate those who are drawn to us on their merits. For someone to love us doesn't automatically mean that they're deluded. It might simply mean that they love us.

If I don't love and value myself, I won't really be able to love back someone who does.

We saw endurance, chance, and law. We knew transi-
ence but glimpsed eternity. We learned that nature's
flux is constancy and we were at ease.
—Edna Hong and Howard Hong

Precious are the glimpses we get into the nature of things. But we must be ready for them, or the most exquisite lessons will be lost on us. Anxiety, regret, or egotism can cloud our perceptions. We only learn when we can set aside our preoccupations.

To be hung-up is to be caught, like a coat on a hook, unfree. When we're hung-up, our attention is somewhere else; we can't learn anything. And hang-ups are a choice we make. If we choose the freedom to experience nature's flux, we can slip off the hook.

Mainly we choose to stay hung-up out of fear—fear of the unknown and perhaps fear of freedom. If we've spent most of our lives on one hook or another, we may not have much confidence that we can get along by ourselves. But we can.

Today I'll choose freedom and groundedness. I'll choose to learn ease.

The change of one simple behavior can affect other behaviors and thus change many things.
—Jean Baer

The effects on every action are far-reaching. Our response to a particular set of circumstances will influence its outcome and the lives of all persons concerned. Harsh words one time, a smile and praise another, will make their mark in the system that includes us all. Our actions and interactions are interdependent, each one having been affected by preceding actions and in turn affecting those that follow.

A single action has impact on our subsequent actions. An angry retort is likely to influence our behavior toward the next unsuspecting person who gains our attention.

A grateful attitude expressed will soften the harsh realities of life for the giver as well as the receiver. The principle underlying all behavior is that it breeds itself repeatedly. Positive, respectful action can become habitual.

Let me remember that I'm creating habits by my every action today. I can make them good ones as easily as bad ones.

To live is not merely to breathe, it is to act; it is to make use of our organs, senses, faculties, of all those parts of ourselves which give us the feeling of existence.

—*Jean-Jacques Rousseau*

We are gifted with talents that need encouragement in order to blossom. Few of us fully appreciate our talents. Many of us fail to utilize them. And yet they are waiting for the invitation to present themselves.

We have been blessed with particular talents because the world we live in needs our individual involvement. Each of us is charged with a responsibility to contribute to the lives around us. Our shared talents make the road smooth, when each of us has acted as the need arose.

We are called to participate by our talents. They help define who we are. They affirm that we count, that we are needed. No one is without a capability, a characteristic that lends just the right flavor to a situation involving others. Whether it's a sense of humor, the ability to write or paint, or a talent for settling disputes, we each have a calling card, and we are asked, daily, to make our contribution.

Am I willing today to participate fully in the life around me?

Out of every crisis comes the chance to be reborn. . . .
—*Nena O'Neill*

It is not our smooth passages that reveal new understandings, but the strenuous, uphill battles that benefit us with the knowledge we need to grow. Looking on our challenges as gifts whose resolution promises greater comfort makes them agreeable, perhaps even prized. Without them we stagnate, and life's joys are few.

Life is a series of lessons. And our crises are our homework. The patience and the trust we developed while living through last week's crisis has prepared us for greater benefits from those that lie ahead. Knowing that a crisis guarantees us the growth we deserve makes its sting endurable.

Every crisis is followed by a time of easy stepping. These restful periods let us adjust to our new stage of development, and they invite us to store up our strength, our energy for the tests that lie ahead.

Every stage of an experience has its roots in the past and leans toward the future. I'll trust that whatever I encounter today I'm prepared for and will benefit from.

It is astounding . . . how much energy the body is
capable of pouring out and then replenishing. That is
a magical act, because you never really understand
where all that energy comes from.

—Robert Bly

The energy and persistence of a motivated person are truly marvelous. The work that nourishes us, the work that is a form of rapture, a form of praise, is magical. Where does our energy come from? Surely not from breakfast cereal, sandwiches, or coffee. It is a magical transformation of earthly food into pure spirit.

Rapture isn't our daily state, but we can achieve it. We achieve this rapt state when we forget ourselves, when we're totally immersed in the work that transforms us—whether it's clearing a field, playing a cello, collecting stamps, factoring an equation, or kneading dough.

If we're lucky, we discover this capacity for transformation while we're young. Some of us spend our whole lives searching for it. Most of us come upon it somehow: the key to releasing our limitless energy of mind or body. Self-forgetfulness is basic to it. The strength of the spirit does the rest.

When energy flags, it's often because I'm preoccupied with self.
To renew my energy, all I need do is get out of my own way.

We are not educated: most of us cannot read or write. But we are strong because we are close to the earth and we know what matters.

—Mie Amano

The important thing in life is to know what matters for us. Our reality and values are our own; no one else can dictate them to us. They come out of our experiences and observation, and our spiritual health asks that we be true to them.

Similarly, we must be true to what matters for us. We won't try to win anyone over. Nor will we let someone else sway us. We will respect each other's reality, for that's how we will live in peace.

Further, if we're open and frank with each other, and with everyone else, we can spread integrity, respect, and peace. Quakers have a saying, "Let it begin with me." Integrity will spread outward, in concentric rings, for we are connected with one another.

Strength and growth come from knowing ourselves, knowing what matters for us. If we respect each other, we will find the way to fit any apparent conflict into a broader system that can accommodate us both.

If I am honest with myself, I can be my own best teacher.

Things are in the saddle
And ride mankind.
                              —*Ralph Waldo Emerson*

Some of us buy expensive toys on impulse; tire of them quickly; and let ourselves feel hopeless and inadequate because the impulsive wish was a shallow one. To ease our pain, we buy new toys—and so it goes.

Each new thing we acquire means new responsibilities: insurance policies, computer software, installment payments, safe deposit boxes. Deadlines and taxes oppress us; we dream of "getting away from it all."

At some point, we chose everything in our lives. If we wish, we can choose to do without it. When we feel suffocated by our possessions and obligations, it's good to clear our minds and think about what we really want. Many of us don't think about our values consciously until they become a source of pain.

We'd be kinder to ourselves if we were fully aware of our values when we make choices in our lives. Are we choosing things as a shortcut to happiness—or a substitute for it? If we feel an emptiness that we've tried to fill with things, we'd do better to tend our spirits.

Let me learn to trust myself; then I know I'll like what I do.

We are only as sick as the secrets we keep.
                                        —*Anonymous*

Not letting others know who we really are keeps us continually off balance while in their presence. Risking full openness, even with friends, is not easy; however, the pain that accompanies secret-keeping far exceeds the potential pain of self-revelation.

There are unexpected gifts for our complete honesty. One is discovering that we're like others. We're not unique in our shame nor our self-abhorrence. And the attachments to others inspired by our decision to share ourselves strengthen us. The pain of alienation diminishes. We begin to sense our equality, one with another, and we experience trust.

Sharing secrets, our own and others', lessens the burden of guilt that diminishes each of us. But more than that, our freedom from secrets nurtures healthy personal growth. Hiding nothing convinces us that we have nothing to hide; thus, we're free to try new behaviors, move in unfamiliar directions.

My burdens are only as heavy as the secrets I hang on to.

It isn't for the moment you are stuck that you need courage, but for the long uphill climb back to sanity and faith and security.

—Anne Morrow Lindbergh

It's not just major challenges that require courage. Even the minor skirmishes with life demand some deep breaths, perhaps hushed prayers, and lots of hope. We'd glide more easily through every day if we'd accept that struggle is part of the process of life; that it offers more opportunities for us to realize our individual potential than any other dimension of life.

Struggles strengthen us, enrich our character, temper our emotions. They enhance our being in untold ways, and yet we plead to be spared them. How ironic that we each long for greater success, at least some recognition for our accomplishments, but recoil from the very experiences that guarantee these personal satisfactions.

My struggles today are my gifts in disguise. I will grow accordingly.

We succeed in enterprises which demand the positive qualities we possess, but we excel in those which can also make use of our defects.

—Alexis de Tocqueville

Those areas of our lives we struggle with the most, such as impatience, control, energy, or procrastination, offer us opportunities for great victories. But even more, they offer greater learning, and the greatest chance for further growth and development when we relinquish our struggle. We can be certain that any activity attracting our involvement will provide chances to demonstrate both our positive qualities and our defects.

Our human need to be rid of defects can hamper our progress, keeping us stuck in old behavior. But when we've come to accept defects as normal we can even capitalize on them. They define who we are momentarily. We need to remember that defects are generally assets that have become twisted with use. Therefore, we can understand their origin and smooth off the rough edges. Assets and defects will switch places in our repertoire. We can use each for the greater good of the enterprise deserving our attention.

Defects have so much to teach us. They offer us meaningful opportunities for growth and mature action. Today's assets were yesterday's defects and where we stumble today, tomorrow we'll glide.

My defects will offer me new learning today if I relinquish my incessant urge to be free of them.

To expect life to be tailored to our specifications is to invite frustration.

—*Anonymous*

Life is what it is. It seldom matches our hopes and dreams, but it never fails to be exactly what we need. We are short-sighted, really. Reflections on the past can enlighten us to this fact. Seldom does any plan develop as we'd assumed.

Perhaps we are only beginning to realize that there exists a carefully orchestrated plan that each of us has been invited to experience. Our contributions help to form the plan which enhances our personal development. We are privy to the tiniest segment at any one moment, however. We must trust that the plan has our best interests at heart, even though our sights may be focused elsewhere. The evolution of our lives, often in spite of our own misguided efforts, should convince us that we can let go of the reins.

What life offers today is what I need—no matter what I may think!

Speak your truth quietly and clearly; and listen to others, even to the dull and the ignorant; they too have their story.

—Max Ehrmann

We have been invited to share ourselves in this phenomenon called life. We are not fully cognizant of the value of our gifts to one another. We don't know which words we mutter might be the pearls of wisdom for another. However, we can be certain that we'll show the way to someone else. Each of us is acting as a guide for another, perhaps a friend, perhaps an enemy. Whenever the student is ready, a teacher will appear. We are all students. We are all teachers.

How reassuring to know that we have a story that counts in someone else's unfolding. And it's equally exciting to contemplate how another's progress will nurture our own. But we need another's attention in order to be certain that our movements are in the right direction.

I can't be certain whose story I need most to hear today. I can only be attentive to them all.

. . . we both want a joy of undeep and unabiding things . . .

—*Gwendolyn Brooks*

When I can live fully in each moment, I can open myself to beauties that might otherwise escape me entirely. The more attuned I am to what is really going on right now, which means unhooking my mind from preoccupation with the past and worry about the future, the freer I am to catch fleeting perceptions and subtle shifts in the world about me.

We know that we only use about 10 percent of our brain's capacity for the ordinary business of living, which includes building space shuttles and filing tax returns. The more fully we can bring all of ourselves to each moment, the more of our capacity is available for living.

Life isn't last year, or ten minutes from now; it's now, this moment, which will pass and be followed by more passing moments, a flow of time in which we're carried forward. Our journey is smoothed when we learn to let go, and it's eased by the joy we learn to take in "undeep and unabiding things."

Paradoxical but true: I'll find lasting happiness only when I let go of the notion of permanence.

Happiness is an endowment and not an acquisition. It depends more upon temperament and disposition than environment.

—John J. Ingalls

We carry within us the ingredient which assures smooth travel today, if that's our choice. In our exchanges with life, we can project an attitude of gladness or regret. We can be grateful for our blessings or resentful that we have only what we have. We can offer love to our fellow travelers or harbor envy. However, when we choose to enter a situation, a discussion perhaps, offering loving acceptance of whatever we encounter, we'll discover the prevailing inner happiness.

Becoming aware that the power to be happy is at our fingertips is profoundly exhilarating. At first it may also be frightening because we can no longer deny responsibility for our feelings. Every moment of our lives we are making a choice about how to feel.

Emotional maturity follows on the coattails of responsible choice-making. Never again must I wait for another to make me happy. It's in my power to be happy, today.

Old things were stirring: the old illness of remembering was going to start again.
—Rosamond Lehmann

Does the act of remembering ever resemble an illness? Yes, if it causes pain. For many of us, memories of our past behavior seem to live in cages, like wild animals; if we enter the cages, the beasts attack us.

Why do we give memory this power to wound? We sometimes seem to want the unproductive pain of a shameful remembrance, as though we had sentenced ourselves to feel badly, as if our pain could alter the past—or pay for it.

It's time to forgive ourselves. We know what's past is past, and the only time we have is the present. We may feel as though we carry a complicated weight of guilt and shame, but the act of releasing ourselves is simple—an act of self-acceptance. Let us greet the present in the best way we know, and let go of regrets.

I will tame my memories, so that they become my companions if I choose.

*To love is to place our happiness in the happiness of
another.*

—*G. W. von Leibnitz*

Broadening our vision beyond our self-serving needs and
acknowledging the importance of others in our lives not only
lifts their spirits, but also fosters positive feelings within
ourselves. Our personal happiness grows when we nourish
someone else's.

That which we give to others will be given to us in time.
In order to find peace, we must behave peacefully toward
others. And to receive love, we must willingly and unconditionally offer it. When we try to control others' behavior,
we meet resistance. We can be certain an aggressive stance
invites adversity. How true is the axiom "we reap that which
we sow."

*My own behavior invites the treatment I'll receive today. I am
free to act lovingly, respectfully, and peacefully.*

But one of the attributes of love, like art, is to bring harmony and order out of chaos.
—*Molly Haskell*

The offer of love to the person sharing this time in our lives softens them, ourselves, and the events we share. Giving and receiving loving thoughts eases any momentary difficulty; loving and feeling loved reminds us that we are never alone in our struggles. In partnership we can survive any troubling circumstance.

Love of self, of family, of enemies, increases the harmonious conditions that affect us all. Like the ripples from a pebble dropped in a stream, the act of loving moves beyond the object receiving the love at this moment. In fact, the love we give is the love we'll receive.

It is a demonstrable fact that hatred breeds hatred. Just as absolute is the knowledge that the love we offer another makes easier their gift of love to yet another. Love multiplies itself and the harmony created nurtures us all.

Love makes partners of us all. No circumstances can fell me when I'm in company with another. I will look among my associates today for willing partners.

Honor: what a spiky, uncomfortable thing it can be. I expect the young are wise to be dropping it.
—Rose Macaulay

Each generation looks at its children with mingled pride and horror and thinks they are destroying standards, overturning values, and generally going to wrack and ruin. In Greece, in the fourth century B.C., Plato complained that young people had no morals and that their music was barbaric.

What we've not understood, for 2500 years and more, is that each new generation simply renames the old truths in the process of making them their own. Love, courage, honesty, generosity of the spirit—these values don't change, although they may turn up in unfamiliar shapes.

Virtues may seem spiky and uncomfortable to young people, who need to claim their own experience. But each generation will discover the truth for itself. We needn't fear that the new will destroy the old; it will simply make it new.

I will keep in mind that the young people of each age seek an identity that sets them apart from their elders—without realizing that in this way, too, they resemble them.

Even a happy life cannot be without a measure of darkness, and the word "happiness" would lose its meaning if it were not balanced by sadness.
—*Carl Gustav Jung*

Life is full of contrasts. What we perceive or feel at this moment is often heightened by an experience we just passed through. It's the sum and substance of all experiences and our feelings about them that give meaning to any single moment.

Joy is understood only in a life where discouragement has made its mark. Our lives are recharged, even glorified, by every moving experience, no matter what kind of emotion is evoked. In fact, our very existence is verified each time an encounter invites an emotional response.

When we are sad, it is because it satisfies a need to feel that way. If we accept this fact, our acceptance of every emotion grounds our lives in a serenity which embraces and transcends all our feelings.

Whatever I may feel today is cause for celebration. It's a sign of my vitality.

Mistakes are a fact of life.
It is the response to error that counts.
—Nikki Giovanni

We're not perfect. Our mistakes are consistent with the lessons we've been assigned to learn. We strive for perfection in ourselves and sometimes we demand it of others. And when we fall short of the mark, we frequently feel that all is lost. The most important and timely lesson any of us can learn today is that doing our best is as close to perfect as we need to get.

Since falling short of the mark is the norm among us, a second lesson is to learn to accept this fact. What counts is the effort. And even with our best efforts we can't be sure of the outcome. However, the outcome will be more satisfying if we are confident that we've done all we were able to do.

Shame over mistakes, or over shortcomings in general, is certain to exaggerate and multiply the negative self-opinions that generally haunt those of us who demand perfection. And the result is even more mistakes, because our attention is diverted from the task at hand. We must believe that mistakes are the guideposts to the destination we're headed for.

All is not lost if I err today. Mistakes help me stay on course, providing I'm willing to learn from them.

Two birds fly past.
They are needed somewhere.

—*Robert Bly*

Our lives touch the lives of thousands of other people in ever widening circles. Every act of ours has a public dimension, even something as private as sharpening a pencil or filling a teakettle. We all are needed by everyone, and our chosen lives become a necessary part of the larger pattern woven by all other lives.

Even by becoming a recluse or a hermit, we don't leave the pattern. We may change it, so that others direct their lives in a different way with respect to our own. But this is true of all choices.

And we don't see the pattern as a whole; it's too complex, too vast for us to grasp. About the best we can hope for is the optimistic detachment that lets us see that those birds are needed. The squirrels in our attic, the ants at the picnic, the angry driver honking behind us, are all needed. What can we learn from them?

———————————

Today I'll rejoice in my connectedness.

*The sky changes every minute . . . on the plains side of
the Divide most people have visions or go mad.*
—*Sandra Alcosser*

Our adaptability is a constant source of amazement. We
can learn to live and even thrive in such radically differing
settings as a high-rise apartment in New York City and
a sheepskin hut in Mongolia. We live in deserts, near
swamps; on boats, in trees, and even underground. We can
eat almost anything that any animal eats, and a lot of other
things that no animal would touch. Our instinct for survival
takes expression in our marvelous ability to adapt.

Some brain scientists believe that what we call madness
is an adaptation, a technique for getting what we need. It's
possible that visions are adaptive, too. Extraordinary behavior expresses extraordinary states of mind.

We're often hard on ourselves if we catch ourselves
behaving oddly—humming aloud or weeping or staring in
amazement at a spot on the wall. We want to be normal;
we'll suppress the odd behavior. But we should pay attention; unusual behavior often means that something's going
on inside us that needs attention. Maybe we're grieving a
loss, or sitting on some anger. Self-acceptance and self-love
will heal us better than scoldings.

*I can accept even the unusual in myself. It is only one variety
of humanness.*

There is nothing so moving—not even acts of love or hate—as the discovery that one is not alone.
—*Robert Ardrey*

We live in concert with others, compatibly at times and at other times not so well, but always with others. We don't always acknowledge our togetherness, but when we are moved to, we quickly sense the comforts of a shared journey. We belong to more than just our neighborhood, our families, our circle of friends. The concert that has captured us is greater, and it has a conductor with whom we travel a path as well. It's this journey that encourages us to appreciate the steps we take with others.

The whole of creation depends on the contribution of each part for its completion. Interdependently, never singly and alone, we exist. We are at one with another, and this oneness is eternal.

I may not feel our oneness today, but I will trust that it is so.

I search in these words and find nothing more than myself, caught between the grapes and the thorns.
—Anne Sexton

We are frequently afraid to look into ourselves, to probe our depths. We've feared that if we examined our basic motives and desires, we'd find a swamp of evil: corrupt, selfish, and full of hate. But we've learned—to our considerable relief—that those fears were unfounded. We're human, that's all; not better or worse than everyone else.

We all have particular traits that we struggle with, parts of ourselves that make us unhappy. When we're feeling down on ourselves, it may seem that we're the only person in the world with that fault. "Why am I so insecure?" "No one else talks too loud!" "l hate being so competitive." If we could see into the hearts of our friends and associates, we would find virtually the same struggles.

And yet we go on fearing the monster lurking in those woods. Let's bring that specter into the light; it's only ourselves, constant traveler between pain and joy.

I only fear what I don't know; self-knowledge is my real life's work.

My mission on earth is to recognize the void—inside and outside of me—and fill it.
                                    —*Rabbi Menahem*

Emptiness often haunts us. The alienation we feel that accompanies us to work, to parties, even among friends, is letting us know that we need to nurture our inner selves. Within each of us lives the small child who feels fear, fear about a particular outcome, or our ability to handle a situation. As we practice caring for our inner child in all of our experiences we'll discover a spiritual strength and a calmness that eluded us in the past. Consciously developing a connection to the inner child at first lessens the brunt of the external world, then removes it.

The spirit-child becomes our strength and our hope when we turn to it. It fills us; it comforts us as we comfort it. We no longer doubt our place in this life.

If I go within today to offer comfort, I'll find it. I will not feel alone or fearful if I reach within and take the hand of strength.

I was taught that the way of progress is neither swift nor easy.

—Marie Curie

Some of our goals are easily attained. Others demand stamina and resourcefulness. And still others require a commitment of long standing, a willingness to postpone gratification, but most of all, an acceptance of possible failure. We can never be certain of a final outcome. We can only be sure of our effort. However, we can be assured that honest effort will allow us to make measurable progress.

Life is a process. We learn and grow and move toward our goals little by little. The choice to quit moving is also available to us. In fact, a breather from the path we're on is occasionally in order. Recommitment is necessary, however, to begin the growth process again.

Charging ahead takes energy—emotional, mental, spiritual, even physical energy. The whole person is involved in the process of growth; our progress is in direct correlation to the process.

Today may challenge me, but I will make progress.

The battle to keep up appearance unnecessarily, the mask—whatever name you give creeping perfectionism—robs us of our energies.
                                        —Robin Worthington

Because we fear we're inadequate, and because our expectations of ourselves are inflated along with our assumptions about others' expectations of us, we live in the realm of pretense. However, the truth of existence is that we're exactly who we need to be. None of us is inadequate, yet all of us fall short of being perfect. Our journeys are designed to introduce us to new information, new possibilities for growth and development.

We must trust that we are at the right place, at the right time, with all the preparation we need to succeed, here and now. Fretting takes our focus away from the moment and the rich invitation for personal involvement that it's extending. Remember, it's through the full interaction with the present that we are nurtured emotionally and spiritually and encouraged to attain our full potential.

Today I'll remember that I'm all I need to be.

*With nothing to do but expect the hour of setting off,
the afternoon was long. . . .*
                                                —Jane Austen

The most important single determinant of how we feel at
any given time is our attitude. If we live in the moment, use
the moment to the full, we will never be bored and seldom
depressed. The surest way to bring on a negative mood is to
deny the present, whether by dwelling on the past or by
fantasizing about the future.

The past is unalterable; the future, beyond our control.
All we have is now, and all we can work with is our present
attitude and behavior. Everything that we value, our dreams,
plans, and hopes, dwindle to insignificance before the moment. How we act right now is how we are right now. If we
let ourselves dodge the moment, longing for a phone call
that might not come or eating a candy bar because we'll diet
tomorrow, we're negating all our best intentions.

---

*I will look to the moment, and miraculously, the future will take
care of itself. If I can achieve clarity and honesty right here,
today, I'll give my future a good start.*

We have our brush and colors—paint Paradise and in we go.

—Nikos Kazantzakis

We find in our experiences and in our daily reveries just what we anticipate. If we greet the day wearing a smile, confident that we are needed and able to make a contribution, we'll discover that the day holds great promise. What we need to understand is that every day holds just as much promise as we're capable of expecting. We carry within ourselves the image of the picture we're creating.

Since the choice to find happiness rather than sorrow and regret is our own, why does the latter even attract us? For no other reason than we fail to believe that we're deserving of happiness. We know our own shortcomings; we're aware of the details in our lives for which we feel shame. We think only the pure of heart deserve happiness. But we're human. And this means mistakes are normal and expected. With wisdom comes full understanding of this fact. In the meantime, we can trust that happiness is our birthright. All that's requested is our belief in it.

———————

Today will offer me all that I truly desire. Happiness attracts itself.

Imagination has always had powers of resurrection that no science can match.
—Ingrid Bengis

Imagining the successful completion of a goal increases the likelihood of its attainment. Whether we imagine our success in an athletic event, a college program, or preparing a meal, the image formulates a mind-set that's conducive to the goal's completion.

Seeing ourselves leap with grace to hit a high, wide tennis shot makes the movement familiar when we're on the court. Hearing ourselves answer correctly a committee's queries reduces the anxiety when the test date arrives. Every anticipated event can be prepared for if we use our imagination creatively. However, we need to be aware that imagination can run wild if we're not responsibly in the driver's seat. At no time does someone else have the power to put wild, fearful ideas in our minds. And yet, we're each capable of absorbing someone else's negative suggestions if we're not actively imagining our own positive ones.

No day is free from some level of anxiety about an impending situation. Relief from this anxiety lies in my mind. I'll use my imagination wisely today.

Woe to him that is alone when he falleth, for he hath not another to help him up.

—*Ecclesiastes*

If we are stepping through this life, indifferent to those around us and thus separate from our fellow human beings, it is by conscious choice. It may be hard to reach out to someone close, but there will always be a willing hand to receive our own. Each of us has been created to offer others our unique gifts. When we choose a posture of indifference, we are denying to the universe what we have to give.

There is magic in the realization that our acquaintances, our co-workers and neighbors, are presented to us by design. We are here to learn lessons and we play teacher to each other. When we have stepped away from the circle of people calling to us, we are denying them the opportunities for growth they may need and preventing it in ourselves as well. We need one another, and being helped by someone else fulfills more needs than our own.

We are in one another's world by design. I will enjoy the magic of that meaning, today.

Nobody can hurt you but yourself. Every experience
you have makes you all the more fit for life.
—*"Box-Car Bertha"*

We commonly say, "She hurt me," or "I'm afraid of hurting him." Yet no one can hurt us without our cooperation.
Other people's actions don't affect us unless we choose to let
them; and no words can wound unless we turn them into
weapons.

Some of what we call hurt is really learning. Because our
pride may stiffen us against change, especially when we're
young, any learning that brings about a change in our behavior will hurt. As we learn humility, we bend more easily.
And we learn not to accept pain from others.

All experience teaches us something, if we'll learn. There
will be pain along with wisdom; perhaps the price of wisdom is pain. But everything we learn enhances our life.

I'll come to understand my pain and find its value for my life.

Every physician almost hath his favorite disease.
—Henry Fielding

We wouldn't go to a dentist for corns or bunions, just as we wouldn't go looking for fresh fruit at a hardware store. By and large, we know where to go for what we want. Why is it, then, that sometimes we persist in asking something from one who cannot give it?

We recognize unreasonable demands when we meet them, but not always when we make them. Parents expect mature judgment from young children; children expect saintly patience or flexibility from their parents. Commonly, we expect our friends or lovers to show us their loyalty and affection without our asking.

Reality teaches us that if we want something, we should go to a likely source and ask for what we want. If we're not willing to ask, we'll have to settle for every physician's favorite treatment—whether or not we have the disease.

Today I'll remember to ask for what I want from an appropriate source.

Every human being has, like Socrates, an attendant
spirit; and wise are they who obey its signals.
—*Lydia M. Child*

At no instant are we honestly at a loss about what steps to take, what decision to make. Each of us is both guarded and guided by an inner voice that we occasionally tune in on, but more frequently tune out. We may have defined the inner voice as conscience. However, it's not important what we think it is; it's only important that we acknowledge it. The inner voice is our special connection to the spiritual realm, a network that links us all, whether we acknowledge it or not.

The choice to listen to the inner message is a ready option, and it will never fail to benefit us. As we familiarize ourselves with it, and trust it enough to act as directed, we'll glory in both the comfort and the sureness of the action we take. We sense that we're not alone. Even when no other human is present, we're not alone. Always we are connected to the spirit-energy that inspires us all to right action.

Every dreaded circumstance is made easier if I'm accustomed to going within for guidance. Today can run as smoothly as I want. I'll seek my inner voice.

No man is an island entire of itself. Each is a piece of the continent, a part of the main.

—John Donne

Our problems seem so singular; we often feel alone with our struggles. And it's true that each of us must come to our own terms with whatever situation faces us. But no struggle facing us is free from the influence of other people and their struggles. We have a shared destiny which is accompanied by individual perceptions and both singular and mutual responses to the ebb and flow enfolding us all.

Knowing that we share this journey offers comfort when we need it in our daily struggles. We are not alone, forgotten, unimportant to the destiny of others. Nor are others without meaning in the experiences we're gifted with. Our existences are mutual—we are interdependent contributors to the total life cycle.

What each of us learns eases the struggles of another. All experiences are meant for the good of us all.

Today I may feel alone, but I'm not. My life is fully in concert with those around me, and all is as it should be.

. . . it wasn't sin that was born on the day when Eve picked an apple: what was born on that day was a splendid virtue called disobedience.
—*Oriana Fallaci*

Liberty of conscience is precious to us. We need to feel that we are doing the right thing; sometimes, this may mean disobeying authority, as abolitionists, suffragists, and conscientious objectors have done.

Yet when we search our hearts, it is our own authority, or the authority of a spiritual source outside ourselves, that commands our true loyalty. And others must trust this authority, for themselves. Trust in ourselves teaches us to be respectful of others' beliefs.

Obedience must be based on trust. If this is true for us, we can understand that it's equally true for others. Our spirit is larger than our beliefs, and more generous.

Today I'll try to understand that everyone wishes to do what is right for themselves.

Always I've found resisting temptation easier than
yielding—it's more practical and requires no initiative.
—Alice B. Toklas

If a temptation is easy to set aside, it can't tempt us very strongly. The real, insidious temptations are the ones to which we yield unthinkingly: temptations to inertia, for example, or to stinginess or self-punishment.

It's part of our puritan heritage that makes us equate "temptation" with "indulgence." We're armed against sensuous indulgence; we can be strong in resisting a casual romance, a piece of pecan pie, or an extra hour's sleep. We don't feel tempted by the small meannesses that nibble away at our souls, and therefore we yield without examining alternatives.

Can we learn to recognize these little temptations to anger, to a closed heart? Can we learn to see the feelings that we're tempted to suppress—feelings of love, pity, or communion with others—as occasions for spiritual growth and deliverance?

I needn't deprive myself of joy. Learning to recognize what tempts me to joylessness will help me to develop my spiritual wealth.

Some day science may have the existence of mankind in its power, and the human race (may) commit suicide by blowing up the world.
—Henry Adams

One hundred years ago, Henry Adams foresaw the plight we're in today. Some observers believe that people in positions of power won't be able to refrain from the awful destruction of a nuclear war.

If we believe that the glory of the human spirit is our ability to choose our future, it's important for us to refuse to agree. We must do everything we can to prevent this murderous suicide of our species, and the first thing we must do is to choose to leave war behind us. Our slow progress on this planet, from naked apes to technicians in clothing, has prepared us to make the noble choice of peace. We owe it to our humanity.

Among those who despair of our capacity to make this choice are people with brilliant intellects. They may not, however, be our wisest counselors. Each of us must listen to the truth within our hearts; there lies the wisdom that we need. Let's not confuse war with patriotism; we're all citizens of the whole world, and war hurts our human family.

When my spirit is tranquil, I can listen to the peace in my heart.

The evening star
is the most
beautiful of all stars.
               —*Sappho*

The first star in the evening sky shines with a special brightness, because it is the first. We see it as a signal; the first sign that afternoon has turned to evening.

The first of anything is touched with special glamour; first love, a baby's first words or steps, first day of school, first job. They're signals of change, profound and irreversible. When day turns to evening, that day will never come again. Tomorrow is a new day, unique and never-to-be-repeated.

If we could meet each new day, each new person, each new experience, as though it were the first, our lives could be touched by the excitement and discovery of adventure. We're not the same as we were yesterday. Each moment we change; each new event in our lives can be a cusp between two different states. Today, let's give ourselves that special gift.

Each moment is the first of a new series. I will be attentive.

. . . What is in one's life stays there to the end of one's days.

—*Harrison Salisbury*

Young people often try to pretend they're other than they truly are; they're pleased to be taken for natives in a strange place, or tourists at home. People try to change their hair color, their body shape, or their voice—trying on identities, escaping from themselves.

It's natural to play around with external signs of who we are. We all look for a style that will let us express who we want to be. But we're indelibly marked by our genes and our upbringing. We're made so that virtually nothing we've ever cared about is lost to us. Although we can choose our behavior, we can't choose our antecedents.

We may rail against this in our youth, but by middle age, most of us will be glad for it. One secret of happiness is liking who we are. And that's where our power to choose is important: since we can't change who we are, we gracefully choose to be the best possible us.

I shall be grateful for this day, in which I can make the most of what I have.

Humor is such a strong weapon, such a strong answer.
—Agnes Varda

We take life so seriously, certain that the situation confronting us, or at least the next one, will doom us. We gravely anticipate what lies ahead and assuredly we'll experience what we expect. The power to lighten our load rests within. We're only a decision away from an easier life, one that's built with laughter rather than perpetual gloom.

Few of us are aware of the therapeutic effects of laughter. As Norman Cousins demonstrated in his battle with illness, laughter can activate our total being, recharging the whole system. Besides the positive visceral effects, laughter grants a balanced perspective in life that encourages greater emotional health. Laughing at our human foibles takes away their sting, reducing them to minor irritants, the kind that are easily forgotten when we've developed a healthier perspective.

Nothing has power over us except by our consent. No problem, no difficult person, assumes command unless we've abdicated our own position of power. Remember the strength laughter lends us when a situation gets snarled.

Every situation has a humorous interpretation. My day will be lengthened if I look for reasons to laugh. Without fail, they are present.

> If you want knowledge, you must take part in the practice of changing reality. If you want to know the taste of a pear, you must change the pear by eating it yourself.
>
> —Mao Tse-tung

Our language is poor in words that convey emotional meaning. To know, for instance, with the intellect, is not the same as knowing with all our being. We can "know" in our heads that the universe is infinite, but until we experience that knowledge in our hearts, our spirits, in the pit of our stomachs—we can't really know it.

Full knowledge means change. Experience of the infinite changes us; once we have experienced awe, we are not the same. We can understand oppression or injustice, but until we experience it in our bones and breath, the knowledge is not truly available to us.

The knowledge that changes is the knowledge we seek. And sometimes we must change in order to obtain it. If we find ourselves living in a way that contradicts what we know, we change our lives.

We are continually changing as we grow. Our spiritual progress is a record of small changes that bring us closer to the truth our spirit recognizes.

I will not fear change; I will trust that it brings the knowledge I need.

To wait for someone else, or to expect someone else to make my life richer, or fuller, or more satisfying, puts me in a constant state of suspension.
—*Kathleen Tierney Andrus*

How tempting it is to make another person responsible for our happiness, and how absurd. To give such power to others means we're at their mercy; it does not mean we're happy. Whereas, accepting full responsibility for our own acts and feelings does give us the power to be as happy as we choose, as often as we choose.

Emotional maturity precludes our blaming or praising another for our personal well-being. There is reason to be exhilarated that we are blessed with as much control as we choose to have over our own growth, happiness, and commitment to change. We're in another's control only by choice—never by necessity. And when we've given our precious power away, we're reduced to waiting—waiting for someone else's nod of approval, waiting for their invitation to live.

The time is now to decide for myself who I am, where I'm going, and why! The time is now.

The true use of speech is not so much to express our wants as to conceal them.

—Oliver Goldsmith

Learning to communicate, for little children, means squeezing huge desires into little words, like "hurt" or "cookie." We learn early that we're only going to get part of what we want.

Some of us never recover from this disappointment. We use words to manipulate others, to hide our feelings. We may imagine that we have the power to control others, and so we tell ingenious stories to mask what we think is our naked strength.

But we're deluding ourselves, rather than other people. The strategy of falsehood and control finally traps us in a web of lies, where even we don't know what we want. Clarity is a choice, and so is happiness, if we want to choose them.

Asking for something is risky: I might be refused. But if I don't even ask, I'll never hear "yes."

The game of life is a game of boomerangs. Our thoughts, deeds, and words return to us sooner or later, with astounding accuracy.

—Florence Scovel Shinn

We plant the seeds of the bounty we'll reap by every action we take. We teach others how to treat us by our treatment of them coupled with our own level of self-respect. Never should we be surprised at the level of comfort or discomfort we experience in our interactions with others. We have invited it.

Fortunately, we are in control of our own behavior, which means we have the choice to act responsibly and with respect for others every moment of our lives. We can be certain that we'll be treated in similar fashion throughout the day. The terms of life are simple when defined in this way. We get what's our due—and we've prearranged it ourselves.

It's seldom that circumstances discourage us as much as our relations with others. Most often our frustrations or depression are people-centered. The good news is that we have the capability to favorably influence all outcomes that involve other persons. At every opportunity, remember the treatment we each desire and offer that to others.

I am in command of my behavior today. It will invite similar reaction. I'll put my best foot forward.

Though the seas threaten, they are merciful,
I have cursed them without cause.
                                    —William Shakespeare

To each of us, our own self is the most important person in the world. I am the only person who can get what I want; you are the only person who can make you happy or unhappy. This doesn't mean that the world revolves around us, though.

When we were infants, we believed it did. We valued things according to how they affected us. A rainstorm was good if it meant we didn't have to visit relatives who bored us, but it was bad if it spoiled a picnic. We took everything personally.

It's not easy to give up being the center of the universe; some of us cling to the notion long after we've given up bottles and diapers. But once we acknowledge the impersonality of most events, we can stop taking responsibility for the weather, foreign policy, the outcome of labor negotiations. We can even stop taking other people's actions personally. Other people don't really get sick of us, succeed or fail for our benefit, or live or die because of us. It's wonderful to take the pressure off.

The only thing I need to take personally is my person.

The sun, the hero of every day, the impersonal old man that beams as brightly on death as on birth, came up every morning. . . .

—Zora Neale Hurston

Details bog us down. When we count the trees, we never breathe in the forest. Keeping our focus close means escaping the wider ranges of perception and robbing ourselves of the chance to see more than one little slice of life.

When we're children, everything is near and far at the same time. So many things are new that we need to anchor our perceptions with small bits of the familiar: security blankets, familiar toys, a well-loved thumb.

Grown-ups presumably learn to do without these "transitional objects." Yet we need some certainties in a life of shifting priorities and relative values. We're lucky if we can find our anchor within ourselves. We are the real heroes of every day; we come up every morning out of the individual details of our sleeping minds, and it's given to us to shine brightly on the events that touch us, whatever they may be.

Today may I find both zest in living and detachment from the petty details of life.

*. . . my work was so long so little appreciated that I
learned not to care a scrap for either blame or praise.*
—James Murray

It's instructive to look at important figures of the past.
So many have fallen into utter obscurity, and people who
were quite obscure are now seen as important. Who re-
members newspaper columnists or many best-selling writers
of forty years ago? Yet at the time, their names were on
everyone's lips.

We have an idea that life has speeded up, that history has
accelerated, in that we live faster now than people did in the
past. But this is a function of the media; the experiences we
hear about are other people's experiences. We know more,
sooner, about more people; we know when royal babies are
born and when border wars are fought. But these events
have always occurred, and have always totally engrossed
those who are immediately concerned. Their true import for
the world, history must discover.

When we have a staunch purpose, it's possible to ignore
the praise or blame of those we don't care about. Whereas
people who bloom early may be early sidetracked, the pace
of our own lives is under our direction; so is our real significance in the lives of others.

Obscurity can be a blessing. It will never warp my values.

I think that most of us become self-critical as soon as we become self-conscious.

—Ellen Goodman

It seems all too common that we reject our own best efforts as not good enough. Few of us are satisfied with anything less than perfection in ourselves or others. Criticism is second nature to us, and it does an injustice to both giver and receiver.

The self-image of all humanity could stand a lift. Negativity has gained a strong foothold in our minds, and it digs its talons deeper with every barb given or received. Fortunately, we have the individual and collective power to change our thoughts and the direction we are heading, as individuals and in concert with others. Being positive toward ourselves and others wields great power. Positive strokes encourage greater efforts which guarantee positive results.

I can be self-critical or self-congratulating today. My choice will determine the day's success.

Who would care to question the ground of forgiveness or compassion?

—Joseph Conrad

Some people don't seem able to accept the things that come to them; they always want to go back and dwell on how it was before and what mistakes were made by them and others. Sometimes they want to prove, by this recital of past errors, that they were right; sometimes they seem to want to dwell on their own fallibility.

We can't make much progress toward serenity of the spirit without reconciling the past. If old wounds or conflicts rankle, we need to accept them, forgive them, and let them go. Above all, let's forgive ourselves. Those past errors turned into valuable lessons, didn't they? Life is too short to hold grudges, and they take up energy and time that we could use for spiritual growth.

Each day is new, and this new day is all of time for us, right now. This day can flow pure and clear or we can choke it with old grudges, regrets, or fears—the choice is ours.

The ground of forgiveness and compassion is fertile; from it comes my harvest of the future.

Adventure is something you seek for pleasure . . . but experience is what really happens to you in the long run; the truth that finally overtakes you.
                              —Katherine Anne Porter

In our search for new thrills, for unfamiliar ventures, we will become privy to situations and experiences designed for our personal growth. Our desires to chart new courses, to travel untrammeled paths, are consistent with the inner source of truth and knowledge that subtly and gracefully guide our movements.

Whatever the occurrences in our lives, the circumstances we'd rather shun as well as those that absorb us, we can relish the knowledge that they've sought us out to introduce us to new levels of truth. We can be secure that what we need to learn, we'll be taught. The experiences promising the opportunities needed to fulfill our personal potential will be present today and the days ahead.

I will trust today's experiences, secure in the knowledge that they are meant for me at this time.

Order is a lovely thing;
On disarray it lays its wing,
Teaching simplicity to sing.
                                    —*Anna Hempstead Branch*

Things and events have their own order. It's human to want to impose order from the outside—our order; but often, our attempt to put things in order resembles the old man who tried to push the river. It never went any faster, and if he stopped pushing, it got there just the same.

Some people seem to have a knack for order. It could be that they've learned to let things take their own shape. If order is natural, then maybe disorder is what we create with our human fussing. It could be, too, that disorder is in the eye of the beholder—especially if the beholder is a perfectionist.

Serenity is the ability to appreciate natural order.

Today I'll try to be light on my feet and get out of my own way.

*Putting a question correctly is one thing and finding
the answer to it is something quite different.*
—Anton Chekhov

Questions and answers lie within us. Unfortunately, they
don't come in matched sets, numbered or color-keyed so we
can match them up. Sometimes we think we have all the
answers and we wish we knew the questions.

In fact, the questions are often more difficult to find,
especially questions that have to do with our deepest feelings. What do we want? How do we feel about it? Such questions threaten to expose us—to lay bare our vulnerable selves.

For once we acknowledge that we want something, we
risk not getting it. But if we can remain deaf even to question, we protect our vulnerability. The other side of that, of
course, is that we'll never get what we want until we acknowledge that question. We must work to choose the risk
of hearing the wrong answer over the certainty of deafness.

———————————

*Is lack of pain worth shutting down my capacity for pleasure?
Let me strengthen myself to risk joy.*

Getting started can be very hard for people who have trouble with beginnings. After all, where do beginnings begin?

—Dorothy Bryant

Most of us have trouble getting started at one time or another. It's a common phenomenon, whether the project is Christmas cookies, an annual report, or cleaning the attic: "I just don't know where to begin."

It's a good rule to begin with ourselves, in the moment that is. Start the project where we are now. The other things that are necessary—details from the past and plans for the future—will reveal themselves as the project takes shape.

Sometimes we will begin, like writers, by talking about how hard it is to begin. This seems to oil the wheels; they start to turn, and before we know it, we've begun (though we may have to throw away the first paragraph).

Trying to begin at the beginning is a good way to drive myself mad. I will grasp the tools that are at hand: myself and the moment.

Together is a road travelled by the brave.
—*George Betts*

Moving through life fully in concert with others requires commitment and much energy. It demands self-love, unconditional acceptance of others, patience, the ability to be vulnerable and to take risks, and the decision to stay put even when the desire to run is great. And this assortment of characteristics is only the beginning. More is required of us, much more, if we want a real experience of belonging to those around us. But even more than that is guaranteed for us if we are willing to *be present always.*

If we've chosen to go it alone in the past, we can quickly recall the frequent uncertainty, the defensiveness when questioned by others, the absence of emotional support when the going was rough. But then, we may have believed we were free—others didn't have to be counted on. However, real freedom to be who we are can only be found among a circle of friends who have committed themselves to us, just as we've committed ourselves likewise.

Together we'll grow, find happiness, and gain strength.

I will lock arms today and move forward in the company of those who need me. I need them also.

We have a tradition in my family: We wash our own laundry, we raise our own children, and we clean up our own dirt.

—*Alice Silverman*

One life is all we have, and it's enough. One life contains plenty of joy, sorrow, exaltation, despair, astonishment, and cruelty. Why then do we borrow trouble? Every time we take responsibility for someone else's deeds, whether they're failures or successes, we're borrowing trouble—just as we rob ourselves when we refuse to take responsibility for our own.

Somehow we learn to give away our powers of independent choice. Somewhere we learned to say, "You make me miserable," and "Look what you made me do." But we can unlearn these twisted borrowings; we can learn to stand straight, be ourselves, and own our own lives. The power to be happy or miserable lies within us; when we give away our power to choose, we should be very sure we know what we're getting in return.

If I feel trapped, let me look at how I built the trap, and how I can take it apart. Where I used to say, "I can't," let me practice saying, "I won't."

The nature of consciousness is to flow. It seems ever changing. States of mind succeed one another. . . . We can direct consciousness to an idea or impulse, but we cannot lock it in place.

—Dr. George Weinberg

Our minds are marvelous, always moving, growing, absorbing, discarding, storing. And we are in control of the direction our minds take. Thus, it's by choice, either conscious or unconscious, that we dwell on negative outcomes rather than positive projections.

Claiming ownership of and responsibility for the direction of our minds and our lives develops a sense of individual power and, in turn, enhances self-esteem. *We are what we think.* We can think ourselves into becoming better selves.

We are free, at last, from the overwhelming feelings of powerlessness and impotence. The decision to take control of our thoughts and attitudes will be the turning point. When we complement that decision by offering positive direction to our minds, we'll quickly benefit from the advantageous outcomes.

———

I will utilize my personal power today. I will believe in positive outcomes. I will have hope.

There are two ways of spreading light: to be the candle or the mirror that receives it.

—Edith Wharton

Each of us carries within us the power to illuminate others. Likewise, we are enlightened by others' gifts of perception. Every exchange of ideas, each expression of feeling, instructs us when our restraints against new information are broken down.

It is an awesome realization that whoever and whatever engage us are purposeful, having their place in our development at the moment. Nothing is for naught, and what we are inspired to share with another, too, fits into their scheme.

There is a message to be gleaned every moment. The choice to be enlightened awaits us.

Today will offer me lessons and information that I need. Will I accept enlightenment?

The most blessed thing in the world is to live by faith without imputation of guilt; having the kingdom within.

—Paul Goodman

What does it mean, to have the kingdom within? At those times when we're happiest, we also feel most blessed. The kingdom is one name for a peaceful spirit.

There are times, though, when we doubt whether anyone could live this way, in hope and joy. No regrets, no fears, no guilty conscience: how can it be? So often we feel we have to cover our happiness with misery, to feel bad in order to feel good. But the inner kingdom is built of self-acceptance. When we learn to love ourselves for the good people we are, that kingdom is ours.

Even when happiness is not our condition, even when sadness clouds our lives, we can be peaceful. By knowing ourselves to be good, and by believing we deserve goodness in return, we will acquire the strength to endure. The faith we live by is a peaceful, hopeful faith in the goodness of our spirit.

I'll work to free myself from the shadow of old shame and guilt. I can be as blessed as I choose to become.

I was to give a child security and tenderness, but didn't feel I received enough of this myself.
—Liv Ullman

We can increase our level of serenity by learning to nurture ourselves. The child in us continues to need security and tenderness, even while other children in our lives may call on our reserves. We can ask for nurturing from others, but our surest source is ourselves.

People who have never learned to love themselves may not be able to tap their source of security and tenderness. It's never too late to start loving ourselves, fortunately. Neglect and abuse in early life may have damaged us; we may have to unlearn many years of mistaken lessons. What better time than the present?

Self-nurturing is a great adventure. We must remember to have patience with ourselves, for deep trust and security, the kind we all need, don't happen in a moment. Especially if we're unlearning some damage, we must go slowly. We are a precious gift, to ourselves and others, and we deserve love and nurture.

Today I will love myself, and patiently care for my needs so that my security soon will grow to include others.

To be what we are, and to become what we are capable of becoming is the only end of life.
                                    —*Robert Louis Stevenson*

Our creation was our invitation to contribute that which is uniquely our own to the life process. Our brothers and sisters have been likewise invited. Our experiences are not without purpose. They offer us opportunities to practice the contributions we have been created to make.

Realizing potential is possible when we are committed to stepping forward to meet the challenges head on. No challenge is beyond our capability; every challenge promises new growth and a measure of serenity. Our search for security, for self-worth, if it's sincere, pledges us to stay with the daily challenges. They will teach us all that we are prepared to learn.

I go forth today with anticipation and gratitude for the opportunities to be wholly one. My experiences will be exactly what I'm ready for.

Miracles do not happen.
          —*Matthew Arnold*

Many of us will insist that miracles *do* happen. We've seen transformations in ourselves or our loved ones that have seemed miraculous, strokes of fate, demonstrations of divine intervention.

Yet, we must do our part. If we look at the history of our personal miracles, we can usually see that time, pain, and patience prepared the way. Nothing comes from nothing. The changes that transform our lives are born from the suffering that is itself a reason for change.

Whether or not we believe that a higher power intervenes directly in this world's affairs, we realize, if we think about it, that humans must be ready. To catch a falling star, we must be standing under it.

Today I'll try to position myself in readiness for whatever miracle might come my way.

. . . the function of freedom is to free somebody else.
—Toni Morrison

We all struggle over the issue of freedom—how much we want; how much we're comfortable with; how able we are to accept others' freedom. We cannot grow and create unless free to do so; in fact, our progress will be proportional to the freedom we feel to breathe, to move, to live fully.

Control is the opposite of freedom. It steals the freedom of the controller as well as the one controlled. No one grows emotionally, intellectually, or spiritually if energy is being expended controlling. And yet, the human condition is such that we passively, if not willingly, practice the game of control with the many principal characters in our lives. It's a game no one wins. Even when we're seemingly in control we lose our freedom, too, when our attention is given over to the control of someone else.

No one is free until we are all free, and, when free, we will find joy in our work, at home, and with friends. We, too, will discover the measure of joy we encourage others to experience.

If I reach out to love, I'll find love. If I mete out control, I'll be diminished in turn.

God's most lordly gift to man is decency of mind.
                                        —*Aeschylus*

"Decent" means appropriate, proper, becoming. Decency of mind means to think appropriate thoughts, to respond properly to events and people, neither exaggerating nor trivializing their importance. What a consolation it must be to have a mind always in balance, always ready to dwell on the good and let the negative aspects go!

It's possible to achieve such decency. Perhaps it is a gift from a higher power; but we must ready ourselves to receive a gift like that. Becoming ready for the gift of a balanced outlook entails work: the work of overcoming our tendencies to, on the one hand, ignore, postpone, and forget unpleasantness, and on the other, to dwell on misfortune until we let it blot out the sun.

Decency is another name for the middle way, the true road. When we achieve decency of mind, we'll know it by the serenity of our outlook. Obstacles won't melt, but they will assume their true proportions.

———

Today I'll ready myself to receive the gift of a decent mind.

In soloing—as in other activities—it is far easier to start something than it is to finish it.
—Amelia Earhart

Our inspiration to master any art, to attain any goal, to tackle any project, comes from within—the center of all knowledge. All of us are gifted with all knowledge. When the desire to pursue a particular avenue keeps presenting itself, we should pay heed, trusting that we will be shown the way to succeed. This desire is our invitation to develop our talents in ways that may even be foreign to our conscious minds.

The decision to trust the desire is only the first step in tackling a new project. What comes after is effort and daily recommitment to completion of the goal or project. It is much easier to switch goals or projects than to see them to their end, but it's in their doing that we develop our talents to their fullest. Each time we back off, letting our commitment die, we are opting for less than a full life. No one else can handle a project in just our way.

Today I'll be faced with the choice to stay on top of my goals. I must remember the source of my inspiration and trust it.

To be happy means to be free, not from pain or fear,
but from care or anxiety.

—W. H. Auden

The ancient meaning of "happy" comes from "hap," or chance—as in mis-hap, or hap-pening. Happy meant fortunate or lucky, and we still call people happy who manage to turn life's unpredictability to their advantage.

Could happiness be a matter of attitude? If we persist in calling our cups half full instead of half empty, if we re-value setbacks as opportunities, aren't we behaving happily? Happiness of attitude is like a muscle: use strengthens it. Whatever *happens* to us, we should be determined to meet it positively.

Happiness can't protect us from life's woes, but it can ensure that we won't double those woes by worry or regret. We can't control other people or events; all we're responsible for is our own behavior. The decision to behave happily could change our life.

Anxiety shuts me in. I'll let it go and be free to respond happily to whatever comes.

Continuous effort—not strength or intelligence—is the key to unlocking our potential.

—Liane Cordes

Perseverance is the plus that assures us of goal completion. Unquestionably, every one of us is capable of achievement. All that's required is that we commit ourselves with determination to the task before us, one moment at a time, one day at a time. Our rewards will be many. Among them will be accomplished goals, high self-esteem, and a secure sense of well-being.

It's probable that we sometimes fail to recognize our worth or understand the real value of our talents. It's likely, too, that on occasion we shut out of our consciousness the knowledge that our very existence validates our necessity to the whole of creation. Self-reminders are important. They're like vitamins; they contribute to our nourishment.

When we have lost sight of our ability to make valuable contributions to society, we slow down our efforts. We close ourselves off from others and our potential is stifled. To move forward once again requires only our attention to the moment engulfing us. We can handle what lies before us.

Today my efforts are needed, in the here and now. That's all.

> . . . *be patient toward all that is unsolved in your heart and try to love the questions themselves like locked rooms and like books that are written in a very foreign tongue.*
>
> —*Rainer Maria Rilke*

We strive to know ourselves, yet we all have unsolved questions in our hearts. We don't need to answer them to achieve self-understanding; all we need do is accept them and understand ourselves as creatures with questioning hearts.

When we're ready to receive it, the answer will come within our grasp. Perhaps a lot of work will be required of us: as much as learning a foreign tongue. Or perhaps the answer will be as simple as a key that fits the door of a locked room. But no effort will get it until we're ready.

Patience seems like such a dull virtue, especially when we're young and eager for accomplishment. But patience is another name for love. If we're patient with ourselves, it's because we've achieved self-acceptance, and because we trust that, when we need it, the secret language and the locked room will be open to us.

I know I need not fear whatever lies hidden in my heart.

One is happy as the result of one's own efforts.
—George Sand

Our attitude about our circumstances or our hopes determines the tenor of a moment, eventually of the whole day.

No attitude, no feeling or emotion, is foisted upon us. We have always made the choice. Perhaps our passivity regarding choices has all too often eased us into situations detrimental to our emotional health. Nevertheless, responsibility for the pain that accompanies poor choice is always our own. Conversely, the joy that is ushered in by certain other choices is also our responsibility.

Personal power commands our lives, and the fruits are as bountiful as are our choices, selectively made. We will be as happy as our choices make us, and as we decide to be.

Today is all mine, and whatever I make of it is by personal choice.

When we are no longer children, we are already dead.
—Konstantin Brancusi

Children are born into a world whose rules they must learn. As part of the learning process, children always question rules. For simplicity's sake, we stop questioning most rules. We'll walk on sidewalks, eat with forks, talk in sentences, and keep our clothes buttoned. But the child inside us looks out with eager eyes and stands ready to question any rule that seems absurd.

Sometimes we bully that interior child into silence, for its questions embarrass us. Sometimes we hide it, sit on it, punish it—but it's always there. If we put that child to sleep, we lose one of the best parts of ourselves. We are right to question, to want to see for ourselves, especially when we're asked to do something that troubles our conscience. The child needn't always have its way, but it deserves our love. It was a young child in the crowd of people who said, "But the emperor is naked!"

I will love and nurture the child within me, and I will heed its questions, which may bring me to new answers.

Death, when it approaches, ought not to take one by surprise. It should be part of the full expectancy of life.

—*Muriel Spark*

The process of living includes many dimensions. We can joyfully anticipate high periods and we must expect pain. We won't escape sorrow over wrongs we've committed nor grief for the departure of a dear one. Anxiety over what may transpire is a given. But working to develop a balanced perception of all the events of our lives will ease our way. It's our overreactions to the ups and downs that make all of our daily steps uncertain.

Fearing the unknown wastes our time. How much better to trust that life will offer us exactly what we need to develop as healthy human beings. No event will be more than we can handle. All events are necessities of life, and each event needs simple acceptance.

If I understand that every situation carries a blessing, today will offer me comfort throughout.

Life is a battle in which we fall from wounds we receive in running away.
—William L. Sullivan

Our experience in this life is a composite of many lessons—lessons which will ease our personal growth and offer us the opportunities necessary to encourage our unique contributions. Clearly, not all lessons are easy or pleasurable when we first encounter them, but their rewards are great if we choose to learn from them, and we can be certain that no lesson is without its reward.

Those things we need to experience, to learn, to understand, will present themselves again and again until we have attended to them. We may choose to close our minds one time, and even close them again, but the lesson will not be put off for long. Another experience will surround us, offering once again the opportunity necessary for the personal growth we're destined to realize.

We must trust that our lives are unfolding in ways that will evoke our full potential, and that no challenge comes that earlier lessons haven't prepared us for.

Tackling my lessons head-on is a decision I can make today.

We cannot fail to meet the same problems as did our forefathers, and learning their answers may help us to act upon them as intelligently as they did, and may even, perhaps, teach us to avoid making always the same mistakes.

—Anne Fremantle

As youth, we are impatient and don't always believe in the value of elders' experience. A few mistakes, however, and most of us will acknowledge that we can learn something from the wisdom of the past.

As parents, we want to protect our children from suffering the same pain we have gone through. We may have forgotten that some risks are healthy. Fear teaches only more fear. We must experience some failure and some pain if we are to grow and learn.

The balance between safety and exploration isn't easy to strike, but everyone needs to find it. If we listen to the stillness within, we'll discover what is right for us to do—when to hang on and when to let go. We will be able to trust ourselves in both caution and bravery, and we will learn from history all it can teach us. The choices in our lives are ours to make.

If I am patient, I can understand and use the experience of others.

A man that studieth revenge keeps his own wounds green.

—*Francis Bacon*

Our progress along the path of human growth is measurable by the exercise we encourage of our forgiving spirit. Each time we harbor a resentment toward another, we block our own growth.

Preoccupation with a troublesome situation or person prevents our responding to the thrill and possibilities of the moment. Stepping out of the flow of events to stay stuck on an old hurt guarantees us a stifled existence. Forgiveness of self and others frees us, frees our spirit to soar ahead. And we'll do so with a glad heart.

The act of forgiveness lightens whatever burden we may be carrying. Forgiveness heals the soul; it energizes the spirit. It makes possible our forward movement once again.

My hope for a good life is proportionate to my forgiving heart. Happiness is within my power.

Life is not always what one wants it to be, but to make the best of it as it is, is the only way of being happy.
—Jennie Jerome Churchill

The posture we take while performing our tasks today, and the attitude we project toward those who cross our path, will emphatically influence what the day brings. No one else can decide for any one of us what we'll feel or think about the day. We have the power to be as content or as discontent as we make up our minds to be.

A sign of maturity is acceptance of the full responsibility for the failures as well as the successes of a day. Another sign is the willingness to let go of the day's outcomes, whatever they are, and ready ourselves instead to face tomorrow, confident and hopeful. Carrying yesterday's baggage into today will only distort the size and shape of any bundle we must handle in the twenty-four hours ahead.

I begin the day free of yesterday, unburdened, hopeful, cheerful, confident, if I so choose.

Some people are so fond of ill-luck that they run half-way to meet it.

—Douglas William Jerrold

It's not wholly true in this world that we make our own luck, but we certainly have a share in it. Opportunity shakes out pretty evenly for most people, but what we do with it, whether we're willing or able to grasp a chance when we see one, is an individual matter. Some of us even have trouble seeing opportunities for growth.

When we feel abused or resentful, we need to examine our own part. Have we so mistrusted our own powers that we've not let ourselves see the chances life has dealt us? It's important for us to recognize that we have a choice. If we're dissatisfied, we can choose to change. We can also choose not to change, and to complain about being stuck; but we should realize the choice is our own.

If we've had a long string of bad luck, maybe we need to look at what we're doing. If our self-esteem is very low, we may want to punish ourselves somehow, to prove that we're no good. The knowledge that we're lovable and necessary people may have slipped away, and we may need to do some structural repair. But that's okay; we're worth the effort.

I deserve to be happy and I know how—whether I'm using the knowledge or not.

It is not until our own hearts are pierced that we can begin to know the suffering.
                                    —Sarah Minturn Sedgewick

Our own painful experiences serve a worthy purpose. They make possible our understanding of another's pain. In turn, we are able healers to one another because we have shared the experience of pain.

Being present to another's sorrow or suffering is like a healing balm, lessening the burden, the intensity of pain. However, healing is only possible after the pain has been acknowledged, internally embraced, and then released by the injured person.

Frequently, we seek freedom from all pain. But pain stretches us, pushes us to grow, to develop new levels of ourselves. Pain promises us unexpected pleasure. It also requires patience of us. We have many lessons to learn in life, and each one is generally punctuated by a stab of pain. It's within our power to rejoice even when the pain is felt. It isn't without purpose.

The pain I may experience today can teach me and heal me, if I allow it to.

Living well is the best revenge.
—Anonymous

Because we're human, and thus imperfect beings, we'll often be less than serene. In fact, tension and upset may commonly characterize us. However, the anger or resentment we too frequently feel toward others generally causes the greatest harm to our own lives. Although we may wish ill to others, it returns, like a boomerang, to ourselves.

We let others assume command over our lives when we give energy to our resentments. Those who are the objects of our focus gradually control all of our moves. We are no longer free to grow, to determine our actions, when we have given over our power to those we resent. Our attention goes toward them, and we forsake the steps toward our personal goals that need to be taken.

Wanting revenge is human, though always unproductive. We should understand, however, that those who have triggered our anger have garnered the greatest revenge. They've managed to pull us off course. It's up to us to take back our power and go about our lives with joy and direction. How much sweeter is this response to the ones who deserve our greatest consideration: ourselves.

Today I'll live well and productively; having a resentment is a choice that I never need to make.

It is only by forgetting yourself that you draw near to God.

—Henry David Thoreau

There is a spiritual presence which can aptly cushion our every fall, bringing comfort and subtle meaning to our lives. However, we'll not feel this gentle comfort unless we attune ourselves to the others in our company. It's within another's soul that we sense the beacon of light which illuminates the way we're traveling.

Broadening our vision so that we may see life from a stranger's perspective heightens the clarity of our own, and sharing the view bonds us, deepens all meaning, and closes the gap that lies between.

We must think and dream beyond ourselves if we are ever to sense the vast network that includes us all. We can be certain there is a rhythm to the unfolding of our experiences; a symphony which knows its own end.

Today I'll listen to the notes of others, and find my harmony with them.

If you have been put in your place long enough, you begin to act like the place.

—Randall Jarrell

Others can't put us in our place all by themselves; we have to go there. Our cooperation is required for snubs or for blame or for glorification. If we don't choose to accept the role another has found for us, we don't have to play it.

Sometimes it's difficult to accept the choices life offers us. It seems easier to go along with the roles that others assign. How many people do we know who seem to drift through important areas of their lives, neither fully cooperating nor asserting their own choices? They might not like to admit it, but in "going along," they've accepted someone else's definition of who they are.

Some of us comply out of a desire to cooperate—but there's a big difference. Compliance means refusing to exercise our own power to choose; cooperation means using our power together with others to achieve more than any of us can alone. If we accept the responsibility for our lives, we forego the luxury of saying, "Look what you made me do"; but in exchange we may get to do what we want.

I will remember that anything that happens between us is half mine and half yours.

He who does not start life well will finish badly, one can tell.

—*Great Calendar of 1500, quoted by*
Philippe Aries

As a species, we're obsessed with the future. We spend time, energy, and money on horoscopes, almanacs, and sophisticated statistical "predictors," all of which, we think, will enable us to foretell the future. But life, economics, and the weather resist most of our efforts to control them.

In the case of children, predictions are more complicated. If a child's parents decide "this one's going to be a loser," that child has a lot of overcoming to do.

Can we escape the noose of a self-fulfilling prediction? Yes, probably. Health, self-respect, and a balanced outlook are easier to achieve for us if we have had loving nurturance and support in early life. But even if our early life has been filled with neglect or abuse, we can learn to love and nurture ourselves. And we can pass along the blessing by refusing to predict the future for others in ways that damage or confine them.

All we really have is here and now. All we can control is our own behavior. When we surrender to these limits on our human power, we can begin to tap the sources of a power greater than ourselves.

I will surrender to the moment today.

The still mind of the sage is a mirror of heaven and earth—the glass of all things.

—*Chuang Tzu*

In our own personal stillness, we find the solutions to the challenges facing us. We need to be willing to be quiet and turn our attention inward. No information we need eludes us for long when we dwell in the stillness.

Our opportunities for growth are hidden within the challenges that attract our attention. We need these if we are to contribute to the world. No challenge is beyond our capabilities or strength, and every one can be handled with relative ease if we have sought the comfort of the stillness.

The wisdom we admire in others is the birthright of us all. Each of us is a channel to full knowledge; any of us may be gifted with the wisdom to understand the present clearly, if we choose to exercise the commitment to move within ourselves—to the stillness, to the heart of all knowledge of the past, the present, and the future.

I'll have the answers I need, when I need them, if I turn within for them.

We should have much peace if we would not busy ourselves with the sayings and doings of others.
                                        —Thomas À Kempis

We can go forth peacefully today if we pay close attention to our inner urgings; they will direct our steps safely and justly. The choice is forever ours to respect this inner voice— rather than be nudged off course or have our progress severely hindered by the strength of another's self-serving tug.

Action that is clearly our own, rather than reaction to another's laments, is certain to bring personal satisfaction. This will strengthen even more the connection between the self we offer to the world and the voice that nurtures, guides, and safeguards us from within.

With practice we will develop an appreciation for all the people in our lives, and yet be free of their influence when it's not complementary to our own efforts. Taking full responsibility for who we are and where we're going is exhilarating. But even more, it's the only way we're certain of arriving at our most meaningful destination.

I will listen to and respect the men and women I meet today, but I will be most attentive to the friend within.

The first element of greatness is fundamental humbleness.

—Margot Asquith

Recognition of the magnitude of creation heightens our awareness of the small but essential contribution that we each offer to the whole. We come to know that we are necessary to *its* completion, thus we are special. With that knowledge we are quieted, softened, and secure. We are at peace.

Sensing the meaning of our own existence enlightens us about others' value as well. This knowledge fosters love, respect, and acceptance of another's unique personhood. Each attempt at nurturing another is, in turn, an act of self-nurture.

The road stretching before us looks long and will often be rocky. We'll inch along at times. But when we remember our value, our unique necessity to the whole, the rocks will easily be sidestepped and our pace will quicken.

I will breathe deeply the realization of my meaning today. I am needed by the people I meet. And I will recognize their value to me.

We are a feelingless people. If we could really feel, the pain would be so great that we would stop all the suffering.

—Julian Beck

Other people's suffering is painful to us, but we have skins that protect us from the continual awareness of pain. We know that we are connected to all other life forms on the planet; yet we are distinct beings who can disregard the suffering of the torture victim, the slaughtered animal, or the starving child.

The thickness of our skins is good in one sense; it lets some of us be whole and happy in a world where many are not. But if it is too thick, we become callous. We shut out reality and pretend—successfully, sometimes—that everyone is as well off as we are.

It's difficult to respond to the suffering of others in a balanced way. The Serenity Prayer can show us how:

Grant me the serenity
To accept the things I cannot change,
Courage to change the things I can,
And wisdom to know the difference.

Much suffering can be lightened. Many decide to work, in some way, for the welfare of others. Our "feelinglessness" is only as deep as we decide.

My skin is a membrane that receives information from both sides. I will pay attention to both kinds of messages today.

At every step the child should be allowed to meet the real experiences of life: the thorns should never be plucked from the roses.

—Ellen Key

Reality is not always pleasant. More often it's painful. Accepting that pain, as well as pleasure, is part of the process of growth evens our responses to their presence in our daily lives. Being shielded or shielding another from pain directly hinders the rapture of pleasure.

Maturity is measurable by our response to the ebb and flow of the day, the season, even our lifetime. The vibrancy of life lies in the truth of experience. Myriad opportunities for growth, for rapture, for pensive meditation will present themselves every day. Absorbing from every experience will strengthen our character and prepare us for whatever lies ahead.

We cannot hide from pain. And we can grow from pain, whenever it appears.

Today may offer me pleasure and also pain. I need experiences of both to meet tomorrow.

*Women who have reached positions of prominence . . .
have not always been the best supporters of new
measures to encourage female activism.*
—Anna Coote and Beatrix Campbell

Generosity is a problem for some; they feel resentful. Giving to others seems unfair to them: "Nobody gave anything to me," they'll say. "I had to fight for everything I got." As if that were a reason to deny others.

Giving to others takes nothing away from us; on the contrary, it refreshes the soul. Yet the fear that someone else's success will mean our failure can keep us resentful and competitive.

Competition is drummed into us as children. It's a hard lesson to unlearn. But there aren't many traits that are so unsuitable—and so frustrating—as cutthroat competition. The person who must compete is doomed to unhappiness and to a sense of inadequacy. We'll stop the hopeless attempt to best others only when we achieve the serenity of knowing that each of us is the best at one thing: being ourselves.

Being the best me I can often involves my helping others.

Every worthwhile accomplishment, big or little, has its stages of drudgery and triumph; a beginning, a struggle, and a victory.

—*Anonymous*

Every goal that offers us pleasure on completion has triggered periods of pain. The lessons we need to learn are seldom simple. Nonetheless, our development has relied on successfully tackling them. We can be certain that goals we are inspired to set for ourselves are tied closely to the lessons we're in this life to learn.

It's not unusual for us to want an easier life, one free from turmoil and pain. We'd rather not know that a life with no bumps falls short of the fulfillment we desire. But it does. We need struggles to stretch our capabilities. We need sorrow to appreciate the laughter. We need boredom to discover joy in small blessings.

Every worthy task will avail us of opportunities to grow, to think new thoughts, and to hone the skills we already possess. Every worthy task is destined to clear new ground for us.

Today I can celebrate, I'm on the road to victory. Every step leads toward the goal I've chosen.

Alienation is essentially experiencing the world and oneself passively, receptively, as the subject separated from the object.

—*Erich Fromm*

The goal of our spiritual quest is to put ourselves back together, reintegrating the self that acts and the self that observes. To be split is to be in pain. We feel our inner separation as a wound, and we try to dull our pain with frantic or self-destructive methods.

The pain won't yield to pleasure nor to danger or violence. These sensational methods leave us as alienated as we were before. We seek wholeness, and we'll achieve it only by surrendering to our sense of a reality beyond ourselves. Whatever we choose to call the great oneness, we must acknowledge it as a higher power or we'll continue to suffer the anguish of alienation.

Achieving serenity is a lifelong process. While we have this goal in view, our efforts will be unified and our attention not easily distracted by setbacks.

Today I'll resolve to focus on my spiritual goal and let it heal me.

When you hold resentment toward another, you are bound to that person or condition by an emotional link that is stronger than steel.

—Catherine Ponder

Our attention is consumed by what we want to control. Like a magnet, we are attracted to it; preoccupation sets in, and our freedom to live in the moment is gone. We give up living when we try to control others.

Our resentments grow out of our failure to control others, a failure that heightens our personal insecurities. When we need others to fall into line, to buy our plan, we have set ourselves up for failure. We have guaranteed that we'll experience the feelings of inadequacy that we dread.

Each one of us is on a path that is landscaped according to our inner needs. Accepting that will relieve us of the anger triggered when other people behave according to their own dictates rather than ours.

Resentment stifles us. To respond creatively to the fluctuation of the day, we need to make the most of our personal power.

Let me follow my path today, knowing it's right for me. I will work on letting others walk their own paths, too.

Eternity is called whole, not because it has parts, but because it is lacking in nothing.

—*Thomas Aquinas*

We all learn in geometry that the circle is a perfect form, but there's no such thing as a perfect circle. Straight lines aren't perfectly straight; a flat floor can never be perfectly flat. Perfection is an idea that can never be realized.

The idea of eternity is beautiful, like the idea of perfection. It expresses the striving of the human spirit for perfect unity; the fulfillment, the perfect satisfaction, of all desire, perfect wholeness, "lacking in nothing."

Of course, eternity is an impossible standard to attain. Civilizations aren't eternal, nor are laws, nor are works of art. We make ourselves miserable if we try to measure our achievements against such a standard. We invent techniques and gadgets to help us overcome our human weakness and awkwardness. And we cooperate with others, both weaker and stronger than ourselves, to multiply our efforts manyfold. How much kinder it would be to love the idea, as an expression of longing, and to love ourselves because we do the best we can. It's because we lack many things that human beings are so creative and ingenious.

My fullest expression of myself is in my reaching out to others.

It is not often given in a noisy world to come to the places of great grief and silence.

—Sarah Orne Jewett

Many of us live with energy and gusto, tackling our lives like wrestling partners, busy earning a living, caring for our homes and families, serving our communities. Are we forgetting something?

Often, we forget to nourish our spirits at the deep well of grief and silence. Grief is a nourishing emotion, because in grieving we experience fully the inevitable losses of our lives. Only after grieving can we heal. Only after knowing fully the dimensions of our loss can we summon the vitality to continue our lives.

Parents, friends, children, trusted leaders, die and cannot be replaced. Their loss may have deep meaning for us; we deserve to take the time and care to learn what that meaning may be.

Grief can change people; we may become more detached, quieter, more feeling, more deeply appreciative of life's gifts. One of these gifts is silence—the silence of tranquility. Through plumbing our feelings, we may come to be at peace.

Not all gifts are gaiety, love, and joy. Let me respect the gifts of grief and silence, that I may learn from them.

Pain is inevitable. Suffering is optional.
—M. Kathleen Casey

Every day is a series of experiences; some we'll greet with relief, laughter, or anger. However, all experiences, even those most dreaded, encompass the very lessons we're ready to undertake. And the people in our lives are here to serve as our mentors.

The pinch of any experience lives on in the mind. We sometimes savor the wound, letting it feed our self-pity or fester our resentment. Likewise, we often hang on to a fond memory, replaying the action over and over again in our minds. Whether it's a good or a bad memory, we neglect the present if our minds are locked in to the past.

Our freedom to let go of an experience, to laugh at ourselves, to accentuate the positive in our lives, exhilarates us. It also heightens our anticipation for every moment a day promises.

I am personally in charge of all responses to all experiences today. I can feel however I choose every minute of the day.

Some day science may have the existence of mankind in its power, and the human race [may] commit suicide by blowing up the world.

—Henry Adams

One hundred years ago, Henry Adams foretold a modern predicament, one we all must live with. Science has indeed given us the power to destroy ourselves. How, in such a hazardous world, are we to find serenity?

Peace begins within. Each one of us knows what conflict is, and so each of us possesses the power of reconciliation. The glory of the human spirit lies in our ability to choose, to let go of despair, to turn our energies to creative uses. Peace begins with resolution of our inner wars.

The whole history of our species on the planet has prepared us for the noble choice of peace; it's the fulfillment of our humanity. Each of us must listen to the truth within our hearts; there lies the wisdom we need, and there lies our capacity for love and creativity.

When I listen to the peace within my heart, my spirit is soothed.

The cruelest lies are often told in silence.
—*Robert Louis Stevenson*

Is it frequent that we fail to come forth to explain, defend, or offer support? Remaining silent is always our option, no matter how grave the situation. Holding back information that would ease another's pain or shed light on a hateful experience is cruel. The effects of cruel acts will find their way back to the actor. The axiom, "As we sow so shall we reap," is true.

Perhaps we need reminding that our performance is unique and essential to those around us. Together we move forward, in concert. When any one of us falters or misses a cue, another of us will likely miss one, too.

We're alive to honor one another's presence, and only when we're fully present, honest, and straightforward are we fulfilling our role.

Today I share center stage. Let me speak my lines fully.

Eat and carouse with Bacchus, or munch dry bread
with Jesus, but don't sit down without one of the gods.
—D. H. Lawrence

In religious communities, as in tribal societies, the
ordinary events of life are sanctified. Orthodox Jews and
Benedictine monks are alike in this, and so are devout
Buddhists, Hindus, or animists. Prayer and ritual observance
aren't reserved for special occasions; they accompany sleeping, waking, the daily washing of the body, the simplest meal.

Whatever our beliefs, it's possible for us to express the
spiritual dimension of our lives in simple, everyday ways.
And each expression strengthens our spirituality and extends
it to flood more of our life with light. Whatever names we
give to the truths of the spirits, our least act can connect us
with them.

The stronger our spiritual connection, the less we'll be
held back by our fears and self-doubts. If we can invoke a
trusted guide for the ordinary gestures of life, then we'll
never lack guidance in perplexity.

I will feed my spirit and it will grow strong.

Our awesome responsibility to ourselves, to our children, and to the future is to create ourselves in the image of goodness, because the future depends on the nobility of our imaginings.
—*Barbara Grizzuti Harrison*

The world we live in depends on the responsible contributions each of us makes. And this world is just as good as are the many talents we commit ourselves to developing and offering. None of us is without obligation to offer our best to our family, friends, or strangers, if our hope is to live in a good world. The world can only be as good as each of us makes it.

Individually and collectively our power to mold the outer circumstances of our lives is profound. Our personal responses to one another and our reactions to events that touch us combine with the actions of others to create a changed environment that affects us. No action, no thought goes unnoticed, unfelt, in this interdependent system of humanity. We share this universe. We are the force behind all that the universe offers.

Whether I acknowledge the depth of my contribution is irrelevant. It is still profound and making an impact every moment and eternally.

Some things you must always be unable to bear.
—William Faulkner

The strong spirit cannot bear lies; the free spirit cannot bear shackles. To tend our spirit with love and rigor means weeding it like a garden, cleaning it of false values and fake pride. We must never bear those things that violate our integrity.

Sometimes, for the sake of peace or a secret doubt that we deserve excellence, we violate ourselves. We give away pieces of our truth and we tell ourselves it doesn't matter. But it does. And we deserve excellence; we deserve the best quality of life. Peace bought at the price of spiritual violation is no true peace; it is a form of oppression.

Meditation can strengthen the spirit against violation. Today and every day, we will practice becoming the person we deserve to be.

When I listen to my own truth I will be guided truly.

*. . . I am incapable of conceiving infinity, and yet I do
not accept finity. I want this adventure that is the
context of my life to go on without end.*
                                        —Simone de Beauvoir

The paradox of life is that we cannot conceive of its ending, but we also can't conceive of its not ending. We have
the image of the circle to help us out of this dilemma. And if
we think of the vast cycles of time and generation, the image
of a spiral comes to mind.

The rich web, the adventure of life, goes on without end. It
preceded us and will outlast us, and humans will go on
struggling and surrendering. A related paradox is that we live
in a moment of time that is constantly becoming the past, yet
will affect a future that we cannot really predict or control. All
we have to work with is our brief arc of life, now.

Yet how precious it is, and how vast, and how it is extended by our ties with others. The web of our relatedness to
others brings us into their lives, them into ours. As we share
our attention, we enrich our spirits, and we're enriched again
by the gifts of others.

A further paradox: every individual is alone, yet none of
us is unaccompanied on the curving journey that takes us
through this life.

Only by letting go of life do I most profoundly enhance it.

Gift, like genius, I often think only means an infinite capacity for taking pains.
—Jane Ellice Hopkins

There is no easy way through this life. Few days are void of struggle. Some days are fraught with it. Each day presses us in some manner. Our opportunities for growth, whether on the job or in relationships, are generally accompanied by the pinch of a difficult decision or the push of an unwelcome thought.

Often we need reminding that we're unlikely to attain personal growth without the experience of pain. Pain first beckons and then pushes us forward to new solutions for tired old situations. But these new solutions will always surface if we trust ourselves to move through the pain.

No problem is beyond solving. The process of living, when experienced with care and patience, will reveal the solution that any problem contains.

I will take today slowly and easily. If a struggle develops, I will cherish it. It means growth.

Injustice anywhere is a threat to justice everywhere.
We are caught in an inescapable network of mu-
tuality, tied in a single garment of destiny.
—Martin Luther King

Safe in our own homes, or deep into our jobs, it's difficult to remember that we're part of the indivisible life of each, and that everything we do affects that "network of mutuality," just as we're affected by it. Stop and think of the beautiful image of the Arctic tundra, or the atmospheric envelope. These are parts of the world that we may have thought of as inert, nonliving, until we learned how delicate is their sensitivity to everything that touches them.

And everything touches them, as everything touches us. We are as much a part of the rhythm of life as the delicate web of roots that hold the permafrost in place. The same over-arching world spirit inhabits us, and we are as necessary as molecules of oxygen.

At last, we have achieved the capacity to communicate with our fellow human beings. Let us hope we can do it as well as sparrows do, or grass does, for we can shape our destiny even as we're shaped by it.

I will try to live today so as to answer for it to all my fellow creatures.

Now in the middle of my days I glean
this truth that has a flower's freshness:
life is the gold and sweetness of wheat,
hate is brief and love immense.

—*Gabriella Mistral*

Eternal truths are always fresh. That's why so many people treasure a daily spiritual guide as an occasion for meditation. Each day we can refresh our spirits with the help of such a guide.

Meditation is a process of simplifying, emptying out, concentrating our minds. We won't achieve much spiritual progress from simply reading these words; they're just the beginning, just the signpost. Growth comes from the work we do, transforming spiritual nourishment into the strength we need.

Some of us are skeptical at first. We don't believe we need to acquire any more disciplines; our spirits are in fine shape, thanks very much. But then we notice a change in our friends or intimates; they've made a discovery. Mysteriously, their lives are straightening out. Maybe we ought to try some of whatever they've got.

It doesn't matter how we come to a program of spiritual growth. The truth was here all the time, waiting for us.

I can't speak the truth too often; it's new every day.

Whensoever a man desires anything inordinately, he is presently disquieted within himself.
—*Thomas À Kempis*

We are at peace when we cherish the gifts of the present moment. And gratitude for the moment enhances the value of what is to come next. When we take our focus off the present, longing only for another time or place or experience, we'll never reap the rewards that offer themselves to us moment by moment. The longing heart guarantees little peace, infrequent moments of joy, and stunted growth. The soul's nourishment is here, now, with these people who surround us and within these activities inviting our involvement.

So few people understand the benefits of celebrating life as it's received. Finding pleasure in the ordinary occurrences heightens our awareness that indeed, no occurrence is truly ordinary. Every moment is special.

I can answer yes to today and all it offers, and be at peace.

Women and men in the crowd meet and mingle.
Yet with itself every soul standeth single.
                                    —Alice Carey

Joy for living depends on the level of intimacy with others whom we've grown comfortable with: sharing our grief, our fears, and our glories with others relieves their power over us and fosters a healthier perspective on all the situations in our lives. Yet, even the deepest level of sharing doesn't relieve us of the need to come to full acceptance, solely alone, of the turmoil, the trauma, the tension in our lives.

Interdependently we share this universe, each of us giving to its continuance and receiving sustenance in turn. With little thought, really, we are living our lives bonded in myriad ways, great and small, to one another and to the cycles of the earth housing us all. Just as absolute as is our interdependence, so sure is our need to be at peace. This means to be alone, but not lonely, with our soul's relentless search for understanding, for serenity, for certainty about the direction we are taking. Together and yet alone we are traveling the path of life.

I will find a listener today if I want closeness with someone. And I'll need time alone, away, to understand the life I've been given.

. . . [To] take something from yourself, to give to another, that is humane and gentle and never takes away as much comfort as it brings again.
—Thomas More

We take different kinds of pleasure in giving. Perhaps the purest is the gift to a child so young it doesn't really know who the gift came from; the pure joy that the teddy bear or pull-toy produces is our reward, unmixed by any expectation of return.

When children get older, we want something back from them: gratitude, respect. The gift is less pure. When lovers exchange gifts, their pleasure is often tinged with anxiety: Did I give more than I got? Did I get more than I gave? Or with power: He'll always remember where he got that shirt; she owes me something for the fur jacket.

To friends and relations our gifts reflect many things: our appreciation of their lives, our shared memories, our prosperity. We tend to give in a spirit of *self*-expression.

Perhaps the closest we can come to a pure gift is an anonymous one: a gift of volunteer work, of blood, or a contribution to a charity. Such a gift, which can never be acknowledged or returned by those it comforts, can heal our spirits when they are wearied by too much ego.

The gift of myself can be a gift to myself.

That life is a fragile shell on the beach I have thought of before. This Christmas I am thinking big basic wonders as if I were just born.

—Naomi Shihab Nye

The big basic wonders about our origin, and that of the stars, must still occur to us all, even though we're grown up and knowledgeable about astronomy and human reproduction. The germination of a seed is still much more wonderful, in a strict sense, than the mere electronic marvel of a calculator that makes twelve thousand computations in a second.

Do we ever let ourselves simply wonder? Do we still open ourselves to the awe that filled us once, when we first realized the vast intricacies of the solar system or of human physiology?

Every great ritual surrounds a story that is wonderful: the presence of a god; the deliverance of a people; the transformation of life or death. It's appropriate that we should respond to them with a thrill of wonder. Wonder is a gift; it contains the germs of reverence and of knowledge.

Life is frail and intricate, and it contains everything I need for fulfillment.

A holiday is a permitted—or rather a prescribed—
excess, a solemn violation of a prohibition.
                                    —Sigmund Freud

Breaking our own small rules is a luxury that we some-times forget to indulge. How pleasant it can be to stay in bed late on a Sunday, not get dressed or shaved, to let clutter accumulate. On our days off, we can get a thrill from such "solemn violations" as going to a film in the afternoon, eating an unscheduled treat, jogging twice around the track.

It's probably important to give ourselves these little ex-travagances, especially if our usual lives involve a highly organized routine. Just breaking up the day differently—reversing daytime and nighttime activities, for example—can give a special flavor to a day off.

Routine is consoling for many of us. We feel good about ourselves as long as we keep to the schedule, obey the rules. But we need to break some rules to get a different kind of good feeling about ourselves; above all, to know that we can choose to return to our former law-abiding selves. Some-times we fear that if we step out of line once, we'll never get our lives together again. We need to know that we can re-new ourselves on a holiday.

Giving myself a holiday by breaking my routine can make it stronger—because I choose to resume it.

Anger repressed can poison a relationship as surely as the cruelest words.

—Joyce Brothers

Anger toward a mate, a co-worker, a friend, or neighbor, builds a strong wall, separating us from everyone if we don't acknowledge the cause of the anger. Like any secret, denied anger festers and infects relations with friends, acquaintances, even strangers. It dominates our attention and pollutes every emotion. But more importantly, if not checked it controls us, and this all-consuming power then decides our destiny.

Anger doesn't need to be a major force in our lives. Like any emotion, we can learn from it, but we must let it go if we are to grow. It helps to remember the sweet aftertaste when an angry encounter is resolved.

Anger acknowledged and resolved tightens understanding between people, and encourages intimacy. Anger is bittersweet when squarely faced.

My anger need not own me today.

How magnificently you tossed away this God who plagues and helps man so much! But you did not and could not toss out of your heart that part of you from which the God notion had come.

—*Richard Wright*

Each of us accommodates "the God notion" in our own way, but we all have it. Although we may not all worship a great Mother or Father figure, our spiritual dimension makes us all kin.

To deny our spiritual selves will bring us unrest; our life's journey is always toward serenity, and serenity means finding peace within, answering those searching questions of the spirit. Some of us will seek answers in many forms, in different languages, but our quest is as real and as simple if we stay at home and explore within ourselves.

When we're honest with ourselves, we find this radiant truth: an authentic search for spiritual wholeness can be successful.

Let me honor "the God notion" and never use it against myself or any fellow being.

• DECEMBER 29 •

---

*The way in which we think of ourselves has everything
to do with how our world sees us and how we can see
ourselves successfully acknowledged by that world.*
—*Arlene Raven*

Our self-perception determines how we present ourselves.
The posture we've assumed invites others' praise, interest, or
criticism. What others think of us accurately reflects our
personal self-assessment, a message we've conveyed directly
or subtly.

It behooves us to acknowledge the power we each master
over others' judgments and opinions of our worth. It's with
absolute certainty that those opinions are molded by our
own. When our personal opinions are negative, it's likely to
be because we've lost touch with the rhythm of this life we're
sharing with others. Perhaps we've forgotten what is essential to the completion of the whole. Perhaps a gentle
reminder is needed, day by day.

---

*How I grade myself today will he imitated by the men and
women who share my experiences. I can earn high marks if I
want to.*

*. . . Is not all the world beyond these four little walls
pitiless enough, but that thou must need enter here—
thou, O Death?*

—*W. E. B. Du Bois*

The concept of a refuge strengthens us. For some of us,
it's a dark basement and headphones, or a workbench; for
others, a garden or a bedroom.

Some of us take refuge outside ourselves, in our spiritual
faith. There we find a death-defying certainty and a reminder
that our being is a gift. Some of us find this refuge in service
to others; we feel the benign power of creation stream
through us, and we're strengthened.

Death is part of life, and it belongs on the same plane as
life's other events: birth, nurturing, and sickness. But spiritual refuge lifts us to another plane, where the powers of life
and death join to form the whole of existence. This higher
truth, like all real refuge, lies within us. We can summon it
as the need arises.

The more I turn outward to others, the stronger I become within.

• DECEMBER 31 •

Despite my geographical love of mankind, I would be
attacked by local fears.

—Grace Paley

We may have the highest principles, be generous, trusting, and public-spirited, and still find ourselves assailed at times by doubts and fears. The "local fears" don't mean that we've betrayed our "geographical" principles; only that, this time, we're afraid.

The wonderful thing about being human is that we can choose how we act at any given moment. If we find ourselves behaving in a way we don't like, we can choose to change; either to change our behavior or—if that doesn't seem possible—to change the way we look at it. It's wisely said: "You can do something for twelve hours that you could never think of doing your whole life long."

It's a waste of time and effort to disapprove of ourselves. If we won't change our behavior, let's change our standards. Many of us have impossibly high expectations for ourselves, and when we don't measure up, we feel guilty.

Guilt is unproductive. When we keep everything in the moment—the "geographical" as well as the "local"—we can accept ourselves as we are. We are as good, right now, as we can be.

Scaling down my expectations closer to what I'm capable of will
aid my spiritual growth.

SUBJECT INDEX

AUTHOR INDEX

B

You do build in darkness if you have faith. When the light returns you have made of yourself a fortress which is impregnable to certain kinds of trouble; you may even find yourself needed and sought by others as a beacon in their dark.

—*Olga Rosmanith*

Hazelden Publishing and Education is a division of the Hazelden Foundation, a not-for-profit organization. Since 1949, Hazelden has been a leader in promoting the dignity and treatment of people afflicted with the disease of chemical dependency.

The mission of the Foundation is to improve the quality of life for individuals, families, and communities by providing a national continuum of information, education, and recovery services that are widely accessible; to advance the field through research and training; and to improve quality and effectiveness through continuous improvement and innovation.

Stemming from that, the mission of the Publishing division is to provide quality information and support to people wherever they may be in their personal journey—from education and early intervention, through treatment and recovery, to personal and spiritual growth.

Although our treatment programs do not necessarily use everything Hazelden publishes, our bibliotherapeutic materials support our mission and the Twelve Step philosophy upon which it is based. We encourage your comments and feedback.

The headquarters of the Hazelden Foundation is in Center City, Minnesota. Additional treatment facilities are located in Chicago, Illinois; New York, New York; Plymouth, Minnesota; St. Paul, Minnesota; and West Palm Beach, Florida. At these sites we provide a continuum of care for men and women of all ages. Our Plymouth facility is designed specifically for youth and families.

For more information on Hazelden, please call **1-800-257-7800**, or access our World Wide Web site on the Internet **[http://www.hazelden.org]**.

INTRODUCTION

When I entered the program in May 1983, I suddenly discovered I had incredible feelings I had never allowed myself to feel. Those feelings were fear, anxiety, and loneliness. For years I had built up walls and defenses that repelled those feelings, but the program took away my defenses.

I found those negative feelings particularly prevalent at night. I would be fine all day and even at an evening meeting. But after the meeting I would come home and have overwhelming feelings of loneliness and fear. Sometimes I had a difficult time getting to sleep. Sometimes I would wake up in the middle of the night and stay up for hours with anxious feelings. What was it about the nighttime that was so difficult?

I soon discovered daylight chased away many of my fears because of the hustle-bustle of the day. There were things to do, people to see, and—as Robert Frost says— "miles to go before I sleep." Each new dawn held new promises and new beginnings. But what did the sunset hold? What was there to focus on at night? The meditations on the following pages are designed to help keep your program in focus at night. Each meditation focuses on a particular issue or feeling you may feel at the end of the day. The meditation then provides you with program tools to ease your mind gently into a relaxed state at bedtime.

It's so true that the program works, but only if you work it. None of us can get better without the help of the Twelve Steps, sponsors, slogans, the fellowship, our Higher Power, prayer, and meditation. Each of these nightly meditations reminds you of the marvelous tools you have available and helps you keep them ever-present. With them, you are truly never alone, no matter what time of day ... or night.

—Amy E. Dean

It is as important to relax our minds as it is to concentrate them.
                                                    —*Charles B. Newcomb*

After a day of activity, our bodies naturally need to slow down. We yawn, our muscles stiffen, our eyes want to close. Yet our minds can be racing at top speed. How do we learn to slow down our thoughts and relax? We first need to realize we don't have to do it all ourselves. We can ask for help from a book, a relaxation tape, a class or workshop, a movie, or music. And we can learn how to unwind from others.

For most of our lives, we learned how to be tense. Now we need to learn how to relax. Just as we didn't learn our tension in one night, we also won't learn relaxation in one night. But we can begin tonight to find some methods that will work for us. We can try, a little bit at a time, to become familiar with how it feels to have a more relaxed mind. Tonight can be a beginning.

Am I willing to unlearn my tensions? What resources can I use tonight to help me relax my mind?

But where was I to start? The world is so vast, I shall start with the country I knew best, my own. But my country is so very large. I had better start with my town. But my town, too, is large. I had best start with my street. No, my home. No, my family. Never mind, I shall start with myself.
—Elie Wiesel

How many times have we tried to change things outside of ourselves, like a parent, a loved one, a drinking or drug-using pattern, or a boss? Perhaps we felt if we changed someone or something, we would be better off. But we soon discovered we were powerless to change people, places, or things.

All we can change is ourselves. Yet we can't do that by five-minute overhauls. Nor can we go to bed at night and expect to wake up the next day as the person we always wanted to be.

We need to *keep it simple* as we change ourselves. We need to start slowly. If we imagine ourselves as a big puzzle with many pieces, we may understand we can only see our whole selves by joining together one piece at a time.

Did I try to change others today? How can I keep it simple as I try to change myself—just a little bit at a time?

Strange feelings. . . . Just a sort of unexplained sadness that comes each afternoon when the new day is gone forever and there's nothing ahead but increasing darkness.
—*Robert M. Pirsig*

Just as each day is a new beginning, so is each night also a new start. Each night can be a chance to recharge ourselves after our day's batteries have run down. Each night can be a chance to start anew on our goals, our growth, our good thoughts.

Instead of reflecting on the past events of the day, we can look forward to the moments to come. We can be unafraid of the darkness of the night as we prepare for tomorrow by using positive energy.

Although the day is done, tomorrow is yet to come. There are plans to make, places to go, people to see, and projects to do. Tomorrow can begin with hope and strength and energy directed to all our forthcoming events.

I can see tomorrow as a new beginning.

Happiness is not pleasure. Happiness is victory.
—Zig Ziglar

Many people believe happiness is measured in material terms: a house, money, lots of clothes. Others believe it's found in enjoyable moments: a sunset, dinner with friends, a walk in the woods. Although happiness is all these things, it's also the feeling we get when we have achieved something we've longed for and worked hard for. Happiness can be a personal victory.

To be victorious doesn't mean we have to win. It can mean we've gone beyond an expected outcome and gained more than we hoped for. There have been times when we've experienced victory: passing a test, buying our first car, graduating from college, landing a job, living on our own. But all victories don't have to be big. They can be as small and insignificant as losing a few pounds, going a few hours without a drink or other drug, not arguing with a family member, or taking an hour for ourselves.

Big or small, our victories are our happiness. Each one shows us we can do what we set out to do. Each helps build confidence in our abilities and is a boon to our self-esteem. With each victory, we can be assured there will be another.

I can be happy for all my victories.

You will forget your misery; you will remember
it as waters that have passed away.
—Job 11:16

Many of us have painful memories we carry with us like pictures in a wallet. We keep these memories alive through feelings generated by those moments. Why are we so attached to unpleasant memories?

It's difficult to let go of memories, no matter how unpleasant. Sometimes they're a reminder of the past, but more often we clutch them because we're afraid to feel pleasant feelings today. Because the program is working in our lives, we have fewer painful times now. That may not be comfortable, so we invent new pain or dredge up the sludge of the past. As ugly as it may be, it's still familiar.

Tonight we don't have to look back. We don't have to feel misery or pain because it's familiar. We don't have to drag out that wallet and look at the images of unhappy times again. Tonight we can leave those spaces in our wallets empty, ready to be filled with new moments to remember.

I can try to make some new moments to remember. I don't need to look back anymore.

So every faithful heart shall pray to Thee in the hour of anxiety, when great floods threaten. Thou art a refuge to me from distress so that it cannot touch me; Thou dost guard me in salvation beyond all reach of harm.
—Psalm 32

It's difficult to focus on the present when our minds are thinking of events yet to come. We may be so obsessed with an upcoming happening that we forget to stay in the present.

Perhaps we've been asked to speak at a meeting. Or maybe we have a big test tomorrow. Or maybe we have some plans days from now for a party, a family get-together, or a trip, that are already sending us into a whirlwind of tension and anxiety.

To stay in the present, we need to ask for help. Our Higher Power can help us with our anxiety about a future event, whether the event will happen five minutes, five days, or five years from now. Tonight and tomorrow will happen, no matter how much anxiety we have. But future events may turn out a little better if we take some serenity from our Higher Power with us.

Is an upcoming event causing me a lot of anxiety? How can I use the program to help me let go of this anxiety?

Prayer should be the key of the day and the lock of the night.

—*Old proverb*

Many of us believe prayer has to be scheduled—a once-in-the-morning and once-at-night routine. Yet few of us remember prayer is merely a conversation with our Higher Power. We can pray anytime and as often as we'd like.

Prayer in the morning is a wonderful way to open the day. Yet do we continue to keep the door open by renewing our conversation with our Higher Power? Do we turn to our Higher Power during times of stress, joy, sadness, or peace? We may be so busy in our daily tasks that we forget to keep that door open.

Tonight the door is still open. Our Higher Power is still there to listen. We can share our feelings of the day as though we were talking to a close friend. We don't have to prostrate ourselves before our Higher Power. All we have to do is start talking. Then we can close the door with prayer, knowing we have with us the good, warm feelings that faith brings. And as we finally lay down to sleep tonight, we can say goodnight to our Higher Power and give thanks for the day.

Now I lay me down to sleep, I pray the Lord my soul to keep.

Don't be afraid to take a big step. You can't cross a chasm in two small jumps.
—David Lloyd George

Taking a risk can be scary. Whether the risk involves a new relationship, asking for a raise, being honest, or changing a behavior, it's still pretty hard to do. Sometimes we may wish we could approach a risk with only partial involvement, almost as if we had one foot inside a door and one outside. That way, if things get too difficult, we can always run away.

But we can't take a risk unless we commit ourselves to it. And we can't commit ourselves unless we have faith that no matter what happens, we're okay. We may feel vulnerable, but we don't have to feel alone if we remember our Higher Power is with us.

Perhaps we took a risk today and are still feeling scared and exposed. Or maybe we're planning on taking a risk tomorrow and are filled with fear. Remember it's okay to have feelings of fear, doubt, and insecurity.

Tonight I will relax and know I never approach a risk without my Higher Power to guide me.

Later. I'm still young. I'll think of spiritual things when I'm older. On my deathbed.
— *Garrison Keillor*

Too often we've thought prayer is for the aged, the sick, or the dying. If we are young, healthy, and successful, we may think we don't need to communicate with a Higher Power. "I'm fine right now," we may say. "I will . . . later on."

The time to establish contact with a Higher Power is now. From the minute we come kicking and screaming into this world until our last breath, there is a Power greater than ourselves watching over us. This Power guides us, strengthens us, and helps us grow even without our acknowledging it is there. But it is because we don't acknowledge its presence that we become lost, confused, depressed, angry, hopeless, or unforgiving.

Our time to reach out to our Higher Power is not when our bodies stop running. Now is the time to ask for direction, seek knowledge, become open to receiving divine guidance. If we open ourselves now to developing our spirituality, we will open a valuable door to our growth.

Can I begin to develop my spiritual beliefs? Can I open my mind and heart to a Higher Power?

Great Spirit, help me never to judge another until I have walked in his moccasins for two weeks.

—*Sioux Indian prayer*

How many times do we see someone who dresses or acts differently? How do we usually react to such a person? Do we stare or make a comment to someone next to us? Meetings are excellent places to come in contact with those who come from different backgrounds. Do we greet each person we meet with care and attention, or do we pass judgments and make jokes?

Our Higher Power has given each of us a diverse background and personality. Some of us have known incredible hardship or handicap. Some of us have limited education. Some of us live in crowded spaces. But some of us have had opportunities. Some of us have an educational degree. Some of us live in large homes. Yet is there any one of us who is better than another?

If we are prone to judge or criticize, tonight we can decide to take a first step toward silence. Remember that education and economics do not make someone better. We are the same, no matter how much, or how little, we have.

I can learn not to judge others.

Example is not the main thing in influencing others. It is the only thing.
—*Albert Schweitzer*

Imagine how useless meetings would be without examples of how well the program works. There would be no one who was clean and no one with the strength to cope with another's problem. Surely we could use the Steps and principles ourselves, but we'd feel lost and alone without the positive influences of others.

All around us are people who succeed in the program. Their strength and positive energy, their kind words and understanding nature, and their no-nonsense approach to living with faith and perseverance are an inspiration. The fact that they have changed for the better is the best illustration of how we can change.

Ask old-timers what they were like when they first came into the program. They'll say they were unhappy, confused, and near despair. But in the program they met others who had been there, too. It won't take us long to replace our frowns with smiles, our tension with relaxation, our anger with forgiveness. If we look to the examples around us, we will find strength.

Help me remember where I came from, and help me be grateful for how the program has guided me.

The first thing I had to conquer was fear. I realized what a debilitating thing fear is. It can render you absolutely helpless. I know now that fear breeds fear.

—Byron Janis

The future can be scary, especially if we try to predict what will happen. Sometimes we may even go further, not only predicting what may happen but also anticipating our reactions to those events. If only we knew what will happen, then we wouldn't have to be afraid of the future.

If we're not careful, we will allow every fearful feeling to overtake us until the fear extends into other parts of our lives. Fear can be like a hidden trap, catching us whenever we try to go anywhere or do anything. We cannot see, hear, or touch fear, but we can give it so much power that it almost has a life of its own.

We can get rid of the traps fear has set for us. We can do that by having faith in our Higher Power. We can have faith that our way has been prepared for us, faith that we are safe wherever we are.

I can cut the ties with which fear binds me. Without fear, I will only feel the safety of faith.

When health is absent, wisdom cannot reveal itself, art cannot manifest, strength cannot fight, wealth becomes useless, and intelligence cannot be applied.

—Herophilus

If we have ceased an obsessive behavior, we may think we are now healthy. Yet we may not be paying enough attention to our needs for sleep, good food, and exercise. We may also be ignoring our spiritual and mental health needs by not taking time to meditate or communicate with others.

Taking away an obsession doesn't mean we're cured. Instead, the work is just beginning. Now is the time to structure our days and nights to include time to be alone, time to listen to ourselves, and time to listen and talk with others.

We are now in the process of rebuilding ourselves into better people. We need to work on our outer appearances and our inner healthiness. Good nutrition, plenty of rest, a balance of exercise and play, meditation time, and a balance between work hours and home hours is needed for our best health. We can take the first healthy step toward building a better self.

Higher Power, help me look at my health. Can I identify areas that need improvement?

The doors we open and close each day decide the lives we live.

—Flora Whittemore

We often hear the phrase, "When one door shuts, another opens." It means everything has a beginning and an end. When our travels on one path are completed, another path lies ahead.

It's not easy to feel a door close. Relationships, friendships, careers, and lives end. Although we may not understand why a door closes, it's important to remember our Higher Power has everything to do with it. By the same token, we may not understand why certain doors open, revealing opportunities we may have longed for. Again, our Higher Power feels we are ready to pursue that new experience.

The doors that opened and closed today helped prepare us for our experiences tonight. The doors that opened and closed tonight will help us grow toward tomorrow. We are not mice in a maze, randomly pursuing paths for a reward of cheese. We are children of our Higher Power, guided towards our chosen goal through the many doors we open and close along the way.

Have I learned there is a reason for everything in my life? Can I trust that my path has been prepared for me by my Higher Power?

What was completely forbidden for me to do would be to kill myself. . . . If I were to commit suicide, I would be throwing God's gift back in his face.

—Dr. Raymond A. Moody

Many of us have had suicidal thoughts at one time or another. We hear at meetings how others have tried suicide in the past. We may have tried it ourselves or our lives may have been touched by the suicide of someone we knew. We may now find that living a clean, sober, spiritual life is overwhelming. Sometimes we may feel like giving up.

That's when we need to call someone. Talk it out. Or get to a meeting and be honest with the group about our feelings. There are people who care. Our friends and our peers are God's human messengers, ready to give understanding to those in need.

If a friend of ours felt down on life, wouldn't we want to help? Now is the time to open ourselves up to caring and love from another human being.

Do I think about giving up? Who can I open up to for caring and love?

Let everyone sweep in front of his [or her] own
door, and the whole world will be clean.
—*Goethe*

Taking care of ourselves rather than trying to control others may be difficult. Our character defects may lead us to believe we should take responsibility for the actions of others. Sometimes we may feel we know how a spouse, co-worker, or friend should act. We may even go so far as to tell someone what he or she should do or do it for them.

Tonight we can reflect on our actions of today. Did we cover up another's behavior, or tell someone what to do, or take control of something that was not our responsibility? We need to realize that taking charge of another's life is not beneficial to anyone. Focusing on another's life keeps us from looking at ours. Doing for others what they should be doing for themselves takes away valuable lessons for growth.

What would happen if everyone in a classroom were the teacher? Who would listen and learn? Who would mature and grow? The teacher in our lives is our Higher Power. Let us respect our instructor and let our Higher Power do the guiding while we grow.

Help me listen and learn and let go of controlling others.

Enthusiasm is the yeast that makes your hopes rise to the stars. Enthusiasm is the sparkle in your eyes, the swing in your gait, the grip of your hand, the irresistible surge of will and energy to execute your ideas.

—Henry Ford

The automobile is just one of many inventions based on someone's enthusiasm to realize a dream. From the persistence came a machine that has since improved our lives by bringing people closer together.

Enthusiasm is a catalyst for improvement. If we think back to those times when we've felt enthusiasm in our lives, we'll realize its benefits. Perhaps we secured a job promotion or pitched a no-hitter or completed an intricate quilt.

Enthusiasm in the program is also a catalyst for change. If we observe those who truly work their program with passion, we'll see them making positive changes, gathering a greater sense of self-esteem. Their enthusiasm can be contagious if we open up our minds to their belief that all things are possible.

Have I been enthusiastic today? Can I learn from the enthusiasm of someone close to me?

Children do not know how their parents love them, and they never will till the grave closes over those parents, or till they have children of their own.

—*Edmund Vance Cooke*

As adults, we may feel we were cheated out of a "normal" childhood because of our parents' emotional, physical, or spiritual failings. We may think they should never be forgiven for their actions or inactions when we were young.

Yet imagine what our lives would be like today if we did not forgive. We would be bitter, stomping angrily through life with a clipboard in hand, ready to write down the name of the next person who crosses us. It's time to throw away the clipboard and the names on it—including the names of our parents.

The program teaches us to love those who come into our lives, even if we don't like them. It teaches us forgiveness through our Higher Power. We do not have to like our parents, but we can love them. By the same token, we need to realize our parents love us in their special way. They aren't perfect—and neither are we.

Help me remember my parents did the best they could with what they had. That's all anyone can really do.

And if not now, when?

—The Talmud

It's so easy to put things off. Sometimes we're like Scarlet O'Hara, who hoped and dreamed for a better life by saying, "There's always tomorrow." But is there always a tomorrow? If we live too many of our days counting on tomorrows, we may find ourselves putting off achievements and growth now.

What if tomorrow never came? What if all of our time to do what we wanted was put in the hours left in today? We'd be scurrying around like mice trying to cram as much as we could into this short period of time. But today, not having such a deadline, we believe our time is endless and no goal or task is so important that it can't be put off.

The time to achieve is now. The time to live is now. For as long as we believe tomorrow will come, we'll be living for tomorrow. If we don't believe today is the greatest gift we could receive, we'll never know how to live for today. Everything we want to achieve, to learn, to share can begin today. If we don't live the best we can right now, then when?

Higher Power, help me learn to use my time wisely. Help me avoid putting things off.

*I came to understand that it was all right to do
things for people as long as I did it for the sake of
doing it . . . the value being more in the act than
in the result.*

—Joanna Field

We've all heard the sentiment that it is better to give
than to receive. Yet we may find it difficult to give to
others, whether that giving involves an actual gift or
an act of giving of ourselves: caring for someone who
is ill, running an errand for someone, giving a back-
rub, or extending an invitation to someone who is
alone.

We may feel afraid to do for others without any expectations of receiving something in return. To give
unselfishly exposes our feelings and shows we care.
Yet if we can look beyond our fears to the selflessness
of our giving actions, there is a great reward: knowing
we had the courage to risk giving to someone.

The risks we take in giving to others are lessons for
ourselves as well as for those whose lives we touch.
The gift of giving opens doors to the homes of our
souls.

*Did I take time today to give to others? Can I risk giving to
someone close to me?*

I am bigger than anything that can happen to me. All these things, sorrow, misfortune, and suffering are outside my door. I am in the house and I have the key.
—*Charles Fletcher Lummis*

So many things seem to loom over us. There's our addiction to alcohol or other drugs, food, or people. There are our fears of expressing love, of feeling, of being alone, of being abandoned, of being rejected, of failing. There are the miseries of childhood, unhappy relationships, a failed marriage, or death. Sometimes there's even the world in general—all people, places, and things. Some days just about everything seems ready to swallow us up.

Yet nothing has absolute power over us if we have a strong belief in ourselves and a Higher Power. Our Higher Power strengthens us and helps us stay in good condition.

The negative conditions we see are not lurking in the shadows, ready to spring upon us at any moment. There are not people "out to get us," nor traps set to foil our goals. We are secure because of the faith we have in our Higher Power.

The only thing in this life bigger than me is my Higher Power. Tonight I can feel safe and secure no matter where I am.

Be yourself. Who else is better qualified?
—*Frank J. Giblin, II*

Almost every magazine devotes its cover to movie stars and famous personalities. We are taught that we need to look like the most attractive and glamorous people. We need to wear what they wear, eat what they eat, and fix our hair like theirs. The message we are given is: Don't be yourself, be like someone else.

There will always be someone who looks better than we do, has more money, scores better on tests, or has more creative skills. If we're always trying to mimic other people, we won't be looking at ourselves. Imitation may be the sincerest form of flattery, but it keeps us from being ourselves.

We need to stop focusing on what others have that we don't have. We need to look inward at our good qualities as well as our imperfections. We need to see who we are by being ourselves. Life is not made up of people who are good and bad, happy and sad, rich and poor, beautiful and ugly. Life is made up of people being themselves.

I will start to be myself. Help me show others the real me, not an imitation.

The darkness was encumbering only because I relied upon my sight for everything I did, not knowing that another way was to let power be the guide.

—*Carlos Castaneda*

We don't need to be blind in order not to see. Remember how long it took for us to "see" our addictions? Remember how the blindfold of denial kept us from seeing the reality of our lives?

But it took a person or people to help us "see" our way into the program. And now that we are members, we still need others to guide us in our recovery. Sometimes pride gets in the way and tells us we can do it alone, yet those are the times when we stumble and fall. Perhaps today was a day when we refused the guidance of others. We may have felt we were strong enough to "go it alone." But we will feel the effects of such blind gropings if we don't remember that we need others.

Even the blind person has a cane or a companion or an animal for guidance. So we must rely upon the power of the group and our Higher Power to help us "see" our way.

Have I been blind today to the help offered by others? Tonight, can I ask for help to "see"?

It's all right to hold a conversation, but you should let go of it now and then.
—*Richard Armour*

Do we pay close attention to those who talk to us, or do we spend more time talking to them? How well do we listen to others? Do we hear only what we want to hear, mentally editing out comments and statements from others?

A good exercise to improve listening is to repeat statements said to us, almost as if we were parroting the speaker. It may sound easy, but try it first! Too many of us pay more attention to our thoughts and don't let in words spoken to us. As we think back over the conversations of the day, we may find we cannot recall the things discussed with co-workers, friends, or relatives. We may only recall our parts of the conversations. Can we remember things said at last night's meeting or today's noontime meeting? If we can't, we probably didn't carry much healing or strength away with us. If we begin the listening exercise and use it every day, we may find our growth improving by leaps and bounds, because we've started listening to others.

Help me begin the listening exercise. I will listen as closely as I can to those around me and learn from them.

Some people regard discipline as a chore. For me, it is a kind of order that sets me free to fly.
—Julie Andrews

If we think of the word *discipline,* we might visualize forms of punishment or reprimand from teachers, parents, or bosses. Yet discipline doesn't have to be negative or an effort in blood, sweat, and tears. Discipline can be the structure we need in order to achieve our goals.

Within the program are disciplines to follow to achieve our goal of a renewed outlook on life. The Steps are probably the greatest discipline, for they provide a framework to formulate more positive beliefs about ourselves and our lives. Going to meetings is another discipline that helps keep us on track as we learn and grow. There are other disciplines, too—sharing with others, reading literature, becoming committed to a group, and practicing the program's principles in all our affairs. All these disciplines keep us focused on our ultimate goal: freedom from all past obsessions and negativity. With the discipline of the program, we can learn to fly.

I can discipline myself to remain focused on the program. I know the benefits of such discipline.

• JANUARY 26 •

*It is a matter first of beginning—and then
following through.*

—*Richard L. Evans*

How many times have we started a project or a new
path of living only to abandon it after a short time? We
may have thought it wasn't what we wanted or there
wasn't enough time. Instead of following through, we
usually gave up just when it was getting challenging
and difficult.

What are our dreams today? Do we wish we could
speak a second language, know how to operate a computer, exercise regularly, or attend more meetings?
What's stopping us? Each task we'd like to accomplish
can only be done by persistence and dedication. We
learn a new language one word at a time, learn how to
operate a computer one step at a time, exercise regularly one day at a time, and attend more meetings one
night at a time.

We don't have to give up an endeavor just because
the hard work has begun. Instead of looking down the
road where we want to be, we need to look at this moment. If we take a step toward our goals, we'll be
closer than if we never took that step.

---

*I can walk toward my goal, remembering each step I take
will bring me closer to achievement and personal reward.*

Iron rusts from disuse, water loses its purity from stagnation . . . even so does inaction sap the vigors of the mind.
—*Leonardo da Vinci*

After a long day of working or doing errands, we may want to sit and not do a thing. But although our bodies may be physically tired, our minds may be just the opposite.

If we're plagued by tired, cranky thoughts after a day's activity, we might discover our minds are too hooked into our feelings. We can separate the mind from the body and learn to chase away stinking thinking. We might treat our tired bodies to a bath while we treat our minds to a good book. While we're soaking our feet or resting in an easy chair, we can put on some music. Or we can put aside the hectic pace of the day and throw our creative energies into preparing a new recipe.

There are countless ways to wake up our minds even if our bodies are tired. Instead of collapsing in front of the television or eating junk food, we can change our focus. We can tune out the signals of the day and turn on our minds.

Did I exercise my mind tonight?

Either you reach a higher point today, or you exercise your strength in order to be able to climb higher tomorrow.

—Nietzsche

It has been said truth will set us free. Truth is not simply being honest with ourselves and others. It is also the ideals by which we would like to live. Some people spend their lifetimes never knowing truth, while others search for it in vain. To find truth, we must set out on individual journeys.

In many Eastern countries, people believe truth is found after scaling a high mountain peak and consulting with the guru. In a way, that's what we must do—set off on a tiring journey to consult our Higher Power. Yet our goal is not to reach the top, but to realize truth on the way. As we gain such knowledge, the journey becomes easier and less painful.

No matter how good or bad today was, we have gained ground in our search for truth. We may now have some insights to our lives. Even if we didn't come as far in our journey as we would have liked to today, we still have tomorrow. The search for truth is an ongoing quest filled with great rewards.

Help me find the strength to press onward and upward for truth.

Whatever men attempt, they seem driven to overdo.

—Bernard Baruch

It's usually very difficult for us to bring balance into our lives. We may find it hard not to put in overtime at work. We may be obsessed about housework or yardwork to the extent that we work long hours at it. Whatever we do, whatever we have, whatever we want, it's usually not enough for us.

Any activity or commitment needs a certain amount of time, concentration, and energy. But some of us may be too absorbed in physical fitness to notice we are always tense, always on the go. Some of us may be so obsessed with money that we take on additional work, not noticing we are often hard to get along with. Some of us may be so fascinated by a hobby that we ignore people in our lives who need our time and attention, too.

Tonight we need to recognize the obsessive areas of our lives and begin to make changes. It may mean assigning time limits to different activities. Or it may mean altering our schedules, even letting go of an activity. Tonight is the time to begin to bring balance into our lives, gently and gradually.

I know I need more balance in my life. What are some changes I can make to bring the scales more in balance?

So long as we believe we are only human, we are going to experience pain, suffering, tears, disease, and death.

—*Donald Curtis*

Imagine what our lives would be like without negative feelings—fear, worry, anxiety, selfishness, tension, sadness. At first we might feel a great sense of release. But what will we replace those feelings with? What will we feel? Can it be possible to feel happy and joyous and free all the time?

It has been said we experience what we believe in. Do we believe to succeed in this world we have to suffer? We might even believe our sufferings are good: "If I hadn't been hurting so bad, I never would have made that change."

We can try to release the powerful hold our negative ties have on our lives. We can replace those negative ties with warm and loving thoughts, a kind and forgiving nature, and an ability to see good instead of bad. Life doesn't have to be a struggle. We don't have to suffer to be happy.

I can turn over worries, jealousies, fearfulness, and dissatisfactions and look at the other side of living. It is filled with serenity, hope, and light.

Hitch your wagon to a star.
—*Ralph Waldo Emerson*

How often have we struggled to do something alone, refusing to have another help us? Maybe we single-handedly cooked a meal for a family get-together or moved a piece of furniture or plodded slowly through some confusing work without assistance. Instead of asking for help to make our job go smoother, we chose to take care of it all ourselves. While we probably accomplished what was needed, where did that get us?

Our ancestors settled this land by helping one another. Lands were discovered by bands of exploration parties; barns were raised by communities; crops were harvested by many hands. That same pioneer spirit extends today to the program, where each member pulls another through good times and bad.

Succeeding alone means we have survived; succeeding with others means we have truly lived. We were not put into this life to survive without others, but to live with them. By joining ourselves with the humanity around us, we have joined that spirit which connects us all.

I can be a pioneer and share my humanity with others. How are my brothers and sisters tonight?

The Bookshop has a thousand books,
All colors, hues, and tinges,
And every cover is a door
That turns on magic hinges.
— Nancy Byrd Turner

When we start our day, we have a wealth of meditation books to help lead our focus to faith, strength, and hope. Throughout each day, we have pamphlets and books to enrich our minds and expand our understanding of the disease that affects our lives. We learn we are not alone in our struggles and triumphs; there are many before us, many now, and many to come who will ask the same questions, have the same struggles, find the same hope.

Our literature is written by those who, through the help of their Higher Power, can communicate their feelings and thoughts. By keeping a journal to record our thoughts, dreams, feelings, goals, and daily events, we can create our personal book to use for a better understanding of ourselves. This, combined with the literature of the program, will enrich our lives with valuable and inspiring words.

I can begin my record of growth and goals, plans and dreams, and all my feelings. I can be the author of the book of my life.

We should be careful to get out of an experience only the wisdom that is in it—and stay there, lest we be like the cat that sits down on a hot stove-lid. She will never sit down on a hot stove-lid again . . . but also, she will never sit down on a cold one any more.

—*Mark Twain*

"Last night I asked for help, but the person couldn't give it to me. Tonight I'm not going to ask because I'll be refused." Poor us! One person has rejected us, so now we've got the whole world rejecting us. We believe if one person lets us down, everyone else will too.

Such thinking, as negative as it is, can provide safety. If we believe we can't trust anymore, then we won't. But there won't be any growth in this kind of safety. By condemning everyone, we won't see those who want to help.

To find help we may have to ask several people. If we get turned away by a few people, we shouldn't give up hope. There are many flowers in the field of life, but to pick the best, we need to look at them all.

If I get rejected it doesn't mean I'm a bad person or no one can be trusted. It means I need to take another risk or maybe two.

Be strong and of good courage; be not frightened,
neither be dismayed. . . .

—*Joshua 1:9*

It has been said when we are at the end of our rope, we can do one of three things: let go, tie a knot and hang on, or splice the rope and begin again. Whenever we feel there's nowhere to go but down and nobody to turn to, that's when we can start all over again. If we can learn to look beyond the end of something, we'll always see an exciting, fresh beginning.

At the end of every storm is calm. At the end of every argument is silence. At the end of one relationship there is another. Although life is composed of many endings, there are just as many new beginnings. "Life goes on" is even assured by the passage of time—at the end of each minute there's another.

Nights may have many endings, but they will also have just as many beginnings. Just as the sun will set, so the moon will rise and the stars will appear. Just as the day's activities will end, so the evening's activities will begin. And when those activities are over, there will be new experiences the next day.

I can be unafraid of endings because I know they are only the first half of beginnings.

"You silly thing," said Fritz, my eldest son, sharply, *"don't you know that we must not settle what God is to do for us? We must have patience and wait His time."*

—Johann R. Wyss

The story of the shipwrecked Robinson family is a lesson in patience. It was years before their rescue. They didn't know what their fate would be on the unfamiliar island. Yet they survived every day by working together and keeping strong faith in a Power greater than themselves.

We are certainly far from the adversities faced by that family. But at times we may feel our lives would be better if our Higher Power would do what *we* wanted. How many times have we prayed as hard as we could for something we felt we needed?

Today might have been one of those days where we felt our prayers weren't answered. But we need to remember our prayers are heard. Now it is up to us to *Let Go and Let God* work His will in His own time.

Have I tried to be in control of my Higher Power today? How can I Let Go and Let God tonight?

You have to live on this twenty-four hours of daily time. Out of it you have to spin health, pleasure, money, content, respect, and the evolution of your mortal soul. Its right use, its most effective use, is a matter of highest urgency.
—Arnold Bennett

We have twenty-four hours to accomplish all we need for mental, physical, and spiritual growth. Just because morning meditations have been read, the work or school day is completed, and the day is waning doesn't mean growth time is over.

The first twelve hours of a day are usually spent housecleaning, raising children, working, running errands, and so on. By the time the activities have ended, we're ready for the second twelve hours: contemplation, relaxation, communication with family and friends, socializing, eating dinner, going to a meeting, sleeping.

Our most effective use of each day means believing we can accomplish something. There is time to be grateful for each day's experiences. There is time to build relationships with ourselves and others. Each day there is time to grow.

How can I use tomorrow to the best benefit?

God give[s] us a mind that can or can't believe,
but not even God can make us believe. . . . You
have to believe first before you can pray.
—Harriet Arnow

Sometimes it's difficult to focus on our Higher Power after a hard day at work, after an argument with a loved one, after the frustrating experience of a flat tire, long bank line, or after any of the other nuisances that are part of each and every day. "Why me?" we may cry out in frustration. On a day like today, it may be easier to believe that a Power greater than ourselves is out to get us.

But God does not choose sides. We have not been singled out for punishment. God is on our side, if we only choose to open our hearts and believe that.

As we reflect back on the events of the day, we need to remember the times we asked God for help and the times we didn't. And we need to believe first—before we pray tonight—that God is there to help us every minute of every day.

Did I ask my Higher Power for help today, or did I decide to "go it alone"? Which do I choose to do tonight?

Do not consider anything for your interest which makes you break your word, quit your modesty, or inclines you to any practice which will not bear the light, or look the world in the face.
—Marcus Antonius

Being honest with ourselves and others may be difficult for us. Honesty does not always mean telling the truth. Honesty can also mean knowing our limitations so we don't make promises we can't keep. It can mean letting our actions support our statements. It can mean living for today and not becoming wrapped up in the promises of tomorrow.

How do we feel when people are dishonest? No matter who they are, we probably lose a little trust in them. We doubt their word and don't depend upon them for support. When we are less than honest with others, they may feel the same about us.

Dishonesty may be a quick fix at that moment, but it will never provide a solid foundation for the future. Instead, we can try to be more honest with our abilities and limitations. Honest people attract those who respect them for their honesty.

I can be honest with myself and others about the events of the day and my part in them.

All miseries derive from not being able to sit quietly in a room alone.
—*Blaise Pascal*

When we are alone, what's the first thing we do? Do we turn on the radio, call a friend, invite someone over, make plans to go out, or turn on the television? How easy is it for us to be in silence for a period of time?

Perhaps we grew up in homes filled with confusion and yelling and everyone talking at once. Silence may be uncomfortable for us. Perhaps we prefer to fill our rooms with noise so we don't feel alone. Whatever method we choose to drown out the sounds of silence, we are also drowning out another sound—the inner self.

How can we possibly think, read, meditate, or write in a journal with noise bombarding us? To learn to sit comfortably alone in silence, we need to try it in small steps. We can start with five minutes, then ten, then fifteen, then a half-hour. By gently easing ourselves into quiet moments, we will allow our inner selves the time and space in which to grow.

I can spend a short time alone in silence, and listen to my inner self.

Life is like a library owned by an author. In it are a few books which he wrote himself, but most of them were written for him.
—Harry Emerson Fosdick

In our minds there are multitudes of stored memories, knowledge, and skills. Some of these are the results of living and learning, but most are information given to us by others. Our family, friends, co-workers, teachers, and children are the greatest sources for our storehouses of information.

Most of our learning comes from others. Teachers give us much in the way of facts. Our family instructs us in morals. Friends show us different personalities and lifestyles. Our children reflect what we've taught them and give us their views of the world.

All the information we have is valuable to our growth and maturity. Every person we meet, each place we visit, and everything we try contribute to our library of knowledge and experience. At times we may borrow from what is on our shelves, but we must keep our shelves stocked with fresh material. Each night we can write a new volume based on the day's experiences.

I have more valuable contributions to make to my library of knowledge and experience.

*When folks have allotted themselves a task
and work together in unison, they escape
unhappiness.*

—*Emile Zola*

We may have been loners in the past, preferring solitude to the company of others. We may have spent time as children buried in books instead of outside playing with other children. We may have endured high school without lots of dates. We may now feel more comfortable with people in one-on-one situations rather than in large groups.

A meeting is an ideal place to learn how to interact with others. We don't have to act a certain way or hide our feelings, because our group will understand us no matter what. We can give as much as we choose and they will neither harm us, nor ask for more.

By attending meetings regularly, we'll learn they exist because people are working together in unison. Someone "opens up," others make coffee, one will chair and one will speak, and some will clean up at the end. We can learn that the strength of our group lies in the ability of each member to do what is comfortable for him or her. Such coexistence can help us learn we can gather strength from numbers.

I can do something to add to the strength of the group.

If I can stop one heart from breaking, I shall not live in vain.

—Emily Dickinson

Many times we may say, "I need a meeting," or "I need to call someone." There are times when other people say the same things because they, too, are in need. The purpose of the program is to help ourselves, but we need to remember others are there to help themselves too. Do we know someone who needs help?

There are so many great rewards in helping another through a time of need. Probably the greatest reward is that we lose our self-centeredness. Helping another through pain or sorrow also lets us help ourselves through our pain and sorrow. We say some helpful things to another that we, too, benefit from hearing.

A third reward is seeing another person's vulnerability. We may find it easier to take risks and expose our humanness by seeing another do the same. Finally, helping another is a way of showing love in a nonphysical way. Many of us may need to learn love isn't only a relationship or sex. Love is gently showing concern and compassion with no thoughts of reciprocation.

I can help another and know there are great rewards in reaching out.

Be aware of yourself and validate your experience. Pay attention to your world, to what's happening, and why. . . . Feel your strength. Value it, and use it.
—*Alexandra G. Kaplan*

To truly exist in the here and now, we need to feel ourselves in the present. We need to enter each moment without the excess baggage of the past, nor the anticipation of the future.

How do we think or feel in the present? Take away thoughts of other times and we may feel lost and confused. It takes time to learn to live in the present and to trust it. We need to learn that, for as long as we're in the present, we exist. We are.

Imagine the moment as a brand new car. All we need to do is open the door, hop in, and drive away. For that moment, our thoughts will not be focused on cars we used to own or on those we're going to buy in the future. Instead, for that moment, we are in the here and now. That's how each of our moments can be: fresh and clean and exciting.

I can sit in the driver's seat and experience each moment as it occurs. Therein lies my strength.

Have you learned lessons only of those who admired you, and were tender with you, and stood aside for you? Have you not learned great lessons from those who braced themselves against you, and disputed the passage with you?
—Walt Whitman

Wouldn't it be grand if we could have everything our way! We'd have people at our beck and call. We'd never have to take responsibility for ourselves, never have to struggle for anything, never be refused any wish or want.

But how would we mature? Learning involves gains based on the effort we expend. We learned early that we couldn't listen to a music box unless we wound it. We learned we couldn't get good grades unless we studied. And now we've learned we can't change our behaviors without working the program.

If we can't see the results of the energy we put into things, then our motivation, determination, and confidence can't grow. Some things will come easily, some won't. But the things we work on now will mean the most in the end.

I am not afraid to put energy into something I really want. I need to do this for my self-esteem.

*I will love you no matter what. I will love you if
you are stupid, if you slip and fall on your face,
if you do the wrong thing, if you make mistakes,
if you behave like a human being—I will love
you no matter.*

—Leo Buscaglia

Wouldn't it be nice if there were just one person in
our lives who loved us no matter what our faults? And
wouldn't it be equally nice if we, too, could love just
one person in the same way?

Love is not an easy emotion for us to feel. In the
past we may have associated feelings of love with negative feelings such as pain, hurt, rejection, or disappointment. But we can put the negative feelings aside
and learn how to feel love as a positive emotion.

Love does not necessarily mean sexual attraction or
commitment. Love can simply be seeing someone for
who he or she is, whether that person is a friend, co-
worker, boss, family member, or lover. To show love,
we can keep our actions simple—by making a phone
call, writing a letter, or sharing a hug. Let's show
someone we care.

How can I use Keep It Simple *to show someone I care?*

People are lonely because they build walls instead of bridges.

—*Joseph Fort Newton*

Remember building snow forts? After a sticky snowfall we'd build a big snow wall. Then we'd mass-produce snowballs, preparing for battle. The team who built the best snow fort usually won, for their wall provided the best protection.

Are we still playing snow fort when we meet new people or spend time with family? Each of us has a wall we started building in our childhood. Each time we were hurt, we would fortify the wall to offer greater protection. We may not even realize it now, but we may have such strong, high walls in front of us that even the most ardent friends can't get over them.

We may feel protected behind our wall, but we may also feel lonely. Walls are built to keep people out. To feel less lonely, we need to make a little crawl space to let people in. We don't have to destroy our walls in one day, but perhaps we can let at least one person in. We will learn, one person at a time, what it feels like to be less protected, and less lonely.

I can make an opening in my wall of protection and let someone get to know me. I will be safe.

'Tis the human touch in this world that counts,
the touch of your hand and mine.
                                    —Spencer Michael Free

There once was a girl so afraid of people seeing her sad and lonely that she learned to excel at everything she did. She studied when others were playing so she could get good marks. She practiced sports alone trying to become the best. With all her diligent training, she earned excellent marks and made first-string softball. Her parents thought she was happy and well-adjusted. Yet she was miserable and didn't know how to say it.

How many of us relate to that girl's story? We may have learned at an early age not to share our feelings. Some of us became superachievers; some of us became addicted to alcohol or other drugs, food, or sex; some of us became rescuers for addicts. Yet whatever we became, we always made certain no one touched us or came too close.

We may now accept our feelings, acknowledge them, and share them. We may now be able to let another hold our hands or hug us. We know it's okay to need the human touch.

I can let myself touch and be touched by someone who understands.

We must constantly build dykes of courage to hold back the flood of fear.
—*Martin Luther King, Jr.*

The definition of courage is the ability to conquer fear or despair. In the past we may have been called courageous because we stayed in circumstances that were difficult or nearly unbearable. We may have felt that walking away from family, children, or friends was cowardly or displayed weakness. We may have felt that by holding back our tears we were stronger people.

Yet all the things we may have viewed as weakness are really signs of courage. All the things we believed to be acts of courage were really not courageous at all. If we walked away from difficult or unbearable circumstances, we would be conquering despair. If we cried, we would have been courageous by letting go of our fear, pain, or sadness.

Courage doesn't mean putting ourselves in stressful or unpleasant situations. Courage doesn't mean controlling our emotions. Courage is the ability to strengthen ourselves against the fear and despair of life, rather than be drowned by it.

What have I done today that took courage? I can be grateful for my courage and strengthen it.

*Be glad you can suffer, be glad you can feel. . . .
How can you tell if you're feeling good unless
you've felt bad, so you have something to
compare it with?*
—Thomas Tryon

How many times have we come home at the end of
a day ranting and raving about how horrible the day
was? Or perhaps our spouse, lover, roommate, or
child has carried home the burden of a bad day. How
can we feel good when the day has felt so bad?

First, we have to change our way of thinking. We
need to apply the old saying "opposites attract" to
those times of stress and unhappiness. We wouldn't
know how to smile if we didn't know how to frown.
We wouldn't know how to cry if we didn't know how
to laugh. We wouldn't even know when we were sick
if we didn't already know what it feels like to be well.

By knowing how things feel—both the good and
the bad—we can be more aware of ourselves. If today
was bad, it's okay to let it go now and know there will
be days that will be good.

*Higher Power, help me to let go of the bad feelings of the
day. Help me to feel grateful for today, no matter how it
has been.*

Reputation is what you have when you come to a new community; character is what you have when you go away.

—William Hersey Davis

All of us in the program have a reputation. We are the children or spouses of alcoholics, or are alcoholics or addicts ourselves. But even though we may introduce ourselves at meetings by our reputations, that in no way reflects upon our character—who we are as people.

As people begin to know us, they learn how we think, what we feel, why we do what we do, what we like or dislike. These things make up character. When we refer to someone as "quite a character," we are referring to a unique personality, a person who stands taller than a reputation.

Do we show others our reputation or our character? Sometimes it's easier to hide behind the walls of a reputation by being snobbish, silent, or sarcastic. Yet it's our character that is far more important. Our character allows us to be who we are and lets us show how we feel. Reputation can make someone look at us, but character can make someone look twice and notice us.

How can I show my character instead of my reputation?

The strength you've insisted on assigning to others is actually within yourself.
—*Lisa Alther*

If we think right now about people we admire and respect, we'll usually find that their enviable qualities involve a certain degree of strength. So we admire these people, wishing we, too, could be as strong as they are.

Yet each of us has inner strength. This strength defines us as we are and makes us different. We cannot share the same amount of strength in all areas of our life—mental, physical, and spiritual—because we are all different.

Let us think back over the events of today and find our inner strengths. We may work well with people; we may be a good employee or student. As we look around our homes, we may find further clues—handiwork, a tasty meal, flourishing plants, a set of weights, a shelf full of books, a completed crossword puzzle. If we spend less time envying another's strengths and look instead to ourselves, we will have more time and energy to develop our own inner strengths.

What are my inner strengths? How can I make them even stronger?

The twilight, in fact, had several stages, and several times after it had grown dusky, acquired a new transparency, and the trees on the hillsides were lit up again.
—Henry David Thoreau

There are small candles of light we can bring into our lives to take away some of the darkness. These are the candles of the program—soft, warm lights given to us each time we open our faith and trust to the fellowship.

There is the candle we can take home from a meeting, kindled by the caring and sharing of those around us. There is the candle given to us by our sponsors and friends, which burns brighter each time we ask for help. And there is the candle given to us by our Higher Power—an eternal light reflecting strength, hope, and salvation.

It's true that it's darkest before the dawn, but we have countless candles to brighten our night.

How can these candles help me through the night?

*Prayer is neither black magic nor is it a form of
demand note. Prayer is a relationship.*
—*John Heuss*

A conversation requires two parts: talking and listening. When only we are talking, that is a monologue. When someone lectures, we listen. Prayer can be a form of conversation, yet if we examine the way we pray we may find it's a monologue.

We pray to ask for answers or guidance, to express our gratitude, and to bless those we care for. It's wonderful to open up a channel to our Higher Power by beginning the conversation, but unless we allow time to listen we will never really develop a dialogue.

We can begin to change our way of praying. We can limit our requests so we are not listing a series of wishes or demands. We can ask for patience to listen and then allow a few moments to listen. The answers will come to us and our guidance will be given when we are truly ready to receive them. An equal balance of talking and listening will help strengthen our relationship with our Higher Power.

---

*I will pray and then listen, to allow my Higher Power some
time to communicate with me.*

More important than learning how to recall things is finding ways to forget things that are cluttering the mind. Before going to sleep at night, empty your consciousness of unwanted things, even as you empty your pockets.
—Eric Butterworth

Many of us may make lists of things we need to do. We may refer to a calendar for our scribbled notations of places to go and people to see. We may look over our course syllabus for chapters to read or papers to write. Or we may keep it all in our heads, mentally checking off each item as it's done.

But tonight we can put away the lists, close the calendar book, put away the course syllabus, and empty our minds of obligations, tasks, and duties. Unless we want to keep our heads spinning during a sleepless night, we must learn to turn off the achieving and doing sides of our minds and give room to the relaxing and spiritual sides. We can take away the items cluttering our minds, one at a time. Tomorrow will arrive in its own time; tonight is the time for us to relax.

Tonight I can close my eyes and visualize putting aside each item. I will achieve total relaxation and peace.

*Be patient with the faults of others; they have to
be patient with yours.*

—Our Daily Bread

How do we feel when someone we know makes a mistake? What happens when the boss makes an error and we have to work overtime to straighten it out? How do we feel when a cashier overcharges us, the post office loses our package, or the mechanic doesn't fix a problem?

Most of us become angry. Since we have been brought up from childhood to believe we are victims, it seems only natural in adult life to feel the same way. We imagine all those people had it in for us; they were all in league somehow to make us suffer.

But everybody makes mistakes. Who among us is perfect? We have made many mistakes in our lives that have probably brought inconveniences to others. If we can learn to treat the faults of others with patience and understanding instead of anger and resentment, we may find others treating us accordingly.

I can overlook the mistakes of others as I would want them to overlook mine.

Love doesn't just sit there, like a stone; it has to be made, like bread, remade all the time, made new.

—Ursula K. Leguin

In the first phases of a relationship, everything is new and exciting. It seems as though nothing could ever go wrong.

Yet as we move out of this "honeymoon" phase of the relationship, problems begin. Suddenly we notice things about the other person that bother us. We seem to have more disagreements and more difficulties that take longer to solve. We may even silently choose corners, put up walls, and back away from each other.

It's easy at this stage to want to end the relationship. But now is when the outcome of the relationship is most critical. If we run away from renewing our love and rebuilding the foundations of trust and faith in each other, we will deprive our love of its nourishment for growth. Love takes constant work and needs plenty of patience. Each day can reveal a new layer of love; each stage in a relationship moves us to a new plateau. But only if we are willing.

I can look at my relationships and see the potential for growth. Help me renew my feelings of love through faith.

People often say that this or that person has not yet found himself or herself. But the self is not something that one finds. It is something one creates.

—Thomas Szasz

In the late sixties, people used drugs and politics to find themselves. The flower children advocated love, not war; they listened to hard rock and political ballads; they looked inward to find out who they were. Yet instead of finding themselves, many seemed to escape from themselves and life.

Many of us today look frantically for ways to discover who we are. We may dress differently or wear makeup. We may consult horoscopes or psychics to gain insight into our being. We may trace our family origins or isolate ourselves in cabin retreats to discover our roots and meaning.

Yet we are not the result of dress or psychic insight or family patterns. We are blank pages upon which we draw who we want to be. Just as an architect draws blueprints for a building, so must we draw blueprints for who we want to be. We are the creators, not the created. We are the artists. Now grab the pencils and let the sketching begin!

I have all the tools I need to create the very best me possible.

We fear to trust our wings. We plume and feather them, but dare not throw our weight upon them. We cling too often to the perch.
—*Charles B. Newcomb*

Even before it has learned to fly, a baby bird is pushed from its nest. It will totter upon the ground, stubby wings outstretched from its body, following the guiding cries of its parents to flap its wings and take flight.

When we were young, our wings hadn't even developed before we began tottering through life. We may have received little direction about how to fly. As we grew, we may have built a nest and retreated within it, still not knowing how to fly.

Although our wings have not been used, we can still learn to fly. There are those who can teach us at meetings. They, too, have had to learn to fly after years of nest-sitting. It isn't easy at first. In fact, it may be quite painful and tiring. But by trying out our wings every day, they will grow stronger and more familiar to us. Our nest will always be there, but we won't have to visit it as often. We'll be too busy flying and testing our wings.

Tonight I can begin to learn the freedom of flight and trust my wings.

When one knows Thee, then alien there is none,
then no door is shut. Oh, grant me my prayer
that I may never lose the touch of the one in the
play of many.

—*Rabindranath Tagore*

When we make a person-to-person telephone call, we want to be connected with one particular person. If that person is not in, we make no connection.

Are we taking time to make person-to-person connections? Or are we seeking situations with groups of people so we don't have to be open and honest with just one person? We all need at least one person with whom to share confidences, laughter, tears, hugs, plans, and dreams. If we don't have this special person, we are like one bird in a nest: safe and warm, but isolated and alone.

We can attend a meeting every night and still be isolated and alone. Being around people doesn't necessarily mean we're making connections with them. To truly share ourselves, we need to open the doors to our lives and let at least one person in. Just one person can make the difference between isolation and connection.

I need to connect with a special friend. How can I open the door to this one person?

The preservation of health is duty. Few seem conscious that there is such a thing as physical morality.

—*Herbert Spencer*

How often do we allow ourselves to become hungry, angry, lonely, and tired? When we are feeling those feelings, we are not taking good care of ourselves. And when we're not in good physical health, our emotional health also suffers.

Our past may have been filled with fast food and empty calories or sleepless, caffeine-filled nights. Just as we need to take steps today for our emotional well-being, so must we take steps for our physical being. The first step is good nutrition. We can become conscious of the foods we eat and the vitamins we need. The second step is to exercise our bodies. The third step is to break lonely isolation by making wise choices: attend meetings or spend time with friends. The fourth step is unloading our feelings of anger, frustration, or sadness. The fifth step is to get plenty of sleep.

We can change hungry, angry, lonely, and tired—HALT—with these five steps. We can be renewed!

Tonight I will sleep soundly, for with a healthy mind and body, I can make healthy choices tomorrow.

There are no rules of architecture for a castle in the clouds.

—*Gilbert Keith Chesterton*

When we were children and were asked, "What do you want to be when you grow up?" our answers were usually delivered quickly. There was no reason for us to believe our dreams couldn't come true, for we hadn't yet learned fear, doubt, and insecurity.

As we grew older, we began to lose our dreams. We either became overly practical or highly irresponsible. Our fantasies were unable to fly because they were weighted down by doubts. We became negative and cynical. How could we possibly dream of castles in the clouds? Our highly practical side said clouds couldn't hold castles; our irresponsible nature said someone else would have to build them.

We are learning many things are possible now, if we will only believe. We are learning to live without constant fear, insecurity, or hopelessness. We are slowly building health and happiness. Right now, we are also building the foundations to our castles in the clouds. Through time and belief in ourselves, we will be able to build anything we want.

I can be whoever I want to be; dream whatever I want to dream.

For the whole law is fulfilled in one word, "You shall love your neighbor as yourself."
—*Galations 5:14*

Happy and harmonious relationships are essential. If we treat people with uncaring concern and indifference, they will think there are no paths to our hearts. If we meet people with the expectation that they will do more for us than we will do for them, they will turn away from us.

How did we treat people today? Were we short with co-workers or customers; impatient with students, patients, or children; unloving toward friends or relatives? Were we so wrapped up in ourselves that we weren't aware when people around us needed a bit of attention?

We can repair the roads to our hearts so the paths are straight and true. We can rebuild relationships with those around us. If we can help others feel safe, comfortable, and at ease in our presence, we will encourage positive feelings. Then people will feel safe and will turn to us in friendliness and in safety.

What are the messages on the road to my heart? Help me firm the road's foundation with love, peace, and safety.

Here is a mental treatment guaranteed to cure every ill that flesh is heir to: sit for half an hour every night and mentally forgive everyone against whom you have any ill will or antipathy.
—*Charles Fillmore*

What is forgiveness? In a way, it's the ability to let go of negative feelings toward ourselves or others and replace them with good, positive feelings. Are we forgiving to others?

In retrospect, we may discover ill will toward people with whom we had contact today. Perhaps some driver cut us off in traffic and we shouted in anger. Or maybe we snapped at friends, co-workers, or family members. Maybe we nagged at someone whose behavior bothered us. Maybe we carried some resentful feelings toward someone in our past.

Tomorrow, and maybe for several days, we can take time to forgive people for their negative behaviors. After we've done that, we can forgive ourselves for our reactions towards others. Letting go and forgiving is the best way to cleanse ourselves, leaving more room for positive feelings.

Who do I need to forgive? Right now, I can let go of my negative feelings and replace them with good feelings.

*Walk with the wise and be wise; mix with the
stupid and be misled.*

—*Proverbs*

We may not believe we are wise. We may ask, "How
could I be wise if I got myself into so much trouble
and pain? How can I be wise if I now need the help of
others to stay out of trouble and feel less pain?"

But what is wisdom? Very simply, it is good sense. It
is the ability to make a choice that will be good for us.
No one is born with wisdom. It is learned through
trial and error. Just a glance into our past will assure
us we have certainly had our share of trials and errors.

We have made a wise decision by joining the program. Because of this decision, our lives have become
more manageable and less insane. We have learned of
an all-wise Power greater than ourselves. We have become willing to turn our lives and our wills over to
this Power.

We have become wise, for those who walk with this
Power are wise.

*Have I made wise decisions today? How can I use the
program to gain greater wisdom?*

Remember that you may have and not have. You may receive a property and not enjoy it. You may inherit wealth and not use it. To grasp the great promises of what God can do for you . . . is the way to possess the possessions and realize the wealth.

—H.C.G. Moule

There is so much we have that we take for granted. We seem to focus more upon material things than the wonders of what we already possess. Today we may have wished for more clothes or more money or a bigger house. We may believe more material things will make us better, more powerful, or happier.

Yet we own a wealth of things we never had to buy. We can survive with these things and become a better person. We can take more control of our life and add to our happiness. We were given these things without working overtime or taking out a second mortgage. The wealth we have within us is a gold mine of health, intelligence, and faith. Without these God-given gifts, we are poor in mind, spirit, and body. With these gifts, we truly do have more than money can buy.

Do I realize the value of my mind, health, and faith? I can give thanks for these gifts and learn to appreciate them more.

*It used to be that, if I had a good working day, I
thought I was a wonderful person, but otherwise
I thought I was a terrible person.*
—*Byron Janis*

How often are we buoyed up by successes and
achievements, only to be let down on an unsuccessful
day? If we do well or have a good day, then we may
feel we're good people. But if our day has gone badly
or we've made a mistake, then our self-image becomes
negative and critical.

No matter what happens, no matter what our
achievements, we're still good people inside. No one
can be wonderful all the time. A good day on the job
doesn't mean we're good, and a bad day doesn't mean
we're bad.

We can look at our self-image and see how we really
feel. Then we can remember we are good, no matter
what we feel. We may not be who we want to be; we
may not act the way we want to act; we may not live
the way we want to live. But we have the power to
change all those things as long as we look inside and
see the way we are. We are good inside.

*How do I see myself? Tonight, I can look within and ask for
the courage to see good.*

That's the risk you take if you change: that the people you've been involved with won't like the new you. But other people who do will come along.

—Lisa Alther

When we made the decision to enter the program, it was only a short time before we started making changes. As a result, many of our friends may have become only passing acquaintances; committed relationships may have changed or ended; family members may have become difficult to deal with or may have abandoned us.

Mostly, we have sensed that we "outgrew" those we knew in the past. And we may have been told, "You've changed! I don't like the new you." The excitement and hopefulness we gained with our new way of life were not shared by those who were once close to us. We soon felt alone and rejected instead of supported and accepted by the ones we cared about.

Making changes is risky. But as we become more honest with ourselves and with others, we will soon discover that new people will come into our lives and give us the support we need.

I can become willing to let new people into my life.

Nothing in life is to be feared. It is only to be understood.

—Marie Curie

Most of us have heard older relatives tell of the fears we had in childhood. Many were natural childhood fears; the first day of school, big dogs, even the dark. As we grew older, we understood the fears and grew out of them. Now when we hear reminiscences of those fears, we can laugh.

But what happens when we confront today's fears: meeting new people, attending a social event, giving up an obsession, spending time with our parents? Instead of understanding the cause of our fear, we may let the fear overrun us.

We can put things in perspective by questioning, "What's the worst thing that can happen?" Maybe what we fear isn't always negative. Maybe we fear we'll get that promotion or we won't have an argument with our parents. Whatever our fears may be, we need to see them as lessons to study. Once we understand each new lesson, we'll become masters of our lives. We will run our actions instead of our fears.

I can study at least one of my fears to understand it better.

If one only wished to be happy, this could be easily accomplished; but we wish to be happier than other people, and this is always difficult, for we believe others to be happier than they are.
—*Charles de Secondat Montesquieu*

How many times have we gone out to dinner with friends and ordered what they ordered? Or bought a pair of shoes or some clothing because we liked the item on someone else? Imitation can be the sincerest form of flattery, but it can also be a way of trying to capture the same things we admire in another person.

How often do we compare our emotions? "If only I were as happy as she is," we might say. It may be easier to look at how others feel instead of looking at ourselves. We may not even know how we feel unless we look at someone else for comparison.

Yet appearances are not always the true story. Someone can seem like the happiest person, yet be miserable inside. Happiness has to come from within us. It's okay if our expressions of happiness don't reflect the expressions of others. The only reflections we need to see are our own.

I can look in the mirror and see happiness the way it really is. If I want to be happier, that's up to me.

Little do [we] perceive what solitude is, and how far it extendeth, for a crowd is not company, and faces are but a gallery of pictures, and talk but a tinkling cymbal where there is no love.
—Sir John Lubbock

Today we may be learning what friendship means to us. We may have found that time and the changes we've made have changed the cast of characters in our lives. Friends from the past may no longer be friends; people we never thought we would be close to may now be meaningful to us. Yet we may find it difficult to open up to these people and may hesitate to form friendships beyond a meeting hall or cup of coffee.

Friendship is based totally on trust of another person. Today we are working on trust issues. We are learning we need to take risks to feel comfortable with ourselves and others. Extending the hand of friendship to another or touching the hand extended toward us is the first step in getting to know others and letting them know us.

I can be a friend to another. I can take a risk to share myself and also let someone share with me.

For it is not physical solitude that actually separates one from other men, not physical isolation, but spiritual isolation.
—Anne Morrow Lindbergh

We've discovered that our growth today depends on our mental, physical, and spiritual health. If we picture these as the three legs of a stool, we can see that shortchanging the importance of one or taking one of them away will upset the balance.

We can be at a meeting, for example, yet be unwilling to listen and learn. Or we can bow our heads in prayer at the end of the meeting, yet be unwilling to feel the spiritual strength flowing through the circle of joined hands. By blocking the flow of any aspect of our growth, we are isolating ourselves without even being physically alone.

The remedy to physical isolation is being with others. The remedy to spiritual isolation is opening ourselves to the spirit of life and love that exists everywhere. We can be open to that spirit whether we are alone or with others.

How can I end my spiritual isolation tonight?

Most of us spend 59 minutes in an hour living in the past with regret for lost joys, or shame for things badly done ... or in a future which we either long for or dread.

—Storm Jameson

Do we often travel through life accompanied by the ghosts of our past, present, and future? Instead of focusing on the events in our present journey, we may find ourselves diverted by thoughts of what once was, what we haven't done, and what we may never do.

As long as we travel this way, we will miss a good part of each minute. We will not learn to use our present time to its utmost: to experience, listen, feel, learn, plan, and grow.

The ghosts of the past, present, and future are crutches we lean on when we're too weak to use our own resources. We can be strong if we learn to rely on ourselves, our Higher Power, and our companions in life.

How can I live in each minute without thoughts of the past or future?

The secret to not being hurt like this again, I decided, was never depending on anyone, never needing, never loving. It is the last dream of children, to be forever untouched.
—Audre Lorde

How wonderful it would be if we could never be hurt for the rest of our lives! Imagine never again having to experience the physical and emotional pain of death or loss or change. We might think that all would be well for us, once the potential for any hurt is removed.

Yet hurt is part of the cycle of growth and learning. We had to skin our knees in order to finally ride a bicycle. We had to miss a longed-for event in order to learn how much it meant to us. We had to grieve over the loss of someone dear to us in order to learn how much love we felt.

There are no assurances that we'll never be hurt again. We all feel physical and emotional pain at one time or another. What is assured is that we can ease our pain through the faith and trust we have in ourselves and in our Higher Power.

Have I been living in a never-never land today, shutting myself off from people for fear I'll be hurt?

In returning and rest you shall be saved; in quietness and in trust shall be your strength.
—Isaiah 30:15

By lifting and stretching we stimulate our cardiovascular system, firm up muscles, and add to our strength. But how do we build our spiritual power, increase our strength of belief, build firm foundations of faith, and shape our ability to hope?

Increasing physical power takes time, dedication, and work. So does increasing spiritual power. We need to spend more time in prayer and meditation with our Higher Power, building a strong relationship. We need to work hard at relying upon our spiritual guide to help us in times of need.

We need to awaken and exercise our spiritual muscles by taking Step Eleven every day and night. Prayer once a day does little to improve spiritual power, as sure as one deep knee bend each morning does little to improve leg strength. Just as we would set up an exercise program, we need to schedule our spiritual program. At first it will be hard, but through patience and practice, we will become spiritually stronger every day.

Higher Power, I want to lift the weight in my heart. Help me find ways to develop and exercise my spiritual strength.

Joy enters the room. It settles tentatively on the windowsill, waiting to see whether it will be welcome here.

—*Kim Chernin*

Is joy a welcome feeling for us, or do we find it hard to express positive feelings? If we grew up in an alcoholic home, we learned early not to trust positive feelings because they usually wouldn't last long. We may have lived with or were familiar with people who had emotional mood swings, and we learned positive feelings didn't have a beginning or end.

Is joy welcome in our lives or do we still fear it? Even if we're still living in an uncomfortable situation, we now have tools to detach ourselves from the behaviors of others. We now have a concept of a greater Power. If we trust the tools and the Power, we can relax and let positive feelings into our lives.

There can be laughter now, perhaps even from us. There are smiles we can respond to and we can initiate some. There are peaceful, loving moments we can experience with others. There can be much joy in our lives, if we can only begin to let it in.

There is joy to feel, if I let myself. What can I feel joyful about in my life tonight?

Few begin with anything like a clear view of what they want to do, and the fortune they seek may come in a very different form from that which they have kept in view.
—The Independent, *August 1898*

Take a look at the most focused and purposeful people we know, and we'll find one common trait. Although most worked toward some goal, they all simply *began* without knowing what would happen. Christopher Columbus set out to prove the world wasn't flat, not to discover the New World. Alexander Graham Bell was fascinated with recording and projecting human voices, not creating a worldwide communications network.

What those people share is the fact that they started. They didn't just sit back and dream. They chose an objective and had faith to begin and follow through, despite repeated failures and years of work. We can dream and fantasize to our heart's content. But we will never realize our aspirations until we take that first step.

What would I like to achieve? Higher Power, I ask for faith to take the first step toward this achievement.

The great rhythms of nature, today so dully disregarded, wounded even, have here their spacious and primeval liberty. . . . Journeying birds alight here and fly away again all unseen, schools of fish move beneath the waves, the surf flings its spray against the sun.

—Henry Beston

We think about the many things that are happening around the world. Tonight it is tomorrow somewhere. A new day is dawning, birds are awakening. A rhythm is starting unlike our rhythm now.

Somewhere on the ocean, a supertanker is delivering products to a new location. Beneath it are miles of depth teeming with many varieties of fish. A rhythm is happening that is unobserved.

Birds are flying somewhere in the world right now. There is a nest of eggs with a parent patiently maintaining their warmth. Somewhere there are farmers plowing, children playing, musicians creating, teachers teaching. We are a part of it all. We belong to every creature and every place. We are here—and we are everywhere.

Tonight I can close my eyes and imagine all the life around me and know I am part of it all.

I cannot give you the formula for success, but I can give you the formula for failure—try to please everybody.
—Herbert Bayard Swope

Principles are rules or codes of conduct we set for ourselves; like being honest, striving to be on time, and taking responsibility for bills and expenses. It is up to us to abide by these principles.

When we compromise a principle for someone else's benefit, we jeopardize the strength of that principle and its importance to us. If we want to be honest, then lying to cover up another's actions compromises that principle. If we want to be on time and someone makes demands that cause us to arrive late, we have compromised ourselves and let someone else's desire dominate.

We need to set certain standards for ourselves and abide by them, even if another person will not be pleased. To let principles triumph over the demands and desires of another is a victory for our inner peace. If we are true to ourselves, we will learn we can count on ourselves no matter what.

Is anyone making demands upon my principles? Help me be true to myself and not make compromises I will regret.

Like the body that is made up of different limbs and organs, all mortal creatures exist depending upon one another.

—Hindu proverb

We may have believed only we could solve our problems and satisfy our needs. Or we may have been super-responsible about caring for others, yet negligent in caring for ourselves. "I'll take care of it," may have been our most-used phrase.

There are some things only we can do for our emotional, physical, and spiritual health: eat right, exercise, get plenty of rest, pray and meditate on a daily basis. Yet there are needs we cannot take care of alone: solving all our problems, comforting ourselves, developing intimacy with others, feeling loved and cared for. Those things need to come from others.

Imagine how dependent we would be on others if we lost our eyesight or hearing or mobility. We don't need a physical handicap to ask for help. We have invisible handicaps that are linked to our emotional and spiritual needs. To mend them, we must ask others for help and guidance. We cannot do it alone.

Tonight instead of saying, "I'll take care of it," I can ask, "Will you help me?"

*You telling me God love you, and you ain't never
done nothing for Him? I mean, not go to church,
sing in a choir, feed the preacher and all that?
. . . if God love me, I don't have to do all that.
There's lots of other things I can do that I speck
God likes. . . . I can lay back and just admire
stuff. Be happy.*

—Alice Walker
The Color Purple

When we were younger, we learned bad people go
to hell when they die. So we may have helped old ladies across the street, or didn't kick our brother, or
didn't talk back, or went to church so we could get
"good marks" from the great Power in the heavens.

Today we might still believe our Higher Power
needs material evidence of our faith. We might still go
to church because we think that's what we should do.
We may get down on our knees twice a day because
we feel we should.

All the program asks of us is that we come to believe in a Power greater than ourselves. It doesn't tell
us how to pray or when to pray or the things we need
to do to win our Higher Power's approval. All we need
to do is make our Higher Power a part of our world.

*I can remember that everything is a result of a Power
greater than myself. Can I include this Power in my life?*

Do not lose your inward peace for anything whatsoever, even if your whole world seems upset.

—*Saint Francis de Sales*

Today may have been filled with tense people, hectic schedules, or confusion and anger from those around us. We live and interact with a variety of situations that can range from slightly stressful to very stressful. How we handle ourselves in those situations can determine our inner peace. We can be like an amoeba and suck up the surrounding mood and conform to it, or we can remain detached from the situation and be in touch with ourselves.

Just because the environment around us is like a battlefield or is so uncomfortable we want to squirm, that doesn't mean we have to prepare for battle or move about restlessly. Whatever is happening outside of us is somebody else's issue. Our most important issue is us and our own inner peace. The only way our inner peace can change is if we allow it. We are in control of our inner selves—not the world around us.

I can remain calm and serene in the face of any crises because of my strong faith. I believe all is well with me.

Success is to be measured not so much by the position that one has reached in life as by the obstacles which [were] overcome while trying to succeed.

—Booker T. Washington

When hurdlers race, they look ahead to see each hurdle that must be leaped. High-jumpers see the height of the bar they have to clear. Businesspeople look at charts to see their positions and the number of positions they must pass in order to reach their goals. Students are well aware of the number of credits and course requirements needed for a degree.

Not all of the obstacles in life are as easy to see. Those of us who grew up in alcoholic homes had to overcome tremendous obstacles just to survive. Some of us may have such a low self-image that by just feeling satisfied with an accomplishment, we have overcome tremendous blocks to our growth.

As we measure each day's successes, we need to keep in mind the obstacles we have to face. When we have leaped over a hurdle in life, we have earned a great success. Overcoming one obstacle means there is one less hurdle to stand in our way.

Tonight I can review my day and look for my small successes. I know I have overcome some obstacles today and have done well.

There are parts of a ship which, taken by themselves, would sink. . . . But when the parts of a ship are built together, they float. So with the events in my life. Some have been tragic. Some have been happy. But when they are built together, they form a craft that floats and is going someplace. And I am comforted.
—*Ralph W. Sockman*

If we only remembered the unhappy times we've had, we'd sink into depression. Likewise, if we saw only happiness, we'd have a limited vision of our lives. When we take the good along with the bad, we see reality. When we strive for a balance of opposites, we move closer to maturity. When we accept that for every bad day there will be a good one, we accept life as it is.

There is a saying, *a ship in harbor is safe,* but ships weren't built to stay in harbors. We captain our own ships. When we sail, we are taking risks. There will be calm sailing, but there will also be ferocious storms. We can weather anything with a supportive crew and a determined belief to guide us.

I am not afraid to be captain of my ship. Tonight I can bless all the things in my life that help keep me afloat.

We cannot swing up a rope that is attached only to our own belt.

—William Ernest Hocking

Imagine a drowning person waving for help. A passerby picks up a bundle of rope, tosses it all to the victim, then walks away. That drowning person has no way of reaching safety without another's help. To many of us, that may be a scene from our childhood, where we reached out and asked for help many times, to no avail. Who do we depend on today?

We may not want to place any dependency on anyone but ourselves. But do we truly believe we can provide all the guidance, strength, and hope we need? Even if it is difficult to trust others, we can trust in a Higher Power. That Higher Power doesn't have to be a god; it can be a belief that all is well, that we are doing just what we need to, that we are safe.

By making a connection with someone or something, we can learn to depend on something other than ourselves. When we call for help, we can be rescued only if we believe we can trust another to answer our call.

I can believe I cannot save myself without help. I need to depend upon something or somebody else.

Do not look to small advantages. Desire to have things done quickly prevents their being done thoroughly. Looking at small advantages prevents great things being accomplished.
—*Confucius*

The best work we can do is that which takes time. The ceiling of the Sistine Chapel is the result of years of work. Barns built centuries ago still stand firm. The finest and most brilliant gems are the results of hours of study, cutting, and polishing.

Doing anything well means not merely getting the job done. We are probably very capable of quantity work when we want to be. But it's the quality work—the kind we can step back from and admire today and for years to come—that really counts.

Whether we are working on ourselves, improving our relations with others, or restoring a fine piece of furniture, our best effort is the one that takes time and lasts.

I can work on one thing patiently and thoroughly, knowing the results will be better with time.

One of the most tragic things I know about human nature is that all of us tend to put off living. We are all dreaming of some magical rose garden over the horizon—instead of enjoying the roses that are blooming outside our windows today.

—Dale Carnegie

How we love to think about all the things we want to do! Our lists are probably quite long to include all the things we want, when we have the time or the money.

What are we waiting for? What are our excuses? Many times we make excuses to avoid planning, saving money, or changing schedules. Many times we use our excuses like bricks, building a higher and higher wall until it's impossible to scale. To live is to experience new, exciting, interesting, and diverse things.

To live is to break schedules and change patterns and do things out of the ordinary. To live is to participate in all the fun, all the travel, all the people, all the activities. Are we going to live—starting tomorrow?

I will think about one thing I really want to do and write down what I need to do to accomplish it. To help achieve it, I'll then share this plan with another.

When, against one's will, one is high-pressured into making a hurried decision the best answer is always no because no is more easily changed to yes than yes is changed to no.
                                        —*Charles E. Nielson*

There are many people we have never refused a favor or help. We may have even sacrificed our time, our schedules, or a friendship to accommodate as many people as possible. Then we entered the program and learned we didn't have to do what everyone wanted. We could say no and that would be okay.

But there may be one or two people we find hard to refuse: a parent or a spouse or an ex-lover or someone we feel we owe. No matter what they ask us, no matter what our schedules, needs, or prior commitments, we may find it almost impossible to say no.

What are we afraid of if we say no? Do we think we'll lose their love or approval, or they'll say bad things about us? We aren't working the program if we can say no to some people and not to others. To be our own persons, we need courage to refuse when we feel it is in our best interest.

I can practice saying no to someone who is difficult for me to refuse.

My world is composed of takers and givers. The takers may eat better but the givers sleep better.
—Byron Frederick

At the end of every Perry Mason show the murderers were caught. Whether their motives were greed, revenge, or justice, their guilt would surface and right would prevail.

Before the program, we may have refused to see our guilt. We may have taken from others because we believed they owed us. But after we entered the program we learned nobody owes us anything. We now tell the store clerks when we're undercharged for a purchase. Our guilt over the dishonesty of taking what wasn't ours would be too much for us.

The giver inside us isn't bothered by guilt and shame. Because we aren't taking from others today, we're only receiving what we deserve. Today, we haven't stolen, lied, or cheated. Tonight we can sleep better because we're givers instead of takers.

How did I give to others or myself today? Tonight I can have a clear conscience knowing I was a giver and not a taker.

I must slowly learn to lose control, to let go the petals when it is time ... learn step by softly-treading step, that what I am, what we are, is this Power to move and be moved, to change and be changed.

—Linda Roach

Letting go doesn't mean releasing our grip on life and falling into the abyss below. Letting go is a gentle process of easing the grip on some facet of our lives: an obsession, a character defect, or negative feelings toward someone.

We can think of ourselves as pilots flying a plane full of passengers. As we take off and begin our flying pattern, we need to gradually ease the plane into the right coordinates. We can't make a sudden turn, or our passengers will be tossed about. Instead, we need to gently shift directions, bearing in mind the wind as we work our way into the correct path.

We must guide ourselves gradually. We cannot resolve that tomorrow morning we're going to totally eliminate a character defect. But what we can do is become willing to let go. We need to prepare ourselves to change gently, step by step.

I need to remember letting go is a gradual process. With the help of my Higher Power, I can begin to let go.

Here the people seem to possess the secret of tranquility. . . . Perhaps it is only by going up the old back roads leading to the lost little hamlets of the mountains or the seagirt islands and peninsulas of the world that you can still find it. Perhaps even in such places it has not long to last.

—*Louise Dickinson Rich*

As a child we may have had a secret place we went to be alone or when we were hurt or confused. Wherever it was, we knew we could be safe there.

As an adult we may have lost our secret places. Instead of hiding maybe we learned to run or build up defenses. We learned to cope without secret spaces, but look how we suffered for it! Now we yearn for serenity as we stop running or defending.

We can make a secret space again. Our secret space can be in a favorite chair or even in our minds when we listen to a favorite song. Wherever or whatever we use for times of need, our secret spaces should provide safety and security. It's okay to let the child in us run to secret spaces in times of need. In doing so, we're taking care of ourselves.

Do I have a secret space where I am safe and secure?

Why hoard your troubles? They have no market value, so just throw them away.
—Ann Schade

Some people can't stop talking about their troubles. We innocently ask them how they are, then have to listen to a monologue about this problem and that problem. After a time, we learn to ignore these people and don't dare ask them how they are. We know exactly how they are because they've told us so many times.

We may wonder what those people would say if all their troubles disappeared. They might be speechless, not knowing what to say. Are we, too, afraid to say we're fine? Do we feel uncomfortable not having something to gripe about or focus our energy on?

Troubles are like strings of bangles and beads. They're worthless, don't add much to our appearance, and make a lot of noise. We aren't losing anything by taking off the bangles and beads. In fact, we'll probably look and feel better. We can get rid of the troubles we carry with us as if they were so many bangles and beads. We won't lose a thing by losing them.

I can look at all the troubles I drag around with me and get rid of at least one of them. I'll feel much better without it.

*There's sometimes a good hearty tree growin'
right out of the bare rock, out o' some crack that
just holds the roots; right on the pitch o' them
bare stony hills where you can't seem to see a
wheel-barrowful o' good earth in a place, but
that tree'll keep a green top in the driest summer.*
—Sarah Orne Jewett

When our meetings end, we join hands or place our arms around each other in a circle of prayer. This circle gives us nourishment for our growth, even in adverse conditions.

Without this circle of strength and nourishment, we would be like we were before the program: a tree growing shallow roots, searching far for nourishment. The program grounds us and helps us grow deep and secure roots.

Whether we choose to grow in a forest or out on our own, we're never alone. We can survive because of the spirit that flows through the hearts of program members into our hearts. Within the protection of the circle and outside, our needs for growth are answered and provided for by the program.

Tonight I can push my roots down deeply and hold securely onto my space. I've found the place that provides for my needs.

A well-timed silence is more eloquent than words.

—Our Daily Bread

How do we handle ourselves when someone is yelling at us for things we consider inconsequential? Do we turn away from words delivered in anger or sarcasm? Do we forgive for hurtful statements? Do we go to another room or leave the scene?

Many of us find it easy to feed into arguments generated by another. Our buttons can easily be pushed by others, and they know it. They expect us to react, screaming at them in anger or crying or defending ourselves. When we're not in the heat of the situation, it's easy to say we'll make changes. But once the scene has started again, our best-laid plans are forgotten.

We can strengthen this change in behavior by learning the power of silence. Responding to a hurtful comment with silence, turning away from another's ire without a word, or walking quietly away from one who is on a tirade can be quite effective. Instead of adding more fuel to an already raging fire, we can cool ourselves off by walking away from the heat without comment. Silence can truly speak louder than words.

I can practice silence in the face of anger or outrage. I can turn away from an unhealthy situation.

Sometimes we need to look hard at a person and remember that he is doing the best he can. He's just trying to find his way. That's all.
—Ernest Thompson

Sometimes we need to look hard at ourselves at the end of a day and give ourselves credit for doing our best. We need to look at our actions and reactions as objectively as possible. Now is the time to review and focus on the positive outcomes, not the negative.

The mere fact that we got out of bed, got dressed, and faced the day are sometimes acts of courage and strength. We didn't run from the day; we faced it, even with feelings of anxiety or sadness or fear. What matters is this—that we tried to do the best we could.

Let's look back over the events of the day and remember we did the very best we could to find our own way today.

How did I do the best I could today? What good things have I learned about me?

Sometimes the readiness to be sorry can appear in a flash of insight; other times it may cost a sleepless night or a long sulk. Either way, you've got to go through the process.
—*Laurence Shames*

Making amends—admitting a wrong or apologizing to someone—is never easy. If we are not ready, it really doesn't accomplish much. In order for us to become willing to make an amend, we need to do some work.

We need to feel our way through anger, bitterness, or guilt. We need to recognize and try to put aside our ego issues. We need to become ready to shift from a defensive, battle-ready position to one that is open and honest and sincere.

Sometimes a good night's sleep will help us through even the most difficult of amends. The time spent in quiet rest may help energize us and give us courage and strength to effectively communicate our amends without traces of leftover negative feelings.

Tonight I can let rest and quiet contemplation prepare me to make an amend.

For peace of mind, resign as general manager of the universe.

—Larry Eisenberg

How much did we try to control today? Perhaps on our way to work we shouted in frustration at how other people drove. Later we may have attempted to control our boss, co-workers, bank teller, children, or spouse, telling them to do what we wanted. Perhaps now we're ready to collapse in exhaustion from a day of trying to be director of everyone else's play.

Instead of managing everyone else, we should be managing only ourselves. First we have to catch ourselves when we feel the urge to control others. We have to discover what is best for us, instead of someone else, and do it. We have to stop focusing on people's problems, even if they want us to. We have to look in the mirror and see ourselves for who we are.

Tonight we need to realize our director is our Higher Power, who gives us the play we're in and the ability to act. Although many other people may share the stage with us, it's not up to us to direct them. They have their own direction.

I will ask my Higher Power for direction, and I will not control others.

Often the test of courage is not to die but to live.
—*Vittorio Alfieri*

"Against all odds" is an apt phrase for survival despite the worst conditions. For those of us who have lived in an alcoholic home or with abuse or emotional starkness or poverty or handicap, it has been courageous for us to survive despite the difficulties. Yet many times we may feel it would be easier to give up.

But isn't courage survival—despite the odds? When we listen to the stories of our program's members, we need to think of each person as courageous. To live is to grow. To grow well is to strengthen our faith. To have faith is to see beyond ourselves to the completeness of life and our part in it. To be a part of life is to accept what we have and strive to bring what we want into it. To do so is to survive by using the beautiful tools that give us life: hope, faith, and trust.

I am grateful for all I have survived and all I will survive because of my trust and faith in a Higher Power.

I have to laugh at the times I've knocked myself out over a tough spot only to find out afterwards there was an easier way through.
—Robert Franklin Leslie

We receive messages throughout the day that tell us ways of doing things. The door to the store says "pull." The red light tells us not to drive through the intersection. The cereal box says "lift tab and open." Our car gas gauge tells us "empty." With these messages, we are given the guidance on which to base our decisions.

We can choose not to pull the door. Then we'll spend a lot of time and energy pushing until we finally read the sign. All that effort expended, just because we couldn't stop to get some guidance!

The Twelve Steps offer guidance for an easier way through life. We don't have to knock ourselves out over these Steps; all we have to do is follow the direction they give us.

How can I use the Steps to make my life easier?

Each one of us has walked through storm and fled the wolves along the road; but here the hearth is wide and warm, and for this shelter and this light accept, O Lord, our thanks tonight.
—*Sara Teasdale*

We made it through another day! Sometimes we may feel relief at this statement, other times disappointment, still other times peace.

Tonight we can be grateful for this day. This doesn't mean just giving thanks or recognition for getting something we wanted. Being grateful means recognizing all the events and the people who came our way. It means seeing through disappointments or pain in order to gain understanding of its meaning in our lives. It means trusting everything that happened was given by our Higher Power. We can trust there was a reason for it all.

Giving thanks begins now. We can replay today's events like a tape—watching, listening, and feeling. And at the end of the tape, we can thank our Higher Power for our day, for the people in it, and for the knowledge and experience we gained.

Thank you, Higher Power, for this day. I trust everything in my life today was a gift from You.

We struggle after ideas. We read this book and that, and go from place to place ... instead of pausing to make our own the few great but profoundly simple laws and truths of the spirit.
—Dr. Horatio Dresser

Right now, all we have to remember is that the program teaches us many slogans: *Easy Does It, Keep It Simple, Let Go and Let God, Live and Let Live.* These slogans are more than simple statements. They are truths for our spiritual well-being.

Today may have been a day of intense activity. We may have worked at a frantic pace, but felt we accomplished little. We may then have rushed home to eat a quick meal only to rush somewhere else.

Now is the time to slow down, to stop our frantic pace, if only for a few minutes. We can breathe deeply, let go of all the worries and tensions of the day, then think of a slogan. We can picture how simple it is, yet how truthful its meaning. Now is the time to rest and feel some serenity.

What is my favorite slogan? How can this slogan help me relax tonight?

"And this, too, shall pass away." How much it expresses! How chastening in the hour of pride! How consoling in the depths of affliction! "And this, too, shall pass away."

—Abraham Lincoln

Sometimes, when we're in a dark hour, we may believe time has suddenly stopped. Forever after, we shall always have this pain or sadness or despair. From here on, we think, this is how it's going to be—minute after minute of pain.

But we need to remember time passes quickly when we're enjoying ourselves. When we're in the midst of a negative feeling, every hour seems like two. But this present hour will not endure. Nor the next. Sorrows pass, just as happiness does. Pain passes, just as pleasure does. Nothing really stays the same, nothing ever stands still.

All we need to do, right now, is endure this moment. It, too, shall pass. We need to have strength, patience, faith, and a strong belief that this ˌ ˑnt—and the feelings in this moment—wil'   ˑe. Time passes, and so will the pain.

Tonight I may need help rememb
pass. How can I let my High

I can say ,

We need the courage to start and continue what we should do, and courage to stop what we shouldn't do.

—*Richard L. Evans*

What is courage? Many of us think it involves surviving against all odds. Some of us believe courage is personified by an individual like Helen Keller, who coped with many physical defects to vastly change her life and the lives of those around her. Others of us believe courage is personified by people like astronaut John Glenn, who took risks trying something new knowing he could fail.

Are we courageous? Compared to those people we would probably say no. Yet we *are* because we have taken risks to change our lives. Being willing to change is an act of courage. Believing in change and forging ahead on the new, uncharted path is an act of courage.

We are the only ones who can change ourselves. Just as Helen Keller and John Glenn made decisions to alter their lives, so do we make decisions to risk changes. Whether we started on our new way of life years ago, days ago, or even hours ago, we are filled with courage because of the decisions we made.

[t]he Serenity Prayer and remember my courage.

I have wept in the night
For the shortness of sight
That to somebody's need made me blind;
But I have never yet
Felt a tinge of regret
For being a little too kind.

—*Anonymous*

We have only to turn on the evening news to be deluged by all the unkindnesses in the world. Natural disasters destroy and kill. People murder. Governments oppress and torture. People discriminate against others. But if we turn off the evening news and take a look at our own lives—at our relationships—we can see that unkindness is just as prevalent.

Kindness is like a beautiful flowering plant. Pay attention to it, water it, nourish it, tend to its needs, and it will flourish. One flower will open, then another, with a reward of brilliant colors. Show it no kindness, and it will close up its beauty and die.

There are flowers all around me. I need to cultivate my garden with kindness.

Honesty is the first chapter in the book of wisdom.

—*Thomas Jefferson*

We see our true selves when we don't resculpt our bodies, change the style of our hair, or try to imagine someone else instead of us. If we see ourselves as we honestly are, then we will see the imperfections that make us who we are: perhaps too much weight or not enough, a not-so-clear complexion, or being too short or tall. We will never look the way we really want because our desires are usually impossible to attain. We can certainly make some changes, but we need to learn to see an honest picture of ourselves.

The first step to get to know who we are is to know what we look like. We can start by taking off our clothes and standing naked in front of a mirror. That's us, no matter how much we may want to look away or cry or laugh out loud. We may wish that wasn't what we looked like, but that's because we've learned to look at others rather than ourselves. We can take the first step toward wisdom and maturity by seeing our honest reflection, and accepting it.

I will gather up courage to really look at my reflection. I will accept the good as well as the bad.

When they are alone they want to be with others, and when they are with others they want to be alone. After all, human beings are like that.
—Gertrude Stein

We may get discouraged with ourselves because our moods change from one minute to the next. We may make plans for some event we really want to attend, then come right down to the time we're supposed to leave and not want to go. We may feel content with our job one day, then want to quit and go back to school the next. "What's going on?" we ask ourselves in frustration.

Because we're happy and content one minute doesn't mean we're going to feel the same way later. When we're starting on our recovery, our mood swings will be very dramatic. We aren't accustomed to expressing our feelings, so it's only natural that they all want to be heard at once.

It's okay to change our feelings or opinions about something. As time goes on, our mood swings will lessen. But tonight, we need to remember we are growing and experiencing in a way we never have before. Patience with ourselves and our conflicting feelings will help us accept where we are.

I need to remember it's okay for me to feel.

Let us move on, and step out boldly, though it be into the night, and we can scarcely see the way. A Higher Intelligence than the mortal sees the road before us. We do not have to strive for good, but only to go forward and possess it. Good awaits us at every step.

—Charles B. Newcomb

Remember how energized we feel after a good night's sleep, and how a sunny morning helps us forget the bad thoughts of yesterday? We can feel that same energy and sense of hope right now, even though the night is here. The Higher Power we prayed to this morning for strength, hope, and guidance for the day is with us right now, ready to help us relax tonight.

Take a moment to look upon nightfall as a new beginning. Think of new things to do tomorrow. Try a new meeting or volunteer for a group activity. Resolve to start a Fourth Step inventory or ask someone we respect to be our sponsor. New beginnings can happen, if we keep our eyes and ears and hearts open to the messages of our Higher Power.

What good things would I like to have happen to me? How can I use my Higher Power to help me?

*I am more involved in unlearning than learning.
I'm having to unlearn all the garbage that people
have laid on me.*

—Leo Buscaglia

What are some of the messages we got while growing up? That we were awful people, or stupid, or un-
employable, or lazy, or unlikeable? These messages
may have turned into beliefs as we grew older, and
we've carried these horrible, negative burdens into
adulthood.

Today we may have seen ourselves acting like children again. We may have done or said things to get
approval and acceptance. We may have been less than
honest with others so they wouldn't see the real us—
and perhaps not like what they saw.

We can start to change some of the things we've
learned. We don't have to do anything unless it is
what we need to do for our healthy growth. We don't
have to be someone we aren't. We can be totally honest with ourselves and others even at the risk of possible rejection. We can speak our minds and feel our
feelings.

---

*I am in charge of my lesson plan. Who are the ones I
choose to teach me?*

Finish every day and be done with it. You have done what you could. Some blunders and absurdities no doubt crept in; forget them as soon as you can.

—Ralph Waldo Emerson

Are we living in the present, or are we still reliving the past day? If we're still looking backward, there are no surprises, no new wonders. It's like viewing a television rerun—we already know the plot, the characters, and the dialogue.

Today is done. Whatever mistakes, confusions, disappointments, or problems that occurred are also done. Nothing we do right now can alter the happenings of the day. We can best use our time now by paying attention to the present.

Tonight we can look around us at the here and now. We can turn off the reruns in our minds and get set for the new shows to come. We can start fresh and new— right now.

Can I let go of the events of the day?

Worry often gives a small thing a big shadow.
—Swedish proverb

Worry does absolutely nothing for our emotional, physical, or spiritual health. Worry makes us anxiety-ridden people. Suddenly a small situation or a minor disagreement takes on the proportion of a giant, looming high above us and casting a long, dark shadow over our lives.

"How important is it?" is a good question to ask at times when we are worried. The second question to ask is, "What can I do about this worry right now?" If we stay in the present, we'll soon discover that much of our worry involves something in the past or something yet to happen. For as long as we focus on the object of our worry, we are not living in the here and now.

We have the power within us to make our worries gigantic. We also have the power to make our worries manageable. As we look back over today's events, we don't need to waste our present time worrying over things done or things left undone. Nor do we need to worry over things yet to come. We can choose instead to live for right now and leave our worries where they belong.

I will walk with my own shadow and not one cast by worry.

Cast thy bread upon the waters: for thou shalt find it after many days.

—Ecclesiastes 11:1

There are many conveniences in our lives today. Central heating, instamatic cameras, twenty-four-hour bank tellers, microwave ovens, and shop-by-mail catalogs are just a few of the creations that allow us more time to relax or do what we need to do.

But there are inconveniences, too, that require attention at awkward times. Inconveniences like bank machines that don't work, or hair dryers that break, or airline flights that are delayed. Do we also see people as inconveniences? Perhaps our children need us at inopportune moments or family get-togethers fall during stressful times. If we view such times as impositions, then no time will ever be convenient.

Yet the door we slam may well be the door that is slammed in our face when we are in need. Are we so important that we can't devote a few minutes, a couple of hours, or an evening to someone who needs our attention, comfort, guidance, or companionship? The more we give, the more we shall receive.

Have I viewed people in my life as intruders? Can I learn to give a little to others?

*I know that I am here in a world where nothing
is permanent but change. . . . I can change the
form of things and influence a few people and
that I am influenced by these and other people.*
                                        —*Elbert Hubbard*

We are related to every person we see in a day, from
the bus driver to the family member, from the store
clerk to the boss, from strangers on the sidewalk to
our dear friends. We are constantly changing, in constant motion with the people, places, and things
around us. We are connected like links in a chain.
Each link supports and gets support from those
around it.

This connectedness is especially evident at meetings
when we hear others tell our stories or relate to our
feelings. Yet this same connectedness can be felt outside of a meeting with both program and nonprogram
people. If there are addicted people in our lives, we
can feel a connection with them because of their disease. We can understand them better and see ourselves more clearly through their defects. We are part
of a strong chain made even stronger because of our
differences.

*There are those who know how we feel and can relate to
us. I can learn to feel a part of everything.*

Prayer is one of life's most puzzling mysteries. I have sometimes feared it is presumptuous to take up God's time with my problems.
—Celestine Sibley

For too long, we may have believed there was no God. Or we may have believed there was an omniscient being who was highly judgmental, ready to bless us when we did good things but ready to curse us when we made mistakes. Our sense of spirituality may have been buried deep beneath layers of fear or lack of trust.

The program teaches us there is a Higher Power who's there to listen to our prayers and meditations. But how do we learn to pray? What do we ask for? What do we say? Do we get down on our knees, bow our heads, or lift our faces to the heavens?

We need to remember that our Higher Power hears us, no matter how we choose to pray. Whether we spend several minutes talking aloud about our day or a few moments sitting still and clearing our minds of all thoughts, our Higher Power cares for us. What's important is making the effort to pray.

Higher Power, help me remember there is no mystery to prayer.

The ladder of life is full of splinters, but they always prick the hardest when we're sliding down.
—William L. Brownell

Climbing is usually difficult—shimmying up a tree, climbing stairs, moving up the corporate ladder, or moving ahead in school. All these actions involve effort and hard work and sometimes may not seem worth it for all the energy expended.

Yet if we failed a semester, lost a job, or fell down the stairs, we'd soon feel the effort was harder. The only payoffs we'd gain from such backward movement would be pain, loss, and abandonment. To pick ourselves up and start climbing again would require almost double the effort to regain the lost ground.

We need to keep moving upwards, keep reaching for the top. Keep on working toward higher goals, dreams, and ideals. It won't be easy to constantly struggle to reach higher. But as long as we don't look back or fall back, our lives will be filled with rewards. By moving ever upwards, we cannot fail.

There's no going back to the pain and hurt. I need to keep moving up, up, up.

Man is born broken. He lives by mending. The grace of God is glue!

—*Eugene O'Neill*

Has today been a day when we felt like we've fallen apart, faltered in our sense of direction, or lost confidence in ourselves? Tonight we may feel like we just can't get it together—that it would be better for us to curl up in a tight ball and wait for a new day.

But the dawn of tomorrow will not work miracles upon us. It is up to us to get us back on track. When our shirt loses a button, we don't throw away the shirt. We use a needle and thread and a little bit of patience to sew the button back on. The work we put into the shirt doesn't have to be perfect, it just has to make the shirt wearable again.

Tonight we need to take time to mend ourselves. And we have the tools to do this—our Higher Power, literature, and meditation. These are our needle and thread. Through the grace of God, we've been given all that we need to mend ourselves.

How can I use the tools of the program to rebuild myself?

• APRIL 24 •

Being sorry for myself is a luxury I can't afford.
—Stephen King and Peter Straub

We have surrounded ourselves with many luxuries to enhance our lives: microwave ovens, color televisions, clothes, jewelry, and so on. We may have purchased these items even if we couldn't really afford them—just as long as we could have them and use them.

Some of the things that are also important to us are our negative emotions: depression, self-pity, selfishness, ungratefulness, or anger. But what if we had to pay for the luxury of feeling each of these feelings? Would we be able to afford a week of self-pity? An hour of anger? Or several minutes of selfishness?

The value we place upon the material things in our lives can also be placed on the emotions we feel each day and night. Our positive emotions can enrich us, but our negative emotions will leave us in debt.

Am I rich enough to waste time feeling sorry for myself? How can I use my resources wisely?

Ignorance is the night of the mind, but a night without moon or star.

—*Confucius*

Long ago, before the advent of radar systems, navigators and explorers found it impossible to proceed on cloudy nights. Without the moon or stars to guide them, they lost their sense of direction and the light by which to see. They were powerless and had to accept their inability to progress under such conditions.

Tonight may seem like a cloudy night. We may feel lost or directionless, or we may feel as if we've stayed in the same emotional space. We may pray in desperation for movement and change, only to feel as if our prayers go unanswered. Like a car mired in mud, we may be spinning our wheels and going nowhere.

Acceptance, then, is our answer. Just because our prayers haven't brought the results we've wanted doesn't mean no one has listened. Our prayers were heard, and the answer was to stay where we were and wait. Our journey is being prepared for us. Soon the clouds will roll away, the moon and stars will guide us. Our Higher Power's will, not ours, is what we have to accept.

Even though I may feel like I'm going nowhere, tonight I can turn my life and my will over to the care of my Higher Power.

If you have knowledge, let others light their candles at it.

—Margaret Fuller

We are seen as powerful examples every time we speak at a meeting, offer encouragement, and give support to those in need. The knowledge we've gathered from the strength and hope of the program is a gift to share with others.

If we've ever seen a candlelight ceremony, we know how powerful one candle can be. Countless tapers can be lit until a room is brilliant with light. Our knowledge of the program is kept alive by a tiny candle within us. And each time we share our knowledge, we have the ability to light the candles of others.

Sometimes we may feel our faith and hope lessen and our candlelight begins to flicker and dim. Yet we can light our faltering candles again from the knowledge of another. We are all candlelighters to each other. This gift assures that we'll never be in the dark. We'll always have the ability to gather light and to give it.

I will let others light their candles from mine, thereby sharing the light of the hope in the program.

Everyone needs optimism. If you don't get it inside you get it outside.

—Dr. Denis Waitley

What made us feel optimistic in the past? Perhaps our use of drink, drug, food, or relationship helped us feel optimistic. Perhaps another person's behavior made us feel optimistic. But these feelings probably didn't last long because they were based on persons, places, or things outside of us. As soon as those things changed, so did our feelings.

Today we're learning who we are and what it's like to feel. We're learning to appreciate solitude and our own company. We're learning that feelings come from within. But how can we feel optimism from within us? How can we cultivate feelings of hope?

We can look at how different we are than when we first came into the program. We can also gain optimism by looking at the changes in those around us. Observing abstinence, behavioral changes, and fewer mood shifts are sure signs that the program works. Optimism can grow within us by seeing and hearing growth in ourselves and others.

Can I feel optimism about my growth? Can I see positive changes made by others in the program too?

There is something infinitely healing in the repeated refrains of nature—the assurance that dawn comes after night, and spring after the winter.

—Rachel Carson

Sometimes it seems as though time speeds up during fun-filled hours and slows down during times of idleness, misery, or pain. But time proceeds at a steady, unchanging pace. Because of this, we are assured that with every minute there can be new hope. Bad times will end with the great healer—time.

Time brings summer to a close as well as winter to an end. Time ages the brilliant petals of flowers as well as prepares the new buds. Time brings the end to a life as well as the beginning to another. Because of this continuum, we can trust that time will bring the good to us as well as take away the bad.

Today may have been a trying time. But tomorrow will dawn and along with that dawn comes renewed hope. We can trust in the constancy of one thing—time will always move forward, taking us away from the old and gently guiding us to the new.

Time is always on my side, taking me ever closer to new moments that are fresh and untouched. Tomorrow will give me many such moments, of this I can be assured.

As a girl my temper often got out of bounds. But one day when I became angry at a friend over some trivial matter, my mother told me, "Elizabeth, anyone who angers you conquers you."

—*Sister Elizabeth Kenny*

The phrase "seeing red" is appropriate to describe anger. It may be comfortable for us to feel anger, or it can be excruciatingly painful. But unless we know how to get rid of our angry feelings and bring our lives into balance, anger will dominate us and color everything we come into contact with.

How do we stop feeling angry? The program gives us many ways. First, we can accept our powerlessness over the person, place, or thing that caused our anger. Second, we can ask, "How important is the cause of this anger? Will it be significant enough to remember weeks, months, or even years from now?" Third, we can ask our Higher Power to help us let go of the anger. That may not be easy, for we may want to hold on to it almost as much as we'd like to let it go. But with practice, we can learn to conquer our anger instead of having it conquer us.

Am I angry tonight? I can use the Steps to help conquer my angry feelings and to stop seeing red everywhere I look.

*Keep watch over your ability and prudence, do
not let them slip from sight. . . . Then you will go
your way without a care, and your feet will not
stumble. When you sit, you need have no fear;
when you lie down, your sleep will be pleasant.*
—Proverbs

When we lose our confidence, it's easy for us to
doubt if we're good at anything. Today may have been
a day where nothing seemed to go right. It's easy to
blame ourselves for the people, places, and things that
were out of our control.

As we look back over today, we may find we've
blamed ourselves for things absolutely out of our control: another's anger, poor communication, or a general mix-up of everything. But just because things
didn't work out perfectly doesn't mean we've lost our
God-given abilities and talents.

We have capabilities that make us special. Through
the program, we're beginning to see we are good at
many things. It's not fair to want to throw all those
beautiful talents out the window whenever things go
wrong—not fair to *ourselves.*

---

*Tonight I can affirm that I have special talents and
abilities. Can I list at least five of them?*

The first sight of the lighthouse set boldly on its outer rock, the flash of a gull, the waiting procession of seaward-bound firs on an island, made me feel solid and definite again, instead of a poor, incoherent being. . . . It was a return to happiness.

—Sarah Orne Jewett

Many of us have things that calm us, center us, bring us inner peace. For some it is the ocean, with its smells, sounds, rhythm, vastness. For others it is a spectacular sunset, where luminous colors spark each surrounding cloud into an ethereal hue. Still others may have a song that gives peace and comfort.

These are our positive relaxation "fixes." When we have been away from the ocean for a while, we have an urge to go again. Just seeing the ocean is reassuring and soothing, as is the sunset or song we seek for comfort.

Our ability to recall is a wonderful gift. By closing our eyes we can see relaxation, hear it, touch it. We can create it clearly in our minds. A few minutes of such meditation can do hours of good.

What relaxes me and makes me feel good? Tonight I will think about that pleasant thought and feel the peace and contentment it gives me.

Weigh thy words in a balance, and make a door
and bar for thy mouth.
　　　　　　　　　　—Old Testament apocrypha

What we say can hurt or heal. We may look back at times and wish we hadn't said something to someone. Perhaps we can see the hurt we caused by harsh or insulting words. We may be able to recall a snide or impatient comment delivered to an unsuspecting stranger or friend. Words can be powerful weapons.

By the same token, we may be able to recall when someone said, "Thanks. I really liked what you said to me. It helped." We may have made someone laugh or smile despite tears, or we may have been able to point out a different viewpoint to someone blinded by rage or impatience. Words can be powerful healers.

Freedom of speech doesn't mean we can say anything we want whenever we want. Communication is an action that requires responsibility. Abuse of speech can lead to angry confrontations, severed relationships, and isolation. The responsible use of our gift of speech can lead to healthy relationships and positive emotions. We can listen to ourselves and learn whether our voice helps or hurts.

My words can hurt or heal. Which will I choose?

Go ahead with your life, your plans, your preparation, as fully as you can. Don't waste time by stopping before the interruptions have started.

—Richard L. Evans

Inside each of us is a little voice called "Too Cautious." Too Cautious loves to be the initiator of doom, the forerunner of disaster, the messenger of disappointment. When we start to plan our vacations, for example, Too Cautious will tell us we don't have enough money, or we probably won't get a reservation, or we've got too many other things to do. If we think about going back to school, Too Cautious will tell us we won't have enough time or we'll probably flunk. If we want to ask a friend to do something with us, Too Cautious will whisper in our ears that we aren't likable and will probably get refused.

But we don't have to listen to Too Cautious. We can listen instead to our Higher Power. We'll soon hear inspiring words of faith that will help us take more risks, like "Why not?" or "Wouldn't that be nice?" or "What a wonderful idea." We can listen to our Higher Power for strength, hope, and guidance in all our affairs.

What's stopping me from making plans or taking a risk?

My father taught me that a bill is like a crying
baby and must be attended to at once.
—Anne Morrow Lindbergh

In the past, we may have faced our bills with denial or justification that we needed the things we had purchased. We may have abused credit cards so much that we are still paying for items we purchased months or years ago. And we may have problems today with spending more than we earn.

Many times material wants are based on emotional needs we don't know how to satisfy. In the past we may have thought we could ease our pains and troubles by buying new clothes or a bigger stereo. Our emotional needs are still screaming for attention and it may be difficult to stop using material purchases as pacifiers.

Like the recovering alcoholic who avoids a drink, we must disregard temptations of credit cards, extravagant purchases, and borrowing. Material things provide only a temporary reprieve, they will not take away our emotions. Emotions can only be eased by things money can't buy: time, love, faith, and understanding.

I don't need to buy anything to take away my feelings. I can attend to my feelings with the tools of the program.

You would do well to budget your time as follows: one-half in work, taking care of personal belongings, etc.; one-fourth in social pastimes with others, both young and old; and one-fourth as an interested, pleased observer of life.
—William B. Terhune

Every life needs a balance of work, play, and rest. When we're not at work, we need to pursue other interests like hobbies, socializing, going to movies. When we're not at work and not pursuing an interest, we need to rest. Resting doesn't mean just sleeping. Resting is also meditating, listening to relaxing music, or watching the birds at our bird feeders.

Our financial budget tells us where our money is spent. Our time budget can do the same thing. By noticing where we spend most of our time, we can make sure all our time isn't spent doing just work, just play, or just rest.

I can look at my time budget and ask: "Where haven't I spent any time lately?" I need to use my time doing something I haven't done to balance my budget.

It has never been, and never will be, easy work! But the road that is built in hope is more pleasant to the traveler than the road built in despair, even though they both lead to the same destination.

—*Marian Zimmer Bradley*

Think for a moment about a city nearby. Now picture the many roads that lead to that city. One may be a winding road. One may be an expressway. No matter which one is taken, it will still reach the same destination. But what will matter is how pleasant the journey is along the way.

Before we entered the program, we probably traveled on the road marked *despair*. We didn't know there were other roads for our journey. But the program has taught us there are many roads to recovery: *strength, hope, peace, happiness, caring,* and *love.*

As long as we keep recovery as our destination, we may choose to travel any road of the program we like. If we've traveled today on the road called *despair*, we can change our road tonight to one of *hope*. As long as the program is our destination, we need not worry about losing our way.

Which road will I travel tonight? Where will this road lead me?

*Don't waste your time striving for perfection;
instead, strive for excellence—doing your best.*
— *Sir Laurence Olivier*

We've all heard that even the most beautiful rose has its thorns. But as that rose was growing, the gardener didn't waste time trying to snip off the thorns. Instead, by using the right combination of sunshine, water, and nutrients, the gardener knew the rose would grow healthy and strong.

We are both the rose and the gardener. We are beautiful, yet we have our thorns—our defects of character. We may have seen some of those thorns showing today. But as gardeners we have some very special tools for our growth: the program, the Twelve Steps, the slogans, and the fellowship. By using these tools, we are assured of healthy growth.

We will always have our thorns. But we can still be beautiful as long as we tend to ourselves with patience, love, and the proper tools.

Did I try to strive for excellence today? How can I use the program to help my growth?

Reach high, for stars lie hidden in your soul.
Dream deep, for every dream precedes the goal.
—Pamela Vaull Starr

It has been said that if we tell ourselves what we'd like to dream about before we go to sleep, we can teach ourselves to dream our own dreams. Rather than letting our confusing dreams puzzle us or our nightmares frighten us, we can train our minds to think positive thoughts while we're resting. After a night of positive dreaming, we are more likely to wake up refreshed and ready to continue thinking positively.

Tonight we can prepare our dream by visualizing what it will be. We can close our eyes and see ourselves doing whatever we want to do or be whoever we want to be. Immediately after this visualization, with it fresh in our minds, we can then lie down to sleep with the positive thoughts of the dream in our heads. Such positive thinking is one giant step toward an affirmation of ourselves.

What will I dream tonight? I can imagine the most positive thing and let it become a part of my sleeping thoughts.

How many times have we heard, "Why? I've given him the shirt off my back and now look what he has done to me," or "I've given him the best years of my life and look what I get in return." If we bestow a gift or favor and expect a return for it, it is not a gift but a trade.

—Anonymous

It's not easy to give to another with no thought of return. In the past we may have given to takers who drained us of money, food, and time. We may have felt we were supposed to give and give some more.

Then in the program we learned we could receive and didn't have to give all the time. We may have then become overly conscious of giving. We may have been so adamant about not being taken advantage of that we became afraid to give.

Through our growth in the program, we may find it easier to see the difference between a taker and a true friend. In so doing, we'll find we don't need to measure our giving. It will come back to us from those who are truly worth giving to.

I can give to the people I know won't hurt me or take advantage of me. I can trust them.

Ozone and friendship will be our stimulants—
let the drugs, tobacco, and strong drink go
forever. Natural joy brings no headaches or
heartaches.

—Elbert Hubbard

The longer we stay in the program, working on bettering ourselves, the more addictions we'll find we've outgrown. The alcoholic and the drug addict learn life can be grand without chemicals. The overeater acquires an appetite for fresh air and companionship rather than food.

When we learn to see our lives without a primary addiction, we can then rid ourselves of secondary addictions like smoking, obsessive exercising, caffeine, and sweets. We can free ourselves from all addictions and have a more serene outlook on the healing power we have over our lives.

However, we need to remember we can be obsessive about change. We don't have to become a natural-food freak or a lecturer on the evils of white sugar or nicotine. But we do need to look at the hold those addictions have on us. When we're ready to let go of an addiction, we'll let go of it freely.

I can look at the addictions in my life and make some changes. I can begin tonight by working on letting go.

A mother's heart is the child's schoolroom.
—Henry Ward Beecher

We've learned much from our mother. That doesn't mean all our learning has been good or wise, just as it has not been all bad or crazy. Where we are right now in our lives is a result of the things we have learned thus far.

Mothers aren't perfect. Our mother had a mother who taught her. What our mother did was cope as best as she could with what she was taught. We probably received the best she had to offer, even if it may not have been the best in our eyes.

As we look back to our school days, we need to keep in mind that we haven't retained all the information we were taught. We've kept the most interesting and beneficial textbook learning so we could make our way in the world. The learning we received from our mother can be treated in the same manner. Tonight, we can recall what we like and leave the rest. The most beneficial learning she gave us could be as simple as knowing how to tie our shoes or bake bread, or as all-encompassing as our ability to believe in ourselves.

Tonight, I can thank my mother for the good things I learned from her.

Love is a great thing, a good above all others,
which alone maketh every burden light. Love is
watchful, and whilst sleeping still keeps watch;
though fatigued, it is not weary; though pressed,
it is not forced.

—*Thomas à Kempis*

Love is not just something we say or write. Love is the face we put on, the clothes we wear, the way we walk and move—our very heart and soul. If we are not made up of love, we will reflect this to others and will feel it within ourselves.

Love isn't just a feeling. Love is a truth filled with forgiveness and kindness; with generosity and honesty. It is the willingness to serve and protect, to cherish and respect, to honor and be strong. We do not have to have feelings of love for everyone we meet, but we do need to love them.

Have we loved those around us today? Have we shown others that we acknowledge their truth and character, in the same way we would want them to acknowledge us? If we can see love as separate from the feelings of falling in love, we will then begin to understand there is love in all of us. And each of us is special enough to be loved.

Tonight I can see love is everywhere and in everyone.

We live on a moving line between past and future. That line is our lifeline.
—*George A. Buttrick*

Live in the present is a good slogan for those of us who grew up in an alcoholic family because many of us find it hard to do. Sometimes it feels like everything we do is a result of the way we were brought up, and those memories can come flooding back no matter what we're doing. Our character defects, fears, actions, and defenses were all constructed before adulthood. These influence us in the present.

Because of our childhood, we are also future-oriented dreamers. We learned to look forward to times when our worries, fears, and pains would be gone. That always seemed to be tomorrow. Everything would be all right—tomorrow.

The past is behind us and the future lies ahead. We are learning the present isn't as painful, as fearful, or as uncomfortable as the past. We may look to the future for hope, but not to place all our faith into a future moment. The present is not so bad, as long as we remember it will never be repeated and our future will never be an unattainable fantasy.

I can place all my faith, trust, and hope in the present.

The pessimist sees the difficulty in every opportunity; the optimist, the opportunity in every difficulty.

—L. P. Jacks

How many times have we opted not to do something and listed countless reasons? Perhaps we've rejected a career change or geographic move or promotion. Or maybe we've passed up get-togethers or renewing friendships. What is it that tells us to say no?

Looking back, we may discover we've refused changes in our lives because we'd lose our security. We may have refused friendly offers because they meant sharing ourselves with others. We may find that all we could see were difficulties coming out of change and not any enjoyment.

Yet there are riches in every opportunity that comes our way. Our Higher Power doesn't put anything in our path that won't help us grow and learn. By seeing opportunities only as difficulties, we are stifling our enjoyment, growth, and pleasure. If we learn to see more opportunities as great learning experiences, we may begin to say yes.

There will be opportunities that come my way. Help me learn to say yes to them.

We owe to our first journeys the discovery that place is nothing. At home I dream that at Naples, at Rome, I can be intoxicated with beauty and lose my sadness. I pack my trunk, embrace my friends, embark on the sea and at last wake up in Naples, and there beside me is the stern Fact, the sad self, unrelenting, identical fact that I fled from.

—Ralph Waldo Emerson

Many times we may not like what we are thinking or feeling or the way we are acting. We may try to run away, hoping a geographical move, or new job, or new set of friends will make being with ourselves more bearable. Yet no matter how we change our environment or lifestyle, those changes will not change us.

We can become more bearable by changing from within. If we don't like the way we think, perhaps we can take one minute tonight and think positive thoughts. If we don't like the way we act, we can begin changing our behaviors. By changing from within, we will deal with the reasons why we want to run from ourselves. We will change the person we are running from.

I can stop running and start looking at myself. How can I make myself more likable to me?

If you don't have such a clear picture of what you want, you may become more humble.
—Carlos Castaneda

When we were growing up, our parents often wished our career definitions would be specific: fire fighter, teacher, police officer, doctor, lawyer, nurse. Yet as we grew older, we may have questioned such cut-and-dried choices. We may have gone to college and majored in a subject not defined by a career. We may have chosen the business world for financial reason. We may have enlisted in the military or gotten married.

Who are we now? We may just be beginning to question who we are and what we want from life. We may be dissatisfied by our choices of the past and are yearning to redefine our goals.

We are changing every day. Such change has given us room to grow because our definitions of ourselves are not so clear, so rigid. Our work on Step Four teaches us to take continual inventory of ourselves. This personal inventory has enabled us to remain forever humble as we realize we are ever-changing, ever-growing persons.

Tonight I can be grateful for the freedom in which the program allows me to grow.

Imagine how little good music there would be if, for example, a conductor refused to play Beethoven's Fifth Symphony on the ground[s] that his audience may have heard it before.
—*A. P. Herbert*

Long ago, before printing presses, telephones, and instant replays, our ancestors kept records of people, information, and history by telling the same stories many times. These stories were passed down from generation to generation. People crowded into caves and huddled around roaring fires to hear the old stories. They never grew tired of hearing them, for with each telling could come a new insight and a renewed interest.

When we hear the same things, we can tune in instead of tuning out. We can listen to each word as if it were the first time, feeling all the feelings and leaving our minds open to new insights. Perhaps we can garner a few lines to include in our own storytelling or that relate to us in particular. Conversations and stories can be the same with each telling. But we can keep them fresh by listening differently each time.

As I lie down tonight, I can imagine I've regained my hearing after years of silence. I can begin to listen as if it were the first time and gain so much more.

After 8,000 unsuccessful trials on a nickel-iron storage battery, Thomas Edison said, "Well, at least we know 8,000 things that won't work."
—*Robert Millikan*

If we don't believe we will be successful, all our efforts are doomed from the start. If we fear success or prefer the norm, we will not want to succeed. If we've been let down many times before, once more will make us want to give up. The bottom line is: How badly do we want to succeed at our goals?

Thomas Edison worked eagerly to discover the battery. He looked at his unsuccessful attempts not as failures but as information. He turned what some may see as failures into successes even though he didn't achieve the results he wanted.

If we want something desperately, we can choose to do all we can to get it. We can change our attitudes about the results by looking at them not as failures but as accomplishments. Then we can try a new way and not give up until we have exhausted all possible ways. If we work hard at it, we will be successful.

Tonight, I can keep a positive outlook and a strong determination.

Happiness is knowing that you do not necessarily require happiness.
—William Saroyan

Do we believe happiness comes from material things? Yet stereos break down, clothes become worn, and cars attract scratches and dents. Do we believe we will be happy with a promotion or move? Yet new jobs and new homes soon become old jobs and old homes. We'll yearn again for another change, another challenge.

The struggle to attain happiness becomes easier when we realize we can be happy without having to struggle for it. We can be happy just by knowing we don't have to have the new car or the new home or perfection in our lives. Our happiness can come from just being ourselves, living each day, doing what we need to do for ourselves. To be happy means we don't need to struggle to find happiness.

Tonight I can be happy with myself and where I am right now.

You just have to learn not to care about the dust-mice under the beds.

—*Margaret Mead*

Perfection is something many of us strive for. We want the perfect marriage or relationship. We want the perfect house and perfect clothes. We want the perfect job and we yearn to be the perfect employee. We want perfection in our personalities and in all our actions.

Perfection means being perfect—no faults or blemishes. Sometimes we see perfection by a gymnast who scores a perfect ten. Yet every time that gymnast performs, she doesn't always score a ten. She is not perfect all the time, or even most of the time.

We can experience momentary perfection. Perhaps we earn an "A" or write a faultless business proposal or complete a knitting project without a dropped stitch. But these accomplishments don't mean we will always be perfect. We need to see ourselves as imperfect and allow the dropped stitches, the "Bs," and the 9.5 scores to exist. They let us see we are perfect in a special way—we are perfectly imperfect human beings!

Nothing has to be perfect, as long as I give it my best effort.

She looked around and found there were no monsters, only shifting shadows from the play of moonlight through the trees outside the window.
—Lisa Alther

How often have we heard a child's bedtime fears are the result of an overactive imagination? Our own imagination can run wild at night, to such an extent that our reality becomes distorted. We begin to imagine things that are not real.

If someone doesn't say hello to us, we may think that person hates us. An unreturned telephone call could signal that another has stopped being our friend. Instead of seeing what really exists, we let our imagination take over. Minor inconveniences become major catastrophes; small sounds become amplified into "things that go bump in the night."

Tonight is as real as today. There is nothing to fear except the thoughts in our own minds. And we can chase those away by remembering to look at things the way they really are, not as we imagine them to be.

Tonight I can use my mind to see clearly. Darkness cannot cloud my thoughts.

Sometimes I feel mad at her. Feel like I could scratch her hair right off her head. But then I think [she] got a right to live too. She got a right to look over the world in whatever company she choose. Just cause I love her don't take away none of her rights.

—Alice Walker,
The Color Purple

When we open ourselves up to caring, sharing, and giving, we also bare our vulnerable spots. We often hear how beautiful it is to be in love, but we also know how painful it can be.

We might not mind being in love if the other person would stop hurting us. Sometimes it seems deliberately done: coming home late for dinner, forgetting an appointment or special event, or falling asleep when we want to be intimate. We may then express our hurt in ways that will hurt the other: yelling, throwing things, hitting, running away, breaking up.

Sometimes we forget important dates or are too tired to express intimacy. If those are our rights, then they must also be the rights of others. To truly express love, we need to have room to grow as two beautiful flowers, instead of one depriving the other of light and nourishment.

I can give space to a loved one.

The soul is dyed the color of its thoughts.
—*Marcus Aurelius*

If we give a group of children paper and crayons and ask them to draw a self-portrait, we will see that their choice of colors will communicate how they feel about themselves. Pastel colors can convey happiness and contentment; bright colors can reveal strong feelings; black or blue can mean sadness or pain.

How would we color a picture of ourselves tonight? If our day has been good and we've kept our thoughts positive and focused in the present, our choice of colors will probably show contentment and serenity. If our thoughts today have been negative or focused on the past or future, we may choose colors that reflect confusion, fear, sadness, or insecurity.

We can steer clear of the blues tonight if we think of ourselves in happy colors. There's a whole rainbow of colors to feel—the choice is up to us.

What color is my soul tonight?

Tension is a habit. Relaxing is a habit. And bad habits can be broken, good habits formed.
—*William James*

Nail biting, foot shaking, hair twirling, finger tapping, and hand wringing are all ways of showing nervous tension. We most likely have these habits unconsciously. To stop, we can use the tools of the program as if we are breaking an obsession. We can use the slogans and Steps to give us first the awareness and then the strength to break the nervous habits. We can also learn good habits with which to replace the old.

For example, we may be very nervous before a meeting starts. So we sit there biting our nails, perpetuating the bad habit. We can replace that bad habit with a good one like volunteering to make the coffee. By doing so, we'll keep our hands and minds busy until the meeting begins. By using the program to deal with bad habits and choosing positive replacements for them, we can change our bad behaviors into good ones.

What are some of my bad habits? Tonight I can think of good habits to replace my bad ones.

There are two things to aim at in life: first, to get what you want; and, after that, to enjoy it. Only the wisest of mankind can achieve the second.
—Logan Pearsall Smith

Through our work in the program, we are learning a new way of life. We may never achieve all we want in life, but along the way we may find ourselves enriched by our progress. Perhaps we didn't argue with our partners last week or maybe we made plans on our own or tried something new. How did we celebrate such great gains? Have we spent time enjoying the good things in our lives?

When we make any gain, we need to stop for a moment and enjoy it. No gain is too small to be recognized and enjoyed. All the time we have to enjoy our progress is right now. Let's take time to enjoy the fruits of our labors.

What gains—big or small—have I made today? Tonight I can enjoy the gains while they are fresh in my mind. I have done well.

I think the important thing is caring about someone. It's being by themselves that does people in, makes them old and bitter.
—*Thomas Tryon*

Isolation is always a choice. We choose the times we wish to be with people and the times we don't. Sometimes we choose to be alone to center ourselves—to "get away from it all." But when we start to spend too much time away from others, it's time to take a look at the reasons for our isolation.

Perhaps we're afraid to take risks with people and expose our vulnerable selves to them. Or maybe we feel people wouldn't really like us if they knew us. We may believe people will only hurt us, and we can look back into our past to recall such times.

But we are different people today. We're involved in a program based on love, trust, faith, and hope. It is a program centered on meetings filled with people caring for one another—exchanging phone numbers, hugging, getting together for coffee, listening, and understanding. It is our choice: isolation or the wonderful benefits of people caring for people.

Do I feel isolated tonight? How can I feel more connected?

I have but one lamp by which my feet are guided, and that is the lamp of experience.
—Patrick Henry

Think what it would be like to walk through the woods at night without a flashlight. We would be at the mercy of every root, stump, tangle, rock, and hole. Though we may have walked the same way in daylight, without the guidance of light it is as if we are walking the path for the first time.

Experience teaches us to use tools when necessary. If something didn't work for us once, it is up to us to keep trying until we find something that will work.

Why stumble in the dark agony of fear, sadness doubt, anxiety, and insecurity? We have many flashlights to light our paths. They are the slogans, such as *Let Go and Let God, First Things First,* and *Easy Does It.* Our experiences and those of others tell us the program works. We can choose to stumble in the dark or walk easily with the light of the program.

Although I may be feeling low tonight, I can trust in the experience that tells me to let go, for all is well.

Everything that is in agreement with our personal desires seems true. Everything that is not puts us into a rage.
—Andre Maurois

There was a woman who prided herself on her ability to achieve. In fact, she bought a button that read: "I want it all—I want the best—and I want it now!" Most of the time she got what she wanted, and that made her very happy. But when she didn't get what she wanted, she would throw temper tantrums. We may be like that woman. It may be difficult to accept less than we desire. Not getting our way may be cause for battle, and we may not give up our fight until we do get our way.

If everyone acted this way, what would the world be like? Not everyone can be a "taker," receiving all the time. And not everyone can be a "giver," giving all the time. Giving once doesn't mean we always have to give, just as receiving once doesn't mean we'll always receive. We need to keep in mind that there is a balance. To achieve that balance, we need to learn we cannot have everything we want. And that's okay.

Do I fly into a rage when I don't get my own way? Help me learn how to receive, as well as how to give.

Lost, yesterday, somewhere between sunrise and sunset, two golden hours, each set with sixty diamond minutes. No reward is offered, for they are gone forever.

—Horace Mann

As we reflect on the day, were there moments we wasted? Was there a chunk of time we idled away, perhaps bored or listless? Those moments are gone now. We can never get them back, but we can be more conscious about wasting time tomorrow.

When we were drinking or using, we probably wasted a lot of time in bars, in front of the television, or passed out. We may have argued constantly with our drunken spouses or parents, wasting precious evenings and weekends. Or we may have spent all our time with our family and not any time with friends.

We don't have to waste time. We can give to others, but not to the extent that it infringes upon our time. We can walk away from an argument and venture out on evenings and weekends. We can put away the bottles and the pills and go to meetings and experience life sober and clean. Time we've wasted is gone, but the time to come we can use. We can let every minute count.

I won't waste any more of my life. I will make the most of every minute and resolve not to let precious time slip away.

The first step in solving a problem is to tell someone about it.
                                        —*John Peter Flynn*

Many times we may believe we should keep our problems to ourselves. Why should we worry others? Or perhaps we don't believe we'll get help and support, only pity and sympathy. Maybe we don't want others to know we have problems.

Everybody has problems, even the people who seem to be all smiles and good cheer. Yet nobody solves problems alone. Many call upon their Higher Power or a close friend. Others use their sponsor or counselor. Some use meetings. All of these people who share their problems will find a solution. It's when we don't use any other sources that our problems become too difficult to handle.

Every problem has a solution, but that answer may not lie within our grasp. When we ask for answers, we are admitting we can't find the answers ourselves. That is the First Step to the program and the first step to living sanely and sensibly. A shared problem is always a solved problem.

I can share my problems with my Higher Power tonight. I can ask for help and thereby find a solution.

The voice of intelligence is soft and weak. It is drowned out by the roar of fear. It is ignored by the voice of desire. It is contradicted by the voice of shame. It is hissed away by hate and extinguished by anger. Most of all, it is silenced by ignorance.

—Karl Menninger

The story of Sybil tells of a woman who sheltered sixteen personalities within her. Her confusion and fear about the many voices made it almost impossible to make decisions and to be herself. Instead of being one person she was sixteen, until she got help.

Many times we may feel like Sybil. Inside, many voices try to tell us what to do, contradict us, knock us down, or make us cringe in fear. Yet we don't have to listen to those voices. We only need listen to the one that is guided by our Higher Power. That voice tells us we're good, we're doing good things for ourselves, and the program gives us all we need to get better. This voice can become louder and more powerful in time, gradually drowning out the other voices we've let run our lives.

Tonight I'll tune in the best voice—the one of my Higher Power. I'll turn my will over to this voice and let it guide me.

As the old man walked the beach at dawn, he noticed a young man ahead of him picking up starfish and flinging them into the sea. Finally catching up with the youth, he asked him why he was doing this. The answer was that the stranded starfish would die if left until the morning sun. "But the beach goes on for miles and there are millions of starfish," countered the other. "How can your effort make any difference?" The young man looked at the starfish in his hand and then threw it to safety in the waves. "It makes a difference to this one," he said.

—Minnesota Literacy Council

Our efforts can make a difference. There will be many starfish on the paths we will travel and how we treat them will make a difference in our growth. The best resolution we can make tonight is to pay attention to the starfish we'll see. If we can reach out to all who need us, we will have made a difference to their lives and to ours.

My efforts can make a difference. I can take the first step toward making changes, taking risks, expressing feelings, and letting in the positive feelings of life.

You're only human, you're supposed to make mistakes.

—*Billy Joel*

Are we determined faultfinders? It may be easy for us to point fingers at others or to cite instances of wrongdoing. It may also be easy for us to misinterpret another's actions, twist words, or make something seem totally opposite to the truth.

Everyone makes mistakes, including us. But somewhere along the path of our growth, we learned we could defend ourselves if we were judge and jury. So we took a defensive stance, clinging to our battle stations as we weathered school, family, relationships, and careers.

We don't have to be so ready to make ourselves blameless and faultless. We can disband our courts of law at any time. But when we do, we will be admitting to ourselves and the people in our lives that we are only human. When we, too, can see ourselves as human, we'll no longer look at life as a battlefield, but as a classroom where everyone is both teacher and student.

I can see myself as human and accept that no human being is blameless.

The ebb and flow of will is like the movements of the tides. . . . If we cease our vain struggles and lamentations long enough to look away from the personal self . . . we realize life is going well with us after all.

—*Charles B. Newcomb*

Everything in nature changes. We can trust the sun and moon will rise and set, the tide will ebb and flow, and the seasons will change. Because we can trust these things to happen, we can learn to trust the fact that extremes in nature are normal.

So it is with people. We laugh and cry, work and play, we are young and we grow old. There will be extremes with us, just as there are in nature. And as nature finds its natural flow even after the worst disasters, so can we find our natural flow.

There is a rhythm in life that leads us to awaken and one that guides us to sleep. Tonight our natural rhythm will lead us to peace and relaxation. If we can flow with that rhythm, we'll give the quiet calmness a chance to revitalize us for tomorrow. Now is the time to follow nature's rhythm and sleep in peace.

Can I rest tonight in quietness of mind, soul, and body and trust I will find my natural flow?

In three words, I can sum up everything I've learned about life: It goes on.

—Robert Frost

If we've ever dug in a garden and unearthed an ants' nest, we can recall their first reaction to our unintended destruction: they do everything possible to save their lives and supplies. The ants scurry around, moving the larvae to an underground room. Exposed contents are then relocated to unseen passages. In a matter of minutes, the ants are again safely underground and ready to resume their daily routines.

How do we react when some catastrophe or unplanned event occurs? Do we want to crawl under a rock or are we as resilient as the ants? Instead of moaning over postponed plans or the loss of something in our lives, we can try to be like the ants and learn how to best work *with* circumstances that come our way.

Life doesn't stop for us to lick wounds or add fuel to grievances. Hours pass, we grow older, nature continues. Every event is part of life's cycle. We can't run away from anything. We must meet life head-on and adjust to its ebb and flow.

I can look at an unplanned event in my life as part of life's cycle. I need to trust that life will go on.

Fear imprisons, faith liberates; fear paralyzes, faith empowers; fear disheartens, faith encourages; fear sickens, faith heals; fear makes useless, faith makes serviceable.
—*Harry Emerson Fosdick*

It has been said that the opposite of fear is faith. But how do we change our fears into faith if we have little or no faith? How do we start having faith? One of the easiest ways to develop an alternative to fear is to ask ourselves during a moment of fear: What is the worst that could happen? Once we know the answer to that question, we have dealt with the source of our fears—the unknown.

What do we fear now? First we need to identify all the unknowns that we fear. Once we recognize all the things that can happen, we will be able to prepare ourselves for possible failure, loss, or sadness. By recognizing the fears, we take away some of their power over us. We can then believe we will be all right.

What do I fear and why do I fear it? I know I am okay because I have identified my fear.

Mankind has advanced in the footsteps of men and women of unshakable faith. Many of these great ones ... have set stars in the heavens to light others through the night.
—Olga Rosmanith

All around us there are wonderful role models. Their faith, hope, strength, courage, and fearlessness can give us guidance during any time of need. But in order to look to those people for inspiration, we first need to be ready to look beyond ourselves.

In our times of need, it's easy to focus solely on ourselves. It's almost as if we climb into our own womb, conscious only of our feelings, thoughts, pains, and needs.

Yet there are those among us who have lived through times just as trying as the ones we're in. However, instead of looking inward, these people looked outward to the solutions and applied them. By using the same solutions, we can bring some light into our darkness.

Where can I find my powers of example?

*The mind is its own place, and in itself—Can
make a heaven of hell, a hell of heaven.*
                                        —John Milton

If we listen to the news, we can hear stories of natural disasters, starvation and deprivation, torture and bloodshed. Yet we may sit in our homes and look at our lives and moan, "Life isn't fair to me. Nothing ever works out the way I want it to."

If we could lose our self-centeredness and look at the powerlessness issues that go on outside of our little world, we would realize our hell is of its own creation. When we see what we don't have and what we can't change, we are building the foundations of a hell memorial. We are striving to preserve the have-nots and are-nots as a fitting tribute to all we cannot be.

We can stop eulogizing such negativity. Sure, there are many bad things in this world and a lot of bad people. Sure, there are many things we cannot do and possibly never will be able to do. But we can tear down the tribute to hell and erect instead a tribute to heaven—to all the things we can have and can do, to all the things we can change.

I can build tributes to my life, not memorials. The Serenity Prayer can help me see blessings, not bitterness tonight.

We ought to hear at least one little song every day, read a good poem, see a first-rate painting, and if possible speak a few sensible words.
—Johann Wolfgang Von Goethe

Schedules! At the end of a day, have we ever felt we've accomplished anything? Maybe we did everything according to our schedules, but were we able to take time to do the things we wanted?

Dinner doesn't have to be eaten at a fixed hour. Work doesn't have to be brought home every night. Chores don't have to be done on the same night every week. A little variation in our evening schedules is healthy, especially if we need a change of pace. It will also help us unwind, center ourselves, be more alert and in touch with life rather than frantically trying to keep pace.

Read a book. Play a record that's been collecting dust. Call a friend. Write a letter. Go for a walk. Prepare a special dessert. Take a hot, luxurious bath. We can break the weekly routine and add a new one—pampering ourselves.

What can I do special for me? I can decide tonight what I'd really like to do—and then tomorrow, I'll do it!

When you worry, you go over the same ground endlessly and come out the same place you started. Thinking makes progress from one place to another. . . . The problem of life is to change worry into thinking and anxiety into creative action.

—Harold B. Walker

The prisoner in a narrow jail cell has one path to pace—walking the same path with the same amount of paces at the same rate. It never changes until that prisoner is released.

When we worry, we are like that prisoner. Worry keeps our minds confined to one set of thoughts and keeps our physical bodies in a state of anxiety. We may believe that by thinking of the problem, we are working on a resolution. But we are really only dwelling on the futility of the problem.

It is only when we are released from worry that we can see solutions clearly. Tonight, let us free ourselves from worry's constraints, change our minds from tunnel vision to clear thoughts. These thoughts are the key to our release from worry and anxiety.

I don't have to stay prisoner to worrisome thoughts. Tonight I can allow clear thinking to give me freedom from worry.

I wish there were windows to my soul, so that you could see some of my feelings.
—*Artemus Ward*

Wouldn't it be great if people could see our feelings? All we'd have to do is walk into a room and someone could say, "I see you're feeling sad right now. Let me help you."

Many of us grew up expecting people to be mind readers. Without voicing our feelings or asking for help, we believed people should be able to see how we felt. When they didn't, we usually became angry, hurt, or depressed. Until someone pointed this out to us, we never recognized how silent we were and how great our expectations were of others.

Unless we voice our feelings, they will never be heard. And unless we ask for help, we will never get assistance. The people in our lives have ears to listen and arms to hold us—if we choose to open the windows to our soul.

I can tell someone how I feel. I can ask for help if I need it. If those around me seem to be upset, I can be there for them but I will not try to be a mind reader.

So I can't sink down and let the time of my real being take me, for if I try and for a moment can see no direction, cannot tell where I am going, I am filled with panic, scared of emptiness. I must be doing something. . . .
—Joanna Field

Imagine for a moment that we have no plans for tomorrow. No job to get up for or classes to attend, no errands to run. At first we may think this is delightful, but we need to think back to the last occasion we had time to spend alone.

Did we sit comfortably, clearing our minds of all thought and tension to listen to our inner selves? Or did we immediately turn on the television, reach for a book, or aimlessly putter?

We may be afraid to sit alone in our stillness. Yet when we allow our inner selves to be heard without background noise or the diversions of projects or hobbies, we will begin to discover our inner thoughts are creative and stimulating and intuitive. We will begin to discover ourselves.

Tonight I can take fifteen minutes to lie quietly with myself. If I have to ask what I will think about, I know I can Let Go and Let God.

Use what talents you have; the woods would have little music if no birds sang their song except those who sang best.
— Rev. Oliver G. Wilson

The perfectionist in all of us gives us some pretty harsh criticism. It tells the photographer in us we'll never be Ansel Adams. It tells the writer in us we'll never be Charles Dickens. It tells the businessperson in us we'll never be Henry Ford. It tells the parent in us we'll never have the perfect family.

This perfectionist has an uncanny way of making us feel inferior to all who have gone before us. Such condemnations may hurt our creativity and abilities so much that we decide to give up trying to be good at anything. So we fail before we begin.

How do we know we won't be good at what we do? We certainly won't be Ansel Adams or anybody else because they've already existed. But we can be ourselves and use our talents to do our best. We may become famous and successful, or we may not. But we won't know unless we try. With our talents and determination, we can achieve splendid things. But we won't know unless we try.

What are my talents? I can develop these talents not in imitation of another but with curiosity about what I can do.

This time, like all times, is a very good one if we but know what to do with it.
—Ralph Waldo Emerson

Is the glass half full or half empty? We know the answer to that question can symbolically reflect whether we have a positive or negative outlook on life. If we see the glass as half empty, we focus on what is gone. But if we say the glass is half full, we see what remains.

If we're full of ideas about how to spend our time, then our outlook is positive and we'll not waste a second. But if we're feeling bored or directionless or lonely, our days may be filled with a lot of negative energy and wasted moments.

Instead of focusing on what we don't have, we can change our attitude and look at what we do have. We have choices about how we want to spend our time. The decisions we make will have a direct bearing on how meaningful each day will be.

How can I change my attitude and make each day full?

A father who cares enough to wait and worry,
who cares enough to counsel and be concerned,
is among the greatest blessings God has given.
—Richard L. Evans

The memories we have of our childhood may be filled with joy, sorrow, happiness, or pain. The child within us may still be crying for a father with whom to share our joys and growth. We may feel cheated out of a wonderful relationship with him or saddened because that relationship has ended.

A loving, healthy father is a great blessing. Yet many of us do not have such a blessing. Instead of thinking back to childhood with feelings of anger or bitterness, we each need to believe our father did the best he could to raise us. Our father had to deal with his imperfections and circumstances at the same time he was also trying to be a father to us.

We can look back and remember the good things about our father. By looking at the good along with the bad, we'll see him as human instead of imperfect.

I need to see my father as another human sharing my path in life. Can I see the good in him?

I wish to live without hate, whim, jealousy, envy, fear. I wish to be simple, honest, frank, natural, clean in mind and clean in body . . . to face any obstacle and meet every difficulty unabashed and unafraid.

—Elbert Hubbard

Growing up, we learned there were many places to make wishes: the first star, a well, candles on a birthday cake. We saw Dorothy return from Oz after she wished she were back home. Fairy tales taught us wishes can come true.

We don't have to stop wishing, even though many of our wishes never came true. We may have wished for the impossible when we said: "I wish things would get better at home." But we may have gotten our way when we said: "I wish this pain would end." Our dreams came true with the program.

Our best wishes can be about ourselves and the lives we want to have. We can wish for riches and find friends with hearts of gold. We can wish for comfort and health, and get a night of uninterrupted sleep. Whatever we wish for, we can receive.

I can read tonight's quotation aloud and apply it to my life. This powerful affirmation can help me tonight and every night.

Love comes unseen; we only see it go.
—*Austin Dobson*

How often are we blind to love shown us by others? Yet we are always aware when love is taken from us. Suddenly we feel helpless, alone, rejected, and full of despair. "No one will ever love me again!" we may cry. Yet all around us are loving people, ready to give their support.

If we only equate love with a sexual relationship, we will never see love's beauty. Love comes in so many forms and from so many people. When we experience the loss of a love, we may believe we have lost all the love that will ever be shown to us.

Love is more than Valentine's Day and passion and giddy feelings of ecstasy. When we desire love in that form, we are like addicts craving a drug. The effects are blissful, but they are only temporary. Love that lasts, that stays with patience and strength, is the love that binds all of humanity. It is what makes us smile at a stranger, it's what makes long-term friendships, it's what makes us feel pain, as well as joy. Love is the connection we have with every person in our lives.

Tonight, I feel the love I have for others and the love they have for me. I can learn to see the love that exists all around me.

When you want to hurry something, that means you no longer care about it and want to get on to other things.

—*Robert M. Pirsig*

At times we may feel pressured to accomplish certain things in a short period of time. We may find ourselves rushing through activities aimlessly, operating under some kind of invisible deadline. Or we may be looking forward to future events and wish the present would hurry up and end.

Now is the time to slow ourselves down. Like a swimmer before a race, we can take time to breathe deeply, relax our tense muscles, and test the waters before we take the plunge.

We can use *Let Go and Let God, Easy Does It,* and *Keep it Simple* as our guidelines. As we let these slogans relax us, we can get a clearer picture about the reasons for our hurrying. By examining these reasons, we can then determine what activities we really need to work on—at a much slower pace.

What slogans will help me relax my hustle-bustle pace?

For the happiest life, days should be rigorously planned, nights left open to chance.
—*Mignon McLaughlin*

How spontaneous are we? Are we more rigid people or more flexible? If our plans suddenly change, do we handle that easily or is it difficult for us? If we're more rigid, change is often difficult for us to deal with. We may feel anger, resentment, hurt, or sadness when a friend calls to cancel an engagement or something happens to interrupt our plans. We may find ourselves so rigid that we have difficulty going to a meeting and parking in a different space or sitting in a different seat.

Rigidity is built over time and so must be loosened up with time. Little changes in our patterns will help us deal with little changes in our lives. By gradually learning to accept smaller changes, we'll learn to deal with bigger ones. To become more flexible on a daily basis, we need to make slow and gentle changes. Over time, we'll learn to change from rigidity to spontaneity and flexibility.

I can make a small change in tomorrow's schedule. Each day I'll make a minor change to help develop flexibility.

The man who makes no mistakes lacks boldness and the spirit of adventure. He never tries anything new. He is a brake on the wheels of progress.

—M. W. Larmour

"Progress, not perfection" is all the program asks of us. Yet our expectations to do everything the right way at the right time—and usually without asking for help—only lead to incredible disappointment and a sense of failure.

When Henry Ford made his first automobile, he forgot to make a reverse gear. Was that a failure? Not if we look at how his next car—the Model T—revolutionized the automobile industry. Ford learned from his mistake and used that knowledge to build something even better.

Tonight we're building something even better—ourselves. But we won't be able to make a perfect model, only a better one. To do so, we need to accept the fact that we're going to make mistakes along the way.

What mistakes have I made today that I can learn from tonight?

Hope is the only bee that makes honey without flowers.

—Robert Ingersoll

Hope is the invisible part of ourselves that can be the difference between getting somewhere and getting nowhere. Hope is the extra set of muscles that allows us to carry on even though our legs can't support us any longer. Hope is the extra heartbeat that gives us positive energy when our senses can't feel, hear, or see beyond negativity. Hope is the nectar that restores health when our bodies feel old and broken-down.

The one thing everyone in the program has is hope. Hope keeps us sane and keeps us trying. For as long as we have hope, we'll always feel a candle burning within us that's ready to light the world.

We increase our supply of hope every time we do something good, even when we don't want to. Hope is the extra push we give ourselves to quench rage, to bolster our reserves of patience, and to feel love when we find it difficult to feel. With hope in our lives, all else is possible.

Do I have hope tonight? Help me remain filled with hope about my life and the lives of those around me.

A person remains immature, whatever his age, as long as he thinks of himself as an exception to the human race.

—Harry A. Overstreet

Most every rule has an exception because of special people or circumstances. We may sometimes believe we are exceptions to the rule when it comes to the program. We may believe our set of circumstances or who we are makes us different. We may feel the slogans and Steps are good for most people, but they don't relate to us because of some unique things we believe no one else has.

Even though each of us is a unique individual with our own lifestyles and set of circumstances, we're no different than anyone else in the program. We are in the program for one purpose: To learn to live a better way of life while coping with the effects of an addiction. Once we realize we're working toward the same solution as everyone else, we won't see ourselves as exceptions. Our growth will occur in leaps and bounds once we're freed from the label of "exception to the rule."

I'm no different than anyone else when I look at the reasons why I'm in the program. I will remember my connection, not my exception.

One must do more, think less, and not watch oneself live.
—*Sebastien Roch Nicolas de Chamfort*

A talk show host was interviewing a new starlet. Every time he asked her a question she watched herself in the monitor, listening more to herself than to him. Midway through the show, she was totally flustered trying to watch herself and keep up with the show's progress.

At times we may be so focused on ourselves that we are unable to see anyone else. We soon become our own greatest fans, watching only ourselves and listening only to our own thoughts. Reflecting on today, we may be conscious of how much time we spent talking about ourselves or focusing attention on ourselves and our issues.

We can start to change this behavior. Instead of spending a few hours focused on us, we can focus on a hobby, a book, a movie, or a family member. We aren't so important that we need to keep a constant watch over ourselves. There are a lot more important and more interesting people, places, and things to see.

I can stop watching myself and start noticing others. Higher Power, help me discover the world around me.

Life is like a ten-speed bike. Most of us have gears we never use.
—Charles M. Schulz

To ride a ten-speed bike, we need to learn to use the gears. If we're going uphill, we should know what gear eases the climb. If we're going downhill, we should know what gear best uses the slope of the hill.

The Twelve Steps of the program are like the bicycle gears. If we know the purpose and benefit of each Step, we can use them to ease our way. Sometimes life may feel like an uphill climb. Steps Two and Three teach us to call on our Higher Power for help. If we're contentedly coasting on a wonderful slope, then others may benefit from our strength and hope if we use Step Twelve. If we're struggling to change our behaviors or character defects, then Steps Four, Five, and Six may ease our struggles.

If we use all the Steps when we need them, we will never have to struggle again. But if we ignore them like never-used gears, they will become rusty and unproductive. Proper maintenance means we must use everything frequently in order to get the best benefit. We must use the Steps as much as we can.

Do I need to study the Steps more so I can use them better?

Don't find fault. Find a remedy.

—*Henry Ford*

A person in need and a listener were on the telephone. "The problem is," began the one in need, "I wouldn't be in this situation if those things hadn't happened." The one in need talked on, listing all the people, places, and things that brought him to such a state.

The listener let him finish, and then replied, "I believe you're blaming people, places, and things for your problems. You can only blame yourself because you're the one who can change things. As long as you hide behind 'causes' you won't take action. It's up to you to act, so do it!"

It may be easier to blame, because finding remedies means we'll have to work. Looking for scapegoats for our current situation won't get us out of our ruts, it will only mire us deeper. To get free, we need to use our talents and wisdom to good benefit. As the listener said, it's up to us to take action, so let's do it!

Tonight I can stop finding scapegoats. It's up to me to find remedies for my current position and to help pull me out of a rut. Let me do it!

Blame yourself if you have no branches or leaves; don't accuse the sun of partiality.
—*Chinese proverb*

How much do we use our past to find reasons for our faults or shortcomings today? Because we may have come from alcoholic homes or impoverished households doesn't give us the license to place blame for the way we are.

We may feel we would be easier to get along with if other people didn't act the way they did. We may believe we would have so many more hours in the day if others didn't take up so much of our valuable time.

If one tree in a forest is thirsty and starved for sunlight, it doesn't blame the other trees around it for drinking its water and basking in its sun. If the tree wants water it spreads its roots wider and deeper to seek water. If it wants sunlight it spreads its branches and reaches higher. Like that tree in the forest, so must we concentrate on the things we need to do for our nourishment and growth. Our health depends on ourselves, not upon the failings of those around us.

I can look at my growth, and do the things I need for me.

It's better to be a lion for a day than a sheep all your life.

—*Sister Elizabeth Kenny*

Following the crowd, going along with the majority, or doing for the approval of others makes us like sheep. Sheep travel in packs behind a leader or are guided by the barks and nips of sheepdogs. Sheep never travel alone and one sheep never leads the others. Are we like sheep?

By following the norm, we've learned life may be easier without arguments or disagreements over bucking the trend. But how has such following helped us grow? Do we really know who we are, or are we more aware of how everyone else is?

To walk against the wind once in a while is healthy. We don't always have to follow the crowd if we don't believe the crowd is right. We can be like a lion once in a while: a leader, unafraid to travel alone or to guide others. We can let out a mighty roar that will set us apart from the din of the crowd. We don't have to be sheep all the time, only when we want to be.

Will I be a leader or a follower? Whichever I choose, let me believe my choice is the best for me.

If we want to keep living with ourselves, we must keep on trying, trying, trying.
                                        —*Robert J. White, M.D.*

Tonight we may feel we failed in some way today. Even though we may have done our best, we may now believe we could have done more, done it better, or tried harder, then things would be different now.

But there are things beyond our control. One of them is the outcome of any circumstance. We cannot expect that, if we do all we can, all will be well. Even the most skilled surgeon loses patients. The surgeon knows the grace of God is with the patient, no matter what the outcome.

The grace of God is in our lives and the lives of those around us. Though we strive to do our best and to make everything better, we need to remember the outcomes are not in our control. How we accept them, however, is in our control.

Higher Power, help me keep trying to do my best, no matter what the outcome.

Anger blows out the lamp of the mind.
—Robert Green Ingersoll

When we feel anger, our hearts pound faster and we feel warmer. We can go through our daily motions and from the outside look as if all was well. But under the surface is a pot of boiling anger that we keep stoked throughout the day.

Remaining angry for more than a few minutes can be as dangerous as letting a cancerous growth go untreated. It will overtake our healthy thoughts and bodies until we become emotionally and physically sick. We'll become sicker the longer we let anger run our mental, spiritual, and physical selves.

The time to deal with anger is the moment we feel it, not later. If we can't confront the source of our anger at the moment, we still need to let go of it. Getting out our anger doesn't necessarily mean yelling, throwing things, or setting ultimatums. Letting our anger go means letting it be felt and expressed, then releasing it. Anger with obsession makes us sick; anger with expression keeps us sane and healthy.

Am I holding on to anger from the past? I can let go of this anger tonight and not let it rule me.

If you can't be thankful for what you receive, be thankful for what you escape.

—Anonymous

Those Jews who were fortunate enough to evade the clutches of the Third Reich were extremely grateful for their escape from family separations, torture, and death. Even though they may have fled their homes, possessions, friends, and businesses, and had little food in their stomachs, they could give thanks for what they did have: their lives and hope for a better future.

How thankful are we for what we have? Many times we aren't grateful for the shirts on our backs and food in our stomachs. We criticize our lives and our family, perhaps even ourselves. We find we aren't happy, healthy, mature, or serene enough. But imagine for a moment what it was like in our pre-recovery days.

Remember pain, sickness, confusion, anger, hopelessness? We've escaped from the bleakness of the past. But if we can't be grateful for the good in our lives tonight, we've not learned a thing from the program. To be grateful for our new path of discovery, all we need to do is look back at the rocky road we used to travel.

Tonight I can be grateful for what I've gained and what is gone.

Victory is not won in miles, but in inches. Win a little now, hold your ground, and later win a little more.

—Louis L'Amour

For athletes to succeed as runners, they must not stop after their first race is won. To become the best, they need constant practice and warm-ups, and race after race. Some races they will win; others they won't. But in each race they will have achieved another step in their success as a runner.

We, too, must set goals and achieve them step by step. When we entered the program, our goal may have been to know ourselves well enough to make decisions. We then entered "little races" that led toward that goal: sharing our feelings, asking for help, taking our Fourth Step, telling a friend what we wanted to do. Each time we accomplished one, we moved closer to our goal.

We need to give ourselves credit for all the "little races" we've won. If we look not to the goal but to the path, we will see we are gaining ground step by step.

I can take another step toward my goals. Each small step deserves recognition and praise.

Why do some people always see beautiful skies and grass and lovely flowers and incredible human beings, while others are hard-pressed to find anything or any place that is beautiful?
—Leo Buscaglia

We may have some pretty strong feelings about those people who come to meetings and say only positive things. We may feel uncomfortable with their smiling faces and warm welcomes. We may wonder how anyone could be so happy. We know they wouldn't be happy if they had a day like we had today!

It's hard to break the pattern of seeing only the negative things. We've spent so long at the bottom of the barrel that it's hard to be at the top. It takes work to think of things in a positive way; that may be a new way of thinking for us.

But we can start thinking positively. Instead of remembering all the negative things that happened today, we can sift through until we find just one positive thing. After a while we may come up with two, or three, or many more. Soon, we may be one of those positive people with a cheery outlook!

Can I think of one positive thing that happened to me today? Can I express this positive thing to others?

*When we stop looking at whatever troubles us,
and turn in faith to God, the source of good, the
difficulty disappears and a new condition takes
its place.*

—William A. Clough

If our garden is choked with weeds, we don't stare
at it and think, "My garden is going to have a lousy
growing season." We start pulling those weeds to give
our plants room to grow and the nutrition they need.
Because we believe clearing the weeds will make the
garden grow, we change a bad condition into a good
one.

But what do we do when we see ourselves being
choked by debts, bad relationships, or health problems? Do we take action to affect change or do we become paralyzed at our view of an unchangeable
situation? We need to learn to take our focus off fears,
doubts, worries, and insecurities and place it instead
upon faith and a belief that all will work out.

We can begin to replace difficulties with faith. No
matter what problems we have, none is too big for
faith to change. Our belief that these conditions can
change is the first step in letting faith work its own
way.

*Tonight I can change my outlook by replacing my
difficulties with faith.*

We can't all be captains, we've got to be crew.
—Douglas Malloch

An old saying tells us, *There is no I in team.* That means there is no one hero, no one member who carries a team or becomes the personality of the team. The team wins or loses because of all its members, not the actions or omissions of one.

There are many of us who don't like to play on a team. We would prefer individual sports or hobbies. We may like to be in control or seek solitude rather than the company of others. We may even try to assume so many responsibilities that we become the only person who can accomplish a task or job.

Sometimes it's good to be a leader. But leaders also need to know how to be led. To work well with other people, we need to know what it feels like to be a member of a group where we are all equal. A ship comprised of only captains may flounder or be tossed against the shore. A ship with one captain and a crew may sail smoothly and safely by the efforts of all.

Let me become a member of my group, not a leader. Help me extend this affirmation into all areas of my life.

Silence propagates itself, and the longer talk has been suspended, the more difficult it is to find anything to say.

—*Samuel Johnson*

Remember growing up with a parent or other family member who showed anger by "the silent treatment"? How infuriating it was to experience this. One person would be attempting to make things right or provoke a response while the other would maintain a "lips sealed" policy.

Forced silence can be as devastating as the most angry, most vicious comment. Forced silence is a wall erected in front of the vocal chords so human communication cannot scale it.

The silent treatment, like inappropriate anger, is not the way to patch rips in the fabric of our human support system. Unless we break the soundless barrier, the wall will become nearly impossible to tear down. Tonight we can look back to any relationship that's in jeopardy and seek to mend it by human communication.

Is there someone in my life with whom I haven't communicated for a while? It's up to me to scale the wall of silence before I lose that person forever.

Patience is a virtue that carries a lot of WAIT!
—Our Daily Bread

Before we came into the program, we may have had little patience. We may have been tired of waiting for our parents to sober up and live up to their promises. We may have impatiently crossed off the days until we were legally free to leave home.

When we entered the program, we again found we had to wait for so many things. We learned the Twelve Steps couldn't be done in twelve days. We listened to people talk about the years of recovery they had. We may have privately thought it wouldn't take us that long. We were going to be in and out of the program in a matter of weeks—and we would be cured!

Good things come to those who wait could be another program slogan because it is so true. To truly master any skill requires long hours of study and continual practice. Like playing the piano, we start out with short, easy chords that build to full-length concertos. Our goal in the program is to play concertos for the rest of our lives. That will not happen today, nor tomorrow, but will come in time.

I can use what I've learned in the program to begin my lifelong study. Higher Power, help me have patience.

Panics, in some cases, have their uses. Their duration is always short; the mind soon grows through them and acquires a firmer habit than before.

—*Thomas Paine*

Any anxious feeling is a signal that needs attention. It means there's something going on, and it's a way our bodies communicate that they are being overwhelmed. If we ask ourselves what's going on, we might hear answers of frustration, shame, guilt, or fear over things that are over and done with or things that have yet to occur.

One of the ways to get through an attack is to center ourselves in the present. We can do this by remembering the date, time, and temperature. Then we can identify objects around us, including what we're wearing. This exercise will bring us back into the present where we won't have the feelings that contributed to our attacks. When our minds are clear, we can learn from anxiety and grow through it.

Tonight I can keep myself in the present by identifying the things and people around me that exist for this moment.

You have learned something. That always feels at first as if you had lost something.
—George Bernard Shaw

We listen as we watch the newcomer cry, "After coming to meetings, I realized my parents couldn't be there for me anymore. They have an addictive disease and I can't get the help I need from them. I feel like I've lost them!" We may nod our heads as we relate these words to our lives.

Didn't we feel like we had lost family, friends, or mates when we began learning the truths in the program? As we learned about addiction, we were faced with just how much we had depended on others to help us. We discovered we weren't who we thought we were. We realized there could be another way of life.

A snake must shed its old skin before the new one can appear. Like furniture, parts of us become worn and uncomfortable. We must replace the old with the new. For every gain, there must be a loss. But instead of mourning our losses tonight, we can rejoice over what we have gained.

I can be grateful for all the gains in my life and in my growth. The losses have allowed me to become stronger and more fruitful.

When we are tired, we are attacked by ideas we conquered long ago.
—Friedrich Wilhelm Nietzsche

Many times our late night thinking is like a late night movie. It can be scary, it's usually of poor quality, and it makes little sense. Trying to understand ourselves or to make decisions during such times only leads to crazy thoughts.

When we can't apply the Steps and the principles of the program because our minds are running like a late night movie, we have only one alternative to insanity. That's to go to bed. Shut off the movie reel and go to sleep. When our bodies are tired, our muscles can't perform and we're left with little energy. This kind of thinking is our mind's only way of telling us that it needs rest. We need to respect this.

The program works for us when we're alert, focused, and able to process healthy thinking. Tired minds breed tired thoughts—thoughts we've been over many times. The cure for a tired mind is an alert one, and the medicine is a good night's sleep!

Tonight I can shut off the late night movie reels of my mind and go to sleep. Sleep is my Higher Power's gift to help my mind get the rest it needs.

You take yourself too seriously! You are too damn important in your own mind. That must be changed!

—*Carlos Castaneda*

How can we appreciate the world around us if we're blinded by our self-importance? Like the horse who wears blinders, we only see ourselves apart from everything else. We miss the natural beauty and the loveliness of human nature if we only have a mirror before our eyes.

Losing self-importance begins by opening our eyes and ears to those around us. By listening to others, we learn our lives and experiences are not unique. By looking around us, we see we have the same good qualities—and bad traits—as others.

Today may have been a day when we were blinded by our own self-importance. Yet tonight we can remember we are no better—and no worse—than anyone else. Tonight we can take off our blinders and become part of the world around us.

What uniqueness can I recall in the people around me today?

You must travel the river, live on it, follow it when there is morning light, and follow it when there is nothing but dark and the banks have blurred into shadows.

—Wil Haygood

Any lifeguard knows a swimmer who tries to swim against the current stands a good chance of becoming tired and drowning. *Go with the flow* is a good reminder to help us stop going against the current of life.

Tonight we may discover that our weariness is a result of swimming against today's current. We may have tried to force changes in people, places, or things. We may have even tried to force ourselves to do things we were incapable of doing.

Going with the flow tonight means accepting the way we feel—right now. It means listening to our inner voices when they tell us whether we're tired, hungry, cold, or lonely. By accepting ourselves and not fighting how we feel, we'll be better able to travel the river tonight.

Tonight I will respect myself and go with the flow.

I never make the mistake of arguing with people for whose opinions I have no respect.

—*Gibbon*

"She just doesn't understand." "He doesn't listen to me." "She can't see my point of view." Do we ever say these things? No matter how much we argue or how convincing our argument, we may never be able to change another's opinion.

It may be our parents. But do we value their opinion, or are we trying to force their approval? It may be a boss or co-worker. But are they people we would choose to have as friends outside work? Before we become tense and angry, we must look at the person with whom we are arguing.

Do we respect these people? Would their opinion benefit us? Are they interested in our best welfare? Sometimes we may struggle to change the opinion of those who have never supported us, rather than talk with those who have always been there for us. To distinguish between the two is the difference between disapproval and tension, and love and acceptance.

Am I driving myself crazy trying to change another's opinion? I can take a look at this and seek those opinions I value and trust.

The highest compact we can make with our fellow is, let there be truth between us two forevermore.

—Ralph Waldo Emerson

When was the last time we told a lie? Do we remember who we lied to and the reason? Did our lying bring us closer to that person, or did it build an invisible wall?

We have chosen to travel on the path of recovery. Because of this, there are certain requirements for our growth and learning. One of them is honesty with ourselves and with others. If we aren't honest with ourselves, we will suffer because the truth will come out. If we aren't honest with others, we will hinder our ability to grow closer to people. Dishonesty doesn't make bonds, it breaks them.

We can make amends for our lies. We can "come clean" to those we lied to and tear down the walls. By doing so we will move further along our path of recovery by learning how to build relationships, not break them. Honesty with others builds trust, trust builds love, and love makes life so much better.

Tonight I will promise to get honest with at least one person to whom I have lied. I will learn how to build a better relationship by doing so.

There is a divine plan of good at work in my life.
I will let go and let it unfold.
—Ruth P. Freedman

There is a lesson to be learned from each person we meet. Our contact, however brief, has happened for some reason. We may feel as if we are part of a play, especially when we meet someone at a particularly meaningful time. Maybe we were laid off from work and for some reason attended a meeting in a different town and sat next to an employer looking for someone with our qualifications.

Yet we may question the meaning behind meeting those who leave us with pain and heartache. We may wonder at the lessons to be learned from those who may treat us badly. Not all the lessons are easy, nor do all our contacts feel wonderful. But there is a purpose that can be seen after the healing of time. We'll always meet new people, just as we'll always be learning. These things we can trust are in the hands of our Higher Power.

Tonight, I will trust that my life is lit by goodness and that all people and events can add to my light.

It was like a revelation to me, taking complete responsibility for one's own actions.
—Cary Grant

All our lives we may have looked for someone to take care of us. This may have begun with our parents, then continued when we formed relationships. We may have found life was easier when someone else took responsibility for our finances, obligations, and emotional health. Whenever someone left us, we may have quickly latched onto someone new so we didn't have to feel the burden of taking responsibility.

The program teaches us that we are the only ones who can take care of us. After entering the program we may feel like we're suddenly stripped bare, vulnerable to the whole world of responsibility: bill paying, social obligations, career decisions, health, and fitness.

We may not know all we need to know about taking responsibility for ourselves, but we're learning. Every time we do something on our own, for ourselves, we are that much closer to responsible living.

I can take responsibility for many parts of my life. When I don't know how to do something, I can ask for help from others.

When I hear somebody sigh, "Life is hard," I am always tempted to ask, "Compared to what?"
—*Sydney J. Harris*

We've probably heard all the negative quotations about life. There was also probably a time when we believed them all. Based on the state of our lives at the time, it was probably no surprise that life was difficult and brutal.

Certainly there are many things in life that are harsh and cruel—we see such things in the paper every day. But there are some very wonderful things, too. It's just that we've been conditioned to believe the horrors instead of the wonders.

Today may have been a long, tiring, boring day. But that doesn't mean all days are long, tiring, and boring. There's much good in life that we can see if we let ourselves. We can get off our "life-is-difficult" soapbox and hear the humor, see the smiles, and feel the caring. Life may be difficult at times, but it is also quite fulfilling.

I need to feel that life is good tonight. What event happened today that I can feel good about? Who did I see today that made me feel good?

When something does not insist on being noticed, when we aren't grabbed by the collar or struck on the skull by a presence or an event, we take for granted the very things that most deserve our gratitude.

—Cynthia Ozick

Was today an ordinary day, one filled with the usual events, the same people, the same routine? If nothing unusual or out-of-the-ordinary happened, are we now feeling a little ho-hum about the day's predictable pattern?

It's easy to recognize the extraordinary events in a day—the ones that break the norm, perhaps add a challenge, or a chuckle, or a bit of chaos. We give those events recognition and tend to belittle the events in an ordinary day.

Tonight we can look back over our day and feel gratitude for every minute of it. We can remember our uneventful commute to work, for instance, and feel grateful that we drove in safety. We can recall the people, places, and things now and be grateful they were a part of our day.

Tonight, I will feel grateful for the good in the ordinary.

The world is full of people looking for spectacular happiness while they snub contentment.
—*Doug Larson*

Before we came into the program, our lives were like roller coaster rides. We'd either be on a downward plunge of despair or an upward lift of ecstasy. When we were on a high, it seemed as if nothing could take that feeling away from us. We kept going from high to high and began calling our highs happiness.

Today our lives aren't so dramatic, nor filled with such radical swings. Because we can't equate our happiness with those highs, we are often uncomfortable with feelings that don't include ecstasy or depression. Today we feel contentment, cheerfulness, serenity, and peace.

Just like we do with a pair of new shoes, we need to try on our new feelings. We need to wear them through our daily routines and our nightly schedules. It won't be long before they fit us well. Then, it won't feel so strange when we feel stability and gentleness. We'll soon learn these feelings have always been within our reach. We've just been too afraid to feel them.

Tonight I am grateful to be off the roller coaster. I am unafraid of the content feelings that I have.

When the cards are dealt and you pick up your hand . . . there's nothing you can do except to play it out for whatever it may be worth. And the way you play your hand is free will.
—*Jawaharlal Nehru*

Playing a card game with a winning hand can be joyful. We gain confidence from the cards and play well, knowing we can be successful. But when we pick up a hand that could be a losing one, we may want to walk away from almost certain defeat.

How we play the hand we're dealt each day will determine the outcome. A hand that requires effort, determination, and skill to play well we may see as too difficult. Rather than play it, we may want to pass it to another and draw a new hand.

But we won't be given another hand tonight. We can pick up the cards and use the tools of the program to work through the difficult ones and try to change the hand into a good one. Win or lose, the best way to stay in the game is to play with what we have.

Tonight I can choose not to fold. I'll continue to face what life has given me today and work through things to the best of my ability.

Three ... are my friends: [One] that loves me, [one] that hates me, [one] that is indifferent to me. Who loves me, teaches me tenderness. Who hates me, teaches me caution. Who is indifferent to me, teaches me self-reliance.

—*Ivan Panin*

Not everyone is going to be a best friend. Some people will choose not to know us. Others may dislike us for whatever reason. Yet we can see these people as our friends by realizing each has something to offer.

We may be hurt when we realize not everyone likes us or wants to be our friend. But do we want to be friends with everyone? Certainly there are those we know who bore us, make us angry, or turn us off.

It's okay that everyone isn't our friend. We can learn from the one who dislikes us that there are aspects about our behaviors that some people won't like. We can learn from those who don't care to pursue a friendship that not everyone can be there for us. Such people will also help us appreciate more the special people in our lives who are unquestionably our friends.

I know I have some very special friends in my life. Tonight I can be grateful for their support.

Sickness tells us what we are.

—Proverb

Our lives are made up of many things that define who we are. Our salaries and savings tell how rich we are. Our clothes tell the colors and styles we like. The cars we drive show our tastes and transportation needs. Our homes reflect our family size and the type of furniture we like.

But those are outer, material reflections. We also have inner, emotional reflections that show who we are. Our feelings reflect whether we are happy or sad. Our muscles show whether we are relaxed or stressed. Our health reflects whether we're taking good care of ourselves or not.

Many of our stressful or emotional times are accurately reflected by a cold or flu, or negative thinking. The sick feeling we may have inside about things we are dealing with can erupt into outward signs of sickness. It's okay to be sick, but it's important to look at the sickness and come in touch with what may be going on inside. Our body defines us and expresses this definition in many ways. By noticing all expressions, we are that much more in touch with who we are.

Tonight I can observe myself and the things that define me.

Sometimes I found that in my happy moments I could not believe that I had ever been miserable; I planned for the future as if happiness were all there was. . . .

—Joanna Field

Wouldn't it be great if we could forget all the miserable times or, better still, never have them again?

In the past, our lives have been like a roller coaster ride. The thrill of going up was something we never wanted to end; when we went down, we never imagined we could leave such depths.

We may still have moments of unhappiness, sadness, or despair, but now we have the tools to trust those moments won't be with us for long. And we don't need to desperately clutch at happiness, joy, and serenity like we used to.

Whatever kind of day we have, we can trust that the bad day can get better and the good day will be back again.

Did I have a good day or a bad one? Can I trust that today was okay, no matter what kind of day it was?

*When wealth is lost, nothing is lost; when health
is lost, something is lost; when character is lost,
all is lost.*

— *German proverb*

Imagine being in a foreign country when you suddenly discover you've lost your traveler's checks. At first you may panic and worry, but after a phone call to your bank, reimbursement will be sent. You have lost nothing.

Then imagine you've eaten a new dish that doesn't agree with you. You become so sick and weak that you're bedridden. Your ill health becomes more difficult to cope with, for you must let rest, medicine, and time restore you. For a time, you cannot sightsee and experience all the festivities of the foreign land.

Now imagine you've lost your passport and all forms of identification. To the authorities you are a nameless person who may need to be detained. You have now experienced the biggest loss of all, that of your character and self. Money can be replaced, health can be restored, but losing who you are and what you stand for cannot easily be regained. Hold fast to your self. It is richer than money and more valuable than good health.

Tonight I can hold dear who I am. I need to learn my possessions and my body are mere supports for myself.

*The measure of success is not whether you have
a tough problem to deal with, but whether it's
the same problem you had last year.*
—John Foster Dulles

Have we been wanting to make changes in our relationships, our careers, our education, our behaviors?
What efforts have we made? How much have we
changed in the last year? Have we truly made the
physical, emotional, and spiritual changes we needed?
Or have we only paid lip service to those changes?
There may be many things we want to alter in our
lives. But unless we stop talking and start doing something, those changes won't happen.

We can start by setting a small, easily attainable
goal. For example, we may wish to change our behavior of raising our voice. We might set this goal: "For
the next twenty-four hours, I will not raise my
voice—no matter what buttons are pushed in me or
reactions I have." When that goal is achieved, then set
another small goal. Breaking down each change into
small, easily attainable steps is like working the program: a step-by-step, gradual process toward greater
health and happiness.

---

*I can set at least one easily attainable goal. I will share
that goal with another and ask for help when I need it.*

This is a delicious evening, when the whole body is one sense, and imbibes delight through every pore.

—Henry David Thoreau

Natural beauty can be spectacular. There is the bright, full moon, glowing orange or ethereal white. Perhaps we see it reflected on shimmering waters of a lake, like silver streaks on a cool, black mirror. City lights transform even the smoggiest and grayest of cities into a magical kingdom of colors. The rhythmical sound of rain on a road, cleansing the night air, lulls us into soothing sleep.

If we use our senses to their fullest, we can come closer to our Higher Power. We can open our eyes to the silhouettes of the trees and buildings around us, to the colorful lights. We can listen to bullfrogs croaking, crickets chirping, or the wind howling. Each night we can breathe deeply of the cool, clean air, almost feeling the evening on our face.

Just as our Higher Power created fall foliage, lush forests, and blue skies, so did our Higher Power create beauty in the night. It is up to us to open our senses and take it in.

I will experience the night's beauty. I can be grateful for the night as well as the day.

Anyhow, I say, the God I been praying and writing to is a man. And act just like all the other mens I know. Trifling, forgetful and lowdown.

—Alice Walker,
The Color Purple

When many of us first came into the program and heard the words "God" or "Higher Power," we may have wanted to walk out. We may have thought God a kind of heavenly scorekeeper who lived by "an eye for an eye; a tooth for a tooth." But we learned in the program that Higher Power could be any image we chose. Some of us found it easier to picture a pleasurable image when we thought of God, like a mountain stream. Some of us began conversing with an "invisible" friend. We learned any image we chose was okay, as long as we believed a Power greater than ourselves could restore our sanity.

Some of us may still have trouble with the concept of a Higher Power. If we remember we don't have to hold the negative images we grew up with, it may be easier to create a spiritual image with which we can be comfortable. Our Higher Power can be whatever or whomever we choose because it is a personal belief.

I can remember my Higher Power is my personal belief, not a religious dogma.

The seed of God is in us. Pear seeds grow into pear trees, nut seeds into nut trees, and God seeds into God.

—Meister Eckhart

Often we may feel critical and judgmental about our maturity or personality. When we read we have God seeds within us, we may find that difficult to believe. How can we have the God seeds within us that other people have? It may seem everyone else has more good within them than we have.

Just as we admire certain qualities about other people, so can we admire qualities about ourselves. We need to remember a good critic looks at both the good and the bad. A good critic doesn't pass judgment, but merely assembles the facts to allow others to make judgments.

The seeds that grow pear trees don't yield perfect trees. Some of the fruit is ripe and juicy; some is hard and dry; some fruit never matures. Yet the pear tree will be a good tree if it's tended with care. So it is with us. Every part of us may not be perfect, but with care we can make the best person possible from the God seed that began us.

I can be a healthy, bountiful person if I give myself plenty of care. Tonight I won't give up on me.

Never let your head hang down. Never give up
and sit down and grieve. Find another way. And
don't pray when it rains if you don't pray when
the sun shines.

—Sachel Paige

When children are tired they make their feelings very clear. They just sit down and start to cry. As adults, we may sometimes feel like a child, ready to sit down and give up. But we're not tired children anymore. We're grown-ups, living with responsibilities and duties.

Instead of giving up, we need to find another way of handling responsibilities. To begin with, we can ask for help. There are others who can help with meals, family care, and household duties. We can also rearrange our schedules so we're not doing too much at one time and not enough at other times. Whenever we feel like giving up under the pressure of responsibilities, we can remember there are always solutions. Nothing is cast in stone, unless we want it to be.

Tonight I can begin thinking about making changes in my
responsibilities. I can ask for help and do some re-
arranging so no day is overwhelming.

You have no idea what a poor opinion I have of myself, and how little I deserve it.
—William Gilbert

Can we say "I like me" and really mean it? To say that statement and mean it we have to like everything about ourselves: our good qualities as well as our bad, our appearance, the way we interact with others, the way we express ourselves. We don't have to love everything about us, but we need to learn to like ourselves.

Liking ourselves doesn't mean we approve of certain traits or behaviors. But we can accept them. We don't deserve the low opinion we may have of ourselves. We aren't so bad. We make mistakes as well as everyone else. We aren't the most perfect companion, lover, friend, or parent. Neither is anyone else.

There are very likable people inside us that struggle to change and become better. We deserve to like ourselves for who we are and who we're becoming.

Tonight I will think of at least five qualities about myself I like. I can say "I like me" and mean it.

The sculptor produces the beautiful statue by chipping away such parts of the marble block as are not needed—it is a process of elimination.
—*Elbert Hubbard*

When people set aside items for a yard sale, they tag things no longer needed. When we look at things we might sell, we might be surprised to remember how badly we felt we needed or wanted a particular item. But over time, or because we grew up, we found we could eliminate the once-treasured item from our lives.

We'll find we can do the same process of elimination with our character defects. Some may be impossible to eliminate now for whatever reason. Yet over time, we may find ourselves outgrowing this defect or gathering courage to eliminate it.

Tonight we're on our way to sculpting beautiful people—ourselves. We may have a long way to go in forming our shapes, but we're in no hurry. Every so often we'll eliminate a piece of marble so more of our beautiful shapes are revealed. Before long, we'll have smooth, striking statues for all to behold.

I'm on my way to sculpting a beautiful me. Every day I will sculpt some more and eliminate things I don't need.

The error of the past is the success of the future. A mistake is evidence that someone tried to do something.

—Anonymous

Remember our high school science fairs? There was always one entry that seemed to be everything the judges wanted: it was perfect, innovative, instructive. Yet there were other entries that would also win awards, and we may have wondered why they won. They seemed to be simplistic and maybe messy. So why did they win recognition?

Most often it was because of the effort someone put into the entry. Not every winner has to be the most perfect, most innovative, and most instructive. Some are winners because the person who did them made his or her best effort.

The important thing to know tonight is that it's the effort that counts. We don't have to have all the answers, or act in the most mature way, or be the best friend ever. There is room for error in everything because nothing is gained in perfection the first time around. We can make mistakes because mistakes are sometimes the only way to reach perfection, and to measure how hard we've tried.

Have I made mistakes today? Tonight I can see my mistakes as valuable evidence of my efforts.

Give us to go blithely on our business this day, bring us to our resting beds weary and content and undishonored, and grant us in the end the gift of sleep.

—Robert Louis Stevenson

Tonight, our reward for the day is sleep. To make sleep peaceful and relaxing, and filled with pleasant thoughts, we can spend time gently closing our minds to the day's events.

We can walk down a pleasant, nature-filled path in our minds. With each step we can move farther away from the day's activities and the many tasks we did or left undone. Look around us. We can see lakes and mountains and hear the soothing sounds of a speeding stream. Nothing is important now except peace of mind and the hours ahead in which our minds will be at peace.

Before we shut off the light we can spend a few minutes visualizing our pleasant nature walks. We can think *Let Go and Let God* and feel the day's tensions and pressures fall from our shoulders. Today has been good. We can close our eyes now and let the reward of sleep drift over us.

My day has been good. I have done well. I am satisfied and ready to let sleep overtake me.

*. . . each cycle of the tide is valid; each cycle of
the wave is valid; each cycle of a relationship is
valid.*

—Anne Morrow Lindbergh

Any photograph will show us a moment frozen in
time. Forever after, anyone who views that picture will
see that moment as it was.

Many things in our lives have cycles. Nothing ever
stays the same from one minute to the next. We may
not like change in our relationships, for we may expect that any variation from our happy moments will
mean pain or loss or rejection. Even in a relationship's
dark moments of anger and pain, we may fear changes
that can bring happiness, hope, and success.

Yet change is a valid measurement of growth and
time. It has as natural a rhythm as the ebb and flow of
the ocean, the change of the seasons, the waxing and
waning of the moon, the rise and set of the sun. Tonight, we can be assured that our relationships are
right where they need to be in their natural places.

---

*Tonight help me experience the natural rhythms in my
relationships without fear.*

Worry is a thin stream of fear trickling through the mind. If encouraged, it cuts a channel into which all other thoughts are drained.
—*Arthur Somers Roche*

A trickle of water that drains down the side of a hill poses no problem to the hill, its vegetation, or the people living in the valley. But if that trickle grows into a stream, the water will erode a path, carrying along plants, rocks, and soil, endangering the lives and property of the people in the valley.

When a worry nags us, it is like that trickle. It poses little threat to us and can be stopped at any time because it is so small. But if we let more worrisome thoughts feed into the stream, we will allow it to grow until all of our thoughts and energy are focused on one worry that has attained great power.

We all have things we worry about. But we don't have to give these worries more than passing acknowledgment. The trickles that run through our minds are okay to have. But to keep them at that size, we need to remember what is important to us at this very moment. We don't need to let the worries grow.

I have worries just like everyone else. However, I don't have to dwell upon my worries or make them any bigger than what they are.

What must I do is all that concerns me—not what people think. It is easy in the world to live after the world's opinion; it is easy in solitude to live after our own—but the great man is he who in the midst of the crowd keeps with perfect sweetness the independence of solitude.
—*Ralph Waldo Emerson*

Many times we are like chameleons, changing colors to please others. We may hide our true feelings and pretend to be happy and content, not wanting to hurt someone close.

Chameleons survive because they are adept at hiding from predators. We may feel we are living well when we hide our true feelings. Yet who is seeing the real side of us? Aren't we ignoring our needs and making someone else's more important?

Today we may have changed colors to please others. But we don't have to be chameleons. There are no predators out there—only people, just like us. Their thoughts and feelings may be different from ours, but that's okay. We all have our own brilliant colors to show.

I have beautiful colors to show off. Tonight, I'll remind myself that I do not need to hide.

The height of wisdom is to take things as they are
. . . to endure what we cannot evade.
—*Montaigne*

What are some of the things we dread? As children we probably dreaded school and occasions when we had to dress up. As students we most likely dreaded tests. As adults we may now dread job performance reviews or visits with our parents. We may have other dreads such as going to a dentist or doctor, purchasing a major appliance, or making changes.

Wisdom is the ability to acknowledge the dread and not run from it. It's okay to feel dread: wanting to postpone, feeling sick, having an anxiety attack, becoming dependent on another to help us out. As long as we don't succumb to those feelings—as powerful as they may be—we will endure the dreaded event.

Nothing lasts forever. Job reviews and dentist visits comprise only a portion of a day. If we can accept these dreaded events as inconveniences, we will have a more mature approach to them instead of magnifying them. The steps to overcoming dread are simple: accept, let go, and do it!

Are there events I dread tonight? I can remember the three steps to overcoming dread and work through my feelings.

I still find each day too short for all the thoughts I want to think, all the walks I want to take, all the books I want to read, and all the friends I want to see.

—*John Burroughs*

We may look upon richness as an abundance of wealth. Some of us may believe if we only made more money our problems would be solved. Yet we've also heard the phrase, "Money doesn't buy everything." And, because we know that's true, we may question just how we get the riches in our lives.

If we put aside all the insignificant things, we may find we have more time and attention to pay to important people and things. By focusing on the things most important to us, we would find ourselves with more time to do what we want.

Worrying over minor details, fretting over some misplaced item, or whining about some unobtainable desire only serves to distract us. We can increase the richness in our lives by eliminating whatever robs us of our peace of mind.

Tonight I can choose between wealth and poverty. What can I give up in order to enrich my life?

I offer you no reward for being loyal to me, and surely I do not threaten you with pain, penalty, and dire disaster if you are indifferent to me.
—Elbert Hubbard

We can learn a great deal about unselfish love from a pet. A cat or dog stays with us despite mixed messages of "Come here, I need you," and "Go away, you're bothering me." They're always there for us and expect nothing in return.

Are we as loyal to our friends, or do we demand they be there for us when we need them? If they don't show up, or they let us down, or they give disapproval, do we write them off? Being a friend or having one doesn't mean making demands. It also doesn't mean seeking retaliation if our demands aren't met.

We can allow others to show us friendship without making demands upon them. This means accepting their attention and love, as well as their lack of attention and their silence. Friends are not promises to be kept or admirers to be courted. Friends are blessings. The more we treat them like blessings, the more friends we'll be blessed with.

How well did I treat my friends today? I can let my friends be themselves, showing their own forms of love and respect.

I been so busy thinking about Him I never truly notice nothing God make. Not a blade of corn (how it do that?) not the color purple (where it come from?). Not the little wildflowers. Nothing.
—Alice Walker,
The Color Purple

Each snowflake that falls from the sky has a different pattern. Every fall foliage season is a spectacular pallet of oranges, reds, and yellows. The height of the giant redwoods is astounding. The rainbow after a rainstorm, the camouflage of nature's insects and animals, and the majesty of the mountains are just a few of the natural wonders of the world.

How often do we notice these wonders? How often do we go out of our way to discover a new path, or vary our schedules to include a new hobby, task, or person in our lives?

Tonight we can slow down the pace and notice the things around us. If we can quietly think about these things for a few minutes, then we have meditated upon them and brought ourselves spiritually closer to them. We can begin to notice the creations of our Higher Power and appreciate their beauty.

Am I grateful for the creations of my Higher Power?

The man who goes alone can start today, but he who travels with another must wait till that other is ready.

—Henry David Thoreau

Do we ever change our minds or our plans, depending on what another person says? Maybe we'd like some time alone, but because another wants us to do something else we bow to those wishes. We may even feel lost unless someone provides us with suggestions of things to do.

It's up to us to undertake our own journeys in life. If we're always waiting to see what someone else will do, we'll be waiting forever. We need to make independent choices and decisions without feeling linked to the wishes or desires of others.

Tonight we can begin our journeys by making our choices. Our desires are important, and it's equally important to stick to them no matter what the wishes of another.

It's okay to change my mind and my plans if I wish, choose to be alone, or ask to be with another. The decision is mine to make.

I have accepted fear as a part of life—specifically the fear of change . . . I have gone ahead despite the pounding in the heart that says: turn back. . . .

—Erica Jong

There comes a time in every horror movie when we know something bad is going to happen. We can feel the tension and the pounding of our hearts, and we may want to scream at the actors to alert them of danger. But that's only a movie.

We will feel fear whenever we see darkness and not light. We will feel fear whenever we imagine someone or something is out to get us. Before the program, our lives were filled with many real dangers, yet we may not have seen them as real. Today our lives can be filled with safety, security, and harmony, if we see and face real dangers and not imaginary ones.

Life isn't a horror movie where danger is always lurking around the corner. There isn't some big monster out to grab us. The only fears we have tonight are those that spring forth from the shadows of the unknown.

Tonight I can remember my fears are based on making changes in myself for the better. It's okay to be afraid, as long as I don't let this fear rule—and ruin—my life.

*. . . We look upon Niagara and say, wonderful—
thinking nothing of all that makes its glory and
majesty possible. We look upon a man or woman
of character; we are lost in admiration, but we
omit to consider the thousand influences,
conscious and unconscious, which have gone to
make up the result.*

—*Stephen S. Wise*

We are molded and influenced by countless people, beginning with our parents. Relatives, friends, lovers, co-workers, and neighbors all play a role in making us who we are.

We may wish to blame others for who we are when we see only our negative sides. But we have positive sides, too, that may be admired. And just like our negative sides, people help shape our positive sides.

A lake at the base of a mountain range gets its origin from the highest mountain, when its snowy cap is melted by the sun. This one trickle of melted snow expands into a stream, and then a river, by the countless trickles that feed into it. We, too, are like that lake. We are beautiful as we stand alone. Yet we must remember all the energy that contributed to our beauty.

Tonight I can be grateful for the people who have had a positive influence on me. I am beautiful because they showed me I am.

Listen, or thy tongues will keep thee deaf.
— *Native American proverb*

The Tower of Babel was so named because all the people who were working on it were speaking different languages all at the same time. Construction didn't succeed because no one listened to one another. With all the babbling, it was as if they were deaf.

Most of us have the ability to hear. Yet we don't make full use of it when we choose to talk constantly, bending someone else's ear as we endlessly babble on. We don't use our ability to listen at meetings or to family members or our lover as well as we could. We can become so wrapped up in listening to ourselves that we can't hear anyone else.

It's our choice to remain deaf to other voices but our own. This self-imposed deafness can deprive us of valuable experience and knowledge from those working on the same issues as we are. To improve our hearing, we need to shut our mouths and open our ears. To hear other voices can be music to our ears!

I can stop being deaf to other voices around me. There is a symphony of strength and serenity if I only stop to hear it!

The biggest lesson I've learned ... was that if you have all the fresh water you want to drink and all the food you want to eat, you ought never to complain about anything.
—Eddie Rickenbacker

For almost twenty-one days, Eddie Rickenbacker floated aimlessly in a life raft in the Pacific Ocean. That experience helped him see life differently than most people, because he learned to focus on the basics of happiness and contentment—food and water.

Are we satisfied with what we have, or do we believe happiness is achieved after we have a new appliance, a new car, a different house, more money, a better partner, or two more years of recovery? Are we always looking to the next thing we need before we'll be satisfied, rather than appreciating the basics around us?

Keep it Simple reminds us that we need very little to survive comfortably. Food to eat, a place to live, a way to make money, and a belief in a Higher Power are some of the things our early settlers gave great thanks for. Have we given thanks today for simple things that help us stay happy, healthy, and hopeful?

Tonight, I can give thanks for the many simple blessings around me.

Nobody grows old merely by a number of years. We grow old by deserting our ideals. Years may wrinkle the skin, but to give up enthusiasm wrinkles the soul.

—Samuel Ullman

Today we see more young people in the program. We may look at them and think, "If only I had found the program at their age. I would have so much more time to live and grow."

We've heard it said, "You are as young as you feel." Although physically we may feel not so young, that phrase refers to our state of mind and the belief in our hearts. To feel younger, imagine the program has given us new life, and we can measure our age in terms of our time since recovery.

Perhaps today we are one year old or five or more. In the program we are all children, not adults. We are all learning for the first time how to walk on our own, how to speak our minds, and how to take care of ourselves. We are not old . . . we are but babes ready to learn and grow!

Tonight I can forget my chronological age and think instead of my youth in the program. I am young, with lots of time to grow.

I am sick and tired of the snivelers, the defeated, and the whiners. I am sick and tired of being expected to believe that ugliness is beauty, that melancholy is man's sole pleasure, that delinquency is delight, that laughter is something to be ashamed of.

—John Mason Brown

Every year businesses go through their files, throwing out old information and papers, and reorganizing remaining files. We can do some cleaning of the message files we keep in our heads.

Stored inside us are messages that no longer hold true: "You're a bad person." "You shouldn't show your feelings." "If you cry, you're not a man." "You'll never amount to anything." "Nobody loves you." We can toss out these old messages. We have learned things are not the way those messages claim they are.

We can start new message files: "I'm a nice person." "Crying is a good way to express my feelings." "It's important for me to show how I feel." "I'm doing wonderful things for myself." "People love me." There's no need to hold on to old files when we have wonderful new ones.

I can start weeding out negative messages in my mind. What are some new messages I can put there instead?

Laughing ... stirs up the blood, expands the chest, electrifies the nerves, clears away the cobwebs from the brain, and gives the whole system a cleansing rehabilitation.
—*Anonymous*

One of the greatest gifts the program gives us is the ability to laugh. Laughter is one of the best forms of relaxation. But unless we allow ourselves to see the humorous things in life, we'll have a difficult time bringing out this delightful release.

One way to begin is to practice laughing when we're alone. A loud "ha, ha, ha" while we're driving can startle us at first. But with a little practice we will see the humor in our laugh sessions and laugh without a cue.

There are a lot of things to laugh about in life. But laughter isn't always easy to find. We may have to go out of our way to look for the humor in some situations. We don't have to be comedians to be able to laugh. All we have to do is want to see the other side of life—the humorous side.

Tonight I can try to see things in a humorous light instead of with a heavy, depressing view. There are things that will make me laugh if I try to find them.

If a ship has been sunk, I can't bring it up. If it is going to be sunk, I can't stop it. I can use my time much better working on tomorrow's problem than by fretting about yesterday's.
—Admiral Ernest J. King

Have we ever really thought about the things we cannot change? We may know we can't change things, but we need to personalize that list. What people can't we change? What places? What things?

Until we make a list, we may spin our wheels trying to change the actions or thoughts of others. We may try to control the lives of our children, relatives, or friends. We may attempt to force attitude changes in the boss, teachers, or co-workers. We may even go so far as to believe we can change traffic patterns, the weather, or the past!

Saying we cannot change things is not enough. We need to recognize what people, places, and things we have been trying to change. By listing them, we will recognize there is only one thing in our lives that we can change—ourselves.

Who are the people and what are the things I cannot change? After I list these things, I can begin working on who I can change—myself.

. . . there are hundreds of tasks we feel we must accomplish in the day, but if we do not take them one at a time and let them pass through the day slowly and evenly, as do the grains of sand passing through the narrow neck of the hourglass, then we are bound to break our own physical or mental structure.

—Ted Bengermino

Our mental and physical states at bedtime are important. If we are tense, edgy, and feel a sense of failure and defeat, our sleep will probably be restless and unpeaceful. But if we go to sleep tonight feeling we have put the day to rest in peace and acceptance, our sleep will likely be restorative and refreshing.

What difference does it make if things are left undone tonight? Will it matter ten years from now? Nothing is so important that we should carry tension and worry into our relaxation time. What is important is our ability to accept the day's events by the time we're ready to sleep. The most important thing right now is to get the rest we need to be in good shape for tomorrow. The day is done, and so is the day's work.

I am ready to relax in a peaceful, restful sleep. I can loosen the day's tension from my shoulders and meditate on acceptance.

For every ailment under the sun,
There is a remedy, or there is none;
If there be one, try to find it;
If there is none, never mind it.
—*Mother Goose*

Long ago peddlers sold instant remedies for everything from illness to baldness. "Miracle" cures did a brisk business because people always wanted to try the next instant solution to persistent ailments and problems.

Are we still looking for a miracle cure, one that will make us that person we always wanted to be? Although those peddlers sold a lot of cures, none beat the time-tested methods of assured success for curing worry and woes: plenty of time, a good deal of effort, and an acceptance of things that can't be changed.

There are miracle cures in the program, but they are not instant. In fact, sometimes we can't even feel the restorative powers until months later. But if we continue to take them, the cures we get in the program are guaranteed for life. Our lives can be free from worries and woes with the program.

Tonight I can plan to get a good, healthy dose of the cure by attending a meeting tomorrow, reading literature, or talking with my sponsor.

When we hate our enemies, we give them power over us—power over our sleep, our appetites, and our unhappiness. Our hate is not hurting them at all, but it is turning our days and nights into hellish turmoil.

—Dale Carnegie

Hate is such a strong feeling, and it may be part of our black-and-white way of looking at things: right or wrong, yes or no, now or never, love or hate.

Spending our precious nights nurturing a strong dislike for a co-worker, boss, teacher, parent, former lover, or even a stranger is a waste of time and energy. It becomes an obsession, and we know how easy it is for us to find an obsession and hold on to it dearly.

Instead of making one person our focus, we can think of all the people who are near and dear to us. We can visualize the faces of those who give us strength and hope and comfort and let their images stay in our minds and hearts.

Instead of seeing one face in the crowd, I will see many.

You can observe a lot just by watchin'.
—*Yogi Berra*

Our sight is one of our most valuable senses. We can lose our hearing and have our senses of smell, taste, and touch eliminated, yet our eyes will provide us with all the information we need for hearing, smelling, tasting, and feeling.

We can picture in our minds a person we admire greatly. We can even visualize that person's expressions. We may be able to see that person's confidence, strength, and unity just in those expressions. We can imagine the person's lips moving and, without hearing a voice, we can see by the body movements how the person presents a being full of confidence and hope.

Can we picture ourselves and how we come across to others just by what they see? Are our words trying to mask the sad expression on our faces? Are we honest with how we feel and show this? We can let people observe us and let them see openness and honesty through all their senses.

Can the words I speak reflect who I am? Let me observe others and myself to truly feel the real person within.

Fear less, hope more, eat less, chew more, whine less, breathe more, talk less, say more, love more, and all good things will be yours.
                                                    —*Swedish proverb*

What do we have to do to get better in the program? Our first response may be to list all the healthy things we need to do: detach, meditate, pray, share, make phone calls, go to meetings, do the Steps, use the slogans, change behaviors. We soon have constructed an incredible list of dos and don'ts.

But we can *Keep It Simple.* All we need to do is live *One Day at a Time* in a different way than before. There are many positive things we can do, but we don't need to do them all at once.

Tonight we can just be ourselves. We don't need to make drastic changes or have dramatic mood swings or create radical resolutions. All that is asked of us is just to *Keep It Simple.*

Tonight I don't need to make radical changes. Help me Keep It Simple *in all the changes I want to make.*

Never measure the height of a mountain until you have reached the top. Then you'll see how low it is.

—*Dag Hammarskjöld*

What happens when we try to pick up a shell or pretty rock that's under water? We may have a difficult time with the play of sunlight and the rippling of water. Because we're outside the water looking in, once our hands enter the water our perspective changes.

Many times the overreacting side of our personalities may blow things out of proportion. Mountains become molehills, and vice versa. Because of our sensitivities, we may find it difficult to be objective during certain situations. Because we're taking risks and feeling more vulnerable, we may blindly build unneeded defenses.

We can try to keep our perspectives in line by pausing before reacting. We can ask ourselves to identify what's happening and what action we need to take, if any. Instead of feeling threatened, subjective, or sensitive, we can use the extra time to get the proper perspective on a situation.

Have I blown anything out of proportion today? I can review the situation in order to get the proper perspective.

You want me to succeed so much.
Could you understand if I failed? . . .
Could you love me if I failed?
—*Sister Mary Paul*

What is it we fear the most about success? Sometimes we fear we'll fail. But failure isn't as scary as losing the admiration, respect, or even the love of those we're trying to impress.

We sometimes look outside of ourselves too much for the love, rewards, and approval for our actions. We may feel we're not good enough, so we set nearly impossible feats in which we strive to succeed.

Tonight, we're a success. No matter what we've done or what we'll do, we are a success. If we've set out to do something today and fallen short of our goals, we haven't lost the admiration, respect, or love of those around us. There are those who will love us whether we fail or succeed, for they are the ones who love us for ourselves and believe in us. Their love will always be there.

Who loves me and believes in me? Tonight I can be grateful for their love and belief and know that is the greatest success I can achieve.

The message is, "It's okay if you mess up. You should give yourself a break."
—*Billy Joel*

The song "You're Only Human" was written to help teens eliminate suicide as an option to life's problems. It tells them it's okay to make mistakes. In fact, because we're human, we're supposed to make mistakes.

Mistakes don't last forever. They are small events in the larger master plan of life. While a mistake may hurt another or affect the outcome of a situation, a mistake is not so earth-shattering and catastrophic that we can't learn something from it, forgive ourselves, and let it go.

There's no reason to feel we need to punish ourselves if we do something wrong. It's the mature person who can look at a mistake and shrug it off easily. It's the perfectionistic, people-pleasing person that demands retribution for mistakes and never wants to forget them. Which is easier for us to be?

Tonight I can look at my mistakes and know they are signs of my humanness. It is healthy to make a mistake every once in a while and be able to accept it as a normal part of living.

To get peace, if you want it, make for yourselves nests of pleasant thoughts.

—*John Ruskin*

A bird builds its nest by first searching for the perfect twigs, string, and papers. Then it patiently interweaves these materials until its nest achieves the right shape, size, depth, and warmth. Once completed, the bird ceases its work and spends its time nestled comfortably in its home.

To be at peace with ourselves, we have to construct our own nest. This nest doesn't always have to be a place. It can also be found in freedom from negative thinking. Or it can be a time we set aside solely for our enjoyment and relaxation.

Without this time or space, peace will be difficult to achieve. We may see evidence of this in our schedules that allow plenty of time to do but not enough time to just be. Tonight we can start to set aside moments, rearrange schedules, and give ourselves the chance to make our own nest of pleasant thoughts.

Tonight I can find pleasure in today and relax. What pleasant thoughts can I use to build my nest?

The real voyage of discovery consists not in seeking new landscapes but in having new eyes.
—*Marcel Proust*

How have we felt when we return to our hometowns, childhood homes, old playgrounds, or high schools after years of absence? Suddenly each place isn't as it once seemed because we're looking through the eyes of someone older and changed. Where we once saw our high school through the eyes of students, we now look at it through the eyes of adults—in a much different way.

So it is with all areas of our lives: our jobs, homes, families, friends, or partners. Many of these people and places haven't changed for a long time. Yet, we change every day. Instead of seeing our job as the same old job or our home as the same old home, we can start to look at them differently.

Tonight we don't need to change things on the outside to feel better on the inside. We can change how we look at things from the inside out. We can start to see who and what are outside of us as if we were looking at them for the first time. Tonight the ho-hums in our lives can turn into ah-has just by changing the way we see them.

There may be many things in my life that haven't changed, but I'm not one of them. Tonight I can see them all with new eyes.

*How poor are they who have not patience. What
wound did ever heal but by degrees?*
—*William Shakespeare*

The broken leg, stitched cut, burned arm, sprained
ankle—even the broken heart—all need time to heal.
Such healing is a process of slow steps. Each day finds
the leg, cut, arm, ankle, or heart a little bit stronger—a
little more capable of functioning at full capacity.

The injured football player who paces the sidelines
during the championship game can do nothing for his
team. He must be patient and know the healing process will allow him to resume his position next season.
Those who wish to speed up the healing process are
trapped by powerlessness and loss of control.

Patience is more than a virtue. It's the ultimate test
in powerlessness. Patience means waiting for people,
places, or things beyond our control. Patience means
letting go and trusting that a Higher Power is in control. Without patience, we're like the injured athlete
filled with pain, misery, and stress. With patience, we
become full of acceptance of our current condition
and trust it will change.

*Do I have patience? Tonight I need to practice patience by
letting go and trusting my Higher Power is in control.*

It takes more than a soft pillow to insure sound sleep.

—*Anonymous*

Our minds may be the most difficult part of our bodies to relax. From our toes to our fingertips, we may find we can easily make the limb and torso muscles grow heavy with relaxation. But when it comes to the muscle that exists above our necks, we may find our heads so loaded with facts and feelings that signals to relax get blocked.

If we were to open the top of our heads and see the crammed things as slips of paper, what would we find? On one slip of paper we might see the word guilt. On another, shame. Others might read anger, stress, jealousy, pressure, fear, or distrust.

All these papers do is clog the channels of creativity, fun, and relaxation. When these channels are clogged, even the most comfortable bed and the softest pillow won't help us have a peaceful sleep. To make the most of our relaxation time tonight, we need to place those papers where they belong—in the trash.

Tonight I can do a little "head cleaning" before I go to sleep. Help me remove all the unwanted messages and let the peaceful channels flow free.

The awareness of the ambiguity of one's highest achievements (as well as one's deepest failures) is a definite symptom of maturity.

—Paul Tillich

While we were still living with the effects of the disease, we may have ridden the roller coaster of highs and lows. But once we got off that crazy ride, we learned life isn't so dramatic. Life has its wonderful moments and its not-so-wonderful ones, but on the whole it takes us on a steady ride.

Once we begin to mature in the program, we learn how to become a passenger of life without gripping the rails and strapping ourselves in. Now we can open our eyes for the whole ride, look around us with wonder and appreciation, and feel less breathless about the movement of it all. Life without the highs and lows is a wonderful trip.

Tonight I can feel the quiet pace of my life and not question whether it is normal. I can relax and trust this quiet pace as a sign of my maturity.

A bit of fragrance always clings to the hand that gives you roses.

—Chinese proverb

Remember reading fairy tales where elves would come in the middle of the night to build toys or repair broken dreams or help another have more free time? They would work furiously, yet happily, knowing they were doing something that person really needed or wanted. They asked for no reward; in fact, they didn't even stay long enough to see the surprised, smiling faces. They knew without seeing the results that they were creating happiness and gratefulness in another.

We can do the same thing for others. We can decide to be more caring, to watch for opportunities to reach out to others. We can bring some flowers to a friend. We can remember someone's special treat. We can write a letter or send a card or make a long-distance phone call.

I will brighten the life of another tomorrow, by doing something special and unexpected. I will feel the joy of giving and brighten my day, too!

The secret of being miserable is to have the leisure to bother about whether you are happy or not.

—*George Bernard Shaw*

How much time do we spend thinking about our problems, our pasts, our miseries? We may spend a great deal of time feeling negative feelings. We may even find ourselves thinking miserably in happy, fun situations.

How much time we spend alone may have a direct bearing on time spent thinking miserable thoughts and feeling miserable about our lives and ourselves. Until we can spend time alone with positive feelings, we may need to depend a great deal on others to spend time with us. We need to change our belief that we will never be happy. To do that, we need to learn from others that things do get better. Tonight, it is up to us to spend our time with good thoughts of including others in our lives. This is the antidote to misery.

Tonight I can choose to be miserable or happy. I can plan some positive actions to avoid misery by including friends and the program in my life.

I like trees because they seem more resigned to the way they have to live than other things do.
—Willa Cather

If a tree's soil becomes dry or low in valuable minerals, it can't pull up its roots and move to a better place. Instead, the tree spreads its roots deeper and wider, seeking fertile ground. It makes the surrounding soil richer by dropping dead branches and leaves to mulch the ground below. It remains firm in the wind, bends but doesn't break under the weight of ice and snow, and gives shade, shelter, and nourishment to the ground below.

Beginning tonight, if we think of ourselves as trees firmly placed, we can learn to be more accepting of our surroundings. We can learn to grow no matter how difficult it may seem. Such growth can enrich our lives and make us stronger so we don't break with the weight of problems or difficulties. We, too, can be as strong and enduring as trees.

I can learn to move with the winds of change and bend with the weight of difficulties—and still stand tall and firm.

And this is my way o' looking at it: there's the sperrit o' God in all things and all times—weekday as well as Sunday—and i' the great works and inventions, and i' the figuring and the mechanics. And God helps us with our headpieces and our hands as well as with our souls. . . .

—George Eliot

The concept of a Higher Power may have been difficult for us to understand as children. But many of us still question the existence of anything beyond us that will help us get well.

A Higher Power's existence can be evidenced in many nonreligious ways. The creative gifts given to an artist, people who smile at us and call us friends—these are evidence of a Higher Power.

The Higher Power of the program is an overriding feeling of peace and serenity. We can take in that feeling when we detach, when we say the Serenity Prayer, when we ask for help, even when we breathe deeply and relax. There is a greater Power for all of us who want to believe, whenever we're ready.

I believe I can find peace and serenity in my life. Tonight I can ask for help to find it.

*Avoid friends and followers who are detrimental
to thy peace of mind and spiritual growth.*
—*Tibetan Rosary of Precious Gems*

Who are the friends we love tonight? Are they
healthy in mind, body, and spirit? Do we learn from
them and grow with them? Are they an important part
of our lives?

Through our growth in the program, we may look
at our friends of the past and recognize they were not
the best influences on us. In fact, they may have been
as needy, sick, confused, obsessive, and miserable as
we were. Perhaps that's why they were our friends:
they were just like us. But now we may have different
friends and they may be like us: healthier, happier,
more mature, and more capable.

The people we choose as our friends validate us and
our growth. If we choose to be around unhealthy
people, then we, too, are unhealthy. Yet if we choose to
be around people concerned about their growth, who
ask for help when necessary, who can receive yet also
give, then we are like those people. They are the mirrors through which we see ourselves.

*When I look in the mirror, what do I see? How can I
improve my image and my personal growth?*

*Loneliness is a bitter thing . . . more bitter when
you think you have been freed from it and find it
returning again.*

—Anne Cameron

It is a rare person indeed who never feels lonely.
Even when we are surrounded by co-workers, friends,
or family, we can still feel lonely. Now that we have the
program and our Higher Power, why shouldn't we
have feelings of loneliness? "What's wrong with me?"
we may cry, thinking we are doing something to cause
these feelings.

But feelings of loneliness can reveal our need to get
out more, to be with people. We may be so withdrawn
into ourselves that we cannot see or hear others
around us. Yet they are there. They have been there all
day today, and they will continue to be there for us.

If we listen to ourselves, we will be able to hear our
needs crying out for attention. If we pay attention to
our lonely feelings, we can open ourselves up to the
"cures"—a phone call, a walk with a friend, a meeting,
or a few hugs!

*Help me listen to my loneliness. I can then open myself up
to others.*

Rest is not a matter of doing absolutely nothing.
Rest is repair.
—Daniel W. Josselyn

When we are sick, it is evident we need rest because our bodies tell us so. But when we are healthy, it is more difficult to hear those messages. So we may work overtime, stay up later, or spend more time on chores or projects.

But if we learn to listen to our bodies, we will pick up subtle messages that signal a need for rest. Tight muscles, a backache, a slight headache, and tired eyes are some of those messages. When the batteries wear down in a flashlight, the light becomes dimmer until it finally goes out. Before our "bulbs" go out and we fall victim to ill health, we need to remember our inner batteries can't run without rest.

Resting doesn't necessarily mean doing nothing. Rest is slowing our pace, becoming less active, less tense. Going to a meeting can be restful. Reading literature, watching television or a movie, listening to music, or talking to friends are all forms of rest. Resting recharges our batteries so we can continue to shine bright and strong.

Tonight I will recharge my batteries so I can shine tomorrow.

Life is an experience of ripening. The green fruit has but small resemblance to that which is matured.

—*Charles B. Newcomb*

When a lion cub is born, it bears little resemblance to its adult form. As it matures, it still is a far cry from being king of the jungle. It has tiny teeth, small paws, and a clumsy sense of balance. With training and time for growth, it learns to stalk and kill. Finally, it becomes a full-grown, mature lion with thick mane, long teeth, and powerful claws.

Sometimes we are like that cub. We are acquiring skills, learning to grow emotionally, spiritually, and physically. Our footing may be clumsy, our efforts not always successful. But there are others who are experienced and can show us the way.

There is a lion inside of each of us: strong, sure, and proud. We are growing and maturing toward this final form. Every day our footing becomes a little surer, our confidence greater, and our beliefs in our abilities stronger. Life is a process of growing from cub to lion, and each day takes us closer.

Tonight I can feel the growth within me. I have strength, sureness, and pride that are just beginning to bud.

*We have loved the stars too fondly to be fearful
of the night.*
—Inscription in crypt of Allegheny
Observatory, University of Pittsburgh

Some people so love their work or hobbies that they almost seem to become different people when they're involved with what they love to do. Their voices becomes animated, their eyes light up, and they feel energized all over. What do we have in our lives that makes us feel that way?

If we don't love doing something—just one thing—then we are missing out on an experience that drives us and challenges us to learn and grow.

Loving what we do teaches us much about our abilities. Through the program of recovery, we may be learning we have a great deal of skill and talent we never knew we had. Developing these skills and talents can yield us more pleasure than we've ever had.

What do I love to do? Tonight I can find pleasure in recognizing my skills and talents.

Don't try to saw sawdust.

—*Dale Carnegie*

The pile of sawdust that gathers under our wood-working can never go back to its previous form. The lumber used to build a house can never return to the forest as a tree. That is a law of nature: whatever takes on a new form can never return to its original state. We may believe this statement as a law of nature, but may not believe it also applies to the past.

We can never go back to the past; the past can never become the present. We are not the same people today that we were when we were five years old, ten years old, or twenty years old. If we are always trying to live in the past, then we are trying to saw sawdust. To live in the present, we must work with new pieces of wood and make new piles of sawdust.

Tonight I can stop living in the past and see the present for what it really is: clean, fresh, and new.

It would all be so beautiful if people were just kind . . . what is more wise than to be kind? And what is more kind than to understand?
—*Thomas Tryon*

Sometimes we may think life is pretty unkind. Such a feeling could have started years ago when we were brought up in an alcoholic home. That feeling might have continued as we agonized through our addictions. Now we may even be able to make mental lists of those unkind things in our lives: family, loved ones, bosses, major disappointments, disease. "Life has dealt me a terrible blow!" we may moan.

But kindness can start with us! How many times today could we have smiled instead of frowned? Couldn't we have let someone ahead of us in traffic instead of barreling on by? Perhaps we could have picked up the telephone and spoken a few kind words to a friend or family member.

We can't change the unkindness of today. But we can make changes in how we behave tomorrow.

Is there someone who needs my kindness and understanding? How can I show this kindness?

Nowadays some people expect the door of opportunity to be opened with an electric eye.
—*Anonymous*

"Great Expectations" may be an appropriate title for certain scenes in our lives. If we act a certain way, do certain things, or think in a certain way, we may believe these actions will have an expected reaction. But we'll have a rude awakening when we find this isn't necessarily so.

It's as if we stepped on the automatic doormat to a grocery store when the mat wasn't operating. We'll crash into the door if we expect it to open every time. Similarly, we can't have expectations about the people in our lives or we'll crash into defeat, hurt, and rejection.

It's okay to behave toward others in a loving and kind manner. In return, others may become more kind and loving toward us. This treatment won't come to us because of our expectations, but because others decide to treat us in this way. If we change our expectations, we may receive many pleasant surprises.

Do I expect people to treat me in a way they don't want to? Tonight I can let go of my expectations. What's most important is my behavior.

Our belief at the beginning of a doubtful undertaking is the one thing that insures the successful outcome of our venture.
—*William James*

How often have we heard ourselves say, "Well, I'll try, but I probably won't do it right." We're setting ourselves up for defeat, right from the start. With that much negative energy, certainly our ventures will turn out just the way we predicted. If pessimists had always been right, we would be living differently. We might still believe the world is flat, because Columbus wouldn't have taken his voyage. We might still be reading by candlelight, because Edison wouldn't have invented the light bulb. It would take us days to cross the country, because the Wright brothers would have believed only birds can fly.

Some things we do will succeed, and some will fail. But in order to make successes happen, we need to believe they can occur. And we also need to believe in ourselves, believe that we can make things happen. Since we've lived for so long without faith in ourselves, what will it hurt to give it a try?

Higher Power, help me fill my mind tonight with thoughts of success and a belief in myself.

Love does not consist of gazing at each other but in looking together in the same direction.
—Antoine de Saint-Exupery

When we're addicted to a person all we can see is that person. Time moves slowly when we're apart, but passes quickly when we're together. We may feel panicky during even the most minor of separations and believe that we are fused into one being.

Loving relationships are not made by taking prisoners. Love is neither hypnotism nor possessiveness. Love is simply a sharing between two people. Many times this sharing involves movement in the same direction toward a mutual goal. Even though we're sharing the same path, we're not sharing the same body and mind.

A successful relationship is one in which we feel it would be okay even if we weren't with the other person. To be able to stand alone as firmly as when we're with another means we've found some sense of self-esteem and self-respect. We can love another and, at the same time, love ourselves.

Is my loving relationship healthy? Tonight I can work on my self-esteem and self-respect and trust I am a good person with or without a partner.

The cure for grief is motion.
                                    —*Elbert Hubbard*

Anniversaries of death, separation, and loss are difficult times. We can be feeling fine one month and then suddenly feel tremendous sadness, pain, and anger during the next. A quick look at our calendars may reveal a reason for our feelings, for we may have experienced something particularly trying at that time.

It's okay to relive an event and our feelings about it, as long as we don't wallow in the past or try to use the event as a reason for all our present difficulties. Grieving is a process that can proceed only when we are in motion.

How do we get in motion? We can imagine we're sitting in a small room of horrible-smelling cigar smoke. We can sit there and feel uncomfortable or even nauseous, or we can leave the room. That's how we get in motion—by simply getting up and moving.

Tonight I can move out of my chair of painful memories. I can think of ways to get in motion and cure these sad feelings. Then I can relax and have a peaceful night's sleep.

Faith is the bird that feels the light when the dawn is still dark.

—*Sir Rabindranath Tagore*

The bird that sings long before the sun has risen is strong evidence of faith. For that bird trusts the sky will soon lighten, the sun will rise, and the world will come alive. It is when the bird won't sing at such a time that we know it has lost faith in the great continuum of things.

Even when things seem darkest for us, we can still sing. Even in our grief or loneliness or fear, we can find a voice within us that will help us have faith that all things change, all wounds heal, all is eased through the passage of time.

We hear people tell us things get better. They do. Of that we can be certain, for it's as sure as the rising sun. There isn't a day that won't have light. There isn't a night that won't have a rising sun at its end. There isn't a problem that won't have a solution, a teardrop that won't have a smile, a weary soul that won't be energized once again. Tonight we can sing, for we can have faith in the rising sun.

Things aren't as bad as they may seem tonight. There is hope, because there is always change.

Whatever course you decide upon, there is always someone to tell you you are wrong. There are always difficulties arising which tempt you to believe that your critics are right. To map out a course of action and follow it to an end requires . . . courage.

—*Ralph Waldo Emerson*

When we first entered the program, someone may have said to us, "Oh, you don't have a problem. You don't need that program." That person may have dismissed our reasons with countless excuses, saying that our decision was silly or foolish, that someday we'd come to our senses.

At first we may have believed our critics. The program certainly wasn't easy. Maybe our circumstances weren't as bad as we thought, compared to others'. Maybe we looked around the meeting room and didn't see people of the same age, the same sex, or the same background. Maybe we felt we didn't belong.

But as we became familiar with the Steps and the principles of the program, we realized we could relate to others and benefit from what they had to say. We, too, belonged.

Tonight, help me be grateful for the courage it took for me to stay in the program.

*Let us not look back in anger, nor forward in
fear, but around us in awareness.*
                                        —James Thurber

What is it we fear the most? Going into a grocery
store or going to a gathering of strangers? If we teach
ourselves to look not in fear but in awareness, we
might see the grocery store's well-stocked delicates-
sen or the lovely outfit worn by someone at a social
gathering.

Who makes us angry? Perhaps the boss does, or
maybe a loved one. If we look at him or her not in
anger but in awareness, we might see the boss has
many tensions and pressures, or a loved one is tired
and can't be supportive.

If we look only at our feelings of anger or fear, then
those are all we'll see. But if we look around and become aware of the issues of anger or fear, suddenly the
anger and fear won't be the focus anymore. Through
awareness, we'll learn more about people and we'll
gain a greater understanding of their behaviors.
Through this awareness, we'll change our reactions of
fear and anger to understanding and acceptance.

---

*I can become aware of my feelings and understand them.
Then I can work on changing these feelings for the better.*

If you make an error, use it as a stepping stone to a new idea you might not otherwise have discovered.

—*Anonymous*

Sometimes we struggle so hard to become perfect human beings that we may view any minor errors of the day as earth-shattering mistakes from which we might never recover. Instead of seeing our errors as entirely human and forgivable, we may sink into feelings of hopelessness and despair.

We can choose to berate ourselves for our errors, or we can see such errors as lessons to learn from. When we were in school, our teachers used tests to measure our capacity for learning. Today, life is our test, and our grades depend upon how well we learn from our errors.

Some of our greatest thinkers used their errors to discover medical cures, time-saving inventions, or scientific theories. The errors of today can become just the stepping stones we need to cross the river of recovery tonight.

Did I make any errors today? How can I learn from them tonight?

Consider the postage stamp: its usefulness consists in the ability to stick to one thing until it gets there.

—Josh Billings

We can go to one store and buy an appliance, a shirt, a fishing pole, perfume, shoes, a stereo, and a saber saw. One-stop shopping is convenient, but it has one major drawback. Because of the diversity of products sold, there's no specialization. The sales clerk's knowledge about the saber saw and the shirt will probably be about the same—just enough to sell, but not enough to provide in-depth information.

If we work on several parts of our personalities at once, we'll be like that clerk. To do our best, we need to spend time, brainpower, and perhaps muscle power on just one task. We need to become a specialist in what we're working on for that moment.

If we're hard at work on many changes in our lives, we'll only be setting ourselves up for defeat. The attention we devote to one change deprives another change of the time and effort it needs. To make a change, we need to become a specialist in that change. Then the change we make will be beneficial and lasting.

What is one change I can work on beginning tonight? I will stay focused on that change, giving it my concentrated effort.

When the friendly lights go out, there is a light by which the heart sees.

—*Olga Rosmanith*

Coming home at night to an unlit house or apartment can be frightening. As we frantically grope for a light switch, we may stumble over tables and chairs that seem to have shifted position in the dark. Yet once the lights go on, we feel an instantaneous burst of relief as we once again view our familiar surroundings.

We do not always need bright lights to find our way in the dark. Faith in a Higher Power that watches over us at all times of our lives is our inner light. This light burns as brightly as our belief. If we are filled with fear, doubt, and insecurity, then we will stumble. But if we are filled with faith, hope, and trust, our feet are always secure.

If we can learn to trust that light within us, we will no longer be frightened of the night. We will not have such a panicked need to flutter from light to light. We will be secure in ourselves, no matter where we are.

Tonight I can remember I am the lighter of my internal lamp.

*What [we] usually ask of God . . . is that two
and two not make four.*

—*Anonymous*

Wouldn't it be nice if . . . If only . . . What I wish
would happen is . . . Imagine if . . . I should have . . .
Don't these unfinished statements sound familiar?
They usually occur when we're looking away from the
reality of a situation to the fantasy of what might have
been.

We may do the same wishful thinking in our
prayers. Do we still ask for our Higher Power to make
our parents or child or brother or sister or lover or
spouse stop drinking or using drugs? Do we ask for
material things?

Our Higher Power isn't a fairy godmother sent to us
to grant us any wish we'd like. Our Higher Power
deals in realities, not wishful thinking. We, too, need
to deal in realities when we pray. That way, we have a
much better chance of having our prayers answered.

*How can I make my prayers more real tonight? I can ask
for things I know are possible instead of impossible.*

The great victories of life are oftenest won in a
quiet way, and not with alarms and trumpets.
—*Benjamin N. Cardozo*

How do we know we're getting better? What do we
think will happen when we exhibit mature behavior
and a positive outlook?

Sometimes we may expect too much from recovery.
The successes we have and the achievements we make
will not be greeted by fanfare and celebration. Sometimes we won't get any recognition. We might even get
disapproval for our mature, positive behaviors.

It's up to us to recognize our victories. We can celebrate such joyous times with a smile or a nod, by
making a notation in a journal, or by sharing it at a
meeting or in a telephone call. Victory after victory,
we will come to realize the most important thing
about our achievements is not the recognition but the
peaceful, satisfied feeling we have inside.

What were my victories today? Tonight I can celebrate
these victories with the wonderful feelings of pride,
satisfaction, and good self-esteem.

Live so that you wouldn't be ashamed to sell the family parrot to the town gossip.
—Will Rogers

We may have been brought up to feel a great deal of guilt and shame over the actions of our alcoholic families. As we grew older we may have chosen to act inappropriately toward others so we could continue to feel the guilt and shame that had become so familiar to us.

Are we ashamed or guilty about our behaviors today? Chances are we have so improved our attitudes and our self-image that we now act in mature, responsible ways. We may feel quite proud today about the good people we are becoming.

Today we may feel a lot less fear about our actions. We may be more confident that we aren't antagonizing people anymore or making a spectacle of ourselves. Tonight we can be proud of who we are and project this pride to others.

Tonight I feel I'm on the right path. I'm no longer filled with guilt or shame about my actions. I'm proud of me!

No one can really pull you up very high—you lose your grip on the rope. But on your own two feet you can climb mountains.

—Louis Brandeis

Depending upon people, places, or things to help us live our lives is a sure setup for disappointment and failure. No one person or geographic location or material item can give us answers. None of them can bring us happiness, security, maturity, or faith.

We have been given everything we need to find our own answers. Although today may have been filled with questions, we can remember now that we have the tools we need.

Our Higher Power has brought people to us who we need to hear. Our path has led us onto a well-traveled road with a foundation of strength. By the Grace of God—and our fellow travelers—we can follow this road to the greatest of heights.

How can I use the resources my Higher Power gave me to find my own two feet?

Worry is most apt to ride you ragged not when you are in action, but when the day's work is done. Your imagination can run riot then . . . your mind is like a motor operating without its load.

—James L. Mursell

Each day we may have full-time activities: jobs, school, family, or hobbies. The hours we spend in those activities are usually focused on the tasks at hand. But when they are done and we're left with free time, we may find ourselves cultivating a new interest: worry.

During the day, we are like a train engine. For as long as we stay on the tracks, keeping busy, we move easily. But when the day's activities are done, we are like a derailed engine. The power still makes the wheels spin, but we are going nowhere.

We don't have to be on full speed, going nowhere, as we fill our minds with worry. When the day's work is done on a railroad, the engines are guided onto sidetracks to cool until morning. Tonight we can guide the engines of our minds onto sidetracks of relaxation and rest. We can cool our activities until morning.

I don't need to fill my mind with worry tonight. I can rest and relax my mind by bringing peace to my heart.

We should think seriously before we slam doors, before we burn bridges, before we saw off the limb on which we find ourselves sitting.
—*Richard L. Evans*

Many of us have difficult days. People disappoint us. Events or circumstances upset us. Anger may be our sole feeling at such times. Unfortunately, we may act upon that anger hastily by saying things we later regret, by making shortsighted decisions, or even by slamming a door in someone's face.

Sometimes a slammed door won't open again. Sometimes people we insult or snap at will back off from us. Sometimes decisions we make in anger and haste cannot be changed—or may take considerable time and effort to undo.

Angry moments do not have to erupt into fiery volcanoes. If we learn to sit with our anger awhile until we are calmer and more rational, we can avoid shameful, regretful results. Today's anger does not need to erupt tonight toward any person, place, or thing. Tonight we can let the dust settle and tempers cool while time helps us get things into perspective. We who wait are both wise and mature.

How can I use time to help heal the sores of anger?

I will not meddle with that which I cannot mend.
—Thomas Fuller

Sometimes we can effect change. Speaking up about something, suggesting an improvement, or learning a new skill can bring about a longed-for change. But we have to change ourselves first, not anyone, anywhere, or anyplace else.

We can take a moment now to think of those people or things we tried to change today. Then we can resolve not to keep trying to cause change or keep wishing things could change. If a button falls off our shirt, we can pick up a needle and thread and sew it back on. But if we see someone on the street without a button, we can't change that situation. By looking to ourselves and mending our own fences, we won't so likely try to mend the fences of others.

Tonight I can think of people, places, and things I cannot change. Then I can resolve to leave them alone and work on me.

You who are letting miserable misunderstandings run on from year to year, meaning to clear them up some day . . . if you could only know and see and feel all of a sudden that time is short, how it would break the spell!

—Phillips Brooks

The story of the Hatfields and the McCoys is an intense lesson in unforgiveness. Generation after generation honored a long-standing feud. After a while, no one was quite sure how it all started. What seemed more important was how to continue it.

Are there people in our lives toward whom we feel bitterness or hatred? Why? Do we remember why our gripe with them started? Does it really matter now? What are the benefits of hanging on to feelings of unforgiveness?

It takes so much energy to remain cold and aloof to those people. We can be feeling relaxed and at peace until they walk into a room. Tonight we can ask ourselves if honoring a long-standing feud is wise or just willful.

Am I holding on to feelings of anger or bitterness when it would be wiser to forgive and let go? Tonight I can make a wise choice for my course of action.

When you have shut the doors and darkened your room, remember never to say that you are alone; for God is within, and your genius is within, and what need have they of light to see what you are doing?

—*Epictetus*

As adults we may feel very secretive about the ways in which we fall asleep. Some of us may have a night-light in our room, fall asleep to music, or tightly hug a stuffed animal. Each of these ways is designed to make us feel safer—less alone in the dark.

None of us is ever alone, especially at night. The methods we use to fall asleep peacefully are good, but we need to remember there are always three angels that guard our sleep.

The first angel is our Higher Power. The second is the positive side of our minds that believes in us. The third is the gentle, hopeful spirit within. Whether we know they are there during the day isn't as important as knowing they are there at night. We are at peace in our sleep because they are there to watch over us.

I know I'm never alone at night. My three angels are watching over me. I'm safe tonight and every night.

Life can only be understood backwards, but it must be lived forwards.

—Søren Kierkegaard

One of Mark Twain's most interesting writings states we should live life backwards from the age of eighty to the time we were just a gleam in someone's eye. How much more we'd learn, he felt, if we already knew how to live before we had to.

We may fantasize sometimes about going back with the tools of the program we're using today to our families, our high schools, or our dating years. It may please us to think of how "together" we would be with such tools, knowing what we know now.

But we can't live backwards. Every year we move along in age, experience, maturity, and wisdom. Sometimes we only see such growth on birthdays, when we look back to a year ago at who we were then and who we are now. As our years advance, so do we. Sometimes we need to take a brief look backward in order to see this.

Tonight I'll remember that to see my growth all I have to do is look at where I was a year ago. I have advanced in age, but I've also advanced in wisdom and maturity.

Our main business is not to see what lies dimly at a distance, but to do what lies clearly at hand.
— *Thomas Carlyle*

"Five years down the road,' says Jack, "I want to have a new job, an intimate relationship, and a bigger house. I want to be earning more money and feel better about myself." What nice dreams! But what is Jack doing for himself now?

"My relationship is not going well," sighs Sarah. "This isn't the first time I've been told I have the same character defects. Someday I really want to make changes and be in a warm, supportive relationship. Then I'll be happy." But how can Sarah expect to have a wonderful relationship if she doesn't begin her work now?

"My family is so messed up," declares Leslie, a parent. "No one communicates. If we had a bigger house we wouldn't argue so much or be so disorganized. When Bill and I start making good money, we can look for that dream house." But when will Bill and Leslie work on the family problems they're having now?

Tonight I can begin to see what lies clearly at hand—not a dream or goal years away from now. All I have is right now. Tonight I can build my future foundations by working on me.

I could tell where the lamplighter was by the trail he left behind him.

—Harry Lauder

Before electricity, people were dependent upon lamplighters to light the gas lamps before dark so people could walk about at night in safety. Without light, the streets were dark and ominous—almost impassable.

How many times have we felt as though we were floundering about in the dark, wishing we had a lamplighter to light our way? Many times we may have been afraid to walk alone and became dependent on others to light the way. But they would grow tired. When our dependency became overpowering, we'd look for another lamplighter, and the cycle would repeat itself.

Then we found the program. We've learned we are all lamplighters at one time or another, both for ourselves and for others. Sometimes it may be dark, but we'll soon find another who has traveled that darkened road before. That person will light our way until we can carry our own light. As long as we see ourselves and others as the lamplighters, we will never have to walk alone again.

Help me light someone's path so I won't walk alone.

There seemed to be endless obstacles preventing me from living with my eyes open, but as I gradually followed up clue after clue it seemed that the root cause of them all was fear.
—Joanna Field

How often have we complained that we would be able to do something if only another thing weren't preventing us. "I can't" is our answer when we look around us and see only potential obstacles to accomplishing something. We need to realize, however, that "I can't" is just another way of saying "I fear."

If we took away our fearfulness, think of all we could do. There would be nothing to prevent us from taking risks, trying new things, going new places, becoming more intimate, changing careers, going back to school, taking a Fourth Step inventory, chairing a meeting, or sponsoring a newcomer.

We can change our response of "I can't" to "I'll try." We can take the first step away from our fear toward trying something new. There are no obstacles in our path—only the ones we put there to protect us from things we fear.

Higher Power, help me take the steps to change from "I can't" to "I can."

The nice thing about football is that you have a scoreboard to show how you've done. In other things in life, you don't. At least, not that you can see.

—*Chuck Noll*

When we entered the program, we learned how much blame we placed on others and how much denial was in our lives. Gradually we began to see our teachers, friends, or coaches weren't against us. As time went on, we learned our bosses weren't against us, or our lovers, or our siblings. In time, we may have even stopped blaming our parents.

We have no scoreboard to measure our progress other than the way we feel. If we feel restless, edgy, anxious, or unhappy, we've got some more work to do, and we can begin that now. If we're content, serene, and peaceful, we need to continue the work we're doing.

Life's ball game is with ourselves. Either we will push on and keep in winning form, or we will ignore our needs and fall behind. It is our choice, for we are the captain and the team.

I can ask my coach—my Higher Power—for help to keep me in winning form. Let it begin with me.

All our actions take their hue from the complexion of the heart, as landscapes their variety from light.

—*Francis Bacon*

Tests have proven color and light play a significant role in influencing our moods. Even if we don't believe such statements, we can recall how we feel at the onset of a brilliant sunrise or breathtaking sunset. We can remember how we feel after two or three days of gray, overcast skies. The bright and vibrant colors stimulate our senses, and we react to them differently than we react to gray, dark colors.

The colors we wear and the way we decorate our living spaces are pretty accurate reflections of how we feel about life and ourselves. Sometimes dressing in a more brilliant or a softer color can subtly change our mood from sad to happy. Sometimes imagining we are surrounded by a healing color—one of our favorite colors, perhaps—can help lift our spirits. Just as we give a coloring book and crayons to a child, so can we give ourselves a palette of beautiful colors with which to paint ourselves.

I can create a wonder of colors within me and around me. I can color me beautiful!

Know what you want to do, hold the thought firmly, and do every day what should be done, and every sunset will see you that much nearer the goal.

—*Elbert Hubbard*

Every good story has a beginning, a middle, and an end. The beginning is like our morning, full of newness and promise and hope. This morning was our introduction to a new day, to new people, and to new experiences.

The middle of the story is how our day progressed. It's the actions and events, the dialogue and the locales, and the conflicts of the day. The middle may have been dull and boring, or it could have raced along.

The ending of the story is our evening. Tonight we may have found resolutions to the conflicts of the day or logical endings to some of the promises and hopes of the morning. The story's conclusion is decided by how we want to end our day. Why not end today's story with hope, gratitude, and peace—a happy ending!

How will I end today's story? I can write a happy ending with gratitude for the peace my Higher Power has given me.

I guess we are now small enough to go to bed.
        —Theodore Roosevelt,
        To his soldiers, after
        gazing at the stars one night

Sometimes after a really "up" day we may feel impervious to troubles and problems. We may even feel a bit cocky if others have depended on us for help and assistance and we've been able to provide what they needed.

It's easy to get off on an ego trip by feeling we're the best when we've solved problem after problem. We may even feel superhuman. But we need to shrink back to our proper size.

Some days are good, and we deserve them. But good days don't prove that we're the greatest or that all our problems are solved. Today we did what we needed to do. We may have had a lot of energy and patience to work with. Tonight we can feel grateful for this positive, constructive energy. But we need to remember we're the same size we were this morning. We're human, not superhuman. Tonight everything is where it belongs. The stars are up in the heavens and we're here looking up at them.

Tonight I can pray for the continued ability to have wonderful days and to feel good about myself.

The great gifts are not got by analysis.
— *Ralph Waldo Emerson*

Lovers often reflect on how they met and when they first realized they were in love. They'll play back the tapes of courtship as if they were analyzing instant replays of a sports play. "Yes, it was then when we first knew we were in love," concludes one. The other disagrees: "No, I still didn't know you well enough and wasn't ready."

The bottom line is they fell in love. Whether it was Tuesday or April or morning, what is most important is that they did grow to love each other. Not by analysis did they learn this love, but by accepting the gift of love they had for each other.

Analyzing people, places, or things may be a great way to reminisce, but we need to remember analysis isn't as important as what we've received. We aren't given gifts for any reasons. We're given gifts because that's what gifts are for.

Tonight I can stop analyzing why I have a nice family, a good job, supportive friends, or great meetings. I can accept them all for what they are—gifts to be appreciated.

The turbulent billows of the fretful surface leave
the deep parts of the ocean undisturbed.
— William James

Picture in your mind a calm lake, its surface like glass reflecting the sky and the full trees along its edge. A short distance from shore a flock of geese float smoothly along the surface. With their long necks extended gracefully, they barely create a ripple on the surface of the lake.

That picture is very serene. But below the surface of the water are a bunch of legs furiously churning. This lake scene teaches us a lesson: things are not always as they appear. A smiling face may not reflect a broken heart. A sleeping child may not reflect nightmares being dreamed. An efficient worker may not reflect the nervous approval-seeker. A responsible adult may not reflect the hurting, angry child within.

Tonight we can think about the appearances we reflect to others. Are we like the smoothly floating geese, not letting anyone see our struggles? Tonight, we can learn that keeping up appearances is really for the birds!

I can let down all appearances and let people see how I really feel. I can be honest and show the emotions that are under my surface.

The ideal day never comes. Today is ideal for him who makes it so.
—*Horatio W. Dresser*

What kind of day did we have today? Are we critical of the day's events or circumstances because they didn't meet our expectations? Based on our standards of perfection, will we ever have the perfect day?

There is no such thing as a perfect day. Today happened just the way it was supposed to, with its imperfections as well as its achievements. If it was a lousy day, it was only because we believed it was a lousy day. By the same token, today was a good day because we believed it was, not because the sun was shining or traffic was light or we got paid.

Every day is different. Some days may be enjoyable experiences while others may be difficult to get through. But each day plays an important part in our development. Instead of judging each day like a teacher grading papers, we can see each day as our teacher. What we learn from the day, as well as the attitude we have about it, is our daily lesson.

Tonight, can I see today as my teacher? What did I learn today?

I think one must learn a different, less urgent sense of time here, one that depends more on small amounts than big ones.
—*Sister Mary Paul*

Up until the beginning of our adult lives, our growth depended on big moments: graduation from high school, leaving home, marriage, or entry into the job force. Now that we're adults, we still may have expectations that our lives will be composed of big moments.

But things aren't always so momentous. Job promotions happen over time, as do salary increases. The move from apartment living to ownership of a condominium or house comes after years of saving or years of training for the job with the big salary.

It's important to take our time and savor the smaller moments. Those are the moments we sometimes don't pay attention to because they seem minor and inconsequential when compared to bigger moments. Little moments, like small gift packages, can contain the richest and most satisfying rewards.

What are some of the small but precious moments that happened today? Tonight I can appreciate their rewards, even if they're not the biggest I could get.

People who fly into a rage always make a bad landing.

—*Will Rogers*

We may have learned rage at a very early age from an alcoholic parent. We may have found we could manipulate people and distance them by taking off at them like a rocket. We found they had no choice but to take cover or speedily undo what they had done to make us angry.

Today, we may feel a need to fly into a rage because we fear someone will see our human, vulnerable side. Now that we're dealing in feelings, our rage may simply be a symptom of our own frustration in the slow process of recovery.

If a mirror were placed in front of us during one of our rages, we probably wouldn't recognize the person in the reflection. We can do far more harm than good, more damage than repair, and generate more feelings of dislike than like. Do we need to fly into a rage anymore? Tonight we can treat raging behavior as a thing of the past and move on to mature, constructive behavior.

Do I remember my last rage? What did it accomplish? Tonight I can work on new scenarios for old, immature behaviors.

If you are too busy to pray, you are too busy.
—*Anonymous*

Our growth depends on our mental, physical, and spiritual health. Yet too often we may spend more time on physical and mental growth than on spiritual growth. When this happens, all three suffer.

Through recovery, we may find we've been able to set aside time for hobbies and relaxation and for eating right and getting enough rest. Yet our spiritual side may be easily sacrificed due to time constraints. A little extra sleep in the morning may mean we have to skip our morning prayer and meditation. A long night of socializing, and our sleepy minds may opt for rest rather than a few moments of prayer.

When we start to cut back or postpone our spiritual times, we're eventually going to harm our mental and physical sides. We need to allow time for prayer and meditation and be able to stick to that time—no matter what!

Do I pray on a regular basis? Tonight let me spend time in prayer and meditation to benefit my mental and physical health.

I could almost dislike the [person] who refuses to plant walnut trees because they do not bear fruit till the second generation. . . .
—*Sir Walter Scott*

There once was a man who wanted to give up his high-salary job to start a Christmas tree farm. He told his friends about his dream. The first thing they asked him is how much money would he make. "A lot," he said, "once it gets started." "How long will that take?" they wondered. "Years," was his reply. "First I have to purchase the land, then prepare the soil, then plant the seedlings, then tend them with care until they mature. By the time I'm forty-five," he concluded, "I'll have my first Christmas trees to sell."

None of his friends could understand why he would want to take a risk on such a long-term venture. But deep down inside he knew this was his dream and this would make him happy. It didn't matter how long it took for him to get what he wanted. What was important was that he was working on his dream.

Do I have any long-range dreams I believe will never happen because they'll take too long? Tonight I can visualize my dream and take the first step toward making it happen.

There are three things that only God knows: the beginning of things, the cause of things, and the end of things.

—*Welsh proverb*

We learn when we enter the program that we didn't cause our disease, we can't control it, and we can't cure it. Those are the only answers we're given. It's up to us, in our hearts, to place trust and faith that a Power greater than ourselves will take care of the rest of the answers.

Many times we may feel overwhelmed by the disease. We may want to scream at the unfairness of the changes we have to make and at the patience and detachment required of us. We find it's not enough to confront the root of our problems; now we need to look at more than just the problem. But we don't have to do all the work in one night. Tonight we can find relaxation amidst the effects of the disease. There's hope tonight, if we'll only open our hearts to believe that.

Tonight I can trust I don't need to feel overwhelmed by my disease. My Higher Power won't ever give me any more than I can handle.

In the midst of winter, I finally learned there was in me an invincible summer.
—*Albert Camus*

When things seem to be going badly and everyone appears to be against us, what do we see? Do we think things will never get better, or is there a ray of hope inside us that believes everything will soon be okay?

In the midst of a long, cold winter, we might only see the gray skies, feel only the biting chill, hear only the crunch of our feet on the frozen earth. Wintertime can be compared to the bottom we first had to hit before we entered the program—a gray, dreary, hopeless, emotional freeze.

Yet we've learned there is hope. Each day of recovery has warmed the emotional chill and brought new life back into our bodies. We can now trust that even in the darkest and coldest of times, there is a warm glowing ray of hope and faith all around us.

I trust there is hope for even the most hopeless of situations. Tonight I have great faith in the healing of the program.

To make one pound of honey one bee would need to travel 50,000 miles, more than twice the distance around the globe. . . . A single teaspoon of honey in six weeks is a bee's entire life quota.
—Margaret T. Applegarth

A grandmother watched her grandchild open birthday presents. All around the child were toys and records and books that had brought smiles to the child's eyes. But after the child opened the large box and saw what was in it, the smile faded.

"What is it?" the child asked. "It's a quilt made to show the story of your eleven years," the grandmother said. "Here's your very first step and here's the first time you lost a tooth. Here's your first time swimming and here's the birth of your baby brother. Each picture shows you growing and maturing. It has taken me eleven years to make this quilt for you, but you will have that quilt for the rest of your life."

The child is now an adult, but goes to sleep every night under a quilt filled with memories of her early life and the loving patience of her grandmother.

Tonight I need to remember the most special things take time to become special.

We come into this world crying while all around us are smiling. May we so live that we go out of this world smiling while everybody around us is weeping.

—Persian proverb

Do we matter to others? Have our lives touched the lives of others? Do we think of ourselves as important and worthwhile?

There are many lives we touch in a day, a week, months, or years. Each of these lives was meant to touch ours. We are meant to exist. We are children of our Higher Power and are watched constantly with love and concern.

We do matter to those around us. Birth, as well as death, heralds the entrance and the exit of a life filled with meaning and purpose. We were meant to be here now, not only for ourselves but for the many lives around us. Our lives are important and worthwhile to all the people we know.

Help me see tonight that my life matters. Just as others have touched me, so have I touched the lives of others.

There is more to life than increasing its speed.
—*Mahatma Gandhi*

We live in an age of instant coffee, one-minute managers, and same-day mail delivery. The speed of living seems to increase every year with improved methods of communication, travel, and manufacturing. Because of this we may feel our daily work in the program and the subtle changes in our behavior are not fast enough. How can we keep pace with the world if we're spending years on recovery?

It is the quality of a thing that is important. Instant coffee is a great convenience, but brewed coffee tastes better. Driving in the fast lane all the way to a destination will get us there faster, but we won't enjoy much of the scenery we pass through.

Life isn't a race won by the fastest. If we set a goal and don't attain it within the time frame we set, we do not fail, we readjust our schedule. Living to the fullest doesn't mean living in the fast lane. It means taking the scenic route, stopping often to appreciate the view, and sharing the ride.

I can slow down my pace and appreciate the road I travel by taking my time and meeting fellow travelers.

Lo! in the middle of the wood,
The folded leaf is wooed from out
  the bud. . . .
With winds upon the branch,
  and there
Grows green and broad,
  and takes no care.
                    —*Alfred, Lord Tennyson*

What does it take for us to be drawn out of our-selves? So many of us have retreated inwardly and are afraid to open up in social situations. We may refuse invitations to gatherings, may be afraid to meet new people, and may want to remain in uncomfortable but stable situations.

When a plant grows a new leaf, we see evidence of a shoot. Then we see the leaf grow longer, curled tight like a cigar. Finally, with nourishment and safety, it be-gins to unfurl. This leaf supports new life, and the healthy plant grows.

We, too, are like that new leaf. As we grow, we learn there are environments where we can open up and be safe. It's okay to close up when there are people or sit-uations around us that are unhealthy. But we need not fear everybody or everything. We can be safe. We can proudly unfurl ourselves for all to see.

Am I withdrawn because of fear? Tonight I can find a safe person, place, or thing and open myself up in safety.

*Happiness grows in our own firesides and is not
to be picked in strangers' gardens.*
—Douglas Jerrold

The old saying "The grass is always greener on the other side of the fence" is an appropriate sentiment for envious people. When we look at another couple or another family, we may only see the good points. We may look for the same good points in our relationships and families and not find them. We then conclude our happiness, security, and contentment can only occur if we have what others have.

In an old comedy routine, a restaurant customer points to another diner and says to the waiter, "I'll have what she's having." The waiter immediately takes the half-eaten food from the other diner and gives it to him. However, we can't take the good things that others have, nor can we share them. We can only learn from them, making things better in our relationships and families. Only we can make things good.

---

*Have I been envious of other people and what they have?
Tonight I can discover what good I'd like to have in my life.
Then I can take steps to bring this good from within me.*

Life is made up of sobs, sniffles, and smiles, with sniffles predominating.

—O. Henry

The balance in life places us between happiness and sadness. Life can't always be ecstatically happy and free from woe, just as it isn't always miserably unhappy. Somewhere in the middle is a gray area where neither smiles nor sobs predominate.

Living life on its terms means accepting the events life brings without overreacting with ecstacy or depression. Acceptance sometimes means we may not feel happy and we may not feel sad—we may just feel. This is the middle ground of feeling that isn't high or low—it seems indefinable.

We don't always have to feel great. Sometimes we can just feel okay. Accepting that middle-of-the-road feeling and not trying to analyze it or define it gives us the freedom to have gray areas in our lives. And sometimes it is the gray area that keeps us from bouncing off walls or riding an emotional roller coaster. Accepting the gray area can give us sanity.

Tonight I can find the gray area in my life and realize not everything has to be good or bad—sometimes it can just be.

Every year I live I am more convinced that the waste of life lies in the love we have not given, the powers we have not used, the selfish prudence that will miss nothing, and which, shirking pain, misses happiness as well.
—Mary Cholomondeley

When we were children our teachers or parents would talk about realizing our full potential. "He's a bright child," they might have said, "but he's not working up to his full potential." What is our full potential? And how do we realize it?

We all have certain abilities. With these we can learn, play, love, mature, take risks, make decisions, and speak our minds. Before the program, we may not have developed abilities to do some of these things.

When we avoid developing an ability, we are not realizing our full potential. If we don't learn to play, we lose social skills and the fun-oriented part of us. If we don't work on our capacity to love, we lose emotional and spiritual growth. By growing to our full potential, we can live life as whole people.

I can begin to include those long-ignored areas and take the first step to becoming a complete and whole person.

I do not know what I appear to the world, but to myself I seem to have been only . . . playing on the seashore . . . whilst the great ocean of truth lay all undiscovered before me.
—Sir Isaac Newton

Before the program we chose to see only what we wanted and turned away from any distractions. We may have been aware of obsessive or addictive problems, but those were off to our left or right. We may have seen the emotional or physical breakdown of a person or family, but this was also off to the side. What lay ahead was just getting through a day and on to a future we hoped would be better.

The program has helped us deal with the problems we always put off. Today we know we must meet every problem face-to-face without running away or avoiding it. What lies ahead of us is no longer as important as what lies right in front of us.

Are there issues I've been avoiding? Tonight I can take one of those issues and see it clearly. I will be unafraid to meet the challenge.

A hug is a perfect gift—one size fits all, and nobody minds if you exchange it.

—Ivern Ball

In the past many of us may have feared physical expressions of friendship. A hug, a touch, or a friend's gentle nudge may have made us want to back away. Or we may have misinterpreted such expressions as overtures to more physical contact. All we knew is that those hugs or touches were confusing.

When we came into the program we saw many people hugging or holding hands in the circle at the end of a meeting. We may even remember the first time someone hugged us; their arms encircled us as our arms lay stiff by our sides. "What can this person possibly mean by hugging me?" we may have thought.

As time went on and we received more hugs, we realized they didn't hurt. It didn't mean someone wanted us sexually; it just meant somebody liked us and wanted to show us that. Pretty soon we started giving hugs instead of just receiving them. We learned to trust them and soon let ourselves feel the wonderful love that encircled us each time we were given one.

I can give a hug to someone I care about. Maybe I can get a hug too!

Our weak and negative states leave us open to 'take on' outside prevailing conditions. . . . We are shaken with the wind and float with the current because we present the negative.
—Henry Wood

A bad day usually begins badly. All it takes sometimes is one thing to go wrong and we run to our battle stations for the rest of the day. Then it seems all that ever comes our way are more bad things. By the end of the day, we're glad it's over.

But our day didn't have to go badly if only we had detached right from the start. Instead of believing we were victims of an unset alarm clock, a ripped shirt, unpressed pants, an angry partner, demanding children, or burnt toast, we could have accepted the upsets and let go of them.

Life is so much better when we aren't drowning in the upsets around us. We don't have to absorb the antics of others or get caught up in the material and mechanical inconveniences. A sure sign of maturity is being able to accept an upset for a few minutes and then let it go.

Tonight, I can let go of minor hassles and upsets and enjoy what lies ahead tomorrow.

When nothing seems to help, I go and look at a stonecutter hammering away at his rock perhaps a hundred times without as much as a crack showing in it. Yet at the hundred and first blow it will split in two, and I know it was not that blow that did it—but all that had gone before.
—*Jacob Riis*

Many times we may hear at a meeting that the length of time in the program isn't as important as the quality of the work we do. Someone with five years of recovery isn't necessarily healthier than someone with three years of recovery.

No one accomplishes everything within a mere amount of time. The greatest achievements are the results of accumulated experience, maturity, and the application of healthy principles.

Today is just a brief entry in our daily journals of recovery. What we do tonight may not draw all the loose ends of our lives together, but may tighten one or two a little more. Tomorrow holds great promise for us if we can see it as another page in our lives instead of as the whole book.

Higher Power, help me forget my destination and remember instead the joy of journeying toward that place.

I observe myself and so I come to know others.
—*Lao-tzu*

If we could view a film of ourselves at the end of the day, we would see ourselves as others see us. We would notice our facial expressions and tone of voice and body language. We would be able to see our actions and reactions. We could study ourselves closely and learn so much more.

How wonderful it would be if we could take an equally close view of those around us! Think of how much we could learn about those close to us if only we paid attention to their facial expressions, their tone of voice, and their body language. We would get to know them and understand them so much sooner if we only paid attention to them the way we sometimes pay attention to ourselves.

If we observe ourselves, we will be able to understand the same actions and reactions in others. The mirror we place before ourselves is but a reflection of those around us.

Can I take the time tonight to observe my actions? How can I use such insight to learn about other people?

Tears may linger at nightfall, but joy comes in the morning. Carefree as I was, I had said, 'I can never be shaken.' But, Lord, it was Thy will to shake my mountain refuge. . . .

—*from Psalm 30*

A great force has shaken us from our caves of isolation. We may have first felt this force at our first meeting. Somehow, we knew we had made the right choice. We belonged.

We next felt this force during a time of incredible need and fear. We may have wanted to run to the farthest reaches of our caves, but once again we felt something telling us to stay vulnerable and remain exposed. We may then have fallen to our knees or simply closed our eyes and silently asked for help.

Our prayers have been answered. Today we know we always have that cave to run into, but we seem to need it less. The great force that shook us from our refuge also gave us refuge. Tonight—as always—we are safe and secure as we stand exposed to the world.

―――――――――――

There is a great force in my life who has saved me from isolation, desolation, and despair. I feel wonderful because of this!

Call on God, but row away from the rocks.
—Indian proverb

Wouldn't it be foolish if we sat in our room tonight and moaned about how dark it is? All we would have to do is reach over and turn on the light. Yet aren't there times when we call on God to help us when we can really help ourselves?

Establishing a conscious contact with our Higher Power doesn't mean we're going to build a dependency on this Power. This Being doesn't exist for us to make request after request for things we can do ourselves. It's okay to ask for God's safety and guidance in the midst of difficult situations, but it's up to us to take the initiative for our own safety and well-being.

Whenever we need guidance, safety, security, peace, and strength, we can certainly call on our Higher Power. But let's make sure we take responsibility when it's needed. God works through us, not *for* us.

What can I take responsibility for in my life tonight? Help me help myself.

One cannot step twice in the same river, for fresh waters are forever flowing around us.
—Heraclitus

Do we sometimes feel bored with our lives? Do we feel like we're doing the same things, following the same schedules, working to get out of the same rut we've been trying to change for a long time? Do we wish to make changes, but don't know where to start?

Imagine living in front of a wide, picturesque river. In the living room of the house is a spacious window that allows a magnificent view of the river. Every day we might see this same scene and believe it is never-changing. But in reality, it is ever-changing.

Each day we see with new eyes. And each day nature astounds us with newness and growth. That water we're watching flow by today isn't the same water we saw yesterday. A stick thrown into the water yesterday is far downstream today. We can see this river in two ways: stagnant or flowing. So too can we see our lives.

Tonight I can look at my life as if it were a river, always changing as it flows.

There are always two voices sounding in our ears—the voice of fear and the voice of confidence. One is the clamor of the senses, the other is the whispering of the higher self.
—*Charles B. Newcomb*

Sometimes we may wish others could hear the station our heads are tuned to. When someone says, "You look nice," our station says, "They're only saying that to get a ride to town." When someone says, "You're fun to be with," our station broadcasts, "If they only knew what a bummer you really are."

The host of our station is Fear; his assistants are Doubt and Insecurity. The trio is always on our airwaves, ready to shoot down any good vibrations we receive. If we start to believe we are good people, then we'll put them out of business.

We can let a new voice onto the airways—Trust. When we hear, "You look nice," Trust can say, "You've been trying to improve your appearance and someone noticed!" If we learn to listen to Trust, we will hear affirmations and motivating statements. With Trust we will always hear the Truth.

Tonight, I will believe I am a much better person than Fear, Doubt, and Insecurity would have me believe.

When it gets dark enough, you can see the stars.
—*Lee Salk*

The tiny points of light in the darkened sky have long been used to plot navigational courses. In fact, sailors trust the stars even more than their most sophisticated instruments. We, too, can look at the sky and find reassurance in its light.

Each star in the sky has meaning. Whether it's part of a major constellation or merely a pulsating, burning mass in the sky, there is a reason for that star to be there.

We are also stars in the night. We are not alone, for we share the expansive heavens with those around us, whether our nearest neighbor is one floor above us or miles away. We are all here for a purpose.

I know I am not alone tonight, for I can see the stars.

Our daily thoughts should be elevated above the ceiling.

—W. W. Loflin

How optimistic are we? Do we see problems as solvable or impossible? Do we see our abilities as expanding or limited? Do we set goals for ourselves, or do we feel goals are unattainable?

Not everyone can scale the highest mountain or find the *Titanic* or survive great disasters. We can't all be president of the country or director of our department. But elevating our daily thoughts above the ceiling doesn't mean we have to strive for recognition or undertake the most difficult tasks. All we really have to do is believe we are good people, capable of enjoying health and happiness. That belief can buoy us up against any obstacle.

We can learn to raise our thoughts whenever they start to go down. First, we can say we are inherently good. Then we can show others our goodness by being kind, friendly, and helpful. Finally, we can ask that our spirits be kept high by the help of our Higher Power. By doing these things, there is no limit to how good we can feel.

I can learn to raise my thoughts when they start to go down.

Do what you can, with what you have, where you are.

—*Theodore Roosevelt*

Suppose we were walking down a street when someone came over to us and said, "I want you for our Olympic volleyball team." We may protest, saying we haven't had the training or haven't developed the skills or even allowed time for this to happen.

Yet we may treat the program as a different kind of example. We may jump right in and expect we'll grasp all the Steps and slogans, suddenly have a marvelous relationship with our Higher Power, and be ready to sponsor every fledgling that walks through the door.

We can't join the Olympics today, and we certainly can't expect to master the work of the program today either. Each takes a great deal of time to develop the necessary skills. Each requires a dedication and perseverance that strengthen us as we grow stronger and more confident. Each requires us to feel like we're part of a team, which can't happen unless we meet all the members of the team and work with them. Tonight we're doing the best we can, with what we have, right where we are in recovery.

Tonight I can participate as a member of an active recovery team, but I'm not ready yet to be the most valuable player. I need more time to work with myself and the team.

Free will is not the liberty to do whatever one likes, but the power of doing whatever one sees ought to be done, even in the very face of otherwise overwhelming impulse.
—George MacDonald

There are certain things we cannot do, whether they are restricted by law, are moral issues, or are safety concerns. We may know this now, but in the past this fact may have meant little to us. We may have driven drunk, beaten partners, or verbally or sexually abused our children.

Free will doesn't mean we can do anything we please. Free will means doing things like changing bad tempers, drinking habits, or unacceptable behaviors. With free will, we have the choice to make changes, even though they may be difficult.

Nothing is impossible if it is within our control. We can use free will to opt for change and improvement. With free will, we can choose when and how we will change. If we choose, we can begin tonight.

Are there changes or improvements I can make in my life? Help me know I'm free to change these things whenever I'm ready.

*One never notices what has been done; one can
only see what remains to be done.*
— Marie Curie

Here's a familiar scene: Several people have come to
our homes ready to sit down to a turkey dinner with
all the fixings. In the kitchen is a dirty oven, messy
pots and pans, cluttered counters. Which do we think
about — the wonderful dinner we have prepared for
family and friends or the kitchen?

Many times we notice what has to be done, not
what has already been done. When we first came into
the program, we learned we had so much to do: detaching, admitting, accepting, working the Steps,
working on ourselves. We may have felt overwhelmed
at what needed to be done, but old-timers may have
pointed out what we already had done — we came to
the program to find help.

Tonight, are we thinking about tomorrow or a week
from now? There are many things left for us to do. But
for right now, we can look at what we have accomplished in our lives, our careers, our families. We have
done so much, if we can only recognize it.

---

*Tonight I can give myself credit for all the growth and
gains. I have done well!*

Constant togetherness is fine—but only for Siamese twins.

—Victoria Billings

Fusion in relationships can be self-destructive. Bonding so tightly with one person, with little time spent apart, is a perfect setup to addiction. When we become addicted to a person, we can be as desperate and suffering as an addict without a fix.

Growing up, we may have spent hours fantasizing about how wonderful relationships were. We may have placed so much hope in dreams of a perfect relationship that once we met someone, we unconsciously smothered the other person and ourselves in togetherness. We may have believed time spent apart meant our partner didn't love us or care to be with us.

Each flower in a garden has a separate set of roots, separate stems, leaves, and buds. Although the flowers may be the same variety, each is different in a subtle way. Similarly, we grow with our partner, like two separate flowers sharing the same garden. Our roots may intertwine and our leaves touch, yet we still grow and flourish separately from the other.

Tonight I can spend time flourishing on my own, relaxing for a peaceful night's sleep.

And if you but listen in the stillness of the night you shall hear. . . . It is Thy urge in us that would turn our nights, which are Thine, into days, which are Thine also.

—Kahlil Gibran

How much would we benefit from the program if we went to meetings with cotton stuffed in our ears? We could use the Steps and read the literature, but how would we learn from others about the strength, hope, and experience of the program?

Listen and Learn may be one of the hardest slogans for us to follow. Many times we come to meetings ready to dump our problems on the group. Sometimes we sit in judgment of those around us. Each of us, no matter what our background or age, shares a commonality. Each of us has something important to share, whether the words be delivered eloquently or with humor, sadness, or simplicity.

We can pause before we speak to listen to others. By opening our ears, we are opening our minds to learn about ourselves through the words of others.

Can I listen to those around me? What can I learn that might help me?

The best prayers have often more groans than words.

—*John Bunyan*

Sometimes we may find it difficult to put into words the thought we'd like to send to our Higher Power. After a day filled with a wide array of emotions, we may find it difficult to summarize in our evening prayers words that will convey our deepest thoughts and innermost reflections.

Rather than attempt to find the words, we can use actions and thoughts to communicate. Our prayers can be filled with visualizations of how we'd like things to be. Our prayers can be a time to cry or yell.

However we're feeling tonight, there's no set of rules for prayer form. We don't have to say, "Higher Power, I'm in pain." We can cry and just as easily and clearly communicate hurt and pain. Unlike people, our Higher Power is a mind reader who always knows how we feel and what we need.

Tonight I don't have to struggle to find the right words for my prayers. How I feel is my best prayer.

I had the blues because I had no shoes, until upon the street I met a man who had no feet.
—Harold Abbott

A young man traveled to the city to apply for jobs. But first he wanted to buy new shoes to assure a good impression. He was so intent on getting to a shoe store that he nearly tripped over another man. This man had no legs and was sitting on a board with wheels, pushing his way along the sidewalk when the two had bumped. But the accident in no way slowed down the disabled man; he waved a cheery greeting to the young man and traveled on.

How often are we so caught up in petty trifles that we don't notice others? The young man so concerned with shoes and a future job learned some people don't have to worry about shoes.

What did we notice today? If we think back to today's events, can we remember little details about people, recall smiles and laughter, or recollect snatches of conversation? We can take time to notice more than our shoes.

Sometimes I pay too much attention to my own issues. Help me notice other people and remember the time I spend with them.

Life consists of opposites in balance.
—*Marian Zimmer Bradley*

Remember playing on a seesaw and trying to achieve the balance that meant we and our friends could sit on opposite ends of the board, suspended in the air without the board moving up or down? To achieve such a balance we had to have only one thing in common with our friend: similar body weight.

Tonight we're still on that seesaw. We've spent our day trying to balance all that came our way. Some things may have weighed us down; others may have buoyed us in the air. Through living each day, we've learned that neither the high nor the low stays around long enough to tip the balance too far.

No matter what sits down on the opposite end of our board of life, we need to remember achieving balance is the important thing. When we are balanced, it means we have equalized both the good and the bad with our strength, hope, faith, and security.

The center of the board of life never moves. Help me to keep this center within me tonight.

A satisfied flower is one whose petals are about to fall. The most beautiful rose is one hardly more than a bud wherein the pangs and ecstacies of desire are working for larger and finer growth.

—*Carl Sandburg*

Every one of us in the program is a flower in a beautiful garden. The ones who move down the road of recovery are blooming right and strong. The newcomer and short-timers are just buds, soon to open in a burst of energy and color.

Our Higher Power tends this garden and provides us with room to grow, rich soil in which to root, ample nourishment, and the company of others. We are not all alike in this garden. We each bloom a different color, have a different petal pattern, and release our own fragrance. Yet our sensuous mixture yields an amazing scene of color, fragrance, and life.

At times we may feel uncomfortable in the garden. We may not feel as wise as some of the older flowers and may think our newness is still too bright. Yet we all belong and we will all be nourished as long as we are within the garden walls.

Do I believe I am unique and beautiful? I will let myself be part of the uniqueness and beauty in the program.

How vastly different a troubled question looks to us at noonday and at midnight. We flinch in the hours of darkness from a problem we can meet bravely when we are on our feet, and under the momentum of the noonday vigor.
—*Charles B. Newcomb*

We've often heard the phrase, "Things will look better in the morning." Somehow in the light of day, in the hustle and bustle of routines, our problems seem to recede from the shores of our minds. But as the hours turn from day to night, shadows lengthen, the stream of life stills, and our problems seem ready to wash up once again at our doors.

Perhaps we trust the day more because of the light and nature's rhythm. As night the darkness shrouds our vision, nature stops its movement, and people seem to be on their own rhythms. Yet we can trust the night by depending upon the light of the program and the natural flow extolled by the slogans. We can create our own rhythm and clear vision to see our way through a problem. Tonight can be secure to us if we will only trust.

I can work out solutions to my problems tonight as easily as if I were in the light of day by using the tools of the program.

The glory of friendship is not the outstretched hand, nor the kindly smile, nor the joy of companionship; it is the spiritual inspiration that comes to one when [one] discovers that someone else believes in [one]. . . .
—*Ralph Waldo Emerson*

Many times we may not totally believe in ourselves. After a bad day or a painful rejection, it may be hard for us to look at ourselves and say, "But I believe in you."

Yet there are people who can tell us that. In our lives we need to have at least one special friend who has a belief in us even when we don't. Sometimes just to hear a friend say, "It's going to be all right. I believe in you," is enough to help us get back on track with our self-esteem.

A friend can be many things: a confidante, a buddy, a good-time pal. In all of these roles, a friend confirms one solid fact: a belief in our goodness as a person. The measure of any person is not by the number of friends, but by the belief any one friend has in that person.

Who is it who believes in my goodness as a person? Tonight I can give thanks for this friend and his or her belief in me.

*Some minds remain open long enough for truth
not only to enter but to pass on through by way
of a ready exit without pausing anywhere along
the route.*

—*Sister Elizabeth Kenny*

Many times what someone says hurts us. If someone is pointing out a character defect or being critical of our work, we may find it difficult to listen. But before we react, we need to ask whether the person is being destructive or constructive in his or her speech. We can ignore destructive words by detaching, but we need to listen to constructive words. There is a reason to hear such words, even though they may hurt or make us feel defensive.

To become a total listener rather than a selective listener, we can let people finish what they need to say. Silence and an open mind can help us hear all their words. By truly listening and then responding maturely, we will grasp the message and perhaps see the love and caring with which it is delivered.

Tomorrow, I will not react to things said to me. I will truly listen and then respond maturely and gently.

*Delegate freely . . . and check on it every chance
you get.*
                                        —*Linda Johnson Rice*

When we ask that something be done, do we let go
and let the job get done, or do we worry it won't be
done on time or how we want it? Part of learning to
trust others is to learn when to let go and let other
people handle something in their own way.

We can look back on today and remember requests
we made. Perhaps we asked an employee for assistance, a child to do a project, or our partner to do
something important. After we made the request, did
we then let go or were we filled with worry and doubt
about whether our request would be honored?

Tonight we can let go of our requests and trust all
will be taken care of. If it is not, that doesn't mean we
can never trust anyone again. It may mean our request
was unreasonable or other circumstances intervened.
It's okay if we make a request and don't get results that
meet our expectations. Trust doesn't mean we will get
what we want when we want it and how we want it.
Trust means having enough faith to ask another—and
to let it go.

Tonight I can let go of requests unhonored today.

What, after all, is a halo? It's only one more thing to keep clean.

—*Christopher Fry*

Those of us who continually strive for perfection may find we place incredible demands upon ourselves. One minute we're working toward serenity, and the next we're busy every night of the week. One minute we say we're going to sit down to read, and the next we're up cleaning the house, rushing from room to room in nervous energy.

Perfection places an incredible demand upon us to do everything right. But what is right? Is there a right way to do something and a wrong way?

The perfectionist in us is always looking for right, but we'll never find it. There really is no right way or wrong way to do anything. It's whatever way we choose. If we choose to try wearing the halo of perfection, we need to know it can be tarnished, tipped to the side, or misplaced every once in a while.

I'm no angel, that's for sure, because I'm not perfect. I'm still working on my halo and wings, and that's a lifelong process.

It is universally admitted that there is a natural healing power resident in the body. . . . Many people have learned to relax and to keep quiet like the animals, giving nature a free opportunity to heal their maladies.
—Horatio W. Dresser

Have we ever met people who never seem to get sick? They eat well, get plenty of rest and exercise, and generally seem to give physical health a priority. Then there are those who always seem sick, and they seem more concerned about their sickness than in getting better.

Medical studies have found a direct correlation between people's emotional and physical states. The person who thinks positive thoughts and expresses emotions usually spends less time being sick than someone who has a mind filled with stinking thinking.

We are our own healers. Our minds and bodies tell us when to eat, sleep, and relax. When we listen, we are in touch with the ways we can help ourselves feel better. It's our choice—we can feel healthy or we can feel sick. Which will it be?

Tonight I can learn to listen to my body and respect its messages. I will take care of myself and get the rest I need.

The past is our cradle, not our prison. . . . The past is for inspiration, not imitation; for continuation, not repetition.

—Israel Zangwill

A history book informs us about the past. It gives us an objective picture of what life was like during particular time periods. With such a view, we can then see how far we've come. How do we apply our own histories to our present lives?

We can learn much from our past. It may tell us about some uninspiring things and some negative experiences. But it can also give us clues about our present behaviors, personalities, and mood swings. It can tell us about our dreams and desires, gifts and goals, talents and tastes.

We can use our past as a springboard for our present way of living. We can look away from the negatives of the past and choose not to imitate or perpetuate such negativity. We can then reflect upon the good parts of our past and use them to inspire our present work.

How can I use the good parts of my history for my best benefit?

Never accuse others to excuse yourself.
— *Anonymous*

How many times have we blamed our feelings at the end of a day on the boss, co-workers, teachers, parents, or even the person who cut us off on the road? It's true we may feel anger or resentment toward any one of those people, but they didn't cause our feelings.

We are the sole owners of our feelings. We're the ones who bought them, and we're the ones who will hold on to them. When we're ready to let go of them, that's when we won't feel them any longer.

There are no excuses we can use to justify our feelings. The program teaches us to look inward at ourselves, not outward at the effects of the universe. Tonight we can look inward and survey the feelings we have. We can choose to keep them, or let them go.

No matter what the circumstances of the day, all the feelings I have are mine. Tonight I can let go of the ones I don't want and hang on to those that feel good.

*Life: a diary in which every [one] means to write
one story, and writes another.*
—*Sir James M. Barrie*

Did our day today live up to our expectations, or
were we greeted by new situations, new knowledge,
and new experiences? Oftentimes what we expect is
not what we're given. Life is not a known substance.
It's many times a delicious new taste we've never had
before.

To go through each day with a set outcome in our
minds will only lead to disappointment and may prevent us from being open to new discoveries. Life cannot be predicted or even imagined. It can only be
experienced each minute.

Let us not try to write the events of tomorrow until
after they've happened. Let us be free to experience all
that's in store for us—fresh and new and exciting.

*What will I write in my diary? Let me meet each new
experience of life on its own terms.*

The first three times you came with the same story [they] would listen and try to help. But if you showed up a fourth time and it was the same old tired things, the others in the circle would just get up and move. . . . It was time you did something about it.

—Anne Cameron

Many of us go to meeting after meeting, talking about the same problem. What are we looking for? What are we asking for? We aren't asking for help, because we usually are given good suggestions that we reject. We aren't looking to make changes, because we keep holding on to the same problem.

We may also have been in the opposite position— listening to one who keeps talking about the same problems. After hearing those people for a while, it's easy to want to tune them out.

But we can change. We can ask whether we use meetings to air the same grievances. If so, we need to stop complaining and do something. If we hear another doing the same thing, we can learn from that person's unwillingness to change. We can learn the difference between stagnation and growth.

I can listen and learn. If I ask for help, let me also be willing to accept it.

No answer is also an answer.
—Danish proverb

Have we ever prayed and felt God must not have heard us because our prayers weren't answered? We may have asked for strength or protection or for things to change. Yet hours, days—even weeks—later we may still be in the same situation, feeling the same way.

God always hears us, but sometimes the answers aren't immediate or guaranteed. Sometimes the best answer is no answer, meaning we need to stay in an uncomfortable situation a little longer. Perhaps there is something we need to learn that can't be learned unless we find it on our own.

We aren't abandoned when our prayers are answered by silence. Silence teaches us to listen closer, observe longer, and learn more in order to find our answers.

Is there anything tonight that confuses me or makes me feel helpless? I can find my answers by remaining open to all the messages I'm given.

I can't write a book commensurate with Shakespeare, but I can write a book by me.
—*Sir Walter Raleigh*

We may have grown up trying to emulate our favorite heroes, wishing we were as strong, as beautiful, as smart, or as self-sufficient as they were. Because our role models in the home may have been poor, we learned to look outside ourselves for people to copy.

Yet we can never be anyone other than ourselves. We may desire to have what someone else has because we don't like what we have. We can change those characteristics we don't like in ourselves, or we can learn to accept them. But we can't disguise our true selves by trying to be the carbon copy of someone we admire.

By striving for imitation, we are ignoring the wonderful person inside. We may not be a great artist like Renoir, a celebrated writer like Shakespeare, a brilliant singer or actor or great athlete or superb politician. We can only be ourselves. And that means we need to write our own book, not copy another's.

Tonight I am proud to be who I am. I have some wonderful qualities and talents that I can develop.

A great obstacle to happiness is to expect too much happiness.

—*Fontenelle*

How happy is happy? When we're laughing and joking, are we happy? Or is happiness doing an activity we really enjoy? Perhaps happiness is a feeling we get when we see a beautiful sight or a happy child.

Who knows what happiness really is? Like love, happiness can't really be defined, for what is true for one person isn't for another. Happiness really comes from within. If we feel a sense of contentment, peace, or joy, then we can bet we're feeling some form of happiness.

As long as we're satisfied with that happy feeling, then we'll feel happiness. It's when we expect happiness to feel differently that we'll lose our happy feelings. To be happy, we need to feel the happiness that exists, even if it isn't the way we've fantasized it to be.

Have I felt happiness today? Help me reflect on the feelings of that happiness and to allow myself to feel similar feelings.

You might as well live.

—Dorothy Parker

Many times we may have thought of quitting this life. We may have experienced close friends or a relative who chose such an end. But suicide isn't a resolution, it's a stop in midsentence. Running away from any pain, whether it be by suicide, drinking or using, or denial, may make distance—but not decisions.

Every life has its hard times, its pitfalls. To feel pain or go through hard times doesn't mean we've got to be hermits. It means we need to seek comfort, compassion, understanding.

When one person in the program is in pain, there are hundreds of others ready to guide that person to peace and serenity. We can let ourselves be guided by those around us.

Tonight, I can remember I am not the only person who has ever felt pain.

Never answer an angry word in kind. It's the second word that makes the quarrel.

—Anonymous

In the past we've probably found it's easy to have an argument. In fact, that may have been how we spent the majority of our time with our spouse, family members, or friends. Arguments may have become so familiar that to have them was to be doing "the right thing."

Today we've learned to detach from angry words. We know now the other person is probably in so much pain that the only way they feel they can alleviate the pain is to hurt another.

Detachment is the only cure for an argument. Once we stop detaching, we are sucked into the tangled web of confusion, pain, and bitterness. We can strengthen our ability to detach by relying on the support of our friends in the program and our Higher Power.

Do I need help detaching? Help me find my strength from those who can help me, not hurt me.

Failure is an event, not a person.
—William D. Brown

We may find it easy to blame disappointing circumstances in our lives on the people in our lives. We might think we wouldn't be so angry with ourselves if we could change bosses or co-workers or partners. We might believe our inability to stay in relationships is caused by the family that brought us up or the circumstances now in our lives.

If we're angry at one boss, chances are we'll be angry at another no matter what company or job we have. The co-workers at a new company can't guarantee our happiness or peace of mind any more than a new relationship will bring us the love we've always searched for.

Once we realize our dissatisfactions come from events, rather than people, we'll be less likely to place blame on people or make them the targets of all our failings.

I can stop trying to discover shortcuts or easy answers to why I feel dissatisfied at times. I am the only one who can make changes, right here and now.

Selfishness always aims at creating around it an absolute uniformity of type. Unselfishness recognizes infinite variety of type as a delightful thing, accepts it, acquiesces in it, enjoys it.
—*Oscar Wilde*

If we think of those who take care of themselves as selfish, we need to look at our definition of selfish. If we want to stay up late and talk and another person doesn't, who is selfish? The person who is tired and wants to sleep, or the one who insists he or she stay up?

Stating a limitation is not selfish; we are taking care of our needs and being honest. Selfishness is when we insist we have our way at the expense of another's needs. Selfishness is dishonest, because it doesn't honor the truth expressed by another.

To be unselfish, we first must be able to listen to others. After we learn to listen, we need to accept what is expressed. And to be truly unselfish, we must be able to enjoy the difference in others. When we can delight in the variety of people around us, we have achieved true unselfishness.

Can I accept the differences in others? I can begin by listening to others and learning just how different we all are.

> *The most important thing in life is not to capitalize on your gains. Any fool can do that. The really important thing is to profit from your losses.*
>
> —William Bolitho

It is easy to see the profit in what we gain, but it is not so easy to see the profit in what we lose. Projects that take shape and collections that expand show the gains we have made. But how can we see profits from the end of a relationship, the loss of a job, or the estrangement from family?

Each loss represents a step we need to take toward maturity and growth. Throughout our lifetimes we will walk up many steps. Sometimes it may seem like we have a never-ending stairway in front of us. Our gains are the level parts of each stair, but the real progress is made when we climb the stairs of our losses.

Although we may feel as though we have nothing when we go through a loss, what we do have is the experience of the loss. We learn to deal with a different lesson. Our profits from a loss may not show up immediately, but we will discover the rich rewards as we learn to accept life on its terms—not on ours.

Tonight I can learn to look at today's losses as gains. What nave I learned? How have I grown?

*Simply to live is a wonderful privilege in itself.
. . . But to what are you alive? Is it merely to a
daily routine? . . . How much do you really live
outside of your chosen profession or occupation?*
—Henry Wood

From an acorn to a tree, the oak puts all its energy
into growing as strong and tall as it can. Moisture,
sunlight, and nutrition are gathered for its leaves,
acorns, branches, and trunk. Yet if our oak tree takes
all the moisture, sunshine, and nutrition, other nearby
trees will be weaker and smaller.

We have within us a forest that demands attention
for its growth: a career tree, a family tree, a recovery
tree, a parent tree, and a friendship tree. If we spend
more time and attention on one than the others, the
neglected ones will not grow strong.

Every part of our lives should be important to us:
our families and friends as well as our recoveries and
careers. It may be commendable to receive lots of promotions at work. But if our families are neglected, the
forest inside us will not flourish. Every part of life
needs attention for us to succeed.

---

*Tonight I can begin to balance my time. All areas of my life
need attention.*

The woods are lovely, dark, and deep,
But I have promises to keep,
And miles to go before I sleep,
And miles to go before I sleep.
                                    —Robert Frost

We made a promise to ourselves when we joined the program—to use the tools of the program, *One Day at a Time,* to stay on the road to recovery.

We need to remember that promise every day. Our program needs come first. After a long day at work or school, it is tempting to turn on the television or take a nap. Instead of calling someone we sponsor or our own sponsor, we may not feel like talking. We may come up with many excuses not to go to a meeting, like doing laundry or balancing the checkbook.

But all these things can wait while we take care of *First Things First.* It may take a lot of energy to stay alert in a meeting, but we'll be doing the best thing we can for ourselves: keeping our promise. Let's keep that promise, beginning tonight with prayer and meditation.

Have I spent time using my program today? What can I do to keep my promise to myself?

There is no royal road to anything. One thing at a time, all things in succession. That which grows fast withers as rapidly; that which grows slowly endures.

—Josiah Gilbert Holland

During winter we can walk through a grocery store and see an array of fresh vegetables and fruits as if it were summer. Chemicals and greenhouses allow farmers to grow food year-round and produce ripe tomatoes even while a snowstorm howls outside.

Yet the tomato that took a few weeks to grow in a climate-controlled, enriched environment doesn't compare to the one that grew to fruition over months in the natural sun and soil. So it is with us. Instant recovery is like instant breakfast—it's satisfying but doesn't last long.

Many times our recovery will seem like it's proceeding at a snail's pace. But emotional growth can't be regulated like temperatures and soil conditions. Our potential for growth is a result of the effort we put into it and the time we give it. The steady regulation of time forces growth to be gradual and balanced. For growth to be good, it must stand the test of time.

I can slow down my desires and not try to push time to move more quickly. I need to accept the pace and grow steadily and surely.

The [person] who is always having . . . feelings hurt is about as pleasant a companion as a pebble in a shoe.

—Elbert Hubbard

Are we overly sensitive or afraid of personal criticism for fear our feelings will be hurt? Sometimes it may seem like no one can say anything to us without us feeling hurt, shameful, guilt-ridden, or rejected. We may find ourselves saying we're sorry so many times in one day that we end up believing we are, indeed, very sorry people.

Our friends and relatives care about us and want to see us healthier, happier people. Because of this, they may give us criticism. This criticism is meant to be helpful, not hurtful.

If we feel attacked by the criticisms of others or always seem to have our feelings hurt, it's because we allow it. No one can make us feel any way unless we let it happen. Although we may have been brought up with criticism and been told we were no good, the only person today who can make us feel worthless is ourselves. We are as good as we'll allow ourselves to be.

I can accept personal criticism and not fear my feelings will be hurt. Tonight and every night, I am a good person, no matter what another says or feels.

*They got scared when they started feeling good,
just because it was so unfamiliar. Like chronic
prisoners facing release from their cells.*
—Lisa Alther

The evening news usually begins with doom-and-
gloom stories and perhaps ends with one positive, uplifting item. If we were to give the evening news of
today, what would it consist of? Stories of disappointment, anger, resentment, and misunderstandings; or
recollections of giving, laughter, closeness, success,
and achievement?

It's scary to focus only on the good things that happen. Many times we're afraid to feel good because we
don't trust the feeling to last long. Perhaps we're very
uncomfortable with good feelings because they're so
unfamiliar. Yet that unfamiliarity can change, over
time, until we grow accustomed to the good.

Accepting good feelings is like meeting someone we
really want to know better. At first we may feel scared
or shy. But in time, we feel more at ease and relaxed as
we spend more time together and share different
things. Feeling good can be a friend that will grow
more important to us every day.

Tonight I will focus on the good in my evening news.

Character builds slowly, but it can be torn down with incredible swiftness.

—Faith Baldwin

Because we are fragile and sensitive, we may feel like our progress is more steps backward than forward. We can take pride in our gains, but losses have a way of throwing us into a tailspin.

We may be progressing nicely in recovery, when one person says, "I don't like what you're doing." Suddenly our self-image changes from that of hope and faith to depression and despair. We become uncertain and confused about where we're going and what we're doing. How much do we value that person's opinion?

Before we let one person break our fragile self-esteem, we need to remember that person's opinion is only one of many. We need to trust our own opinion. Then we need to trust the guidance and support of people familiar with the program and do the character building we wish to do. Then we will find ourselves taking more steps forward and fewer backward.

Tonight I need to remember some people who mean a lot to me but who will never understand or support my new life. I can still care for them, but I don't need to seek their approval.

We either make ourselves miserable, or we make ourselves strong. The amount of work is the same.

—Carlos Castaneda

"Woe is me!" is a familiar cry to many of us, for we have cried it ourselves long and hard. We've placed a lot of energy into feeling our misery, in discussing it, in analyzing it, in living and reliving it. Misery has been our favorite tape recording, to be played over and over.

But our awakening in the program has taught us that we do not have to live in misery. We are learning we have choices, and one of those choices is to hold on to our feelings. If we choose to hold on to pain and despair and misery with both hands, we have no way to grasp on to strength and hope and happiness.

We can let go of misery tonight. Perhaps we won't want to release both hands right away, and that's okay. But we can release the grip of one hand and have it grasp on to positive, strength-giving feelings. Little by little, we'll learn to let go of our misery and use both hands to hold on to the hope of the program to make ourselves strong.

———————

I do not need to fear letting go, for nothing bad will happen to me—only good.

When you get into a tight place and everything goes against you till it seems as though you could not hold on a minute longer, never give up then, for that is just the place and time that the tide will turn.

—Harriet Beecher Stowe

After every downswing there is an upswing. It may not be immediate, like a roller coaster ride with its constant dips and climbs. Sometimes there will be a long stretch of level ground after a downswing, making us feel we are sinking lower and lower. But the leveling off period strives to bring us stability before the upswing.

Listen to those around us. They will talk of bad times and say, "I never thought it would come to an end." But they'll also tell us the end did come and things did get better. Each time that happened they had more faith and the next downswing wasn't as devastating or hopeless. By trusting in the natural up-and-down motion of life, we will be able to say, "Things won't get any worse. In fact, they will get better."

I need to listen to others with experience and trust their stories. Tonight I will believe and trust as they do.

A strong life is like that of a ship of war which has its own place in the fleet and can share in its strength and discipline, but can also go forth alone to the solitude of the infinite sea.
—P. G. Hamerton

We need to achieve a balance between socializing and solitude. If we are around others day in and day out, we will never learn what it feels like to be by ourselves. Likewise, if we are isolated a lot, we will never learn what it's like to be around others. Recovery depends on sound balance between the two.

As we reflect upon today, we can take note of the time we spent with others or in solitude. Then we can better decide how to balance tomorrow's activities. If we've dealt with people all day, it might be good to spend some time alone, traveling in solitude on the infinite sea. If we've spent most of the day in solitude, it might be good to spend time with others, experiencing that we are a part of those around us. We can strive to seek balance and harmony as we steer our ships.

What do I need to balance tomorrow's activities: the company of others or the company of myself?

Risk! Risk anything! . . . Do the hardest thing on earth for you. Act for yourself. Face the truth.
—Katherine Mansfield

Many times when we feel fear we don't realize it's related to a risk that we have the option to take. A risk doesn't have to be as dramatic as climbing a mountain or placing all our money on a bet. A risk can be walking into a new meeting, smiling at a familiar face, or purchasing our first program literature.

In the beginning, we may feel fear taking small risks. As time goes on, we learn there is nothing to fear at a new meeting, at smiling at another, or reading literature that tells us who we are. Then we begin to take greater risks, like asking someone to be our sponsor, going out for coffee, or taking the Fourth Step.

The safety and security we feel when we take risks in the program will help us take risks outside the program. With time, we can learn to trust others, share our needs, and set our limits at home, at work, and with friends. Taking a new risk allows another to soon appear.

What is there to fear in taking a risk? Help me learn that each time I take a risk I open another door.

Actually, these are among the most important times in one's life, when one is alone. Certain springs are tapped only when we are alone. The artist knows he must be alone to create; the writer, to work out his thoughts; the musician, to compose; the saint, to pray.
—Anne Morrow Lindbergh

Most of us are alone for some time at night, whether we're commuting home or sitting down for a few minutes of meditation. Time alone—with ourselves and our Higher Power—is a valuable part of our day. In this stillness, we can listen to ourselves and feel our feelings without the constant distractions of the day.

Being still with ourselves means not running away from the silence around us. It means feeling our feelings, whether they're good or bad. It's a time of reflection and prayer.

For every moment we can be at peace with ourselves, we are that much closer to being a part of life. For as there is peace in nature, so it is in our nature to feel peace.

Am I at peace with myself now? Have I prayed to my Higher Power to help me at this time?

You cannot be anything if you want to be everything.

—*Solomon Schechter*

Sometimes we may feel overwhelmed by the amount of things we believe we have to work on at one time. We may feel stressed under the pressure of working a full-time job, attending school, working on a relationship, caring for ourselves and a family, and growing in recovery. Sometimes we may want to put up an "Out to Lunch" sign and take off for parts unknown.

Anytime we feel overwhelmed it's our mind's way of telling us we need to set limits. We can't do everything and expect to get very far. But we'll get far if we do some things and leave others alone for a while.

Tonight we can look at our overbooked schedules and see where we can make changes. We first need to leave some free time for ourselves. Then we need to prioritize our obligations. Once we try out our new schedules for a while, we may see some changes or find others that need to be made. Starting tonight, we can stop feeling overwhelmed with life and take charge of it.

How can I reorganize my schedule so I'm not so overwhelmed? Tonight I can begin to take charge of my life and mold it to fit my needs.

The reputation of a thousand years may be determined by the conduct of one hour.
—*Japanese proverb*

For the next hour, how will we act or feel? Will we toss and turn filled with fear and worry over the night? Will we be anxious and stressed over our day's activities and unable to sleep? Will we feel lonely and abandoned in our isolation? Or will we be able to sleep peacefully?

If we let this next hour determine how we would feel for the rest of our lives, which feelings would we choose? We might find it easy to let go of the negative feelings we feel right now if we knew we'd have to feel that way all the time.

For the next hour, we can choose how we want to feel just as if we were making a permanent character mold. Chances are we want a good night's sleep, so we can face the new day relaxed and filled with good feelings. Then we can approach the day an hour at a time, maintaining those positive feelings. Imagine what good we can feel if we look at our lives as a series of hours that can be changed and improved as each one is completed!

For the next hour, I would like to relax and begin a peaceful night's sleep. Then I can face tomorrow in a positive mood.

We cannot build until we have laid foundation stones. We add to our foundations every time we meet our difficulties well, however insignificant they may be.

—Charles B. Newcomb

A house without a foundation will not last. As the ground shifts in hot and cold weather, so will the floors. The wood placed upon the ground will rot. The rooms will be cold and damp with no protection from the temperature of the ground. Before the program, we were houses without foundations.

A house built with a strong foundation will provide warmth in the winter and coolness in the summer. Though the ground may shift, the foundation will absorb the movements and keep the rooms level and unharmed. The foundation will protect the precious wood. In the program, we are houses with foundations.

The strength of our foundations will depend on our commitment to recovery. If we keep the program ever in our lives, work the Steps, and take regular inventory of our progress, our foundations will be strong and durable. They will protect our houses through all kinds of weather for a long time.

Tonight I can make repairs upon my foundation and strengthen it.

In the old days, if a person missed the stagecoach he was content to wait a day or two for the next one. Nowadays, we feel frustrated if we miss one section of a revolving door.

—Modern Maturity

Many things today can take place overnight. We can cook a turkey dinner, mail a package several states away, or travel to another continent in a matter of hours. Because the world moves at such a fast pace, it's only natural that we absorb some of that frenetic activity into our own lives.

We become accustomed to wanting change to happen right away. When we share that at a meeting others may laugh, but it's because they, too, have had the same feelings. It's not unusual to want miracles with the blink of an eye.

But just because the outer world is at a frantic pace doesn't mean we, too, have to operate at such a pace. When all the world is a raging stream, we can have a small peaceful stream of serenity flowing within us.

Tonight I can learn patience that things will happen in my time, not the time of the world. Everyone moves at his or her own pace, and I need to move at mine.

When you pray for God's guidance, don't complain when it is different from your preference.

—Our Daily Bread

When we were children we sat on Santa's lap with our lists, or asked the tooth fairy for more money, or begged the Easter Bunny for more candy, or prayed to God for that shiny red bike we wanted. Yet we usually ended up with things we didn't even ask for, but needed, like warm jackets and winter boots or pajamas.

Today we may still pray to God for things we want. Maybe not shiny red bikes, but shiny new cars, more money, better jobs, greater security, or the health of loved ones. Our prayers might not be answered in the way we'd like them to be. We may never win a lottery, we may lose a promotion, or we may experience the death of a loved one.

Yet what we are given is what God feels we need. Though we may be sad or disappointed, those things help us grow in the way we need. Sometimes we may get just what we pray for, and that's wonderful. But if we don't get what we ask for, we must remember that what we get is the gift God feels we need.

I can pray for guidance without any expectations. I know I will get what I need.

Some days confidence shrinks to the size of a pea, and the backbone feels like a feather. We want to be somewhere else, and don't know where—want to be someone else and don't know who.

—Jean Hersey

Who are we? Where are we going? What do we like? Are we happy? What do we want from life?

These certainly are not easy questions to answer. In fact, we may have been struggling with the answers for a long time. We, who thought we knew ourselves so well, are now finding we aren't who we believed we were. We are so much more, but we may not be able to put our finger on the so much more.

We may never get to answer all the questions. For some of us, the answers may change on a daily or even hourly basis. We are just starting to learn who we are without the definitions of people, alcohol or other drugs, or any other addiction. The process of finding out who we are takes time and patience and a whole lot of change from the way we used to be. The answers, like the questions, will come to us when we're ready.

I am just starting to discover who I am. I may not have all the answers tonight, but I know so much more than I did before.

We crucify ourselves between two thieves: regret for yesterday and fear of tomorrow.
—Fulton Oursler

Some women who had been victims of violence banded together to "take back the night" in a series of public demonstrations. Rather than hold regret over the violence or their fear of what might happen, they chose to live in the moment with no fear or regrets.

Tonight we can "take back the night" from our own fears. This can mean easing our minds from the stress of the day so we can have a peaceful sleep. It can mean letting go of any fearful thoughts so we're at peace in our homes. It can mean blocking out crazy thoughts that will make us toss and turn.

This night is ours. It's our time for uninterrupted sleep, pleasant dreams, and gentle rest for our weary bodies.

Tomorrow will be waiting for me, after I've taken back the night to feel peace, trust, and serenity.

The preservation of health is a duty. Few seem conscious that there is such a thing as physical morality.

—*Herbert Spencer*

Do we realize we have an obligation to our bodies to stay healthy? Before we entered the program, we may have abused ourselves with chemicals, diets or binges, little sleep, or chains of cigarettes and coffee. Now that we're in the program, we're beginning to realize our mental health has a direct bearing on how we treat ourselves physically.

If we've been cooped up in an office or home, we need to pay attention to getting fresh air and exercise. We can go for a walk, meditate, or take a warm bath. We can eat a nutritious dinner and get to bed early for a good night's sleep. Just as we have a moral obligation to our mental health, so too do we have a moral obligation to our physical health.

I can eat good foods, breathe in fresh air, and exercise for my best benefit. Tonight I will rest soundly to treat my physical health well.

What is the source of our first suffering? It is in the fact that we hesitated to speak. It was born in the moments when we accumulated silent things within us.

—*Gaston Bachelard*

We may have learned while growing up that it was easier not to communicate. We may have remained silent rather than risk an argument or a reprimand or a misunderstanding. But as adults, we need to unlearn that behavior and learn to give voice to the muted feelings, thoughts, ideas, and grievances within us.

We first need to risk breaking silence, for the silences we hold within us are like cancers. For as long as we ignore them, they will continue to grow and we will suffer. But if we strive to remove them—one at a time—we will become cleansed of their ill effects.

We may discover things we wanted to say, but didn't. We can prevent these silences from growing by taking positive action. There are those who will listen to us—our Higher Power, a trusted friend, a meeting group. But it is up to us to take the first step.

Now is the time to give voice to our inner silences.

'Tis pitiful the things by which we are rich or poor—a matter of coins, coats and carpets, a little more or less stone, wood or paint, the fashion of a cloak or hat. . . .
—*Ralph Waldo Emerson*

What are riches? Are they the luxurious feel of a mink coat, the weight of a bulging wallet, a filled jewelry box, or the size of a bank account or stock portfolio? Or are riches intangibles—things we cannot see or touch or earn or spend? Perhaps riches are happiness, serenity, and faith.

Recalling Dickens's tale *A Christmas Carol*, we remember that even with all the riches imaginable, Ebenezer Scrooge was miserable and friendless. The happiest and most contented man was Bob Cratchit, who was poor in wealth, had a crippled son and other children to feed and keep healthy. Yet his home and his heart were filled with love, peace, and faith.

We can ask our Higher Power for the greatest riches: peace and joy in our hearts and homes. We don't need presents or luxurious finery to make us happy. To become richer, we need to open our hearts to the wealth of wonderful feelings around us.

Tonight, let me give thanks for the riches I have inside. Those are the greatest gifts I can receive from my Higher Power.

It usually happened ... particularly at the beginning of a holiday. Then, when I was hoping for nothing but sleep and peace, the chattering echoes of recent concerns would race through my head, and the more I sought rest the more I could not find it.

—Joanna Field

Stress, anxiety, fear, and worry are especially dominant before holidays. The upcoming family events, gift exchange, cooking, and scheduling seem to take precedence. Yet there are ways to find peace and serenity amidst all the excitement.

Instead of focusing on things we don't like about the upcoming holiday season, we can focus on things we do like. Such things may be as simple as: "I'm looking forward to seeing my sister," or "I like receiving cards from old friends," or "I like the snow on the pine trees."

We can have a nice time this season by putting energy into the things we enjoy. We can go to many meetings, make plans with close friends or our sponsor, and meditate to keep calm and serene. Tonight we can put the stress of the upcoming holidays to rest by remembering ourselves first.

How can I use the program to relax my thoughts tonight?

. . . I finally figured out the only reason to be alive is to enjoy it.

—Rita Mae Brown

We've probably made many changes in our lives since we joined the program. We may have improved our job performance. We may be attending school, struggling to attain the degree we never got when we were using. We may be spending a majority of our evenings at meetings instead of partying as we did in the past. And we may feel life isn't fun anymore—that it just doesn't have the excitement of the past. But did we *enjoy* our lives before the program?

Today we're learning to live in a whole new way. We made a lot of changes in our behavior. And we're learning to enjoy things we never did before—to appreciate a beautiful sunset, to look forward to being around people at a meeting.

If we forget to enjoy today's precious moments, we can change that right now. Tomorrow is full of enjoyment yet to come!

Have I enjoyed my life today? What can I do to enjoy my life tomorrow?

*People disturb us. They sap our vitality from us.
. . . They pile upon us their conditions of fear
and their atmosphere of despondency. In such
cases we must regain our poise by the realization
of the power that is ever within us. Find your
center.*

—Horatio W. Dresser

Did we become wrapped up in the behaviors of
other people today? If we haven't detached from the
problems of our boss, co-worker, or family member,
we feel drained and used—like an old rag that's
choked with years of dust and dirt.

Other people own their behaviors just as we own
ours. If we buy into someone's attitude, then we have
purchased a piece of that attitude. It's ours to feel, and
feel it we usually do. Suddenly we become a reflection
of the other person, displaying whatever emotions he
or she is experiencing.

Now that the daytime is over, we can reflect upon
our feelings and ask if they are ours or ones we purchased from others. To find our center, we need to discover the feelings that are ours alone. As we interact
with people, we can refuse to purchase any more attitudes that are not our own.

---

*I can detach from others and not buy their feelings.
Tonight I will find much serenity from my own feelings.*

If time be of all things most precious, wasting time must be the greatest prodigality, since lost time is never found again.
—Benjamin Franklin

At the beginning of a day we may feel we have so much time ahead of us. But now as we look back on the day, we may feel we never had enough time to do all the things we wanted. Here we are now, ready to say good night to the day, and not satisfied that we did all we wanted to or could do.

Perhaps the day didn't go as we had planned. Perhaps the list of things we wanted to accomplish barely got touched. Perhaps we feel we wasted a great deal of time watching television, shopping, or talking on the telephone.

If we believe now we wasted time today, then we'll view that time as useless. But if we view all of the moments of today as precious and necessary, then we won't feel so critical of how we spent our time. We did what we wanted to do today, in the time we were given. Tonight we can rest—assured—that none of our time was wasted.

I'm satisfied all of my time today was valuable and useful, even if I didn't accomplish everything I set out to do.

When you feel grateful for something others have done for you, why not tell them about it?
—*Anonymous*

It's one thing to express gratitude for the many wonderful things in our lives, whether we do so in our prayers or to our group. But to go one step further and express gratitude directly to the people who help us feel grateful is one of the best ways to show love and kindness.

Our direct contacts with others don't always need to be in making amends. Recognition of the gifts we receive builds a strong bridge that can continually transport positive, loving feelings.

We can enlarge the one-way avenue toward us into a two-lane road that returns to the ones who show us so much patience, kindness, and love. Once we do, we'll find we want to travel this road often, both to receive and to give thanks for what we receive.

Is there someone to whom I can express my gratitude? I need to take time for a prayer of gratitude for the wonderful gifts I have received.

Without prayer, I should have been a lunatic long ago.

—Mahatma Gandhi

How can we make our prayers more satisfying and fulfilling? One of the best ways is to see and hear ourselves as we pray, as if we were getting a bird's-eye view of what we look like and how we sound when we pray.

Seeing from above in this objective way gives a good overview of the strength and the meaning of our prayers. Are we whining and fidgeting as we pray? Maybe we aren't really praying but instead are asking to get our way. Do we sound angry, with fists clenched? Maybe we need to work on letting go first before we pray.

This is how our Higher Power sees and hears us. Our Higher Power know which prayers are serious, meaningful conversations and which are filled with self-pity, resentment, and anger. Tonight we can hear ourselves pray and learn whether we are truly praying or merely taking time for self-centered feelings.

Before I pray tonight, let me run through the things I want to say. Help me keep self-centered feelings at a minimum and true sharing and communication at a maximum.

Life is like playing a violin solo in public and learning the instrument as one goes on.
—*Edward Bulwer-Lytton*

The violin virtuoso whose concerts are sold-out has spent innumerable hours of practice to achieve such fame. That person wouldn't think of inviting the public to a practice session because of the flaws they might hear.

We aren't virtuosos, yet we're always on view to the public. Everyone gets to see our good performances as well as our bad. Because of this, we may often struggle with impatience and disappointment in our striving to "look good" in front of others.

Yet we're all struggling in front of one another. Just as others see our imperfections, so do we see theirs. None of us are virtuosos in life. To become skilled in living, we need to live *One Day at a Time* and learn as we go.

I don't need to strive for perfection and skill. I can just be myself in front of people.

One does not have to believe everything one hears.

—*Cicero*

As we were growing up, we may have been told many things about ourselves. Some may have been complimentary, but others may have been vicious and degrading statements made by a chemically dependent parent or guardian. Because we were caught in the disease, we may have believed all the horrible things that were said.

But today we don't have to buy into anyone's negative comments. We don't have to believe we are no good, we're stupid, lazy, helpless, insecure, inept, or will never amount to anything. Anytime we believe those messages, we're allowing a label to be stuck to our chests.

We can choose to walk around advertising our labels, or we can take them off and rip them up. We can turn away physically and emotionally from the source of the negative comments. The only label we should wear should say we are good people.

Tonight I can affirm I'm a good person and that I deserve the best.

It is important for every one who is trying personally to apply these principles, to understand that all progress is vibratory and uneven. The higher standpoint is only reached through a long series of 'ups and downs.'
—Henry Wood

Are we expecting some magical signal to occur when we're "cured" of the symptoms of our disease? Do we believe once we "master" the tools of the program we won't feel pain, sadness, resentment, or disappointment? Are we still anticipating a happily-ever-after to occur in our lives?

Life is naturally full of ups and downs. Every day isn't all sunshine and perfect temperatures. Nature has its tragedies and destruction as well as its growth and harvest. If we see both good and bad as complements to each other, we will see life is a continuous process.

If we apply the principles of the program, our lives will get better. The ups and downs won't go away, but we will stop focusing on only one or the other. We will see it all as part of the same picture.

My only expectation tonight is to let life flow the way it's meant to.

I wish you the courage to be warm when the world would prefer you to be cool.
—Robert A. Ward

For years we listened to the demands of the world and tried to meet them. We may have listened to our parents and did what they told us to do. We may have heard the needs of a lover or friend and tried to meet them all. We may have even paid heed to absolute strangers, making changes in ourselves to honor their opinions.

Like a reptile, we may have absorbed the temperature of our surroundings and adjusted our body temperature accordingly. We may have found comfort in being warm when the world was warm or being cool when the world was cool.

But tonight we can, in the words of Thoreau, march to a beat of a different drummer. We can say no when others want to hear yes. We can set limits when others ask too much. We can even be warm when the world wants us to be cool. Others don't have power over us anymore. Only we have power over ourselves.

Tonight I won't let anyone or anything have power over the way I feel. I can feel warm or cool—it's my choice.

・ DECEMBER 31 ・

Ring out, wild bells, to the wild sky,
The flying cloud, the frosty light:
The year is dying in the night;
Ring out, wild bells, and let him die.
　　　　　　　—*Alfred, Lord Tennyson*

Past New Year's Eves may have meant times of excessive chemical use. We may have embarrassed ourselves in many ways. We may have chosen New Year's Eve as a time to analyze our past behaviors and write long lists of how that was going to change.

Yet tonight is like any other night. We don't have to feel as though we aren't having a good time unless we're at a party or a bar. We can celebrate the new year tomorrow with those closest to us by doing something we enjoy. The past is gone, the future has not arrived. The present is all we have, here and now.

Look to ourselves and what we want to do, not at what we think we should be doing. We can share our feelings at a meeting, spend quality time with our families and loved ones. We need to focus on ourselves and what we need to do for us, and not be diverted by the craziness around us.

Tonight is an ending; tonight is a beginning. Help me stay in the moment to bid farewell to the old and welcome in the new in my own way.

INDEX